Barnet & Stubbs's
Practical Guide
to Writing

Barnet & Stubbs's Practical Guide to Writing

Fourth Edition

Sylvan Barnet
Tufts University

Marcia Stubbs
Wellesley College

Little, Brown and Company
Boston   Toronto

Library of Congress Cataloging in Publication Data

Barnet, Sylvan.
Barnet & Stubbs's Practical guide to writing.

Includes index.
1. English language — Rhetoric.   I. Stubbs, Marcia.
II. Title.   III. Title: Barnet and Stubbs's Practical guide to writing.
IV. Title: Practical guide to writing.
PE1408.B4314   1983   808'.042   82-23990
ISBN 0-316-08215-5

Library of Congress Catalog Card No. 82-23990

ISBN 0-316-08215-5

10 9 8 7 6 5 4 3 2 1

MV

Published simultaneously in Canada
by Little, Brown & Company (Canada) Limited

Printed in the United States of America

Acknowledgments

Associated Press, "Dodgers Keep Perfect Record in Knocking Out Southpaws," *Michigan Daily*, 29 September 1955, p. 3. Reprinted by permission of the
Associated Press.

Pat Bellanca, "Jimmy Buffett is Going Coconuts." From *The Wellesley News*,
March 13, 1981. Reprinted by permission of the author.

Saul Bellow, *The Victim*. Reprinted from *The Victim* by Saul Bellow by
permission of the publisher, Vanguard Press, Inc. Copyright © 1947 by Saul
Bellow. Copyright renewed 1974 by Saul Bellow.

Barbara R. Bergman, "Here is Why You Lost Your Job." *The New York
Times*, 7 February 1982. © 1982 by The New York Times Company. Reprinted
by permission.

(Continued on page 438)

Preface

Where there is too much,
something is missing.

We have tried to keep this proverb in mind; we hope we have written a compact book rather than an undiscriminating one.

The book is designed for college courses in which students write essays, instructors read them, and students and instructors together discuss them. We hope we offer a practical guide to all three activities. The student, looking for information about choosing a topic, writing an analysis, constructing a paragraph, using a semicolon, can use the text as a guide to writing the week's essay. The instructor, after reading the essay, can suggest chapters or passages the student should consult in revising the essay or in writing the next one. Students and instructors together can discuss the exercises, the techniques used in the reprinted essays, the assumptions we make and the suggestions we offer.

Although we include discussions and examples of description and narration, we emphasize analysis, exposition, and argument because those are the chief activities, usually rolled into one, that we all engage in, both in school and later. When students write papers for a course, or professors write reports for a committee, or psychiatric social workers write case studies, most of what they write is exposition, a statement of what's what; usually they have come to see what's what by analyzing or dividing the subject into parts, and because they want to be believed, they construct as persuasive an argument as possible.

In addition to including many examples from the writing of our students, we have included twelve short essays, as well as numerous paragraphs from books and essays, the work for the most part of first-rate contemporary writers. These essays appear in the chapters on Analysis, Definition, Exposition, Persuasion, Description, Narration, and Acquiring Fluency. There are also a sample book review, a sample record review, an explication, and a research paper. We include all of these readings both to illustrate ways of writing and to provide students with something to write about. Similarly, the suggested exercises often require the students to write about something outside of themselves. The usual Polonian advice, offered to Laertes — "This above all, to thine own self be true" — seems to us as useless to most people of college ages as it is to Laertes. As Erik Erikson has helped us to see, most young people are engaged in a "search for something and somebody to be true to." They experiment with roles in a search for "the rock-bottom of some truth."[1] Asked to write about how they spent last summer, they may feel a profound uneasiness; however necessary last summer was, they are not sure what it added up to, and though they probably would not spend the next summer in the same way, they are not yet distant enough from their experience to be articulate about it. Some of our exercises do present clear opportunities for introspection, and all of them in fact require it, but we think that much of a student's writing should be directed outward, not solely a look into the heart but a look around — at people, at places, and especially at ideas.

We have tried therefore to balance the advice "Trust your feelings," "Ask yourself questions," with prescriptions: "Avoid clichés," "Keep your reader in mind." We have tried to increase the student's awareness that writing is both an exploration of self ("Choose a topic you can write about honestly") and a communication with others ("Revise for clarity").

Chapter 1 includes three essays by students, a brief article by Philip Roth, and some informal exercises. Instructors may find these passages useful for the first few class meetings. During the first week of the semester, we commonly suggest that students browse through the book from beginning to end, reading what interests them, skimming the rest, and generally familiarizing themselves with the book's contents and organization. But because each chapter can stand by itself, the instructor can assign chapters

---

[1] *Identity: Youth and Crisis* (New York: W. W. Norton, 1968), pp. 235–36.

for study in whatever seems a suitable order, probably interweaving chapters on writing, revising, and editing. Similarly, the student can consult whatever passages seem most relevant to writing, revising, or correcting a particular essay. After all, it has never been established that in a college course in English certain topics must be taught before others. Listen to Boswell describing a conversation, more than two hundred years ago, with Dr. Johnson:

> We talked of the education of children; and I asked him what he thought was best to teach them first. JOHNSON: "Sir, it is no matter what you teach them first, any more than what leg you shall put into your breeches first. Sir, you may stand disputing which is best to put in first, but in the meantime your breech is bare. Sir, while you are considering which of two things you should teach your child first, another boy has learnt them both."

A Note to the Fourth Edition

In revising the book we have greatly increased our indebtedness to many colleagues, students, editors, and other friends. These include Barbara Balfour, James Beaton, Kay Berenson, Barbara Jane Berk, Morton Berman, Phyllis Braumlich, Gary Brienzo, Daniel V. Brislane, Pearl L. Brown, Peter Brunette, Carroll Burcham, William Burto, A. Butrym, Terry P. Caesar, Joan Carberg, Thomas Carnicelli, Sally Carson, Charles H. Christensen, Sarah Clark, Michael Cleary, John M. Clum, James Cobb, Phyllis Cole, William F. Coles, S. Cooney, John Covell, Claire Crabtree, Mary Ann Creadon, Leah Creque, Mary Bryan H. Curd, Leopold Damrosch, Robert Dees, Tom De Palma, Imogene De Smet, Aviva Diamond, Pat Dorazio, James Early, Nathaniel Elliott, Marina Femmer, Denise Ferguson, Cathy Fiore, Terry Flaherty, Jan Fontein, C. Denny Freese, John Fugate, Krin Gabbard, Cynthia Galivan, Yolette Garcia, Thomas J. Gasque, Walker Gibson, David Giele, James Gifford, David Goldfaden, Margaret Gooch, John Grass, Jack Guillon, Nigel Hampton, James Hauser, Mark Heidmann, Thomas W. Herzing, Gervase Hittle, Owen Jenkins, Peter M. Johnson, Mary D. Jones, George Kearns, Joseph Keefe, Kathryn Keller, Dr. Frank Kelly, Nancy Kneeland, Judith Kohl, Molly Moore Kohler, Nancy Kolodny, Joseph Komidar, Roberta Kramer, Richard L. Lane, Andrea La Sane, Jonathan Lawson, Elsie

Leach, Helen M. Lewis, Peter Lindblom, Jane Lump, D'Ann Madewell, Bernard McCabe, Victoria McCabe, Donna McCormick, Joan McCoy, Patricia McGowan, George Marcopoulos, Sr. Lynda Martin-Boyle, H.O.O.M., Celeste A. Meister, Michael Meyer, Richard Milburn, George Miller, Gerald Mimno, Nancy Mimno, Melodie Monahan, Joan Moon, Betty Morgan, Rose Moss, Stanley Moss, Denise Muller, Margaret A. Murphy, Robert A. Myers, Barbara Nelson, Thomas Newkirk, Donald Nontelle, Jo Anna Norris, Richard D. Olson, John O'Neill, Mary O'Sullivan, Joan Patrie, Donald Pattow, Douglas Peterson, Russell O. Peterson, Bill Pierce, Elaine Plasberg, Carolyn Potts, Charles Quagliata, S. Quiroz, John Rath, Martha Reid and her colleagues at William and Mary, Stephen Reid, Gerald Richman, Leo Rockas, Judith Root, Zelda Rouillard, Richard Sandler, Frances W. Sauers, Carl Schaffer, Gerald Schiffhorst, William Scott, Patrick W. Shaw, James M. Siddens, Joyce Monroe Simmons, Martha Simonsen, Edward Sims, James Slattery, Audrey Smith, John Smolens, James Sodon, Jay Soldner, David Solheim, Dr. Harold Spicer, Robert Stein, Ann Steinmetz, Gail Stewart, April Stokes, Frances M. Stowe, Elaine Supowitz, Ann M. Tarbell, Larry Uffelman, Kathy Valdespino, Renita Weems, Lisa Wien, Anita C. Wilson, Howard Winn, Elizabeth Wood, Arthur P. Wooley, Haruo Yanagi, Mallory Young, and to all our students, from whose mistakes we hope to profit. It should be noted, too, that several passages in the book appeared earlier in slightly different form in Sylvan Barnet's *A Short Guide to Writing about Literature*.

Sylvan Barnet
Marcia Stubbs

Contents

PART ONE
Writing *1*

1 *From Subject to Essay* *3*

STARTING *3*

How to Write: Writing As a Physical Act *3*
Why Write? Writing As a Mental Activity *4*
Some Ideas about Ideas *5*
Starting to Write by Writing   Asking Questions and Answering Them

Organizing Ideas *10*

FOCUSING *12*

What to Write About: Subject, Topic, Thesis *12*
The Writer As Teacher: Imagining an Audience

CLARIFYING IDEAS *17*

General and Specific Writing *17*
The Groucho Marx Complex

AN OVERVIEW: FROM SUBJECT TO ESSAY *24*

EXERCISES • *28*

2 *Analysis* *30*

SORTING AND THINKING *30*

ANALYSIS AND SUMMARY *38*

COMPARING   *39*

ORGANIZING AN ESSAY DEVOTED TO A COMPARISON   *43*

ARRIVING AT AN ANALYTICAL THESIS   *45*

EXPLAINING AN ANALYSIS: WRITER TO READER   *47*

EXERCISES   *49*

ANALYSIS AT WORK   *57*

Columbo Knows the Butler Didn't Do It   *57*
Jeff Greenfield

Grant and Lee: A Study in Contrasts   *59*
Bruce Catton

3 *Outlining*   *64*

SCRATCH OUTLINE   *64*

PARAGRAPH OUTLINE   *65*

FORMAL OUTLINE   *65*

EXERCISES   *67*

4 *Paragraphs*   *68*

PARAGRAPH FORM AND SUBSTANCE   *68*

PARAGRAPH UNITY: TOPIC SENTENCES, TOPIC IDEAS   *70*

UNIFYING IDEAS INTO PARAGRAPHS   *74*

ORGANIZATION IN PARAGRAPHS   *76*

COHERENCE IN PARAGRAPHS   *79*

Transitions   *80*
Repetition   *82*
Transitions between Paragraphs   *84*

GROUPS OF PARAGRAPHS *84*

PARAGRAPH LENGTH *86*

THE USE AND ABUSE OF SHORT PARAGRAPHS *87*

INTRODUCTORY PARAGRAPHS *90*

CONCLUDING PARAGRAPHS *95*

EXERCISES *97*

5 *Definition* *102*

THE IMPORTANCE OF DEFINITION *103*

DEFINITION BY ORIGIN *104*

DEFINITION BY SYNONYM *105*

STIPULATIVE DEFINITION *106*

FORMAL DEFINITION *107*

LONGER DEFINITIONS *109*

EXERCISES *112*

DEFINITION AT WORK *113*

Mechanic's Feel *113*
Robert M. Pirsig

Sophistication *115*
Bergen Evans

6 *Exposition* *118*

EXPLAINING A PROCESS *123*

ORGANIZING AN EXPOSITORY ESSAY *126*

WRITING SUMMARIES *126*

EXERCISES *128*

EXPOSITION AT WORK   *130*

Indecent Exposure   *130*
Chuck Kraemer

*It's the Portly Penguin That Gets the Girl, French
Biologist Claims*   *132*
Anne Hebald Mandelbaum

7 *Persuasion*   *136*

PRESENTING EVIDENCE   *136*

ARGUMENT   *137*

WIT   *139*

Avoiding Sarcasm   *141*

AVOIDING FALLACIES   *142*

Making Reasonable Assumptions   *147*
Deduction   *148*

ORGANIZING AN ARGUMENT   *149*

A Checklist for Persuasive Essays   *150*

EXERCISES   *151*

PERSUASION AT WORK   *154*

Four Letter Words Can Hurt You   *154*
Barbara Lawrence

Here Is Why You Lost Your Job   *157*
Barbara R. Bergman

8 *Description*   *160*

DESCRIPTION AS PERSUASION   *160*

ORGANIZING A DESCRIPTION   *161*

ESTABLISHING A POINT OF VIEW   *163*

DESCRIPTION AND NARRATION   *165*

DESCRIPTION AND ANALYSIS *167*

EXERCISES *169*

DESCRIPTION AT WORK *172*

Adman's Atlanta *172*
Lynda Martin

Los Angeles Notebook *174*
Joan Didion

9 *Narration* *178*

THE USES OF NARRATIVE *178*

NARRATIVE PACE *181*

ORGANIZING A NARRATIVE *182*

EXERCISES *185*

NARRATION AT WORK *186*

Shooting an Elephant *186*
George Orwell

10 *The Research Paper* *194*

WHAT RESEARCH IS *194*

PRIMARY AND SECONDARY MATERIALS *195*

FROM SUBJECT TO THESIS *196*

FINDING THE MATERIAL *198*

The Card Catalog *198*
Three Notes on the Alphabetic Arrangement of the
    Card Catalog *200*
Scanning Books, Book Reviews, and
    Encyclopedias *201*
Finding Bibliographies *203*
Indexes to Periodicals *203*
Other Guides to Published Material *206*

TAKING BIBLIOGRAPHIC NOTES   *206*

READING AND TAKING NOTES   *207*

WRITING THE PAPER   *211*

SAMPLE RESEARCH PAPER   *213*

EXERCISES (Surviving in the Library)   *230*

A NOTE ON THE USE OF COMPUTERS IN RESEARCH AND WRITING   *231*

11 *Special Assignments*   *234*

WRITING AN EXPLICATION   *234*

WRITING A BOOK REVIEW   *236*

WRITING OTHER REVIEWS   *240*

TAKING ESSAY EXAMINATIONS   *243*

What Examinations Are   *243*
Writing Essay Answers   *244*
Questions on Literature   *245*
Questions on the Social Sciences   *247*
Questions on the Physical Sciences and Mathematics   *248*

PART TWO
Revising   *251*

12 *Revising for Conciseness*   *253*

INSTANT PROSE (ZONKERS)   *254*

How to Avoid Instant Prose   *256*

REVISING FOR CONCISENESS   *257*

Extra Words and Empty Words   *257*
Weak Intensifiers and Qualifiers   *259*
Circumlocutions   *259*
Wordy Beginnings   *260*
Empty Conclusions   *262*
Wordy Uses of the Verbs "To Be," "To Have," and "To Make"   *262*
Redundancy   *264*
Negative Constructions   *265*
Extra Sentences, Extra Clauses: Subordination   *266*

SOME CONCLUDING REMARKS   *269*

EXERCISE   *269*

13 *Revising for Clarity*   *272*

CLARITY   *272*

CLARITY AND EXACTNESS: USING THE RIGHT WORD   *275*

Denotation   *275*
Connotation   *276*
Quotation Marks as Apologies   *278*
Being Specific   *278*
Using Examples   *280*
Jargon and Technical Language   *281*
Clichés   *284*
Mixed Metaphors   *285*
Euphemisms   *286*
A Digression on Public Lying   *287*
Passive or Active Voice?   *289*
The Writer's "I"   *290*

CLARITY AND COHERENCE   *292*

Cats Are Dogs   *292*
False Series   *293*
Modifiers   *294*
Misplaced Modifiers   Squinting Modifiers   Dangling Modifiers

Reference of Pronouns *296*
Vague References   Shift in Pronouns   Ambiguous Reference of Pronouns

Agreement *298*
Noun and Pronoun   Subject and Verb

Repetition and Variation *300*
Euphony *301*
Transitions *302*

CLARITY AND SENTENCE STRUCTURE: PARALLELISM *302*

EXERCISES *305*

14 *Revising for Emphasis* *307*

EMPHASIS BY POSITION *308*

EMPHASIS BY BREVITY AND LENGTH: SHORT AND LONG SENTENCES *309*

EMPHASIS BY REPETITION *312*

EMPHASIS BY SUBORDINATION *313*

Five Kinds of Sentences *313*
Subordination *315*

EXERCISES *317*

PART THREE
Acquiring Style and Fluency *319*

15 *Defining Style* *321*

STYLE AND TONE *323*

STYLE AND LEVELS OF USAGE *325*

Finding the Appropriate Level *327*
Tone: Four Examples *329*

EXERCISES *331*

16 *Acquiring Style* *332*

CLARITY AND TEXTURE *332*

A REPERTORY OF STYLES *333*

ORIGINALITY AND IMITATION *334*

PRACTICE IN ACQUIRING STYLE *334*

Benjamin Franklin's Exercise *334*

EXERCISES *335*

Paraphrasing *335*

EXERCISE *337*

Imitating the Cumulative Sentence *337*

EXERCISE *338*

Transformations *339*

EXERCISE *339*

Finding Poems *340*

EXERCISES *341*

17 *Acquiring Fluency* *342*

KEEPING A JOURNAL *342*

**SOME JOURNAL ENTRIES BY PUBLISHED
WRITERS** *344*

The Pillow Book of Sei Shōnagon *346*

SOME JOURNAL ENTRIES BY STUDENTS *348*

PART FOUR
Editing *351*

18 *Manuscript Form* *353*

BASIC MANUSCRIPT FORM *353*

CORRECTIONS IN THE FINAL COPY *354*

QUOTATIONS AND QUOTATION MARKS *356*

ACKNOWLEDGING SOURCES *360*

Borrowing without Plagiarizing *360*
Fair Use of Common Knowledge *362*
"But How Else Can I Put It?" *362*

FOOTNOTES AND ENDNOTES *363*

Kinds of Notes *363*
Reducing the Number of Footnotes *364*
Footnote Numbers and Position *366*
Footnote Style *366*
*First Reference to a Book   First Reference to a Journal   First Reference
to a Newspaper   Subsequent References   References to Introductions
and to Reprinted Essays   Secondhand References   Footnoting
Interviews, Lectures, Letters*

BIBLIOGRAPHY *373*

**DOCUMENTATION IN FIELDS OTHER THAN
THE HUMANITIES** *376*

19 *Punctuation* *378*

**THREE COMMON ERRORS: FRAGMENTS,
COMMA SPLICES, AND RUN-ON
SENTENCES** *380*

Fragments and How to Correct Them *380*
**Comma Splices and Run-on Sentences, and How to
  Correct Them** *382*

THE PERIOD   *384*

THE COLON   *385*

THE SEMICOLON   *386*

THE COMMA   *388*

THE DASH   *394*

PARENTHESES   *395*

QUOTATION MARKS   *396*

ITALICS   *398*

CAPITAL LETTERS   *399*

THE HYPHEN   *400*

THE APOSTROPHE   *401*

ABBREVIATIONS   *403*

NUMBERS   *404*

EXERCISES   *405*

20 *Spelling*   *407*

21 *Usage*   *413*

A NOTE ON IDIOMS   *414*

GLOSSARY   *415*

LAST WORDS   *437*

Index   *443*

Barnet & Stubbs's
Practical Guide
to Writing

PART ONE
Writing

1

From Subject to Essay

STARTING

How to Write: Writing As a Physical Act

"One takes a piece of paper," William Carlos Williams wrote, "anything, the flat of a shingle, slate, cardboard and with anything handy to the purpose begins to put down the words after the desired expression in mind." Good advice, from a writer who produced novels, plays, articles, book reviews, an autobiography, a voluminous correspondence, and more than twenty-five books of poetry, while raising a family, enjoying a wide circle of friends, and practicing medicine in Rutherford, New Jersey. Not the last word on writing (we have approximately 85,000 of our own to add), but where we would like to begin: "One takes a piece of paper . . . and . . . begins to put down the words. . . ."

Writing is a physical act. It requires materials and energy. And like most physical acts, to be performed skillfully, to bring pleasure to both performer and audience, it requires practice. Talent helps. But few of us are born to become great writers, just as few of us are born to become great athletes. When Mark Spitz won seven gold medals in the 1972 Olympics, *Time* described him as having hands like a "pair of scoop-shovels . . . that can pull him cleanly through the water with scarcely a ripple," and noted his "curious ability to flex his lower legs slightly forward at the knees, which allows him to kick 6 to 12 inches deeper in the water than his opponents." Most of us are not born with the "curious ability" of the great writer or the great swimmer. But we can learn to write, as we can learn to swim, for all practical purposes, including pleasure.

In this book we offer some suggestions, definitions, rules, and examples to help you learn not simply to write, but to write well. We hope they will help you avoid some of the trials and errors — and the fear of drowning — of uninstructed practice. Our first suggestion is this: buy a notebook that you can carry with you (so you won't waste time looking for loose shingles) and write in it regularly. For suggestions about what to write, see "Keeping a Journal," pages 342–44.

Why Write? Writing As a Mental Activity

Born writers often describe their need to write as a compulsion, an inner drive to put their feelings and ideas into words. Despite that compulsion, or because of it, they also regularly complain that writing is hard work: "hard labor for life" was Joseph Conrad's summary of his own career. For the rest of us, perhaps, writing is easier because it is not our vocation; we demand less than perfection from ourselves. But it's still hard work, and we accept the occasional sentence to hard labor only if we have made some commitment or anticipate some reward. In real life (as opposed to school) people are regularly committed by their jobs and other interests to communicating their ideas in writing. Scientists and social scientists, to secure contracts, must put their proposals in writing, and then must report, again in writing, the results of their work to their sponsors and colleagues. Citizens and parents write their petitions and grievances to lawmakers and school boards; through prepared talks and newsletters, volunteers reach the communities they serve. Even television and tape have not diminished the importance of the written word. In short, anyone who is engaged with ideas or who wants to influence the course of events finds it necessary to put what Dr. Williams called "the desired expression in mind" into words.

As students, you may or may not make the connection between the assignment you are given today and the need you will have several years hence to put your ideas in writing. The rewards

— getting the contract, serving your community — are probably a bit distant to motivate you to write five hundred words on a possibly irrelevant topic this week. There is, though, a closer reward. "To be learning something new," said Aristotle, "is ever the chief pleasure of mankind." We believe that. We also believe that writing is not simply a way to express ideas, but a way to acquire them. To quote Aristotle again, "What is expressed is impressed."

We emphasize ideas because we are making some assumptions about you: that you are an adult, that you're acquiring an education, either in school or on your own, and that the writing skill you need most help with is the expression of ideas in clear expository essays. Most of our book will concentrate on that skill. We begin, then, with some ideas about ideas.

Some Ideas about Ideas

Would-be writers have one of two complaints: either "I have the ideas but I don't know how to express them," or "I have nothing to say." They are really the same complaint, known to both professional writers and novices as "writer's block." But let's treat them, to begin with, as if they were indeed separate.

STARTING TO WRITE BY WRITING

If you have the ideas but don't know how to express them, sit down and start writing. It is a universal law that given two tasks, one of which is writing, a person will prefer the other task. You must actively resist the temptation to procrastinate. Resist the temptation to sharpen another pencil, to make yourself a cup of tea, to call your mother. Now is *not* the time to do your laundry or make your bed. Start writing. It doesn't matter where you begin, only that you do begin. Sit down and start putting one word after another. One of the writers of this book finds it useful to start writing notes on three-by-five-inch file cards, then to arrange the cards, and from that arrangement to jot down a sort of outline. Not a formal outline, with capital and lowercase letters and roman and arabic numerals, but simply a list of key phrases in some reasonable order. If that way of starting helps you, fine, do it. It doesn't help me, and I'm writing this chapter.

Let's assume you either have an outline or you don't. Again, start writing. As you write, forget any rules you may have learned. In particular forget anything you've heard about opening paragraphs. If, after writing a sentence, a paragraph, a half page, you find yourself going in the wrong direction (not just a direction you hadn't anticipated — that's probably a good one — but toward a dead end), throw the page away. Take another sheet and start again. After a few false starts, your ideas, if you really have some, will begin to take visible form, and it's much easier to improve ideas once you see them in front of you than it is to do the job in your head.

You may realize, as you near the end of a sentence, that you no longer believe it. Never mind. Be glad that your first idea led you to a better one, pick up the better one and keep going with it. By now, you don't need to throw pages away. Take a pencil and cross out the unwanted sentence if it distracts you. Don't erase it; that takes too much time, and you may make something of that sentence later on if you have a record of it. Again, keep going.

At some point you will begin to see where the words already on paper promise to lead you. That's the point at which I would make a rough outline (and my colleague would be revising his). Now you begin to see which ideas must be developed and which discarded, where ideas must be clarified by specific details and examples and where connections between ideas must be made. When you get these thoughts into notes on paper — and you must write them down or you'll forget them — you are close to having a first draft. We'll have more to say in a while about first drafts and how to pull them into shape. But for the moment, you can go ahead and make your bed and, if you like, climb into it. Meanwhile we have something to say to those who think they have nothing to say.

ASKING QUESTIONS AND ANSWERING THEM

If you think you have nothing to say about a particular topic, ask yourself questions and answer them. You can often get a start by asking these questions:

> Who are my readers? (You can usually assume that you are writing for your classmates.)

What do they need to know?

What do I want them to believe?

These questions will at least help you to recognize some of the things you must say. We'll talk more about your readers later, on pages 15–17, but for the moment let's look at an example of how to go about asking other questions and answering them. First, read the following article from *The New York Times*. We have numbered the paragraphs to facilitate reference to them.

The Newark Public Library
Philip Roth[1]

1   What will the readers of Newark do if the City Council goes ahead with its money-saving plan to shut down the public library system on April 1? Will they loot the stacks as Newarkers looted furniture and appliance stores in the riot of 1967? Will police be called in to Mace down thieves racing off with the *Encyclopaedia Britannica*? Will scholars take up sniping positions at reference room windows and school children "seize" the main Washington Street building in order to complete their term papers? If the City Council locks up the books, will library card holders band together to "liberate" them?

2   I suppose one should hope not. Apparently there must be respect for Law and Order, even where there is none for aspiration and curiosity and quiet pleasure, for language, learning, scholarship, intelligence, reason, wit, beauty, and knowledge.

3   When I was growing up in Newark in the forties we assumed that the books in the public library belonged to the public. Since my family did not own many books, or have much money for a

---

[1] In February 1969, after riots had already destroyed much of Newark's black slum neighborhoods, the Newark City Council voted to strike from the city budget the $2.8 million required to finance the Newark Museum and the Newark Public Library. Hundreds of Newark residents vehemently opposed this move, which would have shut down two exceptional civic institutions. In the face of the protest, the Council eventually rescinded their decision. This article appeared on the editorial page of *The New York Times*, March 1, 1969, about two weeks after the Council had announced the budget cutback [Roth's note].

child to buy them, it was good to know that solely by virtue of my municipal citizenship I had access to any book I wanted from that grandly austere building downtown on Washington Street, or from the branch library I could walk to in my neighborhood. No less satisfying was the idea of communal ownership, property held in common for the common good. Why I had to care for the books I borrowed, return them unscarred and on time, was because they weren't mine alone, they were everybody's. That idea had as much to do with civilizing me as any I was ever to come upon in the books themselves.

If the idea of a *public* library was civilizing so was the place,   4 with its comforting quiet, its tidy shelves, its knowledgeable, dutiful employees who weren't teachers. The library wasn't simply where one had to go to get the books, it was a kind of exacting haven to which a city youngster willingly went for his lesson in restraint and his training in self-control. And then there was the lesson in order, the enormous institution itself serving as instructor. What trust it inspired — in both oneself and in systems — first to decode the catalogue card, then to make it through the corridors and stairwells into the open stacks, and there to discover, exactly where it was supposed to be, the desired book. For a ten-year-old to find he actually can steer himself through tens of thousands of volumes to the very one he wants is not without its satisfactions. Nor did it count for nothing to carry a library card in one's pocket; to pay a fine if need be; to sit in a strange place, beyond the reach of parent and school, and read whatever one chose, in anonymity and peace; finally, to carry home across the city and even into bed at night a book with a local lineage of its own, a family-tree of Newark readers to which one's name had now been added.

In the forties, when Newark was mostly white and I was being   5 raised there, it was simply an unassailable fact of life that the books were "ours" and that the public library had much to teach us about the rules of civilized life, as well as civilized pleasures to offer. It is strange, to put it politely, that now when Newark is mostly black, the City Council (for fiscal reasons, we are told) has reached a decision that suggests that the books don't really belong to the public after all, and that the lessons and pleasures a library provides for the young are no longer essential to an education. In a city seething with social grievances there is, in fact, probably little that could be *more* essential to the development and sanity of the thoughtful and ambitious young than access to those libraries and books. For the moment the Newark City Council may, to be sure, have solved a fiscal problem; it is too bad, however, that they are unable to calculate the frustration, cynicism, and rage that such an insult must inevitably generate, or to imagine what shutting down the libraries may cost the community in the end.

Now answer the following questions.

1. a. What was the occasion for this article? (one sentence)
   b. Summarize Roth's response. (one sentence)
2. a. *How* does he support his position in paragraph 3? Describe his strategy. (one sentence)
   b. What are the two main reasons he gives in paragraph 3 in support of his position? (one or two sentences)
3. Explain what he means by "civilizing" in paragraphs 3 and 4. (two to four sentences)
4. In paragraph 5, what new reasons does he state or imply in support of his position? (two to four sentences)
5. Describe and explain his strategy in paragraph 1 and paragraph 2. (one short paragraph)
6. Optional: Evaluate Philip Roth's article.

If you were now to take your answers and revise them a bit, you'd have an essay something like the student's essay that follows.

On Philip Roth's
"The Newark Public Library"

The City Council of Newark introduced a plan to shut down the public library system in order to save money. (1a) Philip Roth, in his article (The New York Times, March 1, 1969), argues that the closing of the libraries will be a costly mistake, and that the action will be an insult to the citizens of Newark. (1b)

He supports his position by telling how the library helped him when he was young. (2a) He says that the public library gave him a chance to use books that his family couldn't afford, but more important, the very idea of a public library, of the communal ownership of books, played a part in civilizing him. (2b) By civilizing Roth means socializing. The quiet and orderly fashion in which the library was arranged and run taught him restraint, and taught him to value solitude, privacy, and self-control. Looking for books was itself a lesson in order; he learned, for example, that he could find, through the card catalog, one book among the many thousands there. (3)

Roth suggests that since Newark has become predominantly black, the City Council's attitude toward the library's functions and importance has changed. He implies that the Council's plan is irresponsible and discriminatory. He points out that in a city with as many social problems as Newark's, the lessons and plea-sures given to the young by the library are more, not less, essen-tial to their education. He says that although the Council's move may solve an immediate fiscal problem, it will in the end create greater social problems because of the frustration and rage it will generate. (4)

He questions what the readers might do if the library is shut down. He hypothesizes that they might riot and loot the library, or that they might seize the library and liberate the books. His questions are, of course, ironic. By overdramatizing the possible reactions, he gains the interest of the reader, and he shows the senselessness of the Council's plan. Through sarcasm, he dis-closes a further irony: the City Council, whose members are the first to insist on respect for law and order, have no respect themselves for communal as opposed to private property, or for the civilized qualities law and order should foster and support: beauty, knowledge, pleasure, aspiration. (5)

Organizing Ideas

Notice that in the preceding exercise we arranged the ques-tions so that the essay composed of answers to them would be clear and effectively organized. In the essay we chose as an example, the student's first paragraph provides the information a reader who has not read Roth's article will need. It briefly summarizes both the circumstances that provoked Roth's article and the gist of his argument. (It also tells where the article appeared.) The body of the student's essay explains and analyzes the means Roth employs to persuade his readers: first, his use of his own experience growing up in Newark; second, his analysis of Newark's current political and social climate; and finally, his use of irony. Although irony appears in several places in Roth's article, it is especially rich and interesting to analyze in his first two paragraphs. The student's essay, therefore, saves its comment on Roth's opening paragraphs for its concluding paragraph. The essay builds from the beginning to what is most interesting to think about. (But remember, we invented and arranged the questions!)

When, in looking for something to say, *you* ask *yourself* questions, some questions will come to mind at once. They'll pop into your head while you read or while you reflect about an experience, and you'll wisely write them down before you forget them. But if you get stuck, think of the four categories into which our specific questions on Roth's article fall, and see if these generate specific questions about your topic. Here are the four categories of questions and methods of answering them.

1. What happened? — Summarize or narrate
2. What does the happening mean? Or, what do the words mean? — Interpret or paraphrase
3. What is it? How does it work? How does it yield meaning? — Define or analyze
4. How good is it? What makes it good? Or, what makes it bad? — Evaluate

To generate ideas, then, if you have a topic but nothing to say about it, ask yourself questions and answer them. You may write your questions down in whatever order they occur to you, but when you write your essay rearrange your answers with your reader in mind. Your arrangement should be clear: it should make sense to someone who isn't inside your head. And it should be emphatic: it should build to a climax, ending with what you found to be the most interesting questions to answer.

Note that arranging answers to questions in clear and emphatic order is equivalent to arranging note cards, or to writing an outline after the shape of your ideas has become visible to you. So, whether you see your problem as having ideas but not knowing how to express them or as not having any ideas to express, the solution may be either to start writing or to ask yourself questions and answer them. Either way you'll end up with at least a first draft of an essay.

FOCUSING

What to Write About:
Subject, Topic, Thesis

If you're taking a course in composition you will probably receive assignments to write on something you are reading or on something out of your personal experience, which may include your experience of books. In other courses it's usually up to you to choose a *subject* from those covered in the course, to focus on a a *topic* within the subject, and to narrow the topic by adopting a specific *thesis*. Any assignment requires you to narrow the subject so that you can treat it thoroughly in the allotted space and time. Therefore you write not on *Time* magazine, but on a comparison of *Time* and *Newsweek*, based on one or two issues of each, arguing for the superiority of one over the other; not on political primaries (a subject), but on a specific proposal to abolish them (a topic); not on penguins (a subject), but on the male penguin's role in hatching (a topic). A good general rule in finding a topic is to follow your inclinations: focus on something about the subject that interests you.

Suppose you're in a composition course and the class has been assigned to read the Book of Ruth in the Old Testament and to write an essay of 500–1000 words on it. If you start with a topic like "The Book of Ruth, A Charming Idyll" you're in trouble. The topic is much too vague. In writing about it you'll find yourself hopping around from one place in the book to another, and in desperation saying insincere things like "The Book of Ruth is probably one of the most charming idylls in all literature," when you haven't read all literature, have precious little idea of what *idyll* means, and couldn't define *charm* precisely if your life depended on it.

What to do? Focus on something that interested you about the book. (If you read the book with pencil in hand, taking some notes, underlining some passages, putting question marks at others, you'll have some good clues to start with.) The book is named after Ruth, but perhaps you find Naomi the more interesting character. If so, you might say: "Although the Book of Ruth is named after Ruth, I find the character of Naomi more interesting."

Stuck again? Ask yourself questions. Why do you find her more interesting? To answer that question, reread the book, focusing your attention on all the passages in which Naomi acts or speaks or is spoken of by others. Ruth's actions, you may find, are always clearly motivated by her love for Naomi. But Naomi's actions are more complex, more puzzling. If you're puzzled, trust your feeling — *there is something puzzling there*. What motivated Naomi? Convert your question to "Naomi's Motivation" and you have a topic. If you explore Naomi's actions one by one you may conclude that "Although Naomi shows in many of her actions her concern for her daughter-in-law, her actions also reveal self-interest." Now you have a *thesis*, that is, a brief statement of your main point. It's a bit awkwardly worded, but you can work on a smoother, more natural expression later. Now you have other things to do: you must select, clarify, and arrange evidence to support your thesis.

"Naomi's Motivation" is a topic in literary criticism. If you have not been specifically assigned a literary analysis and if you would prefer not to do one, focus on something that interests you more and that you know something about. If your special interest is, for example, economics, or sociology, or law, your topic might be one of these:

> Economic Motivation in the Book of Ruth
> Attitudes toward Intermarriage in the Book of Ruth
> The Status of Women in the Book of Ruth

Any one of these topics can be managed in 500–1000 words. But remember, you were assigned to write on the Book of Ruth.

Formulate a thesis and support it with evidence from that book. Suppress the impulse to put everything you know about economics or intermarriage or the-status-of-women-through-the-ages in between two thin slices, an opening sentence and a concluding sentence, on the Book of Ruth.

Let's take an example of a writing assignment outside of a composition course. Suppose that in a course on Modern Revolutionary Movements you're assigned a term paper on any subject covered by the readings or lectures. A term paper is usually about three thousand words and requires research. You're interested in Mexican history, and after a preliminary search you decide to focus on the Revolution of 1910 or some events leading up to it. Depending on what is available in your library, you might narrow your topic to one of these:

> Mexican Bandits — The First Twentieth-Century Revolutionaries
>
> The Exploits of Joaquin Murieta and Tiburcio Vasquez — Romantic Legend and Fact

(See pages 196–98, on narrowing a topic in research.)
In short, it is not enough to have a subject (the Book of Ruth, revolutions); you must concentrate your vision on a topic, a significant part of the field, just as a landscape painter or photographer selects a portion of the landscape and then focuses on it. Your interests are your most trustworthy guides to which part of the landscape to focus on.

Once you think you know what your topic is, ask yourself questions. We have already suggested that perhaps the first questions are about your audience: Who are my readers? What do they need to know? What do I want them to believe? When you can answer the third question, and have *put your answer in writing*, you have a thesis; for your first draft, at least, you may have a thesis sentence:

> Although we cannot help but admire Ruth, it is Naomi's more complex character that really interests us.
>
> The romantic legends surrounding Murieta and Vasquez have obscured the political significance of their lives and deeds.

THE WRITER AS TEACHER: IMAGINING AN AUDIENCE

Sharing experiences. It will help you to focus on a manageable topic and to develop it thoroughly if you keep in mind that, although you are writing because of an assignment from a teacher, *when you write you are the teacher.* It's your job to clarify your responses to what you have read or otherwise experienced and to share them with another person who is not you and who has something to learn from you. Writing an essay, then, requires that you look not only outside of you and in front of you, but also within you. You not only explore the text or the topic you're writing about, you also explore your responses to it and make them accessible to others.

Imagining your readers. Who are these others for whom the writer writes? Mostly, they are imagined. We might suppose, for example, that Philip Roth in writing about the Newark Public Library (pages 7–9) had in mind the readers of *The New York Times.* But surely he did not think of each reader individually; that would have been impossible. At first, he probably did not think of them consciously at all. Perhaps it occurred to him only late in the game that *The New York Times* might be a good place to submit the piece he was working on. When he began writing he was probably doing something like talking to himself, asking himself questions (in the peculiar shorthand of reverie). Why did he feel so angry about the plan to close the library? Why did it strike him as a personal insult and a threat? Conceivably, he then thought of others like himself, who had benefited from the library without ever before having given the specific benefits much conscious thought. Surely those others would understand, or *should* understand, why the Council's plan was irresponsible, and why it ought to be opposed.

We're only guessing at Roth's mental processes, of course, but we think it a fair guess that, as his essay began to take shape, Roth had no individual readers in mind, but an imagined ideal reader. This imagined reader, being in some ways like Roth, would be interested in what Roth had to say, but would not know exactly how Roth felt, and would not necessarily share his convictions. The imagined reader might not even know some of the facts that were so evident to Roth. Even a reader from Newark might not know, for example, that the Newark City Council planned to save money by shutting down the public library. Thus, to acquaint readers with the facts, Roth, in the article as it finally appeared, does not merely refer to the Council's "plan"; rather, in his first sentence, he cues the reader in by referring to the Council's "money-saving plan to shut down the public library system on April 1."

What we have just attempted to describe is the writer's normal situation. Writers usually write not for themselves but for partly imagined others. *Partly* imagined because the audience is usually in some ways already defined. Film reviewers write for an audience of moviegoers who have not yet seen the new film under review; medical social workers write for the hospital staff who will consult their reports, though they don't think of (or even know) each member of the staff individually. The writers of this book, because we talk to students daily and were once students ourselves, have a general sense of what the readers of this book already know about writing, and what they want to know or need to know more about.

One of the things we know is that *student writers are not in the writer's normal situation.* They face the problem of imagining their readers in a most perplexing form, and we therefore recommend that they face the problem consciously. Who is your reader? The obvious answer — the teacher who assigned you the essay — is, paradoxically, often the least helpful. To learn to write well, you'll have to force that fact out of your mind, pretend it isn't true, or you're likely to feel defeated from the beginning. Write instead for someone who understands your material less well than you. Remember: *when you write you are the teacher.* It's probably easier to assume the role of the teacher if you imagine your reader to be someone in your class, that is, someone intelligent and reasonably well informed who shares some of your interests but who does not happen to be you, and who therefore can't know your thoughts unless you organize them and explain them clearly and thoroughly.

We'll discuss some specific patterns of organization in later chapters, but if you remember that when you write you are teaching, you'll organize your essay so that it will be clear, and you'll present your ideas at a pace that sustains your reader's interest. It's not enough to present your ideas as they happened to occur to you; your reader should profit from the trials and errors of your early drafts, not labor through them.

CLARIFYING IDEAS

On page 6 we wrote "Now you begin to see . . . where ideas must be clarified by specific details and examples." You'll find more discussion of this point on pages 70–74 (about topic ideas) and pages 272–75 (on revising sentences). Here we consider two directions in which the mind of the essayist frequently moves as he expresses and clarifies his ideas.

There must, on the one hand, be ideas or, let us say, generalizations. (Example: "Except for human beings, animals rarely seek to do serious harm to members of their own species.") On the other hand, there must be specific details that support and enliven these generalizations. (Example: "When male rattlesnakes fight among themselves they strike with their heads but they do not bite, and when giraffes fight among themselves they butt but they do not use their hooves, as they do against other attackers.") In a moment we will discuss how to give the reader both generalizations and specific details, but first let us define some terms.

General and Specific Writing

A general word refers to a class or group; a specific (or particular) word refers to a member of the class or group. For example, *vehicle* is general compared with *automobile* or with *motorcycle*. But "general" and "specific" are relative. *Vehicle* is general when compared to *automobile*, but specific when compared to *machine*, for *machine* refers to a class or group that includes not only vehicles but clocks, typewriters, and dynamos. Similarly, although *automobile* is specific in comparison with *vehicle*, it is general in comparison with *Volkswagen* or *sportscar*. Since the aim of writing is to help a reader to see things your way, try to be as specific or as particular as is reasonable. We say "as is reasonable" because your job is not to describe everything in microscopic detail; it may, for example, be entirely reasonable to say "he smoked a pack of cigarettes a day," and not to specify the kind of cigarette. In fact, to specify the kind of cigarette might only get in the way — readers will wonder, why are we being told that he smoked Camels? Again, keep your reader in mind.

Most good writing offers a judicious mixture of the general and the specific. A page of highly general writing may seem to have nothing to get hold of; a page of nothing but specific details may seem a kleptomaniac's trunkful of bric-a-brac. To keep your reader's attention, try to enliven your generalizations with specific examples, and try to unify your details with occasional generalizations. Since students tend to write too generally rather than too specifically, it is good to keep in mind Nietzsche's assertion that the more general the truth you want to teach, the more you must "seduce the senses to accept it." Or, as the Zen saying puts it, "Better to see the face than to hear the name."

Suppose, for example, a writer offered us the following paragraph:

> Certain biological changes which occur as we grow older are apparent whenever you look at an old person. These age changes in the surface of the body are gradual, and vary according to diet, genetic factors, even climate. Like all other aspects of aging, it is not the biological changes themselves (because they are quite natural) but the subsequent changes in self-regard which have the most impact on the individual.

It makes sense, we get the gist of it, and it is even moderately interesting; but could we read many pages of such writing? We hear about "biological changes," but we do not see them in this paragraph.

Now look at what the author really wrote — the previous sentences, but also others rich with details. Notice how the details clarify and add interest to the generalizations. The words we omitted in the previous version we restore in italic.

> Certain biological changes which occur as we grow older are apparent whenever you look at an old person. *The hair becomes thin, brittle, dull, and gray. The skin becomes paler and may become blotchy; it takes on a parchmentlike texture and loses its elasticity. The loss of subcutaneous fat and elastic tissue leads to a wrinkled appearance. Sweat gland activity and oil secretion decrease and the skin may look dry and scaly.*

These age changes in the surface of the body are gradual, and vary according to diet, genetic factors, even climate. Like all other aspects of aging, it is not the biological changes themselves (because they are, after all, quite natural) but the subsequent changes in self-regard which have the most impact on the individual. *Gray hair can be softening and becoming to a woman; and look quite distinguished on a man. Yet the individual may resent the change, and regard gray hair as the external sign of all the internal effects — slowness, muscular weakness, waning sexual powers.*

— Sharon R. Curtin

The generalizations in the first version made all of the points — but how weakly, without the specific details that clarify and enliven them.

Let's look at two essays, each written by a student during the first week of the semester in a composition course. The students were invited to write about something out of their own experience, something they knew or understood well that they could describe or explain to others who were unfamiliar with it. Perhaps you are familiar with such an assignment. You try to think of something interesting you've done, but you've led a most unremarkable life. Your classmates, all strangers, seem to know more than you do about almost everything. They've all been to Europe — well, most of them. All you did last summer was file cards and run errands in an office full of boring people. Here is the first student's essay, on, as it happens, a boring job.

A Lesson

As I look back at it, my first thought is that my job was a waste of time. It consisted of compiling information from the files of the Water and Assessor's Department in a form suitable for putting on the city's computer. Supposedly this would bring the water billing and property taxing to an efficient level. If the job sounds interesting, don't be deceived. After the first week of work, I seriously doubted that I would survive through the summer.

> But I was able to salvage a lesson in the self—discipline of coping with people. Of course we all know how to succeed with friends, family, acquaintances, and employers. But try it in a situation where you have a distinct disadvantage, where you are the seller and they are the customers. And remember, the customer is always right.
>
> By observing the situation, though I was not a participant, I learned that patience, kindness, and understanding can remove the difficulties you cross at the time.

Not a bad topic, really. One can learn something valuable from a boring, menial, frustrating job. Or if not, one can examine boredom (what exactly is it? is it the same as impatience? how does it come about? how does it feel?) and write about it without boring the reader. But this essay doesn't teach us anything about boredom. It doesn't allow us through concrete, specific details to feel with the writer that we too would have doubted we could survive the summer. Instead, it offers generalizations such as "compiling information from the files" and "form suitable for putting on the city's computer," which give us no sense of the tedium of daily transferring numbers from five hundred manila index cards to five hundred gray index cards. In fact, the essay gives us almost no sense of the job. The second paragraph ends "the customer is always right," but nothing in the essay suggests that the writer (whose work "consisted of compiling information from the files") had any contact with customers. We really don't know what she did. Nor does the essay present any evidence that the experience was redeemed by a lesson in "patience, kindness, and understanding."

As it turns out, there was no such lesson. In class discussion, the student frankly admitted that the job *was* a waste of time. She had, out of habit, tried to come up with some pious thought to please the instructor. The habit had short-circuited the connection between the student's feelings and the words she was writing. The class discussion led to some genuinely interesting questions. Why, for example, are we reluctant to admit that something we've done was a waste of time? "The job was a waste of time" would have been, for most of us, a more productive thesis than "I was able to salvage a lesson." What experiences lead to the conclusions: I must write what the instructor expects; the instructor expects a pious thought? (We'd like to hear from a student willing to explore that topic in 500–1000 words.)

The class discussion, as we said, revealed the student's real attitude toward her job. It provided a focus which then allowed us to formulate what would have been a more productive thesis for an essay. It's helpful to think of such discussions as dramatizations, or imitations, of the writer's solitary work in the early stages of writing, as she gropes for what she really has to say on a subject. For although it would be tidy if writers could simply, and in the following order, (1) choose a subject, (2) focus on a topic, (3) formulate a thesis, (4) write the essay, things don't often work out that way. More commonly, writers discover their topics and formulate their theses in the act of writing and revising, in asking questions and in answering them, in discarding the answers, or even the questions, and starting again.

Now look at the second essay, again on a common experience. Ask yourself as you read it, or reread it, what makes it uncommonly interesting.

Dedication Doth Not a Good Teacher Make

The worst teacher I ever had was a brilliant and charming man. Fergy (it was short for Mr. Ferguson) had written the textbook we used for Chemistry. He had designed his house and built it himself, getting professional help only for the electricity and plumbing. He could remember the scores of all the football games he'd seen, and the names of the players on each team. He never kept lists—"Lists rot the memory," he said—so he memorized which type of lab implement he kept in which of fifty drawers, and he could tell you instantly, without pause. Sometimes we would ask him where a certain type of obscure bottle could be found just to test him, but he never failed. "Middle left-hand drawer in Lab Station Six," would say old Fergy, and in that middle left-hand drawer it would be. I never knew him to forget a name, a face, or a formula, either.

That, I think, was his failing as a teacher. Because he had no trouble grasping or recalling a concept, he had trouble in understanding how we could. The one thing his extraordinary mind seemed unable to comprehend was that it was extraordinary, that not everyone could think as completely and as easily as he. If the class had questions he would try to answer them, but he tended to complicate and expand on ideas, rather than to simplify them. He could not believe that we needed not expansion but explanation, with the result that we soon learned not to ask too many questions for fear of extra material to learn. And it did become a fear of learning, because, try as we would, we somehow never managed to pin down concepts like electron shells and the wave theory of gravitation, but we would still have to answer for them on tests—and, ultimately, at home. (I never decided which was worse, knowing that once again I had made a complete fool of myself by taking a chem test, or having to listen to my parents sigh and claim that I could have done better if I'd tried.)

Fergy would have been horrified to know that he had this discouraging effect on us. He loved us and he loved teaching and he loved chemistry. He was always available for outside help, not only for chemistry, but for any problem, whether in English or your social life. He tried to make class interesting by telling little anecdotes and playing with the chemicals. Actually, he was funny, and interesting, and charming, and he kept us hoping that we'd understand chem so that he would approve of us and so we could relax and enjoy him. But although he is one of the best

```
people it has been my good fortune to have known, he never did

manage to teach me a lick of chemistry.
```

As you study this book, you'll frequently find questions following examples of writing. Skills in reading and writing are closely intertwined. If you practice asking and answering questions as you read, as well as when you write, the skills you develop will reinforce each other. Try answering the following questions on "Dedication Doth Not a Good Teacher Make":

What is the writer's thesis?
How does she support the thesis?
If you found the essay interesting, what makes it interesting?
If you found it convincing, what makes it convincing?

THE GROUCHO MARX COMPLEX

Clearly — examining these essays should make it clear — there is no such thing as an uninteresting life, or moment in life. There are only uninteresting ways to talk about them. It's also clear that some people are more interested in introspection and in talking and writing about their personal experiences than others. The others may be suffering from the Groucho Marx Complex: as Groucho put it, "I don't want to belong to any club that would have me as a member." Students who freeze at the notion of writing about themselves often feel that everything they have done is so ordinary, no one else could possibly be interested in it; anything they know is so obvious, everyone else must know it already. If this is your problem, remember that no one else knows exactly what you know; no one else can know what it feels like to live inside your skin. If you work at summoning up from your memory concrete and specific details, and incorporate them in your writing, you can turn the most ordinary experience into a first-rate essay.

Remember too that writing from your own experience does not necessarily mean writing about private experience. We all have areas of experience we'd rather keep private, and have a right to remain private about. The important thing in writing about experience is, as Marianne Moore said, that "we must be as clear as our natural reticence allows us to be." Think, then, of experiences that you are willing to share and to be clear about. If, for example, you have just learned in a psychology course what "operant conditioning" means, define it for someone unfamiliar with the term. You might find yourself narrating an experience of your own to exemplify it; to be clear, you will have to provide an example. Or if an object in a local museum or craft exhibit or store interests you, ask yourself questions — why do I like it? — and you'll probably be able to turn an object into an experience. You'll also be turning an experience into an object — an essay — that will interest your readers.

AN OVERVIEW:
FROM SUBJECT TO ESSAY

We each must work out our own procedures and rituals (John C. Calhoun liked to plough his farm before writing); but the following suggestions may help. The rest of this book will give you more detailed advice.

1. *If a topic is assigned, write on it; if a topic is not assigned, turn a subject into a topic.* Get an early start. The day the assignment is given — or the next day — try to settle on a topic that excites or at least interests you and that you can discuss sensibly in the assigned length. Unfortunately, almost none of us can in a few pages write anything of interest on a large subject. We simply cannot in five hundred words say anything readable (that is, true and interesting to others) on subjects as broad as music, sports, ourselves. Given such subjects, we have nothing to say, probably because we are desperately trying to remember what we have heard other people say. Trying to remember blocks our efforts to look hard and to think. To get going, we must narrow such subjects down to specific topics: from music to country music, from sports to commercialization of athletics, from ourselves to a term with a roommate.

2. *Get a focus.* Once you have turned a subject into a topic, you need to shape the topic by seeing it in a particular focus, by

having a thesis, an attitude, a point: Country music is popular because . . .; College athletes are exploited . . .; How I came to know that I want a single room. Probably you won't find your exact focus or thesis immediately, but you will be able to jot down a few things, including some questions to yourself, that come to mind on the topic you have carved out of the broad subject. For example: Why is country music popular? What kind of people like it? Why are some performers more successful than others? If you ask yourself questions now, you'll probably be able to answer them a day or two later. It doesn't matter whether you make each jotting on a separate card or group them on a sheet of paper as a list or in a few roughly sketched paragraphs; the important thing is to write something, perhaps a few generalizations, perhaps a few striking details, perhaps some of each. You'll probably find that jotting an idea down leads to something else — something you probably would not have thought of if you hadn't jotted down the first thing. Few of us have good ideas about anything at the start, but as we put our ideas into words we find better ideas coming to mind.

3. *Turn your reveries into notes.* Put your jottings aside for a day or two (assuming you have a week to do the essay), but be prepared to add to them at any moment. Useful thoughts — not only general ideas, but details — may come to you while you are at lunch, while you read a newspaper or magazine, while your mind wanders in class. Write down these thoughts: do not assume that you will remember them when you come to draft your essay.

4. *Sort things out.* About two days before the essay is due, look over your jottings (you ought to have at least a dozen phrases by now) and sharpen your thesis, rejecting what is not relevant. Arrange the surviving half-dozen or so jottings into what looks like a reasonable sequence. Perhaps now is the time to give your essay a provisional title. A title will help you to keep your thesis in focus. Don't be afraid to be obvious. If you look back at some of the titles of sections in this book, you will see such things as "Why Write?," "Starting to Write by Writing," and "Clarifying Ideas." Such titles help the writer to keep to the point, while letting readers know what the topic will be. (Leave uninformative titles to the Marx Brothers: *Duck Soup, Horse Feathers.*) Sometimes word-play produces an attractive but still informative title, for

example a student's "If You Have *Time,* Read *Newsweek.*" In any case, whether or not you choose a title at this point, you should now have a focus. Next, look again at your jottings and add what comes to mind. Keep asking yourself questions, and try to jot down the answers. Draw arrows to indicate the sequence you think the phrases should be in.

5. *Write.* Even if you are not sure that you have a thesis and an organization, start writing. Don't delay; you have some jottings, and you have a mind that, however casually, has already been thinking. Don't worry about writing an effective opening paragraph (your opening paragraph will almost surely have to be revised later anyway); just try to state and develop your argument, based on the phrases or sentences you have accumulated, adding all of the new details that flow to mind as you write. If you are stuck, ask yourself questions. Have I supported my assertions with examples? Will a comparison help to clarify the point? Write on one side of the page only, leave lots of space between the lines, and leave wide margins; later you'll fill these spaces in with additional details, additional generalizations, and revisions of sentences. Keep going until you have nothing left to say.

6. *Save what you can.* Immediately after writing the draft, or a few hours later, look it over to see how much you can salvage. Don't worry about getting the exact word here or there; just see whether or not you have a thesis, whether or not you keep the thesis in view, and whether or not the points flow reasonably. Delete irrelevant paragraphs, however interesting; shift paragraphs that are relevant but that should be somewhere else. You can do this best by scissoring the sheets and gluing the pieces onto another paper in the right order. Don't assume that tomorrow you will be able to remember that the paragraph near the bottom of page 3 will go into the middle of page 2. Scissor and glue it now, so that when you next read the essay you will easily be able to tell whether in fact the paragraph does belong in the middle of page 2. Finally, settle on a title. Probably you can't do much more with your manuscript at this moment. Put it aside until tomorrow.

7. *Revise.* Reread your draft, first with an eye toward large matters. Revise your opening paragraph or write one to provide the reader with a focus; make sure each paragraph grows out of the previous one, and make sure you keep the thesis in view. Remember, when you write, you are the teacher. As you revise,

try to imagine that you are the reader, and let this imagined reader tell you where you get off the point, where you are illogical, where you are in any way confusing. Next, after making the necessary large revisions, read the draft with an eye toward smaller matters: make sure that each sentence is clear and readable, and that the necessary details and generalizations are there. (You can do this only by reading slowly — preferably aloud, unless you have developed the ability to hear each sentence, each word, in the mind's ear.) Cross out extra words; recast unclear sentences. Keep pushing the words, the sentences, the paragraphs into shape until they say what you want them to say from the title onward. (This contest between writers and their words is part of what Muhammad Ali had in mind when he said, referring to his work on his autobiography, "Writing is fighting.") Correct anything that disturbs you — for instance, awkward repetitions that grate, inflated utterances that bore.

8. *Edit.* When your draft is as good as you can make it, take care of the mechanical matters: if you are unsure of the spelling of a word, check it in a dictionary; if you are unsure about a matter of punctuation, check it in this book. You will also find footnote form and manuscript form (for example, where to put the title, what margins to leave) in this book in the section on editing. And be sure to acknowledge the source not only of quotations but also of any ideas that you borrowed, even though you summarized or paraphrased them in your own words. (On plagiarism, see pages 360–63.)

9. *Prepare the final copy.* Now write or type the final copy; if you are on schedule, you will be doing this a day before the essay is due. After writing or typing it, you will probably want to proofread it; there is no harm in doing so, but even if you do so now you will have to proofread it again later because at the moment you are too close to your essay. If you put the essay aside for a few hours and then reread it, you will be more likely to catch omitted words, transposed letters, inconsistent spelling of names, and so forth. Change these neatly (see pages 354–55).

10. *Hand the essay in on time.*

In short, the whole business of moving from a subject to a finished essay on a focused topic adds up to Mrs. Beeton's famous recipe: "First catch your hare, then cook it."

EXERCISES

1. Summarize, analyze, and evaluate a current or recent editorial. Include a copy of the editorial with your essay, but write for a reader who does not have access to the editorial. Suggested length: 350 words.

2. Explain something clearly — a process, a concept, a place, an experience — that you know well but that others in your class may not know about or may understand less well than you. Suggested length: 500 words.

3. The following passages are bloodless. Revise them into something with life:

   a. Women are not officially allowed to engage in contact sports, with a few exceptions. Probably this practice reflects our cultural principle of protecting women. But possibly, too, it reflects physical differences between men and women.

   b. What bothers students about nontraditional methods of grading is a concern about their chances of being accepted at the next level of education.

   c. The city has plenty of sights to offer, but greenery is rarely among them. Yet many people have a need for some contact with nature, and of the various ways of satisfying this need one of the cheapest and easiest is growing houseplants.

4. In reading the following passages note which sentences or phrases move toward the general, and which toward the specific.

   a. The really fascinating thing about baby talk is the universality of its linguistic form and content, as demonstrated by a comparison of the way it is spoken in six quite different languages: American English, Spanish, Syrian Arabic, Marathi of India, Gilyak of Siberia, and Comanche Indian of North America. The actual baby-talk vocabularies in the six languages are of course different; nevertheless, the words reveal surprising similarities in linguistic characteristics. All six languages simplify clusters of consonants (as English speakers do when they substitute *tummy* for *stomach*); they reduplicate syllables (*choo-choo*); they alter words in consistent ways to form diminutives (such as the *y* in *doggy*); they eliminate pronouns (*daddy wants* instead of *I want*); and most of the languages drop unstressed syllables (as when *good-bye* becomes *bye* or *bye-bye*). The existence of such similarities in widely different languages suggests that adults with no knowledge of one another's tongues have arrived at much the same linguistic formulas.

— Peter Farb

b. I never really liked the doctrine of Indulgences — the notion that you could say five Hail Marys and knock off a year in Purgatory.

— Mary McCarthy

c. A man is in general better pleased when he has a good dinner upon his table than when his wife talks Greek.

— Samuel Johnson

d. If you saw a bullet hit a bird, and he told you he wasn't shot, you might weep at his courtesy, but you would certainly doubt his word.

— Emily Dickinson

e. Actions speak louder than words.

f. What a country calls its vital economic interests are not the things which enable its citizens to live, but the things which enable it to make war. Gasoline is much more likely than wheat to be a cause of international conflict.

— Simone Weil

g. There is no such thing as a free lunch.

2
Analysis

All there is to writing is having ideas. To learn to write is to learn to have ideas.

— ROBERT FROST

SORTING AND THINKING

Look at this drawing by Pieter Brueghel the Elder, entitled "The Painter and the Connoisseur" (about 1565), and then read the paragraph below.

The painter, standing in front of the connoisseur and given more than two-thirds of the space, dominates this picture. His hand holds the brush with which he creates, while the connoisseur's hand awkwardly fumbles for money in his purse. The connoisseur apparently is pleased with the picture he is looking at, for he is buying it, but his parted lips give him a stupid expression and his eyeglasses imply defective vision. In contrast, the painter looks away from the picture and fixes his eyes on the model (reality) or, more likely, on empty space, his determined expression suggesting that he possesses an imaginative vision beyond his painting and perhaps even beyond earthly reality.

This paragraph is a concise piece of analysis. It doesn't simply tell us that the picture shows two people close together; it separates the parts of the picture, pointing out that the two figures form a contrast. It explains why one figure gets much more space than the other, and says what the contrasting gestures and facial expressions imply. The writer of the caption has "read" the picture by seeing how the parts relate to the whole.

One sometimes hears people say that they don't want to analyze works of art because analysis smashes the works. But a great work can take analysis, and, curiously, it often gets better as one analyzes it. That is, we find that the more we understand a work — the more we see about its construction — the more we like it. But of course the analysis has to be made intelligently; the parts have to be seen for what they are. An architect can analyze the components of a building, seeing the functions of beams, arches, buttresses, and balconies; but a wrecker's ball doesn't analyze a building, it just smashes it into random hunks.

Most of the material that you read in courses, except in literature courses, is chiefly analytic: you read of the various causes of a revolution, of the effects of inflation, or of the relative importance of heredity and environment. Similarly, most of your writing in college will be chiefly analytic: you analyze the characters in a play, the causes and effects of poverty, the strengths and weaknesses of some proposed legislation.

But analysis (literally a separating into parts) is not only a kind of writing, it is a way of thinking, a way of arriving at conclusions (generalizations), or of discovering how conclusions were arrived at. It is, at its simplest, an adult version of sorting out cards with pictures of baseball players on them. Now, if you have identical items — for instance, one hundred bricks to unload from a truck — you can't sort them; you can only divide them for easier handling into groups of, say, ten, or into armloads. But if the items vary in some way you can sort them out. You can, for example, put socks into one drawer, underwear into another, trousers or dresses in a closet — all in an effort to make life a little more manageable. Similarly, you can sort books by size or by color or by topic or by author; you do this, again, in order to make them manageable, to make easier the job of finding the right one later, and so, ultimately, to learn about what is in the book.

When you think seriously or when you talk about almost anything, you also sort or classify. When you think about choosing courses at school, you sort the courses by subject matter, or by degree of difficulty ("Since I'm taking two hard courses, I ought to look for an easy one"), or by the hour at which they are offered, or by their merit as determined through the grapevine, or by the degree to which they interest you. When you sort, you establish categories by breaking down the curriculum into parts, and by then putting into each category courses that significantly resemble each other but that are not identical. We need categories or classifications; we simply cannot get through life treating every object as unique. Almost everything has an almost infinite number of characteristics and can therefore be placed in any number of categories, but for certain purposes (and we must know our purposes) certain characteristics are significant. It is on these significant characteristics that we fasten.

In sorting, the categories must be established on a single basis of division: you cannot sort dogs into purebreds and small dogs, for some dogs belong in both categories. You must sort them into consistent, coordinate categories, let us say either by breeding or by size. Of course you can first sort dogs into purebreds and mutts and *then* sort each of these groups into two subordinate categories, dogs under twelve inches at the shoulder and dogs twelve inches or more at the shoulder. The categories, as we shall see in a few minutes, will depend on your purpose. That the categories into which things are sorted should be coordinate is, alas, a principle unknown to the American Kennel Club, which divides dogs into six groups. The first four seem reasonable enough: (1) sporting dogs (for example, retrievers, pointers, spaniels), (2) hounds (bassets, beagles, whippets), (3) working dogs (sheepdogs, St. Bernards, collies), (4) terriers (airedales, Irish terriers, Scottish terriers). Trouble begins with the fifth classification, toy dogs (Maltese, Chihuahuas, toy poodles), for size has not been a criterion up to now. The sixth category is desperate: nonsporting dogs (chow chow, poodle, dalmatian). Nonsporting! What a category. Why not nonworking or nonhound? And is a poodle really more like a chow chow than like a toy poodle?[1] Still, the classifications are by now established, and every purebred must fit into one and only one, and thus every purebred can be measured against all of the dogs that in significant ways are thought to resemble it.

Thinking, if broadly defined, must include intuitions and even idle reveries, but most of what we normally mean by serious thinking is analysis, separating into parts and seeing how the parts relate to each other. For example, if we turn our minds to thinking about punishment for killers, we will distinguish at least between those killers whose actions are premeditated, and those killers whose actions are not. And in the first category we might distinguish between professional killers who carefully contrive a death, killers who are irrational except in their ability to contrive a death, and robbers who contrive a property crime and who kill only when they believe that killing is necessary in order to commit the robbery. One can hardly talk usefully about capital punishment or imprisonment without making some such analysis of killers. You have, then, taken killers and sorted or separated or classified them, not for the fun of inventing complications but for the sake of educating yourself and those persons with whom you discuss the topic. Unless your attitude is the mad Queen of Hearts's "Off with their heads," you will be satisfied with your conclusion only

---

[1] The American Kennel Club's categories, though, are better than those given in an old Chinese encyclopedia, whose fourteen classifications of dogs (according to Jorge Luis Borges) include "those belonging to the Emperor," "stuffed dogs," "free-running dogs," "those getting madly excited," "those that look like flies from the distance," and "others." Equally zany were the labels on the five cells in the jail at Beaufort, Texas, a few decades ago: White Male, White Female, Colored Male, Colored Female, and U.S. Marines.

after you have tested it by dividing your topic into parts, each clearly distinguished from and then related to the others.

A second example: if you think about examinations, you may see that they can serve several purposes. Examinations may test knowledge, intelligence, or skill in taking examinations; or they may stimulate learning. Therefore, if you wish to discuss what constitutes a good examination, you must decide first what purpose an examination *should* serve. Possibly you will decide that in a particular course an examination should chiefly stimulate learning, but that it should also test the ability to reason. To arrive at a reasonable conclusion, a conclusion worth sharing, and if need be, defending, you must first recognize and sort out the several possibilities.

Often too, the keenest analytic thinking considers not only what parts are in the whole, but what is *not* there — what is missing in relation to a larger context that we can imagine. For example, if we analyze the women in the best-known fairy tales, we will find that most are either sleeping beauties or wicked stepmothers. These categories are general: "sleeping beauties" includes all passive women valued only for their appearance, and "wicked stepmothers" includes Cinderella's cruel older sisters. (Fairy godmothers form another category, but they are not human beings.) Analysis helps us to discover the almost total absence of resourceful, productive women. A thoughtful essay might begin with a general statement to this effect and then support the statement with an analysis of "Cinderella," "Little Red Riding Hood," and "Hansel and Gretel."

Another analysis that forces us to call to mind what is not there is a Chicano saying, "There are only two kinds of Anglos who are interested in us — the sociologists and the police." And, for a third example, notice in the following paragraph, written during World War II, how George Orwell clarifies our understanding of one kind of military march, the goose-step, by calling our attention to how it differs from the march used by English soldiers. (Orwell might have contrasted the goose-step with the march used by American soldiers, but he was an Englishman writing for Englishmen.)

> One rapid but fairly sure guide to the social atmosphere of a
> country is the parade-step of its army. A military parade is really a

kind of ritual dance, something like a ballet, expressing a certain philosophy of life. The goose-step, for instance, is one of the most horrible sights in the world, far more terrifying than a dive-bomber. It is simply an affirmation of naked power; contained in it, quite consciously and intentionally, is the vision of a boot crashing down on a face. Its ugliness is part of its essence, for what it is saying is "Yes, I *am* ugly, and you daren't laugh at me," like the bully who makes faces at his victim. Why is the goose-step not used in England? There are, heaven knows, plenty of army officers who would be only too glad to introduce some such thing. It is not used because the people in the street would laugh. Beyond a certain point, military display is only possible in countries where the common people dare not laugh at the army. The Italians adopted the goose-step at about the time when Italy passed definitely under German control, and, as one would expect, they do it less well than the Germans. The Vichy government, if it survives, is bound to introduce a stiffer parade-ground discipline into what is left of the French army. In the British army the drill is rigid and complicated, full of memories of the eighteenth century, but without definite swagger; the march is merely a formalised walk. It belongs to a society which is ruled by the sword, no doubt, but a sword which must never be taken out of the scabbard.

When we begin to think analytically about a topic, whether it is the appropriate treatment of killers, or women in fairy tales, or a kind of military march, we don't instantly see what the parts are and how we can separate and discuss them. Only when we get into the topic do we begin to see the need for subtle distinctions. Remember, though, you can stimulate your ability to see distinctions (and thus to have ideas) by asking yourself questions:

1. To what group does it belong?
2. How do the parts work together?
3. What are its uses, purposes, functions?
4. What are its causes?
5. What are its consequences?

An essay chiefly devoted to answering such questions is an analytic essay, though of course you may think analytically in preparation for some other kind of writing too. For example, a finished essay may be primarily narrative — a story, true or false — but analytic thinking will help you to decide what episodes to include, whether to give the episodes consecutively or to begin at the end and then use a flashback, whether to quote dialogue or to report it indirectly. But in this chapter we are concerned chiefly with analytic thinking that finally manifests itself in an analytic essay — that is, in an essay chiefly devoted to showing the reader how the parts of a topic are related or how one part functions in relation to the whole.

It is useful to practice with familiar materials. Any subject that you are interested in and already know something about can be treated analytically. Let's say, for example, you are interested in blues. You have noticed that singers of blues often sing about traveling, recalling the lines

> When a woman takes the blues
> She tucks her head and cries
> But when a man catches the blues
> He catches a freight and rides

You wonder, among other things: Why all this talk of traveling? You decide you want to look into this question, so you search your memory of blues, play whatever records are available, perhaps read some anthologies that include blues, and generally try to sort things out: that is, try to set your thoughts in order. You find that blues often talk about traveling, but the travel is not all of the same kind, and you begin to analyze the blues that use this motif. You begin to jot down words or phrases:

disappointed lover
travel to a job
from the South
→ fantasy travel
back to the South
life is a trip
~~my first trip out of the state~~
jail

You are making a scratch outline, for you are establishing categories, fiddling with them until they are as nearly coordinate as possible, and indicating the order in which you will discuss them.

You rearrange them as you refine your thinking, because your essay will not record your thought processes as they occurred, with all the false steps; the finished essay will record your best thoughts in the order that you judge to be best for a reader. Then perhaps you find it useful to describe your categories a bit more fully:

1. travel as an escape from unhappy love
2. travel as an economic necessity when jobs are not available at home
3. travel as an escape from the South to the North
4. travel as an escape from the North back to the South
5. travel as sheer wishful thinking, an image of escape from the unhappiness of life
6. travel as an image of the hard job of living until death releases one, as in "It's a long old road, but I'm gonna find the end"
7. enforced travel to prison

You have now taken the theme of travel and separated it into various parts; you are educating yourself and you will educate your reader. Having made these or similar distinctions you can go on to say some interesting things about one or all of these superficially similar but essentially different motifs of travel. Perhaps you arrived at a generalization about them. You have had to divide the motif of travel into parts before you can answer the question you began with: "Why all this talk about traveling?" Perhaps your answer is that talking about travel is a way of talking about life.

Once you have established your categories and tentatively settled on the order in which you will treat them, your job is half done. You have arrived at a thesis, assembled evidence to persuade your reader to accept the thesis, and begun to organize your essay. Possibly your finished essay will make the following points, in the order given below, but with convincing detail (for example, quotations from some blues) to support them.

1. Singers of blues sing of traveling, but the travel is of various sorts.
2. Often it is because of economic, social, or even physical pressure (to get a job; to get to a more congenial environment in the urban North — or back to the rural South; to go to jail).
3. Most often, however, and perhaps in the most memorable songs, it is for another reason: it is an attempt to reduce the

         pain of some experiences, especially betrayed love, and the hearer senses that the attempt cannot succeed.

4. In such songs it is usually the men who travel, because they are more mobile than women (women are left to take care of the children), but whether it is the man who has deserted the woman, or the woman who has deserted the man, both are pathetic figures because even the deserter will be haunted by the memory of the beloved.

5. But all of these variations on the theme of travel overlap, and almost always there is a sense that the trip — whether to the North or South, to a job or to jail, to a man or to a woman, or to nowhere in particular — is an image or metaphor for the trip through life, the long, painful road that everyone must walk.

ANALYSIS AND SUMMARY

Analysis should be clearly distinguished from summary, though of course, as the essay on Roth's article (pages 9–10) illustrates, an analysis usually includes some summary of information the reader needs. For example, when (in the second sentence) the writer says, "Roth, in his article . . . argues that the closing of the libraries will be a costly mistake, and that the action will be an insult to the citizens of Newark," she is summarizing Roth's essay; she is briefly reporting, without personal comment, what Roth said. But when she says, "Roth supports his position" and goes on to cite those of Roth's points that actually provide the support, she is analyzing; she is not reporting *what* he said but is calling attention to *how* he makes his points, *how* certain parts of the essay function. Similarly, when she says "By overdramatizing the possible reactions, Roth gains the interest of the reader," she is also analyzing, showing how an effect is achieved. Again, she is analyzing when she says "Through sarcasm, he discloses a further irony," but summarizing when she reports what this irony is: the City Council insists on law and order but it does not respect communal property.

Most of your writing about other writing will be chiefly analytical. You will not, in most essays, simply summarize X's report of what happened at the Little Bighorn, or Y's account of role-playing, or Z's arguments on the dangers of cloning. You will try to teach your readers *how* the writings of X, Y, and Z achieve their effects, or how well the writers have used evidence, or what evidence they have omitted, or what initial assumptions their arguments are based on. Similarly, when you write an essay on the function of school vacations, or on the purposes of the gasoline tax, you will be writing an analysis — provided that you don't lapse into a mere summary of the history of these topics or of what other writers have said about them.

COMPARING

Analysis frequently involves comparing; things are examined for their resemblances to and differences from other things. Strictly speaking, if one emphasizes the differences rather than the similarities, one is contrasting rather than comparing, but we need not preserve this distinction; we can call both processes "comparing."

An essay may be devoted entirely to a comparison, say of two kinds of tribal organization, but even an essay that is not devoted entirely to a comparison may include a paragraph or two of comparison, for example, to explain something familiar by comparing it to something unfamiliar. An essay on the heart may, for instance, include a paragraph comparing the heart to a pump. Let us spend a moment discussing how to organize a paragraph that makes a comparison.

The first part of a paragraph making a comparison may announce the topic, the next part may discuss one of the two items being compared, and the last part may discuss the other. Or the discussion of the two items may run throughout the entire paragraph, the writer perhaps devoting alternate sentences to each. Because almost all writing is designed to help the reader *see* what the writer has in mind, it may be especially useful here to illustrate this last structure with a discussion of visible distinctions. The following comparison of a Japanese statue of the Buddha with a Chinese statue of bodhisattva (a slightly lower spiritual being, dedicated to saving humankind) shows how a comparison can run throughout a paragraph.

Buddha (wood, 33½"; Japanese, late tenth century).

The Buddha is recognizable by the cranial bump, representing a super mind. Because the Buddha is free from attachment to things of this world, he wears only a simple monk's robe and his head is unadorned, in contrast to the bodhisattva, whose rich garments and crown symbolize his power as a spiritual creature who still moves on this earth. Moreover, the Buddha is, or was, gilded, symbolizing his heavenly, sun-like nature, whereas the bodhisattva is more or less naturalistically colored. These differences, however, are immediately obvious and, in a sense, superficial. The distinction between the two kinds of spiritual beings, one awesome and one

Bodhisattva (wood, 56½"; Chinese, twelfth century).

compassionate, is chiefly conveyed by the pose and the carving. The Buddha sits erect and austere, in the lotus position (legs crossed, each foot with the sole upward on the opposite thigh), in full control of his body. The carved folds of his garment, equally severe, form a highly disciplined pattern. The more earthly bodhisattva wears naturalistically carved flowing garments, and sits in a languid, sensuous posture known as "royal ease," the head pensively tilted downward, one knee elevated, one leg hanging down. Both figures are spiritual but the Buddha is remote, constrained, and austere; the bodhisattva is accessible, relaxed, and compassionate.

Next, let's think about a comparison that extends through two or three paragraphs. If one is comparing the indoor play and the sports of girls with those of boys, one can, for example, devote a paragraph to girls, and then a separate paragraph to boys. The paragraphs will probably be connected by beginning the second one with "Boys, on the other hand," or some such transitional expression. But one can also devote a paragraph to indoor play (girls and boys), and a separate paragraph to sports (again girls and boys). There is no rule, except that the organization and the point of the comparison be clear. Consider these paragraphs from an essay by Sheila Tobias on the fear of mathematics. The writer's thesis in the essay is that although this fear is more commonly found in females than in males, biology seems not to be the cause. After discussing some findings (for example, that girls compute better than boys in elementary school, and that many girls tend to lose interest in mathematics in junior high school) the writer turns her attention away from the schoolhouse. Notice that whether a paragraph is chiefly about boys or chiefly about girls, the writer keeps us in mind of the overall point: reasons why more females than males fear math.

> Not all the skills that are necessary for learning mathematics are learned in school. Measuring, computing, and manipulating objects that have dimensions and dynamic properties of their own are part of the everyday life of children. Children who miss out on these experiences may not be well primed for math in school.
>
> Feminists have complained for a long time that playing with dolls is one way of convincing impressionable little girls that they may only be mothers or housewives — or, as in the case of the Barbie doll, "pinup girls" — when they grow up. But doll-playing

may have even more serious consequences for little girls than that. Do girls find out about gravity and distance and shapes and sizes playing with dolls? Probably not.

A curious boy, if his parents are tolerant, will have taken apart a number of household and play objects by the time he is ten, and, if his parents are lucky, he may even have put them back together again. In all of this he is learning things that will be useful in physics and math. Taking parts out that have to go back in requires some examination of form. Building something that stays up or at least stays put for some time involves working with structure.

Sports is another source of math-related concepts for children which tends to favor boys. Getting to first base on a not very well hit grounder is a lesson in time, speed, and distance. Intercepting a football thrown through the air requires some rapid intuitive eye calculations based on the ball's direction, speed, and trajectory. Since physics is partly concerned with velocities, trajectories, and collisions of objects, much of the math taught to prepare a student for physics deals with relationships and formulas that can be used to express motion and acceleration.

The first paragraph offers a generalization about "children," that is, about boys and girls. The second paragraph discusses the play of girls with dolls, but discusses it in a context of its relevance, really irrelevance, to mathematics. The third paragraph discusses the household play of boys, again in the context of mathematics. The fourth paragraph discusses the outdoor sports of boys, but notice that girls are not forgotten, for its first sentence is "Sports is another source of math-related concepts for children which tends to favor boys." In short, even when there is a sort of seesaw structure, boys on one end and girls on the other, we never lose sight of the thesis that comprises both halves of the comparison.

ORGANIZING AN ESSAY
DEVOTED TO A COMPARISON

Let us now talk about organizing a comparison or contrast that runs through an entire essay, say a comparison between two political campaigns, or between the characters in two novels. Probably your first thought, after making some jottings, will be to discuss one-half of the comparison and then to go on to the second half. We'll return to this useful method of organization in a moment, but here we want to point out that many instructors and textbooks condemn such an organization, arguing that the essay too often breaks into two parts and that the second part involves a good deal of repetition of categories set up in the first part. Let's say you are comparing the narrator of *Huckleberry Finn* with the narrator of *The Catcher in the Rye*, to show that despite superficial similarities, they are very different, and that the difference is partly the difference between the nineteenth century and the twentieth. An organization often recommended is something like this:

1. first similarity (the narrator and his quest)
   a. Huck
   b. Holden
2. second similarity (the corrupt world surrounding the narrator)
   a. society in *Huckleberry Finn*
   b. society in *The Catcher in the Rye*
3. first difference (degree to which the narrator fulfills his quest and escapes from society)
   a. Huck's plan to "light out" to the frontier
   b. Holden's breakdown

And so on, for as many additional differences as seem relevant. Here is another way of organizing a comparison:

1. first point: the narrator and his quest
   a. similarities between Huck and Holden
   b. differences between Huck and Holden
2. second point: the corrupt world
   a. similarities between the worlds in *Huck* and *The Catcher*
   b. differences between the worlds in *Huck* and *The Catcher*
3. third point: degree of success
   a. similarities between Huck and Holden
   b. differences between Huck and Holden

But a comparison need not employ either of these structures. There is even the danger that an essay employing either of them may not come into focus until the essayist stands back from his seven-layer cake and announces, in the concluding paragraph, that the odd layers taste better. In one's preparatory thinking one may want to make comparisons in pairs, but one must come to some conclusions about what these add up to before writing the final version. The final version should not duplicate the thought processes; rather, it should be organized so as to make the point clearly and effectively. The point of the essay is not to list pairs of similarities or differences, but to illuminate a topic by making thoughtful comparisons. Although in a long essay one cannot postpone until page 30 a discussion of the second half of the comparison, in an essay of, say, less than ten pages, nothing is wrong with setting forth half of the comparison and then, in light of what you've already said, discussing the second half. True, the essay will break into two unrelated parts if the second half makes no use of the first or fails to modify it; but the essay will hang together if the second half looks back to the first half and calls attention to differences that the new material reveals. Students ought to learn how to write an essay with interwoven comparisons, but they also ought to know that there is another, simpler and clearer, way to write a comparison.

The danger of splitting the essay into unrelated parts can be avoided if you remember that the point of a comparison is to call attention to the unique features of something by holding it up against something similar but significantly different. If the differences are great and apparent, a comparison is a waste of effort. ("Blueberries are different from elephants. Blueberries do not have trunks. And elephants do not grow on bushes.") Indeed, a comparison between essentially and evidently unlike things can only obscure, for by making the comparison the writer implies there are significant similarities, and the reader can only wonder why he does not see them. The essays that do break into two halves are essays that make uninstructive comparisons: the first half tells the reader five things about baseball, the second half tells the reader five unrelated things about football.

ARRIVING AT
AN ANALYTICAL THESIS

As we have suggested, the writer of an analytical essay arrives at the idea he will offer as a thesis by asking questions and answering them, by separating the topic into parts and by seeing how those parts relate. Or, we might say, analytic writing presupposes detective work: the writer looks over the evidence, finds some clues, pursues the trail from one place to the next, and makes the arrest. Elementary? Perhaps. Let's observe a famous detective at work.

The Science of Deduction
Arthur Conan Doyle

"I wonder what that fellow is looking for?" I asked, pointing to a stalwart, plainly dressed individual who was walking slowly down the other side of the street, looking anxiously at the numbers. He had a large blue envelope in his hand, and was evidently the bearer of a message.

"You mean the retired sergeant of Marines," said Sherlock Holmes.

"Brag and bounce!" thought I to myself. "He knows that I cannot verify his guess."

The thought had hardly passed through my mind when the man whom we were watching caught site of the number on our door, and ran rapidly across the roadway. We heard a loud knock, a deep voice below, and heavy steps ascending the stair.

"For Mr. Sherlock Holmes," he said, stepping into the room and handing my friend the letter.

Here was an opportunity of taking the conceit out of him. He little thought of this when he made that random shot. "May I ask, my lad," I said, in the blandest voice, "what your trade may be?"

"Commissionaire, sir," he said, gruffly. "Uniform away for repairs."

"And you were?" I asked; with a slightly malicious glance at my companion.

"A sergeant, sir, Royal Marine Light Infantry, sir. No answer? Right, sir."

He clicked his heels together, raised his hand in salute, and was gone.

I confess that I was considerably startled by this fresh proof of the practical nature of my companion's theories. My respect for his powers of analysis increased wondrously. There still remained some lurking suspicion in my mind, however, that the whole thing was a prearranged episode, intended to dazzle me, though what earthly object he could have in taking me in was past my comprehension. When I looked at him, he had finished reading the note, and his eyes had assumed the vacant, lack-lustre expression which showed mental abstraction.

"How in the world did you deduce that?" I asked.

"Deduce what?" said he, petulantly.

"Why, that he was a retired sergeant of Marines."

"I have no time for trifles," he answered, brusquely; then with a smile, "Excuse my rudeness. You broke the thread of my thoughts; but perhaps it is as well. So you actually were not able to see that that man was a sergeant of Marines?"

"No, indeed."

"It was easier to know it than to explain why I know it. If you were asked to prove that two and two made four, you might find some difficulty, and yet you are quite sure of the fact. Even across the street I could see a great blue anchor tattooed on the back of the fellow's hand. That smacked of the sea. He had a military carriage, however, and regulation side whiskers. There we have the marine. He was a man with some amount of self-importance and a certain air of command. You must have observed the way in which he held his head and swung his cane. A steady, respectable, middle-aged man, too, on the face of him — all facts which led me to believe that he had been a sergeant."

"Wonderful!" I ejaculated.

"Commonplace," said Holmes, though I thought from his expression that he was pleased at my evident surprise and admiration.

— From *A Study in Scarlet*

EXPLAINING AN ANALYSIS: WRITER TO READER

Even when, as a writer, you have solved a problem, that is, focused on a topic and formulated a thesis, you are, as we have said before, not yet done. It is, alas, not enough simply to present the results of your analytical thinking to a reader who, like Dr. Watson, will surely want to know "How in the world did you deduce that?" And like Holmes, writers are often impatient; we long to say with him "I have no time for trifles." But the real reason for our impatience is, as Holmes is quick to acknowledge, that "It was easier to know it than to explain why I know it." But explaining why or how, presenting both the reasoning that led to a thesis and the evidence that supports the reasoning, is the writer's job.

In your preliminary detective work (that is, in reading, taking notes, musing, jotting down some thoughts, and writing rough drafts) some insights (perhaps including your thesis) may come swiftly, apparently spontaneously, and in random order. You may be unaware that you have been thinking analytically at all. In preparing your essay for your reader, however, you become aware, in part because you must become aware. To persuade *your* Dr. Watson that what you say is not "brag and bounce," to replace his natural suspicion with respect for your analysis (and for yourself), you must, we repeat, explain your reasoning in an orderly and interesting fashion and you must present your evidence.

In the hypothetical example on pages 36–38, we showed a writer of an essay musing over the frequency of the motif of travel in blues. Perhaps, we imagined, those musings were triggered by a few lines he happened to remember, or to hear. The writer then began to ask himself questions, to listen to some records, to jot down some notes. His thesis (represented by point three in the revised outline on page 37) might have been formulated only in a final draft of the essay. But it might easily have occurred to the writer much earlier. Perhaps the conclusion, that the themes of travel are a metaphor for the trip through life, came almost simultaneously with the writer's first musings. But no matter when or how he arrived at a conclusion interesting enough to offer as the thesis of an essay, he still had the job of explaining to his reader (and perhaps to himself) how he had arrived at it. He probably had to examine his own thought processes carefully — replaying them in slow motion to see each part separately. He would certainly have had to marshal some evidence from available books and records. And he would have had to arrange the parts of his analysis and the supporting evidence clearly and interestingly to demonstrate the accuracy of his conclusion to a reader who knew less about blues than he did.

To turn to a real example of an analytic essay, notice how Jeff Greenfield, on pages 57–59, solves and presents his case, one involving another famous detective. We will never know in what order the thoughts leading to his thesis came to him. But we can observe how Greenfield organized and supported his analysis. How can we do this? Elementary. By asking questions and answering them.

EXERCISES

1. Analyze the seating pattern in a cafeteria or other public room. Are groups, including groups of empty chairs, perceptible?

2. Look over the birthday cards in a store. What images of girls and women are presented? Are they stereotyped images of passivity and domesticity? If such images predominate, what exceptions are there? Do the exceptions fall into categories? What images of boys and men are presented? Are they stereotyped images of vigor and authority? Again, if there are exceptions, do they form a pattern? (After you have studied the rack for a while, and jotted down some notes, you may find it useful to buy two or three cards, so that when you write your essay — of 500–1000 words — you will have some evidence at hand.)

3. Write an essay of 500–1000 words analyzing either why people have houseplants or why people have pets.

4. Write an essay of not more than three paragraphs analyzing the functions of one of the following:

   credit-noncredit grading
   a minor character in a TV series
   the gasoline tax
   the death penalty
   the preface to this book
   the Twenty-fifth Amendment to the Constitution
   pay toilets
   monumental fountains near public buildings
   Mother's Day

5. An aunt has offered to buy you a subscription to *Time* or *Newsweek*. Compare in about 500 words the contents of the current issues and explain which magazine you prefer. (If neither magazine is of interest, try comparing *Sport* and *Sports Illustrated* or *Cosmopolitan* and *Ms.*)

6a. Compare baseball with hockey or soccer as a sport suitable for television. Consider the visual appeals of the sports, the pace — including the degree to which the camera operator can predict the action and thus follow it with the camera, the opportunity for replays and for close-ups — and anything else you think relevant.

b. It is often said that television has had a bad effect on sports. If you believe this, write an essay of 500–1000 words setting forth these effects.

7. Compare the function of the setting in *The Tonight Show* with *Saturday Night Live*.

8. In a paragraph analyze the appeals of an advertisement. An advertisement for a book club may, for example, appeal both to snobbism and frugality; an advertisement for a cigarette may appeal to vanity, and perhaps also to reason, by giving statistics about the relatively low amount of tar. If possible, include a copy of the advertisement with your paper.

9. Write a paragraph comparing a magazine advertisement of the 1980s with a counterpart of the 1950s. (You can easily find ads for cars and cigarettes in old copies of *Time* and *Newsweek* in your library.) How are the appeals similar and how are they different? Include copies of the advertisements with your paper.

10. This photograph of Sitting Bull and Buffalo Bill was taken in 1885 by William McFarlane Notman. Reread the discussion of Brueghel's drawing on pages 30–31, and then write two or three paragraphs describing and analyzing this photograph, paying special attention to the contrasting poses, expressions, and costumes. (Reading brief biographical accounts of Buffalo Bill [William Frederick Cody] and Sitting Bull will help you to understand the photograph. Append a list of "Works Consulted" to your paper, and footnote where appropriate. See pages 373–75 and 363–72.)

Sitting Bull and Buffalo Bill, 1885.

Photographer unknown. Picasso's Son Paul on a Donkey, *c. 1923. Photograph, Collection Pablo Picasso.*

11. Reread the discussion of Brueghel's drawing on pages 30–31, and of the comparison on pages 39–40, and then write a paragraph comparing the photograph of Picasso's son Paul with the painting that Picasso made from it in 1923.

Pablo Picasso. Paul, Son of the Artist. 1923. Gouache, 40 × 32 inches. Collection of Pablo Picasso, Grasse, France. Permission © S.P.A.D.E.M., Paris/V.A.G.A., New York.

12. Study these two drawings, by Francisco Goya (1746–1828), entitled "El amor y la muerte" (Love and Death). They show a woman holding a dying lover, who has fought a duel for her. The first version, at left, is a watercolor; the revision is in chalk. Write a brief essay of one to three paragraphs comparing them.

Robert Frank. Covered Car — Long Beach, California, 1956.

Walker Evans. Westchester, New York, Farm House, 1931.

13. Assume that photographs say something. Compare what it is that these two photographs say.

ANALYSIS AT WORK

*Columbo Knows
the Butler Didn't Do It*

Jeff Greenfield

The popularity of *Columbo* is as intense as it is puzzling. Dinner parties are adjourned, trips to movies postponed, and telephone calls hastily concluded ("It's starting now, I gotta go." "Migod, it's 8:40, what did I miss?"), all for a detective show that tells us whodunit, howhedunit, and whyhedunit all before the first commercial.

Why? Peter Falk's characterization is part of the answer of course; he plays Lieutenant Columbo with sleepy-eyed, slow-footed, crazy-like-a-fox charm. But shtick — even first-class shtick — goes only so far. Nor is it especially fascinating to watch Columbo piece together clues that are often telegraphed far in advance. No, there is something else which gives *Columbo* a special appeal — something almost never seen on commercial television. That something is a strong, healthy dose of class antagonism. The one constant in *Columbo* is that, with every episode, a working-class hero brings to justice a member of America's social and economic elite.

The homicide files in Columbo's office must contain the highest per-capita income group of any criminals outside of antitrust law. We never see a robber shooting a grocery store owner out of panic or savagery; there are no barroom quarrels settled with a Saturday Night Special; no murderous shootouts between drug dealers or numbers runners. The killers in Columbo's world are art collectors, surgeons, high-priced lawyers, sports executives, a symphony conductor of Bernsteinian charisma — even a world chess champion. They are rich and white (if Columbo ever does track down a black killer, it will surely be a famous writer or singer or athlete or politician).

Columbo's villains are not simply rich; they are privileged. They live the lives that are for most of us hopeless daydreams: houses on top of mountains, with pools, servants, and sliding doors; parties with women in slinky dresses, and endless food and drink; plush, enclosed box seats at professional sports events; the envy and admiration of the Crowd. While we choose between Johnny Carson and *Invasion of the Body-Snatchers*, they are at screenings of movies the rest of us wait in line for on Third Avenue three months later.

Into the lives of these privileged rich stumbles Lieutenant Columbo — a dweller in another world. His suspects are Los Angeles paradigms: sleek, shiny, impeccably dressed, tanned by the omnipresent sun. Columbo, on the other hand, appears to have been plucked from Queens Boulevard by helicopter, and set down an instant later in Topanga Canyon. His hair is tousled, not styled and sprayed. His chin is pale and stubbled. He has even forgotten to take off his raincoat, a garment thoroughly out of place in Los Angeles eight months of the year. Columbo is also unabashedly stunned by and envious of the life style of his quarry.

"Geez, that is some car," he tells the symphony conductor. "Ya know, I'll bet that car costs more than I make in a year."

"Say, can I ask you something personal?" he says to a suspect wearing $50-dollar shoes. "Ya know where I can buy a pair of shoes like that for $8.95?"

"Boy, I bet this house musta cost — I dunno, hundred, what, hundred fifty thousand?"

His aristocratic adversaries tolerate Columbo at first because they misjudge him. They are amused by him, scornful of his manners, certain that while he possesses the legal authority to demand their cooperation, he has neither the grace nor wit to discover their misdeeds. Only at the end, in a last look of consternation before the final fadeout, do they comprehend that intelligence may indeed find a home in the Robert Hall set. All of them are done in, in some measure, by their contempt for Columbo's background, breeding, and income. Anyone who has worked the wrong side of the counter at Bergdorf's, or who has waited on tables in high-priced restaurants, must feel a wave of satisfaction. ("Yeah, baby, *that's* how dumb we working stiffs are!")

Further, Columbo knows about these people what the rest of us suspect: that they are on top not because they are smarter or work harder than we do, but because they are more amoral and devious. Time after time, the motive for murder in *Columbo* stems from the shakiness of the villain's own status in high society. The chess champion knows his challenger is his better; murder is his only chance to stay king. The surgeon fears that a cooperative research project will endanger his status; he must do in his chief to retain sole credit. The conductor owes his position to the status of his mother-in-law; he must silence his mistress lest she spill the beans and strip him of his wealth and position.

This is, perhaps, the most thorough-going satisfaction *Columbo* offers us: the assurance that those who dwell in marble and satin, those whose clothes, food, cars, and mates are the very best, *do not deserve it.* They are, instead, driven by fear and compulsion to murder. And they are done in by a man of street wit, who is afraid to fly, who can't stand the sight of blood, and who never uses force to take his prey. They are done in by Mosholu Parkway and P. S. 106, by Fordham U. and a balcony seat at Madison Square Garden, by a man who pulls down $11,800 a year and never ate an anchovy in his life.

It is delicious. I wait only for the ultimate episode: Columbo knocks on the door of 1600 Pennsylvania Avenue one day. "Gee, Mr. President, I really hate to bother you again, but there's *just one thing. . . .*"

QUESTIONS

1. What is Greenfield's thesis? Where does he state it?
2. Describe what Greenfield is doing in his first paragraph; in his second paragraph.
3. Beginning with the third paragraph, Greenfield looks first at the characterization of the hero and villains, then at the underlying conflict, and finally at the implicit meaning of the conflict. Why does he present the parts of his analysis in this order?

Grant and Lee:
A Study in Contrasts
Bruce Catton

When Ulysses S. Grant and Robert E. Lee met in the parlor of a modest house at Appomattox Court House, Virginia, on April 9, 1865 to work out the terms for surrender of Lee's Army of Northern Virginia, a great chapter in American life came to a close, and a great new chapter began.

These men were bringing the Civil War to its virtual finish. To be sure, other armies had yet to surrender, and for a few days the fugitive Confederate government would struggle desperately and vainly, trying to find some way to go on living now that its chief support was gone. But in effect it was all over when Grant and Lee signed the papers. And the little room where they wrote out the terms was the scene of one of the poignant, dramatic contrasts in American history.

They were two strong men, these oddly different generals, and they represented the strengths of two conflicting currents that, through them, had come into final collision.

Back of Robert E. Lee was the notion that the old aristocratic concept might somehow survive and be dominant in American life.

Lee was tidewater Virginia, and in his background were family, culture, and tradition . . . the age of chivalry transplanted to a New World which was making its own legends and its own myths. He embodied a way of life that had come down through the age of knighthood and the English country squire. America was a land that was beginning all over again, dedicated to nothing much more complicated than the rather hazy belief that all men had equal rights, and should have an equal chance in the world. In such a land Lee stood for the feeling that it was somehow of advantage to human society to have a pronounced inequality in the social structure. There should be a leisure class, backed by ownership of land; in turn, society itself should be keyed to the land as the chief source of wealth and influence. It would bring forth (according to this ideal) a class of men with a strong sense of obligation to the community; men who lived not to gain advantage for themselves, but to meet the solemn obligations which had been laid on them by the very fact that they were privileged. From them the country would get its leadership; to them it could look for the higher values — of thought, of conduct, of personal deportment — to give it strength and virtue.

Lee embodied the noblest elements of this aristocratic ideal. Through him, the landed nobility justified itself. For four years, the Southern states had fought a desperate war to uphold the ideals for which Lee stood. In the end, it almost seemed as if the Confederacy fought for Lee; as if he himself was the Confederacy . . . the best thing that the way of life for which the Confederacy stood could ever have to offer. He had passed into legend before Appomattox. Thousands of tired, underfed, poorly clothed Confederate soldiers, long-since past the simple enthusiasm of the early days of the struggle, somehow considered Lee the symbol of everything for which they had been willing to die. But they could not quite put this feeling into words. If the Lost Cause, sanctified by so much heroism and so many deaths, had a living justification, its justification was General Lee.

Grant, the son of a tanner on the Western frontier, was everything Lee was not. He had come up the hard way, and embodied nothing in particular except the eternal toughness and sinewy fiber of the men who grew up beyond the mountains. He was one of a body of men who owed reverence and obeisance to no one, who were self-reliant to a fault, who cared hardly anything for the past but who had a sharp eye for the future.

These frontier men were the precise opposites of the tidewater aristocrats. Back of them, in the great surge that had taken people over the Alleghenies and into the opening Western country, there was a deep, implicit dissatisfaction with a past that had settled into grooves. They stood for democracy, not from any reasoned conclusion about the proper ordering of human society, but simply because they had grown up in the middle of democracy and knew how it worked. Their society might have privileges, but they would be privileges each man had won for himself. Forms and patterns meant nothing. No man was born to anything, except perhaps to a chance to show how far he could rise. Life was competition.

Yet along with this feeling had come a deep sense of belonging to a national community. The Westerner who developed a farm, opened a shop or set up in business as a trader, could hope to prosper only as his own community prospered — and his community ran from the Atlantic to the Pacific and from Canada down to Mexico. If the land was settled, with towns and highways and accessible markets, he could better himself. He saw his fate in terms of the nation's own destiny. As its horizons expanded, so did his. He had, in other words, an acute dollars-and-cents stake in the continued growth and development of his country.

And that, perhaps, is where the contrast between Grant and Lee becomes most striking. The Virginia aristocrat, inevitably, saw himself in relation to his own region. He lived in a static society which could endure almost anything except change. Instinctively, his first loyalty would go to the locality in which that society existed. He would fight to the limit of endurance to defend it, because in defending it he was defending everything that gave his own life its deepest meaning.

The Westerner, on the other hand, would fight with an equal tenacity for the broader concept of society. He fought so because everything he lived by was tied to growth, expansion, and a constantly widening horizon. What he lived by would survive or fall with the nation itself. He could not possibly stand by unmoved in the face of an attempt to destroy the Union. He would combat it with everything he had, because he could only see it as an effort to cut the ground out from under his feet.

So Grant and Lee were in complete contrast, representing two diametrically opposed elements in American life. Grant was the modern man emerging; beyond him, ready to come on the stage, was the great age of steel and machinery, of crowded cities and a restless, burgeoning vitality. Lee might have ridden down from the old age of chivalry, lance in hand, silken banner fluttering over his head. Each man was the perfect champion of his cause, drawing both his strengths and his weaknesses from the people he led.

Yet it was not all contrast, after all. Different as they were — in background, in personality, in underlying aspiration — these two great soldiers had much in common. Under everything else, they were marvelous fighters. Furthermore, their fighting qualities were really very much alike.

Each man had, to begin with, the great virtue of utter tenacity and fidelity. Grant fought his way down the Mississippi Valley in spite of acute personal discouragement and profound military handicaps. Lee hung on in the trenches at Petersburg after hope itself had died. In each man there was an indomitable quality . . . the born fighter's refusal to give up as long as he can still remain on his feet and lift his two fists.

Daring and resourcefulness they had, too; the ability to think faster and move faster than the enemy. These were the qualities which gave Lee the dazzling campaigns of Second Manassas and Chancellorsville and won Vicksburg for Grant.

Lastly, and perhaps greatest of all, there was the ability, at the end, to turn quickly from war to peace once the fighting was over. Out of the way these two men behaved at Appomattox came the possibility of a peace of reconciliation. It was a possibility not wholly realized, in the years to come, but which did, in the end, help the two sections to become one nation again . . . after a war whose bitterness might have seemed to make such a reunion wholly impossible. No part of either man's life became him more than the part he played in their brief meeting in the McLean house at Appomattox. Their behavior there put all succeeding generations of Americans in their debt. Two great Americans, Grant and Lee — very different, yet under everything very much alike. Their encounter at Appomattox was one of the great moments of American history.

QUESTIONS

1. Outline the essay by jotting down for each paragraph, depending on its chief subject, "Grant" or "Lee" or "Grant and Lee." In addition to these key words, jot down next to them a word or two that summarizes the theme of the paragraph. Thus, for the fourth paragraph you would write something like "Lee — aristocratic ideal"; for the fifth, perhaps "Lee — embodiment of aristocratic ideal"; and for the paragraph beginning "So Grant and Lee" (page 62), perhaps "Grant and Lee — summary."

2. A comparison organized along Catton's lines often seems choppy, leaping back and forth from A to B. How does Catton minimize the ping-pong effect? That is, how does he weave together the paragraphs where he moves from one figure to the other?

3. Earlier in the chapter we mentioned that the instruction "compare" can be used to include "contrast." Catton keeps his contrasts separate from his comparisons. Where in the essay does he turn from one to the other? Would the effect of the essay be different if he reversed the position of the contrast and the comparison?

3
Outlining

When you write an outline, you do pretty much what an artist does when he draws an outline: you give, without detail and shading, the general shape of your subject.

An outline is a kind of blueprint, a diagram showing the arrangement of the parts. It is, then, essentially an analysis of your essay, a classification of its parts. Not all writers use outlines, but those who use them report that an outline helps to make clear to them, before or while they labor through a first draft, what their thesis is, what the main points are, and what the subordinate points are. When the outline is drawn, they have a guide that will help them subordinate what is subordinate, and they can easily see if development from part to part is clear, consistent, and reasonable.

An outline drafted before you write, however, is necessarily tentative. Don't assume that once you have constructed an outline your plan is fixed. If, as you begin to write, previously neglected points come to mind, or if you see that in any way the outline is unsatisfactory, revise or scrap the outline. One other caution: an outline does not indicate connections. In your essay be sure to use transitions like "equally important," "less important but still worth mentioning," and "on the other hand" to make clear the relationships between your points.

SCRATCH OUTLINE

The simplest outline is a *scratch outline,* half a dozen phrases jotted down, revised, rearranged, listing the topics to be covered in the most effective and logical order. For an example, see the jottings on page 36. These phrases serve as milestones rather than as a road map. Most writers do at least this much.

PARAGRAPH OUTLINE

A *paragraph outline* is more developed: it states the thesis (usually in a sentence, but sometimes in a phrase) and then it gives the topic sentence (or a phrase summarizing the topic idea) of each paragraph. Thus, a paragraph outline of Jeff Greenfield's "Columbo Knows the Butler Didn't Do It" (pages 57–59) might begin like this:

> Thesis: *Columbo* is popular because it shows a privileged, undeserving elite brought down by a fellow like us.
> I. *Columbo* is popular.
> II. Its popularity is largely due to its hostility toward a social and economic elite.
> III. The killers are all rich and white.
> IV. Their lives are privileged.

And so on, one roman numeral for each remaining paragraph. A paragraph outline has its uses, especially for papers under, say, a thousand words; it can help you to write unified paragraphs, and it can help you to write a reasonably organized essay. But after you write your essay, check to see if your paragraphs really are developments of what you assert to be the topic sentences, and check to see if you have made the organization clear to the reader, chiefly by means of transitional words and phrases (see pages 80–84). If your essay departs from your outline, the departures should be improvements.

FORMAL OUTLINE

For longer papers, such as a research paper (usually at least eight pages of double-spaced typing), a more complicated outline is usually needed. As you can see from the outline preceding the sample research paper on pages 215–16, the *formal outline* shows relationships, distinguishing between major parts of the essay and subordinate parts. Major parts are indicated by capital roman numerals. These should clearly bear on the thesis. Chief divisions within a major part are indicated by capital letters. Subdivisions within these divisions are indicated by arabic numerals. Smaller subdivisions are indicated by lowercase letters. Still smaller subdivisions — although they are rarely needed, because they are apt to provide too much detail for an outline — are indicated by small roman numerals.

Notice that you cannot have a single subdivision. In the example that follows, part I is divided into parts A and B; it cannot have only a part A. Similarly, part B cannot be "divided" into 1 without there being a 2. If you have a single subdivision, eliminate it and work the material into the previous heading. Note also that some authorities require that an outline be consistent in using either sentences or phrases, not a mixture. (Look again at the outline on pages 215–16.) But when you are writing an outline for yourself, you need not worry about mixing phrases with sentences.

Here is a formal outline of Greenfield's "Columbo." Other versions are, of course, possible. In fact, in order to illustrate the form of divisions and subdivisions, we have written a much fuller outline than is usual for such a short essay.

Thesis: *Columbo* is popular because it shows the undeserving rich brought low by a member of the working class.
I. Popularity of *Columbo*
    A.   What it is *not* due to
        1. Acting
        2. Clever detection of surprising criminal plot
    B.   What it is due to
        1. Hostility to privileged elite
        2. Columbo is poor and shoddy.
        3. The high are brought low.
            a. No black (minority) villains
            b. The villains live far above us.
II. The hero
    A.   Physical appearance
        1. Dress
        2. Hair, beard
    B.   Manner

    C.   Success as an investigator
        1. Adversaries mistakenly treat him as negligible.
           a. They assume his lack of wealth indicates lack of intelligence.
           b. They learn too late.
        2. Columbo understands the elite.
           a. They are not superior mentally or in diligence.
           b. They are in a shaky position.
 III. Our satisfaction with the program
    A.   The villains do not deserve their privileges.
    B.   Villains are undone by a man in the street.
    C.   We look forward to an episode when Columbo visits the most privileged house.

There is, of course, no evidence that Greenfield wrote an outline before he wrote his essay. But he may have roughed out something along these lines, thereby providing himself with a ground plan or a roadmap. And while he looked at it he may have readjusted a few parts to give more emphasis here (changing a subdivision into a major division) or to establish a more reasonable connection there (say, reversing A and B in one of the parts). Even if you don't write from an outline, when you complete your final draft you ought to be able to outline it — you ought to be able to sketch its parts. If you have trouble outlining the draft, your reader will certainly have trouble following your ideas. Even a paragraph outline made from what you hope is your final draft may help to reveal disproportion or faulty organization that you can remedy before you write your final copy.

EXERCISES

1. Read the one-paragraph essay in Exercise 9, pages 100–01. Then write a scratch outline of it.
2. Write a paragraph outline of one of the following:
    a. "Indecent Exposure" (pages 130–32)
    b. "A Note on the Use of Computers in Research and Writing" (pages 231–33).

4
Paragraphs

PARAGRAPH FORM
AND SUBSTANCE

It is commonly said that a good paragraph has *unity* (it makes one point, or it indicates where one unit of a topic begins and ends); it has *organization* (the point or unit is developed according to some pattern); and it has *coherence* (the pattern of development, sentence by sentence, is clear to the reader). We will say these things too. Moreover, we will attempt to demonstrate that, generally speaking, they are true. Along the way we also hope to show you how to shape your ideas into effective paragraphs. But first we feel obliged to issue this warning: you can learn to write a unified, organized, coherent paragraph that no one in his right mind would choose to read. Here is an example, which we ask you to force yourself to read through. (It may remind you of many paragraphs you wrote in order to graduate from high school.)

> Charles Darwin's great accomplishments in the field of natural science resulted from many factors. While innate qualities and characteristics played a large part in leading him to his discoveries, various environmental circumstances and events were decisive factors as well. Darwin, himself, considered his voyage on the *Beagle* the most decisive event of his life, precisely because this was to him an educational experience similar to if not more valuable than that of college, in that it determined his whole career and taught him of the world as well.

Notice that the paragraph is unified, organized, and coherent. It has a topic sentence (the first sentence). It uses transitional devices ("while," "as well," "Darwin," "himself") and, as is often helpful, it repeats key words. But notice also that it is wordy, vague, and inflated ("in the field of," "many factors," "qualities and characteristics," "circumstances and events," "precisely because," "educational experience," "similar to if not more valuable than"). It is, in short, thin and boring. Who but a hired sympathy (John Ciardi's definition of an English teacher) would read it? To whom does it teach what?

Consider, by contrast, these two paragraphs from the beginning of another essay on Darwin:

> Charles Darwin's youth was unmarked by signs of genius. Born in 1809 into the well-to-do Darwin and Wedgwood clans (his mother was a Wedgwood, and Darwin himself was to marry another), he led a secure and carefree childhood, happy with his family, indifferent to books, responsive to nature. The son and grandson of impressively successful physicians, he eventually tried medical training himself, but found the studies dull and surgery (before anesthesia) too ghastly even to watch. So, for want of anything better, he followed the advice of his awesome father (6'2", 336 pounds, domineering in temperament) and studied for the ministry, taking his B.A. at Christ's College, Cambridge, in 1831.
>
> Then a remarkable turn of events saved Darwin from a country parsonage. His science teacher at Cambridge, John Stevens Henslow, arranged for Darwin the invitation to be naturalist on H.M.S. *Beagle* during a long voyage of exploration. Despite his father's initial reluctance, Darwin got the position, and at the end of 1831 left England for a five-year voyage around the globe that turned out to be not only a crucial experience for Darwin himself, but a passage of consequence for the whole world.
>
> — Philip Appleman

Notice how full of life these paragraphs are, compared to the paragraph that begins by asserting that "Charles Darwin's great accomplishments in the field of natural science resulted from many factors." These far more interesting paragraphs are filled with specific details, facts and names that combine to convey ideas. We finish reading them with a sense of having learned something worth knowing, from someone fully engaged not only with the topic, but also with conveying it to someone else.

The one indispensable quality of a good paragraph, the quality that the first paragraph on Darwin lacks, is *substance*. A paragraph may define a term, describe a person or a place, make a comparison, tell an anecdote, summarize an opinion, draw a conclusion; it may do almost anything provided that it holds the reader's attention by telling him something he wants or needs to know, or is reminded of with pleasure.

But even a substantial paragraph, as we shall soon see, does not guarantee the reader's attention, because readers (like writers) are lazy and impatient. The important difference is that readers can afford to be. If they find that they must work too hard to understand you, if they are puzzled or confused by what you write, if they find that the difficulty in following your sentences is greater than the difficulty inherent in your material, if, in other words, the effort they must expend is greater than their reward, they can — and will — stop reading you. Because the art of writing is in large part the art of keeping your readers' goodwill while you teach them what you want them to learn, you should learn, among other things, how to write substantial paragraphs that are also unified, organized, and coherent. Now, experienced writers can usually tell — not so much while they are writing as while they are revising — what does or does not make a satisfactory unit, and their paragraphs do not always exactly follow the principles we are going to suggest. But we think that by following these principles, more or less as you might practice finger exercises in learning how to play the piano, you will develop a sense of paragraphing, or, to put it another way, a sense of how to develop an idea.

PARAGRAPH UNITY: TOPIC SENTENCES, TOPIC IDEAS

The idea developed in each paragraph often appears, briefly stated, as a topic sentence. Topic sentences are most useful, and are therefore especially common, in essays that offer arguments; they are much less common, because they are less useful, in narrative and descriptive essays.

A topic sentence often comes at the beginning of a paragraph, but it may come later, even at the end; it may even be dispensed with if the topic idea — the idea that unifies the sentences of the paragraph — is clear without an explicit statement. (You have just read the topic sentence of this paragraph. The rest of the paragraph will develop the threefold point that a topic sentence often begins a paragraph, often ends a paragraph, and often is omitted.) The topic sentence usually is the first sentence in the paragraph — or the second, following a transitional sentence — because writers usually want their readers to know from the start where the paragraph is going. And, because writers want to keep their readers' attention, an opening topic sentence should be as precise and as interesting as possible (*not* "People oppose school busing for several reasons," but "People offer many good reasons for opposing school busing, but seldom offer their real reasons"). Sometimes, though, you may not wish to forecast what is to come; you may prefer to put your topic sentence at the end of the paragraph, summarizing the points that earlier sentences have made, or drawing a generalization based on the earlier details. Even if you do not include a topic sentence anywhere in the paragraph, the paragraph should have a topic idea — an idea that holds the sentences together.

The following paragraph begins with a topic sentence.

> The Marx Brothers' three best films at Paramount — *Monkey Business* (1931), *Horse Feathers* (1932), and *Duck Soup* (1933) — all hurl comic mud at the gleaming marble pillars of the American temple. The target of *Monkey Business* is money and high society, the rich society snobs merely happen to be gangsters who made their money from bootlegging. The target of *Horse Feathers* is the university; knowledge and the pursuit of it are reduced to thievery, bribery, lechery, and foolishness. The target of *Duck Soup* is democracy and government itself; grandiose political ceremonies, governmental bodies, international diplomacy, the law courts, and war are reduced to the absurd. All three films also parody popular "serious" genres — gangster films, college films, and romantic-European-kingdom films. The implication of this spoofing is that the sanctified institution is as hollow and dead as the cinematic cliché; the breezy, chaotic, revolutionary activities of the comic anarchists give society's respectable calcifications a much-deserved comeuppance.
>
> — Gerald Mast

Everything that follows the first sentence develops or amplifies that sentence, first by commenting one by one on the three films named at the outset, then by speaking of the three films as a group, and then by offering a closely related generalization (the films spoof

serious films) and a comment on the implications of this generalization. In short, the writer begins by stating or summarizing his
idea, then offers specific evidence to support it, and then offers a
related idea. The development is from the general to the particular
and then again to the general.

   Next, a paragraph with the topic sentence at the end. A
paragraph that begins with the topic sentence offers readers the
satisfaction of receiving, as they move through the paragraph, what
was promised at the outset; a paragraph with the topic sentence at
the end usually offers readers the pleasure of mild suspense during
most of the paragraph and finally, in the topic sentence, the clarification that they had half anticipated. When the topic sentence is
at the end, the paragraph usually develops from the particular to
the general.

> If we try to recall Boris Karloff's face as the monster in the
> film of *Frankenstein* (1931), most of us probably think of the seams
> holding the pieces together, and if we cannot recall other details we
> assume that the face evokes horror. But when we actually look at
> a picture of the face rather than recall a memory of it, we are perhaps
> chiefly impressed by the high, steep forehead (a feature often asso-
> ciated with intelligence), by the darkness surrounding the eyes (often
> associated with physical or spiritual weariness), and by the gaunt
> cheeks and the thin lips slightly turned down at the corners (asso-
> ciated with deprivation or restraint). The monster's face is of course
> in some ways shocking, but probably our chief impression as we
> look at it is that this is not the face of one who causes suffering but
> of one who himself is heroically undergoing suffering.

This structure, with the topic sentence at the end of the paragraph,
can be especially effective in presenting an argument: the reader
hears, considers, and accepts the evidence before the argument is
explicitly stated, and if the evidence has been effectively presented
the reader willingly accepts the conclusion.

   Next, a paragraph without a topic sentence:

> A few years ago when you mentioned Walt Disney at a re-
> spectable party — or anyway this is how it was in California, where
> I was then — the standard response was a headshake and a groan.
> Intellectuals spoke of how he butchered the classics — from *Pinocchio*
> to *Winnie the Pooh,* how his wildlife pictures were sadistic and coy,
> how the World's Fair sculptures of hippopotamuses were a national

if not international disgrace. A few crazies disagreed, and since crazies are always the people to watch, it began to be admitted that the early Pluto movies had a considerable measure of *je ne sais quoi*, that the background animation in *Snow White* was "quite extraordinary," that *Fantasia* did indeed have *one* great sequence (then it became two; now everyone says three, though there's fierce disagreement on exactly which three).

— John Gardner

The topic here is, roughly, "Intellectuals used to scorn Disney, but recently they have been praising him." Such a sentence could easily begin the paragraph, but it is not necessary because even without it the reader has no difficulty following the discussion. The first two sentences talk about Disney's earlier reputation; then the sentence about the "crazies" introduces the contrary view and the rest of the paragraph illustrates the growing popularity of this contrary view. The paragraph develops its point so clearly and consistently (it is essentially a narrative, in chronological order) that the reader, unlike the reader of a complex analytic paragraph, does not need the help of a topic sentence either at the beginning, to prepare for what follows, or at the end, to pull the whole together.

Finally, we examine another paragraph without a topic sentence, this one from a descriptive essay; it does not have the obvious orderliness of the previous example, but it still hangs together.

I remember my mother's father, called Granddad, as a small silent man, a cabinetmaker and carpenter with a liking for strong drink. For a time I guess he was the town drunk, and my memories of him are as fogged by shame as his mind was by whiskey. When he was working — and he managed to support himself until his death — he was a different man. I remember watching him build a cabinet in our house; his hands were craftsman's hands, marked by his trade. The ends of two fingers were missing, lost in the first power saw brought to the county, when they built a bridge over the North Platte. The nails of the remaining fingers were ridged, horny, discolored, misshapen, not like fingernails but more like the claws of some very old and tough bird. The knuckles had been crushed and mauled until each had its own special shape and size. Every inch of skin was mapped by the building he had done. I can't remember his face and can't forget those hands. When he touched

wood those mutilated old hands would turn into something beautiful, as if pure love was flowing from his fingers into the wood.
— Sharon R. Curtin

A paragraph can make several points; but the points must be related and the nature of the relationship must be indicated so that there is, in effect, a single unifying point to the paragraph. In the example just quoted, we get details about the man's physical appearance and also details about his trade; these two motifs are united by the idea that although he was superficially unattractive, when his maimed hands went to work they became beautiful.

UNIFYING IDEAS
INTO PARAGRAPHS

Although we emphasize unity in paragraphs, don't assume that every development or refinement or alteration of your thought requires a new paragraph. Such an assumption would lead to an essay consisting entirely of one-sentence paragraphs. A good paragraph may, for instance, both ask a question and answer it, or describe an effect and then explain the cause, or set forth details and then offer a generalization. Indeed, if the question or the effect or the details can be set forth in a sentence or two, and the answer or the cause or the generalization can be set forth in a sentence or two, the two halves of the topic should be pulled together into a single paragraph. It is only if the question (for example) is long and complex and the answer equally long or longer that you need two or more paragraphs — or, to put it more precisely, that your reader needs two or more paragraphs.

Let's consider three paragraphs from an essay on ballooning. In the essay from which the following paragraphs were taken, the writer has already explained that ballooning was born in late eighteenth-century France and that almost from its start there were two types of balloons, gas and hot air. Notice that in the paragraphs printed below the first is on gas, the second is chiefly on hot air (but it helpfully makes comparisons with gas), and the third is on the length of flights of both gas and hot-air balloons. In other words, each paragraph is about one thing — gas balloons, hot-air balloons, length of flight — but each paragraph also builds on what the reader has learned in the previous paragraphs. That the third paragraph is about the flights of gas *and* of hot-air balloons does not mean that it lacks unity; it is a unified discussion of flight lengths.

> Gas balloons swim around in air like a sleeping fish in water, because they weigh about the same as the fluid they're in. A good, big, trans-Atlantic balloon will have 2,000 pounds of vehicle, including gas bag and pilot, taking up about 30 cubic feet (as big as a refrigerator), plus 300 pounds of a "nothing" stuff called helium, which fills 30,000 cubic feet (as big as three houses). Air to fill this 30,000 cubic feet would also weigh 2,300 pounds, so the balloon system averages the same as air, floating in it as part of the wind.
>
> Hot-air balloons use the same size bag filled with hot air instead of helium, kept hot by a boot-sized blowtorch riding just over the pilot's head. Hot air is light, but not as light as helium, so you can't carry as much equipment in a hot-air balloon. You also can't fly as long or as far. Helium will carry a balloon for days (three and a half days is the record), until a lot of gas has leaked out. But a hot-air balloon cools down in minutes, like a house as soon as its heat source runs out of fuel; and today's best fuel (heat-for-weight), propane, lasts only several hours.
>
> A good hot-air flight goes a hundred miles, yet the gas record is 1,897 miles, set by a German in 1914 with the junk (by today's standards) they had then. Unmanned scientific gas balloons have flown half a million miles, staying up more than a year. Japan bombed Oregon in World War II with balloons. Two hot-air balloonists, Tracy Barnes and Malcolm Forbes, have made what they called transcontinental flights, but each was the sum of dozens of end-to-end hops, trailed by pick-up trucks, like throwing a frisbee from Hollywood to Atlantic City.
>
> —David Royce

Now contrast the unity of any of the previous three paragraphs on ballooning with the lack of focus in this paragraph from a book on athletic coaching.

> Leadership qualities are a prerequisite for achievement in coaching. A leader is one who is respected for what he says and does, and who is admired by his team. The coach gains respect by giving respect, and by possessing knowledge and skills associated with the sport. There are many "successful" coaches who are domineering, forceful leaders, gaining power more through fear and even hate

than through respect. These military-type men are primarily from the old school of thought, and many younger coaches are achieving their goals through more humanistic approaches.

Something is wrong here. The first half of the paragraph tells us that "a leader is one who is respected for what he says and does," but the second half of the paragraph contradicts that assertion, telling us that "many" leaders hold their position "more through fear and even hate than through respect." The trouble is *not* that the writer is talking about two kinds of leaders; a moment ago we saw that a writer can in one paragraph talk about two kinds of balloons. The trouble here is that we need a unifying idea if these two points are to be given in one paragraph. The idea might be this: "There are two kinds of leaders, those who are respected and those who are feared." This idea might be developed along these lines:

> Leadership qualities are a prerequisite for achievement in coaching, but these qualities can be of two radically different kinds. One kind of leader is respected and admired by his team for what he says and does. The coach gains respect by giving respect, and by possessing knowledge and skills associated with the sport. The other kind of coach is a domineering, forceful leader, gaining power more through fear than through respect. These military-type men are primarily from the old school of thought, whereas most of the younger coaches achieve their goals through the more humane approaches of the first type.

ORGANIZATION IN PARAGRAPHS

A paragraph needs more than a unified point; it needs a reasonable organization or sequence. After all, a box containing all of the materials for a model airplane has unity (all the parts of the plane are there), but not until the parts are joined in the proper relationship do we get a plane. In the following paragraph, a sentence is out of place.

> Leonardo da Vinci's *Mona Lisa* has attracted and puzzled viewers for almost five hundred years, and I don't suffer from the delusion that I can fully account for the spell the picture casts. Still,

Leonardo da Vinci: Mona Lisa.

I think it is easy enough to account for at least part of the mystery. The most expressive features of a face are the mouth and the eyes, and we notice that Leonardo slightly blurred or shaded the corners of the mouth so that its exact expression cannot be characterized, or, if we characterize it, we change our mind when we look again. Lisa herself is something of a mystery, for history tells us nothing about her personality or about her relationship to Leonardo. The corners of her eyes, like the corners of her mouth, are slightly obscured, contributing to her elusive expression.

Which sentence is out of place in the paragraph you have just read? How might you work it into its proper place?

Exactly how the parts of a paragraph will fit together depends, of course, on what the paragraph is doing. If it is describing a place, it may move from a general view to the significant details — or from some immediately striking details to some less obvious but perhaps more important ones. It may move from near to far, or from far to near. Other paragraphs may move from cause to effect, or from effect back to cause, or from past to present. In the following paragraph, written by a student, we move chronologically — from waking at 7:00 A.M., to washing and combing, to readiness for the day's work, and then to a glance at the rest of the day that will undo the 7:00 A.M. cleanup.

> I can remember waking at seven to Ma's call. I'd bound out of bed because Ma just didn't allow people to be lazy. She'd grab me and we'd rush to the bathroom for the morning ritual. Bathing, toothbrushing, lotioning, all overseen by her watchful eyes. She didn't let anything go by. No missing behind the ears, no splashing around and pretending to bathe. I bathed and scrubbed and put that lotion on till my whole body was like butter on a warm pan. After inspection it was back to my room and the day's clothes were selected. A bit of tugging and I was dressed. Then she'd sit me down and pull out the big black comb. That comb would glide through my hair and then the braiding would begin. My head would jerk but I never yelled, never even whimpered. Finally I was ready. Ready to start the day and get dirty and spoil all of Ma's work. But she didn't care. She knew you couldn't keep a child from getting dirty but you could teach it to be respectable.

If a paragraph is classifying (dividing a subject into its parts) it may begin by enumerating the parts and go on to study each, perhaps in climactic order. Here is an example.

> The chief reasons people wear masks are these: to have fun, to protect themselves, to disguise themselves, and to achieve a new identity. At Halloween, children wear masks for fun; they may, of course, also think they are disguising themselves, but chiefly their motive is to experience the joy of saying "boo" to someone. Soldiers wore masks for protection, in ancient times against swords and battle-axes, in more recent times against poison gas. Bank robbers wear masks to disguise themselves, and though of course this dis-

guise is a sort of protection, a robber's reason for wearing a mask is fairly distinct from a soldier's. All of these reasons so far are easily understood, but we may have more trouble grasping the reason that primitive people use masks in religious rituals. Some ritual masks seem merely to be attempts to frighten away evil spirits, and some seem merely to be disguises so that the evil spirits will not know who the wearer is. But most religious masks are worn with the idea that the wearer achieves a new identity, a union with supernatural powers, and thus in effect the wearer becomes — really becomes, not merely pretends to be — a new person.

In short, among the common methods of organizing a paragraph are:

1. general to particular (topic sentence usually at the beginning)
2. particular to general (topic sentence usually at the end)
3. enumeration of parts or details or reasons (probably in climactic order)
4. question and answer
5. cause and effect
6. chronology

The only rule that can cover all paragraphs is this: readers must never feel that they are stumbling as they try to follow the writer to the end of the paragraph. They should not have to go back and read the paragraph again to figure out what the writer had in mind. It is the writer's job, not the reader's, to give the paragraph its unity and organization. A paragraph is not a maze; it should be organized so that the reader can glide through it in seconds, not minutes.

COHERENCE IN PARAGRAPHS

It is not enough to write unified and organized paragraphs; the unity and organization must be coherent, that is, sufficiently clear, so that the reader can unhesitatingly follow your train of thought. Coherence is achieved largely by means of transitions and repetition.

Vladimir Koziakin: Spaghetti.

Transitions

Richard Wagner, commenting on his work as a composer of operas, once said "The art of composition is the art of transition," for his art moved from note to note, measure to measure, scene to scene. Because transitions establish connections between points, they contribute to coherence. Here are some of the most common transitional words and phrases.

1. amplification or likeness: *similarly, likewise, and, also, again, second, third, in addition, furthermore, moreover, finally*
2. emphasis: *chiefly, equally, indeed, even more important*
3. contrast or concession: *but, on the contrary, on the other hand, by contrast, of course, however, still, doubtless, no doubt, nevertheless, granted that, conversely, although, admittedly*

4. example: *for example, for instance, as an example, specifically, consider as an illustration, that is, such as, like*
5. consequence or cause and effect: *thus, so, then, it follows, as a result, therefore, hence*
6. restatement: *in short, that is, in effect, in other words*
7. place: *in the foreground, further back, in the distance*
8. time: *afterward, next, then, as soon as, later, until, when, finally, last, at last*
9. conclusion: *finally, therefore, thus, to sum up*

Make sure that each sentence in a paragraph is properly related to the preceding and the following sentences. Such obvious transitions or roadsigns as "moreover," "however," "but," "for example," "this tendency," "in the next chapter" are useful, but remember that (1) these transitions should not start every sentence (they can be buried: "Smith, moreover . . ."), and (2) explicit transitions need not appear at all in a sentence, so long as the argument proceeds clearly. The gist of a paragraph might run thus: "Speaking broadly, there were two comic traditions. . . . The first. . . . The second. . . . The chief difference between them. . . . But both traditions. . . ."

Consider the following paragraph:

> Folklorists are just beginning to look at Africa. A great quantity of folklore materials has been gathered from African countries in the past century and published by missionaries, travelers, administrators, linguists, and anthropologists incidentally to their main pursuits. No fieldworker has devoted himself exclusively or even largely to the recording and analysis of folklore materials, according to a committee of the African Studies Association reporting in 1966 on the state of research in the African arts. Yet Africa is the continent supreme for traditional cultures that nurture folklore. Why this neglect?
>
> — Richard M. Dorson

The reader gets the point, but the second sentence seems to contradict the first: the first sentence tells us that folklorists are just beginning to look at Africa, but the next tells us that lots of folklore has been collected. An "although" between these sentences would clarify the author's point, especially if the third sentence were hooked on to the second, thus:

Folklorists are just beginning to look at Africa. Although a great quantity of folklore materials has been gathered from African countries in the past century by missionaries, travelers, administrators, linguists, and anthropologists incidentally to their main pursuits, no fieldworker has devoted himself . . .

But this revision gives us an uncomfortably long second sentence. Further revision would help. The real point of the original passage, though it is smothered, is that although many people have incidentally collected folklore materials in Africa, professional folklorists have not been active there. The contrast ought to be sharpened:

Folklorists are just beginning to look at Africa. True, missionaries, travelers, administrators, linguists, and anthropologists have collected a quantity of folklore materials incidentally to their main pursuits, but folklorists have lagged behind. No fieldworker . . .

In this revision the words that clarify are, of course, the small but important words "true" and "but." The original paragraph is a jigsaw puzzle, missing some tiny but necessary pieces.

Repetition

Coherence is achieved not only by means of transitional words and phrases but also through the repetition of key words. When you repeat words or phrases, or when you provide clear substitutes (such as pronouns and demonstrative adjectives), you are helping the reader to keep step with your developing thoughts. Grammatical constructions too can be repeated, the repetitions or parallels linking the sentences or ideas.

The purpose of science is to describe the world in an orderly scheme or language which will help us to look ahead. We want to forecast what we can of the future behavior of the world; particularly we want to forecast how it would behave under several alternative actions of our own between which we are usually trying to choose. This is a very limited purpose. It has nothing whatever to do with bold generalizations about the universal workings of cause and effect. It has nothing to do with the cause and effect at all, or with any other special mechanism. Nothing in this purpose, which is to order the world as an aid to decision and action, implies that the order must be of one kind rather than another. The order is what we find to work, conveniently and instructively. It is not something we stipulate; it is not something we can dogmatize about. It is what we find; it is what we find useful.

— J. Bronowski

Notice the repetition of key words: "purpose," "orderly" ("order"), "world," "behavior" ("behave"), "actions" ("action"), "cause and effect." Notice also the repeated constructions: "we want to forecast," "it has nothing to do with," "it is not something we," "it is what we find."

In the next example the repetitions are less emphatic, but again they provide continuity.

Sir Kenneth Clark's *The Nude* is an important book; and, luckily, it is also most readable; but it is not a bedside book. Each sentence needs attention because each sentence is relevant to the whole, and the incorrigible skipper will sometimes find himself obliged to turn back several pages, chapters even, in order to pick up the thread of the argument. Does this sound stiff? The book is not stiff because it is delightfully written. Let the student have no fears; he is not going to be bored for a moment while he reads these 400 pages; he is going to be excited, amused, instructed, provoked, charmed, irritated and surprised.

Notice not only the exact repetitions ("each sentence," "stiff") but also the slight variations, such as "an important book," "not a bedside book"; "he is not going," "he is going," and the emphatic list of participles ("excited, amused, instructed," and so on) at the conclusion.

Here is one more example of a paragraph that unobtrusively uses repetition.

The main skill is to keep from getting lost. Since the roads are used only by local people who know them by sight nobody complains if the junctions aren't posted. And often they aren't. When they are it's usually a small sign hiding unobtrusively in the weeds and that's all. County-road-sign makers seldom tell you twice. If you miss that sign in the weeds that's *your* problem, not theirs. Moreover, you discover that the highway maps are often inaccurate about county roads. And from time to time you find your "county road" takes you onto a two-rutter and then a single rutter and then into a pasture and stops, or else it takes you into some farmer's backyard.

— Robert M. Pirsig

What repetitions do you note? (For additional comments on repetition and variation as transitions, see pages 300–01.)

Transitions between Paragraphs

As you move from one paragraph to the next — from one step in the development of your thesis to the next — you probably can keep the reader with you if you make the first sentence of each new paragraph a transition, or perhaps a transition and a topic sentence. The first sentence of a paragraph that could follow the paragraph quoted a moment ago on Kenneth Clark's *The Nude* might run thus:

Among the chief delights of these 400 pages are the illustrations.

Clearly "Among the chief delights of these 400 pages" is a transition, picking up the reference to "400 pages" near the end of the previous paragraph, and the rest of the sentence introduces the topic — the illustrations — of the new paragraph. Only if your two paragraphs are extremely complex, and you believe the reader needs lots of help, will you need to devote an entire paragraph to a transition between two other paragraphs. Often a single transitional word or phrase (such as those listed on pages 80–81) will suffice.

GROUPS OF PARAGRAPHS

Since a paragraph is, normally, a developed idea, and each developed idea has its place in explaining your thesis, as one paragraph follows the next the reader feels he is getting somewhere. Consider the neat ordering of ideas in the following four consecutive paragraphs. The paragraph preceding the first of these was chiefly concerned with describing several strategies whereby the Marx Brothers succeeded in making full-length talking films, in contrast to the short silent films of a decade earlier. In the first of the following paragraphs, "also" provides the requisite transition.

The Marx Brothers also overcame the problem of the talkies by revealing individual relationships to talk. Groucho talks so much, so rapidly, and so belligerently that talk becomes a kind of weapon. He shoots word bullets at his listeners, rendering them (and the audience) helpless, gasping for breath, trying to grab hold of some argument long enough to make sense of it. But before anyone can grab a verbal handle, Groucho has already moved on to some other topic and implication that seems to follow from his previous one — but doesn't. Groucho's ceaseless talk leads the listener in intellectual circles, swallowing us in a verbal maze, eventually depositing us back at the starting point without knowing where we have been or how we got there. Groucho's "logic" is really the manipulation of pun, homonym, and equivocation. He substitutes the quantity of sound and the illusion of rational connection for the theoretical purpose of talk — logical communication.

Chico's relationship to talk also substitutes sound for sense and the appearance of meaning for meaning. To Chico, "viaduct" sounds like "why a duck," "wire fence" like "why a fence," "short-cut" like "short cake," "sanity clause" like "Santa Claus," "dollars" like "Dallas," "taxes" like "Texas." He alone can puncture Groucho's verbal spirals by stopping the speeding train of words and forcing Groucho to respond to his own erroneous intrusions. Groucho cannot get away with his coy substitution of sound for sense when Chico makes different (but similar) sounds out of the key terms in Groucho's verbal web. Chico's absurd accent (this Italian burlesque would be considered very impolite by later standards) makes him hear Groucho's words as if he, the Italian who speaks pidgin English, were speaking them.

The substitution of sound for sense reaches its perfection in Harpo, who makes only sounds. Harpo substitutes whistling and beeps on his horn for talk. Ironically, he communicates in the films as well as anybody. He communicates especially well with Chico, who understands Harpo better than Groucho does. Chico continually interprets Harpo's noises for Groucho. The irony that a bumbling foreign speaker renders a mute clown's honks, beeps, and whistles into English so it can be understood by the supreme verbal gymnast plays a role in every Marx Brothers film.

Harpo also substitutes the language of the body for speech. In this system of communication, Harpo uses two powerful allies — props and mime. He gives the password ("swordfish") that admits him to a speakeasy by pulling a swordfish out of his pocket. He impersonates Maurice Chevalier by miming a Chevalier song to a phonograph record, produced out of his coat especially for the occasion. Or he orders a shot of Scotch in the speakeasy by snapping into a Highland fling. In these early talkies, talk became one of the comic subjects of the films as well as one of the primary comic devices. As in the early Chaplin sound films, the Marx Brothers made talk an ally simply by treating it so specially.

— Gerald Mast

A few observations on these paragraphs may be useful. Notice that the first sentence of the first paragraph is, in effect, an introduction to all four paragraphs; because it is too thin to stand by itself, this transition is acceptably attached as a preface to the first paragraph of what is really a unit of four paragraphs. Second, notice that the first paragraph is devoted to Groucho, the second to Chico, and the third and fourth to Harpo. We might think that symmetry requires that Harpo get only one paragraph, like his brothers, but the writer, feeling that each of Harpo's two languages — noises and gestures — is a major point and therefore worth a separate paragraph, rightly allows significance to overrule symmetry. Third, note the simple but adequate transitions at the beginnings of the paragraphs: "Chico's relationship to talk also . . . ," "The substitution of sound for sense reaches its perfection in Harpo," and "Harpo also substitutes the language of the body for speech." Although the repetition of "also" is a trifle mechanical, it serves to let the reader know where he will be going. Finally, notice that this unit discussing the three brothers is arranged climactically; it ends with Harpo, who is said to achieve "perfection" in the matter under discussion. And in this discussion of distorted language, the two paragraphs on Harpo similarly are arranged to form a climax: the second, not the first, gives us the ultimate distortion, language that is not even sound.

PARAGRAPH LENGTH

Of course hard-and-fast rules cannot be made about the lengths of paragraphs, but more often than not a good paragraph is between one hundred and two hundred words, consisting of more than one or two but fewer than eight or ten sentences. It is not a matter, however, of counting words or sentences; paragraphs are coherent blocks, substantial units of your essay, and the spaces between them are brief resting places allowing the reader to take in what you have said. One page of typing (approximately 250 words) is about as much as the reader can take before requiring a slight break. On the other hand, one page of typing with half a dozen paragraphs is probably faulty because the reader is too often interrupted with needless pauses and because the page has too few *developed* ideas: an assertion is made, and then another, and another. They are unconvincing because they are not supported with detail. To put it another way, a paragraph is a room in the house you are building. If your essay is some five hundred words long (about two double-spaced typewritten pages) you probably will not break it down into more than four or five rooms or paragraphs; if you break it down into a dozen paragraphs, readers will feel they are touring a rabbit warren rather than a house.

THE USE AND ABUSE OF SHORT PARAGRAPHS

A short paragraph can be effective when it summarizes a highly detailed previous paragraph or group of paragraphs, or when it serves as a transition between two complicated paragraphs, but unless you are sure that the reader needs a break, avoid thin paragraphs. A paragraph that is nothing but a transition can usually be altered into a transitional phrase or clause or sentence that starts the next paragraph. But of course there are times when a short paragraph is exactly right. Notice the effect of the two-sentence paragraph between two longer paragraphs:

> After I returned to prison, I took a long look at myself and, for the first time in my life, admitted that I was wrong, that I had gone astray — astray not so much from the white man's law as from being human, civilized — for I could not approve the act of rape. Even though I had some insight into my own motivations, I did not feel justified. I lost my self-respect. My pride as a man dissolved and my whole fragile moral structure seemed to collapse, completely shattered.

That is why I started to write. To save myself.

I realized that no one could save me but myself. The prison authorities were both uninterested and unable to help me. I had to seek out the truth and unravel the snarled web of my motivations. I had to find out who I am and what I want to be, what type of man I should be, and what I could do to become the best of which I was capable. I understood that what had happened to me had also happened to countless other blacks and it would happen to many, many more.

— Eldridge Cleaver

If the content of the second paragraph were less momentous, it would hardly merit a paragraph. Here the brevity helps to contribute to the enormous impact; those two simple sentences, set off by themselves, are meant to be equal in weight, so to speak, to the longer paragraphs that precede and follow. They are the hinge on which the door turns.

Now read the following horrible example, a newspaper account — chiefly in paragraphs of one sentence each — of an unfortunate happening.

Fish Eat Brazilian Fisherman

Reuters

MANAUS, BRAZIL — Man-eating piranha fish devoured fisherman Zeca Vicente when he tumbled into the water during a battle with 300 farmers for possession of an Amazon jungle lake.

Vicente, a leader of a group of 30 fishermen, was eaten alive in minutes by shoals of the ferocious fish lurking in Lake Januaca.

He died when the farmers — packed in an armada of small boats — attacked the fishermen with hunting rifles, knives, and bows and arrows after they refused to leave.

The farmers, who claimed the fishermen were depleting the lake's fish stocks, one of their main sources of food, boarded the fishing vessels and destroyed cold storage installations.

Last to give way was Vicente, who tried to cut down the farmers' leader with a knife. But farmers shot him and he fell wounded into the water, and into the jaws of the piranhas.

Fifteen persons have been charged with the attack which caused Vicente's death and the injury of several other fishermen.

> Lake Januaca, about four hours from this Amazon River town by launch, is famous for its pirarucu and tucunare fish which are regarded as table delicacies.

Most marvelously wrong is the final paragraph, with its cool guidebook voice uttering as inappropriate a fact as is imaginable, but what concerns us at the moment is the writer's failure to build his sentences into paragraphs. Probably all six paragraphs (the seventh, final paragraph is irrelevant) can be effectively combined into one paragraph. Better, perhaps, the material can be divided into two paragraphs, one describing the event and another describing the cause or background. At the most, there is the stuff of three paragraphs, one on the background, one on the event itself, and one on the consequences (fifteen people are charged with the attack). Imagine how it could be reorganized into one paragraph, into two paragraphs, and into three. Which do you think would be most effective? Even the present final paragraph can be worked in; how?

If you spend a few minutes revising the newspaper account of the Brazilian fisherman's death, you will notice that sometimes you can make at least a small improvement merely by joining one paragraph to the next, such as the second to the third. But unsatisfactory short paragraphs usually cannot be repaired so simply; most are unsatisfactory not because sentences have been needlessly separated from each other, but because sentences with generalizations have not been supported by details. Consider these two consecutive paragraphs from a student's essay on Leonardo's *Mona Lisa*.

> Leonardo's "Mona Lisa," painted about 1502, has caused many people to wonder about the lady's expression. Different viewers see different things.
>
> The explanation of the puzzle is chiefly in the mysterious expression that Leonardo conveys. The mouth and the eyes are especially important.

If you have read pages 76–78 you know that we have already made some use of Mona Lisa's mysterious expression, but here is another version, strengthening the two feeble paragraphs we have just quoted.

Leonardo's "Mona Lisa," painted about 1502, has caused many people to wonder about the lady's expression. Doubtless she is remarkably life-like, but exactly what experience of life, what mood, does she reveal? Is she sad, or gently mocking, or uncertain or self-satisfied, or lost in daydreams? Why are we never satisfied when we try to name her emotion?

Part of the uncertainty may of course be due to the subject as a whole: What can we make out of the combination of this smiling lady and that utterly unpopulated landscape? But surely a large part of the explanation lies in the way that Leonardo painted the face's two most expressive features, the eyes and the mouth. He slightly obscured the corners of these, so that we cannot precisely characterize them; and although on one viewing we may see them one way, on another viewing we may see them slightly differently. If today we think she looks detached, tomorrow we may think she looks slightly threatening.

This revision is not simply a padded version of the student's earlier paragraphs; it is a necessary clarification of them, for without the details the generalizations mean almost nothing to a reader.

INTRODUCTORY PARAGRAPHS

Beginning a long part of one of his long poems, Byron aptly wrote, "Nothing so difficult as a beginning." Woody Allen thinks so too. In an interview published in the December 1977 issue of *Media & Methods* he says that the toughest part of writing is "to go from nothing to the first draft." Almost all writers — professionals as well as amateurs — find that the first paragraphs in their drafts are false starts. Don't worry too much about the opening paragraphs of your draft; you'll almost surely want to revise your opening later anyway. (Surprisingly often your first paragraph may simply be deleted; your second, you find, is where your essay truly begins.) When writing a first draft you merely need something — almost anything may do — to break the ice. But in your finished paper, the opening cannot be mere throat-clearing. It should be interesting. "Webster says . . ." is not interesting. Nor is a paraphrase of your title, "Anarchism and the Marx Brothers": "This essay will study the anarchic acts of the Marx Brothers." There is no information about the topic here, at least none beyond what the title already gave, and there is no information about you either, that is, no sense of your response to the topic, such as might be present in, say, "The Marx Brothers are funny, but one often has the feeling that under the fun the violence has serious implications." But in your effort to find your voice and to say something interesting, don't yield to irrelevancy ("*Hamlet* is full of violence" is true, but scarcely relevant to the Marx Brothers) or to the grandiloquence that has wickedly but aptly been called Freshman Omniscience ("Ever since the beginning of time, man has been violent").

Your introductory paragraph will be at least moderately interesting if it gives information, and it will be pleasing if the information provides focus: that is, if it lets the reader know exactly what your topic is, and where you will be going. Remember, when you write, *you* are the teacher; it won't do to begin, "Orwell says he shot the elephant because. . . ." We need at least, "George Orwell, in 'Shooting an Elephant,' says he shot the elephant because. . . ." Even better is, "In 'Shooting an Elephant,' George Orwell's uneasy reflections on his service as a policeman in Burma, Orwell suggests that he once shot an elephant because . . . but his final paragraph suggests that we must look for additional reasons."

Compare, for example, the opening sentences from three essays written by students on Anne Moody's *Coming of Age in Mississippi*. The book is the autobiography of a black woman, covering her early years with her sharecropper parents, her schooling, and finally her work in the civil rights movement.

> The environment that surrounds a person from an early age tends to be a major factor in determining their character.

This is what we call a *zonker* (see page 254), an all-purpose sentence that serves no specific purpose well. Notice also the faulty reference of the pronoun (the plural "their" refers to the singular "a person"), the weaseling of "tends to be a major factor," and the vagueness of "early age" and "environment" and "character." These all warn us that the writer will waste our time.

> It is unfortunate but true that racial or color prejudice shows itself early in the life of a child.

Less pretentious than the first example, but a tedious laboring of the obvious, and annoyingly preachy.

> Anne Moody's autobiography, *Coming of Age in Mississippi,* vividly illustrates how she discovered her black identity.

Surely this is the best of the three openings. Informative and focused, it identifies the book's theme and method, and it offers an evaluation. The essayist has been considerate of her readers: if we are interested in women's autobiographies, life in the South, or black identity we will read on. If we aren't, we are grateful to her for letting us off the bus at the first stop.

But of course you can provide interest and focus by other, more indirect means. Among them are:

1. a quotation
2. an anecdote or other short narrative
3. an interesting fact (a statistic, for instance, showing the reader that you know something about your topic)
4. a definition of an important term — but not merely one derived from a desk dictionary
5. a glance at the opposition (disposing of it)
6. a question — but an interesting one, such as "Why do we call some words obscene?"

Many excellent opening paragraphs do not use any of these devices, and you need not use any of them if they seem unnatural to you. But observe in your reading how widely and successfully these devices are used. Here is an example of the second device, an anecdote that makes an effective, indeed an unnerving, introduction to an essay on aging.

> There is an old American folk tale about a wooden bowl. It seems that Grandmother, with her trembling hands, was guilty of occasionally breaking a dish. Her daughter angrily gave her a wooden bowl, and told her that she must eat out of it from now on. The young granddaughter, observing this, asked her mother why Grandmother must eat from a wooden bowl when the rest of the family was given china plates. "Because she is old!" answered her mother. The child thought for a moment and then told her mother, "You must save the wooden bowl when Grandma dies." Her mother asked why, and the child replied, "For when you are old."
>
> — Sharon R. Curtin

The following opening paragraph also is in effect a short narrative, though the point is deliberately obscured — in order to build suspense — until the second paragraph.

> For a couple of days after the thing happened, I moved around Los Angeles with an oddly suspended feeling. It was as if I had not known the city before, and the faces on the street that were once merely blank were more personal in their blankness because I was watching them through different eyes, searching out the fugitive among them, or perhaps the victim, and having the feeling that there were lots of both.
>
> I had joined the brotherhood of the victim, a silent membership with high initiation fees. I got robbed and for a while I thought I was going to be killed.
>
> — Charles T. Powers

The third strategy, an interesting detail, shows the reader that you know something about your topic and that you are worth reading. We have already seen (page 69) a rather quiet example of this device, in a paragraph about Charles Darwin, which began "Charles Darwin's youth was unmarked by signs of genius." Here is a more obvious example, from an essay on blue jeans:

> That blue jeans or denims are not found only in Texas is not surprising if we recall that jeans are named for Genoa (Gene), where the cloth was first made, and that denim is cloth *de Nimes*, that is, from Nimes, a city in France.

(These scraps of learning are to be had by spending thirty seconds with a dictionary.)

The fourth strategy, a definition, is fairly common in analytic essays; the essayist first clears the ground by specifying what the topic really is. Here is the beginning of an essay on primitive art.

> The term "primitive art" has come to be used with at least three distinct meanings. First and most legitimate is its use with reference to the early stages in the development of a particular art, as when one speaks of the Italian primitives. Second is its use to designate works of art executed by persons who have not had formal training in our own art techniques and aesthetic canons. Third is its application to the art works of all but a small group of societies which we have chosen to call civilized. The present discussion will deal only with the last.
>
> — Ralph Linton

The author reviews three meanings of the term, and focuses our attention on the relevant one by putting it last.

We leave it to you to find in your reading examples of the fifth and sixth strategies (a glance at the opposition, and an interesting question), but, lest a reader assume that an opening must be of one of these six kinds, we quote an opening that doesn't fit our list:

> Time and again I wanted to reach out and shake Peter Fonda and Dennis Hopper, the two motorcyclist heroes of *Easy Rider*, until they stopped their damned-fool pompous poeticizing on the subject of doing your own thing and being your own man. I dislike Fonda as an actor; he lacks humor, affects insufferable sensitivity and always seems to be fulfilling a solemn mission instead of playing a part. I didn't believe in these Honda hoboes as intuitive balladeers of the interstate highways, and I had no intention of accepting them as protagonists in a modern myth about the destruction of innocence. To my astonishment, then, the movie reached out and profoundly shook me. (Reprinted by permission; © 1970 The New Yorker Magazine, Inc.)
>
> — Joseph Morgenstern

Here Morgenstern deliberately misleads us in his first three sentences. When he reverses direction in the final sentence, he emphasizes the chief point he wants to make.

Such an opening paragraph is a variation on a surefire method: you cannot go wrong in suggesting your thesis in your opening paragraph, moving from a rather broad view to a narrower one. This kind of introductory paragraph can be conceived as a funnel, wide at the top and narrowing into what will be the body of the essay. A common version of this kind of paragraph offers some background and concludes with the subject at hand. It may, for example, briefly sketch the past that contrasts with the present. The following paragraph is from an essay on the pictorial effects in modern films.

> There are still people who remember when there were no talking pictures, when "movies" were simply moving pictures. In 1927 the first full-length sound film was made, and sound soon took over. Coffee cups rattled, rain pattered, and people talked and talked and talked. But film continues to be an essentially visual medium; films are not dramatic plays frozen on celluloid but are essentially moving *pictures*.

But bear in mind that although the first sentence of an introductory paragraph may be broader, more general than the last, it must nevertheless have substance. "Charles Darwin's great accomplishments in the field of natural science resulted from many factors" (look back at page 68) is so broad, so general, so lacking in substance, that it teaches us nothing either about Darwin or about the writer of the essay. If your opening sentence lacks substance, it will not matter what you say next. No one will bother to read more.

CONCLUDING PARAGRAPHS

Concluding paragraphs, like opening paragraphs, are especially difficult if only because they are so conspicuous. Fortunately, you are not always obliged to write one. Descriptive essays, for example, may end merely with a final paragraph, not with a paragraph that draws a conclusion. In an expository essay explaining a process or mechanism you may simply stop when you have finished. Just check to see that the last sentence is a good one, clear and vigorous, and stop. In such essays there is usually no need for a crescendo signaling your farewell to the reader. Persuasive essays are more likely to need concluding paragraphs, not merely final paragraphs. But even persuasive essays, if they are short enough, may end without a formal conclusion; if the last paragraph sets forth the last step of the argument, that may be conclusion enough.

Let's assume, however, that you do feel the need to write a concluding paragraph. With conclusions, as with introductions, try to say something interesting. It is not of the slightest interest to say "Thus we see . . ." and then echo your title and first paragraph. There is some justification for a summary at the end of a long paper because the reader may have half forgotten some of the ideas presented thirty pages earlier, but a paper that can easily be held in the mind needs something different. A good concluding paragraph does more than provide an echo of what the writer has already said. It rounds out the previous discussion, normally with a few sentences that summarize (without the obviousness of "We may now summarize"), but it also may draw an inference that has not previously been expressed. To draw such an inference is not to introduce a new idea — a concluding paragraph is hardly the place for a new idea — but is to see the previous material in a fresh perspective. A good concluding paragraph closes the issue while enriching it. For example, the essay on being assaulted and robbed (the opening paragraphs are quoted on page 93) ends with these two paragraphs:

> What do they take when they rob you? Maybe a thousand dollars' worth of stuff. A car. A jar of pennies and small change — the jar, which they would probably end up breaking, worth more than the change inside. A portable radio bought years before at an Army PX. Little things that it takes days to discover are missing.
>
> And what else? The ability to easily enter a darkened apartment or to freely open the door after going out. The worst loss is the sense of private space, whether it's in your head or your home, and you can never be certain it will not be invaded again.
>
> — Charles T. Powers

Powers moves from the theft of material objects to the psychological implications of the theft, that is, to a more profound kind of robbery. This is not a new topic because the idea is implicit throughout a discussion of assault and robbery and so it enlarges rather than abandons the topic. It is just that Powers is explicitly stating the idea for the first time.

We hesitate to offer a do-it-yourself kit for final paragraphs, but the following simple devices often work:

1. End with a quotation, especially a quotation that amplifies or varies a quotation used in the opening paragraph.
2. End with some idea or detail from the beginning of the essay and thus bring it full circle.
3. End with an allusion, say to a historical or mythological figure or event, putting your topic in a larger framework.
4. End with a glance at the readers — not with a demand that they mount the barricades, but with a suggestion that the next move is theirs.

If you adopt any of these devices, do so quietly; the aim is not to write a grand finale, but to complete or round out a discussion.

Here are two concluding paragraphs; notice how they wrap things up and at the same time open out by suggesting a larger frame of reference. The first example, from a student's essay on

Anthony Burgess' *A Clockwork Orange*, includes quotations from the book and an allusion to a common expression.

> Both worlds, youthful anarchy and repressive government, are undesirable. For while "you can't run a country with every chelloveck comporting himself in Alex's manner of the night," there should never be a government with the power to "turn you into something other than a human being . . . with no power of choice any longer." What is frightening is that there is no apparent solution to this futuristic society's dilemma. In fact, with the friendly alliance of Alex and the Minister of the Interior at the end of the book come hints that society may soon enjoy the worst of both worlds.

The second is a concluding paragraph from a student's essay on *Black Elk Speaks*, the life story of an Oglala Sioux holy man. The paragraph includes quotations, and then goes on to suggest that the rest is up to the reader.

> "Truth comes into this world with two faces. One is sad with suffering and the other laughs; but it is the same face." The terrible tragedy of the Indian people can never fully be undone. Their "hoop is broken, and there is no center anymore." But perhaps the rising circulation of Black Elk's story will inspire people to look more closely into person-to-person and person-to-nature relationships. Black Elk's message "was given to him for all men and it is true and it is beautiful," but it must be listened to, understood, and acted on.

All essayists will have to find their own ways of ending each essay; the four strategies we have suggested are common but they are not for you if you don't find them comfortable. And so, rather than ending this section with rules about how to end essays, we suggest how not to end them: don't merely summarize, don't say "in conclusion," don't introduce a totally new point, and don't apologize.

EXERCISES

1. Reread the paragraph on page 71, in which a topic sentence (about three films by the Marx Brothers) begins the paragraph. Then write a paragraph with a similar construction, clarifying

the topic sentence with details. You might, for example, begin thus: "When facing a right-handed batter, a left-handed pitcher has a distinct advantage over a right-handed pitcher." Another possible beginning: "All three major television networks offer pretty much the same kinds of entertainment during prime time."

2. Reread the paragraph on page 72, discussing the face of Frankenstein's monster, and then write a paragraph on some other widely known face (Mick Jagger? Jane Fonda?), ending your paragraph with a topic sentence. The cover of a recent issue of *Time* or *Newsweek* may provide you with the face you need.

3. Many people strongly prefer dogs to cats — or the other way round. Write one paragraph in which you express your preference, supporting this preference by a detailed account of the traits of the two kinds of beasts. (If cats and dogs don't interest you, choose some other pair. For ideas about writing a comparison, see pages 39–45.)

4. The following paragraph is unified, but incoherent. How should it be reorganized?

> Abortion, the expulsion of a fetus which could not develop and function alone successfully, is an issue which has caused much discussion in the past decade. There exist mainly two opposing groups concerning this subject, but many people's opinions lie somewhere in the middle. Some believe that abortions should be legalized unconditionally throughout the United States, while others believe that abortions should be illegal in all cases.

5. The following paragraph is both unified and fairly well organized, but it is still lacking in coherence. What would you do to improve it?

> The cyclist must also master prerace tactics. Not only what to wear and what food to bring are important, but how to strip the bike of unnecessary weight. Cycling shoes are specially designed for bike racing. They have a metal sole that puts the energy directly to the pedal, thus efficiently using one's power. The food that one brings is important in a long-distance race. It must not only be useful in refueling the body, but it must be easily eaten while pedaling. Candy bars and fruit, such as bananas, satisfy both requirements. The bike must be stripped of all unnecessary weight, including saddlebags and reflectors. Some cyclists drill holes in parts of the frame, saddle post, and handlebars to lessen the weight of the bike.

6. On pages 75–76 we printed a paragraph on athletic coaches and we also printed a more unified revision of the paragraph. But the revision (on page 76) is still weak, for it lacks supporting details. Revise the revision, giving it life.

7. Here is the opening paragraph of an essay (about 750 words) on the manufacture of paper in the fifteenth century, the days of the earliest printed books. On the whole it is very good, but the unity and the organization can be improved. Revise the paragraph.

> We take paper for granted, but old as it is it did not always exist. In fact, it was invented long after writing was invented, for the earliest writing is painted or scratched on cave walls, shells, rocks, and other natural objects. Paper was not even the first manufactured surface for writing; sheets made from papyrus, a reed-like plant, were produced about 2500 B.C., long before the invention of paper. Although the Chinese may have invented paper as early as the time of Christ, the oldest surviving paper is from early fifth-century China. The Arabs learned the secret of paper-making from the Chinese in the eighth century, but the knowledge traveled slowly to Europe. The oldest European paper, made by the Moors in Spain, is of the twelfth century. Early European paper is of poor quality and so not until the quality improved, around the fourteenth century, did paper become widely used. Most writing was done on parchment, which is the skin of a sheep or goat, and vellum, which is the finer skin of a lamb, kid, or calf. Whatever the animal, the skin was washed, limed, unhaired, scraped, washed again, stretched, and rubbed with pumice until a surface suitable for writing was achieved. Until it was displaced by paper, in the fourteenth century, parchment was the chief writing surface in Europe.

8. Here is the concluding paragraph of a book review. Analyze and evaluate its effectiveness.

> Mr. Flexner's book is more than a political argument. He has written so vividly and involved us so deeply that there are moments when we yearn to lean over into the pages, pull Hamilton aside, and beg him to reconsider, to pity, to trust, to wait, or merely to shut up. Yet the book's effect is not melodramatic. It is tragic — a tragedy not of fate but of character, the spectacle of an immensely gifted man who tried to rule a nation and could not rule himself.
>
> — Naomi Bliven

9. Read the following brief essay (from *The New Yorker*) once through. Then read it again and decide where you would introduce paragraph breaks. For each of your paragraphs identify the topic sentence, or state in a sentence the topic idea.

On the morning the bus and subway fares were raised to fifty cents, we happened to enter the West Side I.R.T. at 110th Street. From the street above, we heard the din of raised voices, and when we got down into the station we found ourself face to face with four or five young people shouting "No fare at this station!" and "Say no to the Rockefeller banks!" and "Don't pay the fare!" Two of the young people held the exit gates to the platform open while the others, without blocking the way to the token window or the turnstiles, pointed to the open gates. The activists, though they were only a foot or two away from the approaching passengers, bellowed their instructions at the top of their voices. We passed through a turnstile and then, while we waited for a train, turned to observe the proceedings. The moment of decision came and passed swiftly for the people descending the stairs. It came as soon as they reached the bottom; most people walked right on to the platform, whether by the paying or the non-paying route, without breaking stride. About four out of five were accepting the invitation to a free ride. In most cases, it was not until people got through to the platform that their grim, set, closed-in subway expressions dissolved into expressions reflecting a reaction to this unexpected experience. Some of those who were taking a free ride looked exhilarated, or were laughing, but sometimes the laughter had a hollow ring to it, and often the laugher's eyes darted around the platform, as though he were looking for companionship in his gaiety. Others who had entered free seemed almost irritated to find themselves on the platform without having gone through the usual procedures. Some of those who had paid had embarrassed looks, and seemed, with deferential glances and smiles, to be apologizing to their fellow-riders. (The command "Don't pay!" was constantly booming in everyone's ears.) Others who had paid looked outraged by what was happening, and stalked away up the platform. We could discern no pattern in the types of those who paid and those who did not pay. Neither age nor race nor style of dress seemed to provide any clue to the choice that a person would make. One young black man loped through the exit gates, but a young black man just behind him paid. A silver-haired, professorial-looking man stopped, scrutinized the scene with a severe look, and then paid. Shortly afterward, three men in suits and carrying attaché cases sailed through without paying. One elderly man held back for a full two minutes, seeming to give the matter the most solemn thought, and then, holding his face in a rigid deadpan, made a beeline at a rapid clip through the open exit gates. Although there was no guessing from examining someone's appearance which choice he might make, we did notice that the numbers of those going in free seemed to increase considerably when the shouting was loudest. Whenever it abated slightly, the people coming down the stairs tended to surge on past the activists and pay the fare. The shouting, which seemed so repellent and so likely to harm the activists' cause, was turning out to be an effective tactic. Every morning, subway riders, held on course, perhaps, by the great inertia that is born of daily habit, had flowed through the turnstiles and onto the platform on their way to work. On this one morning, many were deflected to a new course — through the open exit gates — like a river that has been diverted into a new bed. For when the shouting reached a certain level of loudness more energy appeared to be required to decide to defy the activists and pay than to break the law and go in free, just as on most mornings more energy would have been required to open the exit gates on one's own than pay. No one had really decided to break the law. On that morning, as on others, people had made no decision at all. (Reprinted by permission; © 1975 The New Yorker Magazine, Inc.)

5
Definition

Many things are not what they sound like: a seedless orange is (according to the citrus industry) an orange with five seeds or fewer; there is no lead in a lead pencil; plum pudding contains no plums; a two-by-four is one and five-eighths inches in thickness and three and three-eighths inches in width; peanuts are not nuts (they are vegetables, related to peas and beans); coffee beans are not beans (they are the pits of a fruit). It comes as no surprise, then, to learn that seventeen-year locusts are not locusts, that Vermont Maid Syrup is not produced in Vermont, and that London Fog raincoats come from Baltimore.

Asked to define a word, most of us want to take advantage of St. Augustine's ingenious evasion: "I know what it is when you don't ask me." Or we sound like Polonius talking about Hamlet (II.ii.92–94):

> Your noble son is mad.
> Mad call I it, for, to define true madness,
> What is't but to be nothing else but mad?

A dictionary can be a great help, of course; but don't begin an essay by saying "Webster says. . . ." Because the name Webster is no longer copyrighted, it appears on all sorts of dictionaries, bad as well as good.[1] Moreover, there is no staler opening.

---

[1] Of the five desk dictionaries that we recommend, two have "Webster" in the title: *Webster's New Collegiate Dictionary* and *Webster's New World Dictionary*. The other three recommended desk dictionaries are *The American College Dictionary*, *The American Heritage Dictionary of the English Language*, and *The Random House*

THE IMPORTANCE OF DEFINITION

A course in writing is partly, even largely, a course in thinking. And "thinking" implies getting straight in one's own mind the meanings of the words one is using, and clearly conveying those meanings to readers. Notice how the following passage, the opening paragraph of an essay on the Scholastic Aptitude Test, neatly points out that "ability" can mean two different things. Only when the ground is cleared, by definition of crucial terms, can the writer go on to discuss whether or not the SAT is a useful device. In short, writers often find that they must define their terms at the outset.

> The idea that colleges should choose among applicants on the basis of their "academic ability" appeals to both educators and the public. But "ability" has two distinct meanings, which imply different admissions policies. In one usage academic ability means an *existing* capacity to do academic work. In the other usage academic ability means a *potential* capacity to do such work. To say that an applicant "has the ability to do differential calculus," for example, can mean either that the applicant can already do differential calculus or that the applicant could learn differential calculus given opportunity and motivation. To avoid this ambiguity, psychometricians usually call the ability to learn something an "aptitude" while calling current mastery of a skill or body of knowledge "achievement."
>
> — Christopher Jencks and James Crouse

Dictionary of the English Language: College Edition. If you didn't receive one of these five as a graduation present, you should buy one. "Pocket" dictionaries and "concise" dictionaries, which contain about 55,000 entries, are not adequate substitutes for any of these five, which contain 130,000–170,000 entries. You should also become acquainted, in the library, with the great *New English Dictionary (NED)*, issued in ten volumes, 1888–1928; reissued in twelve volumes with a supplement, in 1933, as the *Oxford English Dictionary (OED)*. Although this dictionary of course does not include recent words, it is unrivaled in its citations of illustrative quotations indicating the meanings of a word over the centuries. Far less exhaustive, but useful, are three American unabridged dictionaries: *Webster's Third New International Dictionary, Funk and Wagnall's New Standard Dictionary of the English Language,* and *The Random House Dictionary of the English Language.*

DEFINITION BY ORIGIN

Sometimes we know the origin of the word, and the origin may be worth recounting for the light it sheds on the present meaning.

> Low Rider. A Los Angeles nickname for ghetto youth. Originally the term was coined to describe the youth who had lowered the bodies of their cars so that they rode low, close to the ground; also implied was the style of driving that these youngsters perfected. Sitting behind the steering wheel and slumped low down in the seat, all that could be seen of them was from their eyes up, which used to be the cool way of driving. When these youthful hipsters alighted from their vehicles, the term *low rider* stuck with them, evolving to the point where all black ghetto youth — but *never* the soft offspring of the black bourgeoisie — are referred to as low riders.
>
> — Eldridge Cleaver

Or we may know the foreign origins of an English word; *pornography*, for example, comes from Greek words meaning "writing of prostitutes." That's interesting enough and relevant enough to be useful. Or take *yoga*. If you are writing an essay on yoga, you may want to say something like this:

> The word "yoga" comes from a Sanskrit root meaning "to join," "to yoke," and indeed our words "join" and "yoke" both come from this same root. Yoga seeks to join or to yoke the individual's consciousness to its spiritual source.

A word's origins, or etymology (from the Greek, meaning "true word"), may be found in any good dictionary. It may be interesting and relevant and therefore worth mentioning — but of course a word's present meaning may be far from its original meaning, or those of its origins. *Doctor*, for instance, is from a medieval Latin word meaning "teacher." Although this etymology is relevant if you are talking about the classroom skills of Ph.D.'s, it is probably irrelevant (and therefore of no use to you or to your reader) if you are talking about the word in its commonest sense today, "physician."

DEFINITION BY SYNONYM

Usually when we are trying to define a word we can come up with at least a single word as a synonym; so we define *helix* by saying "spiral," or *to civilize* by saying "to socialize." Definition by synonym, however, doesn't go very far; it merely equates one word with another. And often no close synonym exists. In any case, definition by synonym is only a beginning.

Often, too, words are used carelessly as synonyms. George Kane argues, for example, that to use the words *terrorist* and *guerrilla* interchangeably blurs a valuable distinction:

> There has been a good deal of discussion of late about the precise difference between a terrorist and a guerrilla. It is not yet generally realized that there has been a major shift of meaning such as often occurs in the development of language. In earlier times the distinction between the two arose from the difference in the choice of objectives and the methods employed. Both used violence, which was illegal, i.e., not exercised by regular armed forces or police. Guerrillas, however, used it against such regular military and police forces or their installations. They did not normally attack ordinary civilians, still less third parties. Terrorists, on the other hand, usually took care to avoid the armed forces and police of the adversary and instead made war on civilians. They preferred identifiable public figures, with a special liking for elderly cabinet ministers, but were willing to settle for supermarkets, bus stations, kindergartens, and similar unmilitary objectives. They preferred, again, to attack the civilians of the adversary, but if, for any reason, this was not feasible they were willing to indulge in the casual murder of travelers or bystanders of other countries. The guerrilla would delay an operation against an enemy force if there was a danger of injuring civilians; the terrorist was willing to blow up a planeload of randomly selected passengers in order to kill one of them or even to get a prime-time spot on television. This was the distinction between guerrillas and terrorists. It is no longer. As these terms are used today in the media and elsewhere, the distinction no longer relates to strategy or tactics or even objectives, but to ideology and sentiment. To put it simply, a terrorist is one who attacks me or my friends; a guerrilla is one who attacks those to whom I am hostile or indifferent.

Is "women's lib" a contemporary synonym for "feminism"? Irving Kristol, in a review of a book on pornography, maintains that there are important differences between the two movements. Here is the opening paragraph of the review:

> It was utterly predictable that freedom of pornographic speech and action would sooner or later come into conflict with the women's movement. Pornography, after all, has long been recognized to be a predominantly male fantasy involving the sadistic humiliation of women. The women's movement itself, however, did not foresee any such conflict. On the contrary: it assumed a perfectly natural congruence between "sexual liberation" and "women's liberation." Indeed, it was this assumption that differentiated what in the 1960s we came to call "women's lib" from the traditional "feminist" movement that is now at least a century and a half old. Whereas feminists demanded more equal treatment and respect for women, corresponding to the more equal status they were in fact achieving in modern society, the movement for women's liberation proposed to create a radically new human condition for both men and women. There was relatively little utopianism in the feminist movement, which was essentially meliorist and adaptive. Women's liberation, in contrast, was utopian in essence, and it was only because it managed to co-opt the feminist impulse that so many were confused as to its ultimate intentions. Today, the unraveling of the movements is well under way. Feminism survives as a sturdy and successful enterprise; women's liberation is enmeshed in intellectual and practical dilemmas.

In using synonyms, a good general rule is "Keep your reader in mind." Use a synonym if it helps your reader to understand a term you wish to introduce; don't use a synonym merely to avoid repeating a word, or especially a key term. (See "repetition and variation," especially "elegant variation," pages 300–01.)

STIPULATIVE DEFINITION

You may stipulate (contract for) a particular meaning of a word, as we saw in the passage on primitive art (page 93), where the writer briefly set forth three meanings of the word, and then announced he would deal only with the third. Similarly, you may stipulate that by vegetarians you mean people who eat only vegetables, fruit, and nuts, or you mean people who eat these and also fish, eggs, and milk products. Or if for instance you are writing about Catholics, you may stipulate that in your essay the word refers to all who have been baptized into the Catholic faith. Or you may stipulate that it refers only to those who consider themselves practicing Catholics. As another example, take the expression "third world people." This term has at least three related but separate meanings:

1. a group of nations, especially in Africa and Asia, that are not aligned with either the Communist or the non-Communist blocs
2. the aggregate of underdeveloped nations of the world
3. the aggregate of minority groups within a larger predominant culture

In fact, a fourth meaning, a variation of the third, seems to be most common in recent American writing: the aggregate of minority groups *other than blacks and Orientals* within the United States. Many discussions of third world people limit themselves to American Indians and to Spanish-speaking people, apparently considering American blacks and Orientals as part of the larger predominant culture. Thus, in an essay you may announce what you mean by "third world": "In this essay, 'third world' refers not to A or B but to C."

It is entirely legitimate to stipulate or contract for a particular meaning. In fact, you often must stipulate a meaning, for although technical words have relatively stable meanings, many of the words that you will be defining — words such as *education* and *society* — have so many meanings that the reader won't know which you're using until you say so.

FORMAL DEFINITION

A formal definition is a kind of analysis. It normally takes a term (for instance, *professor*) and places it within a class or family ("a teacher") and then goes on to differentiate it from other members of the class ("in a college or university"). Such a definition is sometimes called *inclusive/exclusive* because it includes the word in a relevant category and then excludes other members of that category. Plato is said to have defined *man* as "a featherless biped," but a companion pointed out that this definition is not sufficiently exclusive: a plucked chicken fits the definition. Plato therefore amended it satisfactorily by adding "with flat toenails." Another example: in Hitchcock's *Stage Fright*, Marlene Dietrich suggests that "Detectives are merely policemen with smaller feet." If this definition is inaccurate, it is not so because of its structure. Notice, by the way, that a definition demands a parallel form — for example, a noun for a noun: "A *professor* is a *teacher* in a college or university." Avoid saying "A professor is when you teach . . ." or "Love is never having to say you're sorry."

What use can be made of a formal definition? Suppose you are writing about organic food. You may want to clear the ground by saying something like this:

> All foods contain chemicals (milk contains about a hundred, pota-toes about a hundred fifty), and from a chemical point of view, all foods are organic, for they are compounds containing carbon. So-called organic foods do not differ from other foods in their chemical makeup, but they have been grown with the help only of fertilizers or pesticides of animal or vegetable origin rather than with the help of manufactured chemicals.

Or suppose you want to discuss sharks. A desk dictionary will give you something like this: "a cartilaginous (as opposed to bony) fish with a body tapering toward each end." Such a definition puts sharks within the family of a type of fish and then goes on to exclude other members of this family (which happens also to include rays) by calling attention to the distinctive shape of the shark's body. But if you are not writing a strictly formal definition you may want to talk not only about sharks as remote objects but about your sense of them, your response to them:

> Although the shark and the ray are closely related, being cartilagi-nous rather than bony fish, the two could scarcely be more different in appearance. The ray, a floppy pancake-like creature, is grotesque but not terrifying; the shark, its tapering body gliding through the

water, is perhaps the most beautiful and at the same time the most terrifying sight the sea can offer.

In short, a formal definition can structure your definition even if you go beyond it.

LONGER DEFINITIONS

Most of the terms we try to define in college courses require lengthy definitions. If you are going to say anything of interest about machismo or obscenity or freedom or poverty or mother wit you will have to go far beyond a formal definition. If you are writing on a subject you care about, you may find that you will have to write at least several paragraphs until you get to the limits of the word. *Definition,* by the way, is from the Latin *de* "off" and *finis* "end, limit."

One way of getting toward the limits of the word is to spend some sentences, perhaps a paragraph, on a comparison or contrast. In the paragraph on sharks, half of one sentence compares sharks to rays, which are closely related to sharks but different. In a more extended definition of a less easily defined topic, more space might be devoted to establishing distinctions. For example, the writer of an essay on gallows humor (briefly defined as humor that domesticates a terrifying situation by making fun of it) might wish to compare it with black humor (not the humor of black people, but a brutal or sadistic humor). The superficial similarity of gallows humor to black humor might require the essayist to discuss black humor in order to make clear the special quality of gallows humor; but of course the discussion of black humor should be clearly subordinated to the main topic lest the essay lose focus.

The point of such a strategy is to help the reader see something clearly by holding it against something similar but significantly different. The following extended definition of a proverb follows such a strategy.

A proverb is a concise didactic statement that is widely used in an unchanging form. Among the examples that come to mind are "Look before you leap," "A rolling stone gathers no moss," and "Red sky at night, sailors' delight." These, and almost all other proverbs that one can think of, concisely and memorably summarize everyday experience. This everyday experience is usually a matter of conduct; even "Red sky at night, sailors' delight" — which seems purely descriptive — is followed by "Red sky at morning, sailors take warning." Most commonly, proverbs advise the hearer to avoid excess.

We should distinguish proverbs from other concise utterances. Clichés such as "cool as a cucumber," "last but not least," and "a sight for sore eyes," though they may be called proverbial phrases, often do not offer advice implicitly or explicitly. More important, clichés are not complete sentences. He or she or they can be or are or were "cool as a cucumber"; but a proverb has an independent and unvarying form. Proverbs should be distinguished, too, from such conventional utterances as "Good morning," "Thank you," and "Please pass the salt." These are unvarying, but unlike proverbs they are not didactic.

Closer to proverbs, superficially at least, are epigrams, such as Oscar Wilde's "A cynic is a man who knows the price of everything and the value of nothing." Most epigrams are obviously literary; they usually employ a clever contrast (antithesis) that is rare in proverbs. And most epigrams, unlike proverbs, are not really communal property: their authorship is known, and they are not used by ordinary people in ordinary speech. When used by someone other than the author, they are used by educated speakers or writers as conscious quotations. In contrast, the speaker of a proverb, though he knows that he did not invent it, rightly feels that it is part of his own wisdom.

Notice that this extended definition of proverbs begins by including the proverb within a class ("concise didactic statement") and then proceeds to exclude other members of the class by specifying that a proverb is "widely used in an unchanging form." The definition, then, is inclusive and exclusive; it includes the term to be defined within a class, and it excludes other members of the class. Notice too that examples are given throughout. If the examples were omitted, the paragraphs would be less lively and less clear. But of course, a definition cannot be a mere list of examples ("a proverb is a saying such as . . ."); generalizations as well as concrete illustrations are needed.

The definition of a proverb was just that; it was not a focused essay on proverbs. And it was not an attempt to woo the reader to be interested in proverbs or an attempt to persuade the reader that proverbs really have no wisdom to offer because they are often contradictory ("Look before you leap" contradicts "He who hesitates is lost," and "Birds of a feather flock together" contradicts "Opposites attract"). Rather, it was an attempt to make clear the meaning of a word. If more space had been available, especially if the word were a more elusive one, such as *democracy* or *personality* or *feminism,* the essay might have had the following structure:

1. statement of the need for a definition
2. survey of the usual definitions (calling attention to their inadequacy)
3. the writer's definition, set forth with illustrative examples, comparisons, and contrasts

Clearly the heart of such an essay is the third part.

Though some essays seek to do nothing more than to define a term, essays with other purposes often include paragraphs defining a word. Here, from a long essay on the recent fad for country music, are some paragraphs defining country music. Notice how this selection moves from a moderately jocose and obviously imprecise definition ("anything that Grandma can hum, whistle, or sing is country") to a list of the subjects of country music and then to a hypothetical example.

> What is the fuss all about? Glen George, manager of Kansas City's country radio KCKN, says: "Anything that Grandma can hum, whistle or sing is country." Its traditional message is one of despair, hope, loss, death, the land and, often with cloying sentimentality, love. Country lyrics have always been the cry of the common man. They can, and do give comfort to everyone from sharecroppers and truck-stop waitresses to University of Texas Football Coach Darrell Royal, former Energy Czar John Love, Novelist Kurt Vonnegut, Jr. and Operatic Tenor Richard Tucker. Says Moon Mullins, program director of the all-country WINN in Louisville: "If you listen to our station long enough, one of our songs will tell your story."
>
> Cynics like to say that whomever the story belongs to, it will probably deal with trucks, trains, prison, drinking (or moonshine), women misbehaving ("slippin' around" in the country vernacular) or death. The ideal country song might be about a guy who finally

gets out of prison, hops a truck home, finds that his wife is slippin' around, gets drunk, and staggers to his doom in front of a high-balling freight.

The music itself, at least as purveyed by many of the superstars of Nashville and Bakersfield, has a vanilla sameness to it that often does not reflect the pain and sorrow of the words. The voices of the singers are often less charged with emotion than their blues and rock counterparts. Most male country stars have deep bass baritones that seem to say: this man sits tall in the saddle. Women stars tend to have bright, unstrained sopranos — or a Lynn Anderson kind of nasal chirpiness — that rule out not only women's lib but any other kind of defiance. In the past, country lyrics have been astonishingly repressive. Blind loyalty to husband, parents, even political leaders has been a common theme. When men have sung about women, the subject (always excepting long-suffering Mother) has often been the pain, not the pleasure.

Today, however, country is taking on a new sound, a new diversity and message as well. Partly that is due to the influence of rock, partly to the visible softening of the once strong accents of American regionalization. Says Kris Kristofferson, 37, the former Rhodes scholar who is now a leader of country's progressive wing: "There's really more honesty and less bullshit in today's music than ever before."

EXERCISES

1. Define blues or rock or soul or folk music in 250–500 words.
2. Write one paragraph defining one of the following terms: security blanket, twilight zone, holding pattern. Your paragraph should disclose the origin of the term (if you can't find it, make a reasonable guess) and some examples of current use distinct from its original meaning.
3. On July 14, 1789, Louis XVI asked a courtier, "Is it a revolt?" "No, sire," the courtier replied. "It's a revolution." In a paragraph, explain the courtier's reply.
4. Write an opening paragraph for an essay in which you stipulate a meaning for *death,* excluding one or two other meanings. Don't write the essay, just the opening paragraph.

5. If you are fluent in a language other than English, or in a dialect other than Standard American, write a paragraph defining for native speakers of Standard American a word that stands for some concept. Examples: Spanish *machismo*, Yiddish *haimish* or *chutzpa*, Japanese *shibui*, German *Gemütlichkeit*, black English *bad* or *the dozens*.

6. Write an essay of approximately 500 words on the word *natural* as it is used to advertise products such as cereals, yogurt, cosmetics, and cigarettes. Your essay should stipulate a definition of natural, and should have a thesis. An example of a thesis: "Yogurt may be a wholesome food, but most commercial yogurts are not as 'natural' as we are led to believe."

7. Write an essay (about 500 words) explaining one of the following terms: disaster film, situation comedy, soap opera, junk food, underground newspaper, nostalgia, ethnic joke. Your essay will probably include a definition, reference to several examples, and perhaps an extended discussion of one example, explaining the reasons for its popularity, or arguing its merits or lack of merits. Your essay, then, will probably blend exposition with narration, description, and argument.

DEFINITION AT WORK

Mechanic's Feel

Robert M. Pirsig[2]

The mechanic's feel comes from a deep inner kinesthetic feeling for the elasticity of materials. Some materials, like ceramics, have very little, so that when you thread a porcelain fitting you're very careful not to apply great pressures. Other materials, like steel, have

---

[2] Editors' note: This passage is not an independent essay. It is taken from Pirsig's *Zen and the Art of Motorcycle Maintenance* (New York: Bantam, 1975), pp. 317–18. In the previous paragraph Pirsig has mentioned kinesthesia, sensitive muscular response to things.

tremendous elasticity, more than rubber, but in a range in which, unless you're working with large mechanical forces, the elasticity isn't apparent.

With nuts and bolts you're in the range of large mechanical forces and you should understand that within these ranges metals are elastic. When you take up a nut there's a point called "finger-tight" where there's contact but no takeup of elasticity. Then there's "snug," in which the easy surface elasticity is taken up. Then there's a range called "tight," in which all the elasticity is taken up. The force required to reach these three points is different for each size of nut and bolt, and different for lubricated bolts and for locknuts. The forces are different for steel and cast iron and brass and aluminum and plastics and ceramics. But a person with mechanic's feel knows when something's tight and stops. A person without it goes right on past and strips the threads or breaks the assembly.

A "mechanic's feel" implies not only an understanding for the elasticity of metal but for its softness. The insides of a motorcycle contain surfaces that are precise in some cases to as little as one ten-thousandth of an inch. If you drop them or get dirt on them or scratch them or bang them with a hammer they'll lose that precision. It's important to understand that the metal *behind* the surfaces can normally take great shock and stress but that the surfaces themselves cannot. When handling precision parts that are stuck or difficult to manipulate, a person with mechanic's feel will avoid damaging the surfaces and work with his tools on the nonprecision surfaces of the same part whenever possible. If he must work on the surfaces themselves, he'll always use softer surfaces to work them with. Brass hammers, plastic hammers, wood hammers, rubber hammers and lead hammers are all available for this work. Use them. Vise jaws can be fitted with plastic and copper and lead faces. Use these too. Handle precision parts gently. You'll never be sorry. If you have a tendency to bang things around, take more time and try to develop a little more respect for the accomplishment that a precision part represents.

QUESTIONS

1. Is Pirsig sufficiently specific?
2. What is the function of the first sentence in the third paragraph?

Sophistication
Bergen Evans

Words are living, protean things. They grow, take roots, adapt to environmental changes like any plant or animal. Take *sophisticated,* for example. Originally it meant "wise." Then, through its association with the Sophists, it came to mean "over subtle," "marked by specious but fallacious reasoning," "able to make the worse appear the better reason."

While retaining this meaning, it acquired the additional, derivative sense of "adulterated." A tobacconist in Ben Jonson's "The Alchemist" is said to sell good tobacco: "he doesn't sophisticate it," they say, with other materials. Montaigne had the idea of adulteration in mind when he said that philosophy was nothing but "sophisticated poetry." And so did the eleventh edition of *The Encyclopaedia Britannica* when it said (1913) that ground rice was "one of the chief sophistications" of ginger powder.

From adulteration to corruption is a short step and the meaning of corruption ran side by side with that of adulteration. Coryat (1611) called dyed hair "sophisticated." Lear, going mad in the storm, starts to strip off his clothes because they are trappings of civilization and civilized man is "sophisticated." Judge Walter J. LaBuy of the Federal District Court in Chicago, in sentencing an enterprising young woman who was married to twelve sailors and drawing a dependent's allotment from each of them, told her, with stern disapproval, that she was "thoroughly sophisticated" (Chicago *Tribune*). Judge LaBuy may have been blending both meanings.

Up until about thirty years ago, the most common meaning conveyed by the word was of a particular kind of corruption, the corruption of idealism by worldly experience. And this is still given as its principal meaning in most dictionaries.

Then suddenly the attitude implicit in the word was reversed; it ceased to mean unpleasantly worldly-wise and came to mean admirably world-wise. Something — possibly depression-begotten cynicism, urbanization, army experience, the perfume ads, or the glamorous pornography of the picture magazines — had led the populace to revise its estimate of worldly wisdom. For the past fifteen years *sophistication* has been definitely a term of praise.

And even more. "Sophistication," writes Earl Wilson, "means the ability to do almost anything without feeling guilty." Blum's, the celebrated San Francisco candy manufacturers, on opening a branch store in New York, wooed their new clientele by advising them that their "old-fashioned, home-made-type candies" had been "sophisticated" by their master candy maker. Lloyd Shearer informs the readers of *Parade* that a famous movie actress' husband "seemed sophisticatedly impervious to jealousy," losing his wife "graciously, understandingly and philosophically . . . to another man." It is no wonder that — gog-eyed with awe and envy — a sophomore English class at New Trier High School, in Winnetka, Ill., defined sophistication as "a grace acquired with maturity."

The beginnings of this reversal can be seen in the words of Duke Ellington's "Sophisticated Lady" (1933). The lady of the title has "grown wise." Disillusion is "deep in her eyes." She is "nonchalant . . . smoking, drinking . . . dining with some man in a restaurant." She misses "the love of long ago" but, plainly, has no intention of returning to its meager ecstasies. She has lost innocence but has acquired polish, and when she dines some man picks up the tab. In the minds of many rustic maidens this — one gathers from the change in *sophisticated*'s meaning — was to be preferred to dewy freshness that dined alone at home on leftovers or carried lunch in a paper bag. And by 1958 in John O'Hara's *From the Terrace, sophistication* had come to signify not corruption but almost the irreducible minimum of good manners.

Not content with such audacious change, about three years ago *sophisticated* went hog wild and started to mean "delicately responsive to electronic stimuli," "highly complex mechanically," "requiring skilled control," "extraordinarily sensitive in receiving, interpreting and transmitting signals." Or at least that is what one must guess it means in such statements as "Modern radar is vastly more sophisticated than quaint, old-fashioned radar" (*Time*); later "the IL-18 is aeronautically more sophisticated than the giant TU-114." "Pioneer V is exceedingly sophisticated" (Chicago *Sun-Times*) and "The Antikythera mechanism is far more sophisticated than any described in classical scientific texts" (*Scientific American*).

The connections between these and any previously established meanings of the word are not clear, but since they are definitely favorable, they must spring some way from the post-Ellington uses. My own guess would be this: the sophisticated are not unperceiving, insensitive clods; on the contrary, they are particularly aware of nuances, act on the merest hints, are moved by suasion and respond to subtle stimuli. They don't have to be shoved. They know their way around and move with ease in their allotted orbits.

QUESTIONS

1. At the end of his fifth paragraph, Evans (writing in 1961) says "For the past fifteen years sophistication has been definitely a term of praise." Where did he find his evidence?

2. More than twenty years later, is *sophistication* still a term of praise? What is your evidence? What words currently might be considered antonyms for *sophisticated*?

6

Exposition

In our discussion of analytic writing (page 31), we said that most of the essays a student reads and writes are chiefly analytic; that is, by separating something into its parts the essayist draws conclusions and explains those conclusions.

But most writing can also be classified as exposition, persuasion (or argument), description, or narration. This does not mean, of course, that any given essay must belong exclusively to one of these four kinds of writing. More often than not a single essay combines at least two. For example, an expository essay on Zen Buddhism — an essay chiefly concerned with explaining what Zen is — may include a description of a Zen monastery, a narrative of the writer's visit to the monastery, and an argument (that is, a reasoned statement) for the relevance of Zen to us. If the essay is primarily exposition, the descriptive and narrative and argumentative parts will chiefly function to enliven and clarify the explanation of Zen. Similarly, an essay that is primarily an argument for the relevance of Zen to American life may have to sketch the tenets of the creed (exposition) and may tell an anecdote or recount the history of Zen (narration) in order to strengthen the argument.

For the sake of clarity, however, we will talk about relatively pure examples of these four kinds of writing as we take them up one by one in this and the next three chapters. To talk about them all at once would require the skill of Stephen Leacock's knight, who leaped on his horse and rode madly off in all directions.

In a college catalog, the information telling students how to apply or how to register or how to complete the requirements for a degree is exposition (from the Latin *exponere*, "to put forth"), a setting forth of information. It doesn't assume a disagreement, so it doesn't seek to persuade. Note, also, that those paragraphs in the catalog describing the lovely campus are not exposition but description — or, more exactly, description and persuasion combined, because they seek to persuade the reader to come to the campus. Exposition, too, may be permeated by persuasion, because writing that explains something usually at the same time seeks to persuade us that the topic is worth our attention. But exposition in its purest form seeks only to explain — to expose, we might say — what's what.

Here is a short piece, primarily expository. If typed, double-spaced, it would probably be a little more than one page.

In Search of the Elusive Pingo

Canadian scientists are preparing an expedition to the Beaufort Sea to study underwater ice formations that are blocking use of the Northwest Passage as a long-sought commercial route. The formations, called pingoes, are cones of antediluvian ice, coated with frozen muck, that stick up like fingers from the bottom of the sea to within 45 feet of the surface. They could rip the bottom of ships, such as supertankers, that ride deep in the water.

The pingoes are an obstacle to exploitation of oil resources and expansion of trade in the Arctic region that were expected to follow the successful pioneer voyage of the *S.S. Manhattan* through the ice-clogged Northwest Passage five years ago. One tanker ripped open could disrupt the ecological balance of much of the region.

The existence of the pingoes was not known until 1970 when scientists aboard the Canadian scientific ship *Hudson*, using special sonar equipment to plot the shape of the Beaufort Sea's basin, detected batches of them that the *Manhattan* was lucky to miss. Since then, oceanographers have charted about 200 pingoes, and there is no telling how many more there are.

Scientists at the United States Geological Survey and the Bedford Institute of Oceanography in Nova Scotia, where the *Hudson*'s expedition originated, have been exploring the origin of the pingoes and seeking in vain ways to neutralize them. Dynamiting has proved ineffective. So scientists from Bedford are going back this summer for another look.

You may not want to learn much more about pingoes, but we hope you found this brief account clear and interesting. You might ask yourself how the writer sustains your interest:

1. Is the title attractive?
2. What expression in the first paragraph is especially effective? Why?
3. Are the paragraphs given in a reasonable order?
4. Is the final paragraph a satisfactory ending?

By asking such questions and then answering them, you will discover some of the principles of good expository writing.

Exposition need not, of course, explain only the remote or the unfamiliar. Often an expository essay presents in an authoritative way information of interest to a special audience. The following essay, written by a student, serves as a good example.

Tennis Tips to a Beginning Player

by Susan Pope

The beginning player needs tennis tips on the two basic skills of tennis: footwork, the way in which you move to prepare to hit the ball, and form, the way in which you hit the ball. The most important coaching command relevant to both skills is "Concentrate and keep your eye on the ball." As soon as you see the opposing player hit the ball, determine where it will land and move quickly to that spot, never taking your eyes from the ball.

Moving requires footwork, the most subtle and often overlooked aspect of tennis. In order to hit the ball well, you must first reach it in plenty of time. When receiving a serve you should stand behind the point where you expect to receive the ball; you may then run smoothly forward to receive it rather than tripping backwards. Stand, facing the net, with your feet shoulder width apart, knees flexed, and holding the neck of your racket lightly in your free hand. This is called the ready position. Bounce up and down on the balls of your feet and prepare to move.

The instant the server makes contact with the ball, jump; this enables you to move quickly in any direction. Move laterally by jumping and sliding with your feet parallel; never cross your feet. After completing your swing, return immediately to the center of the back court line, assume the ready position, bounce on the balls of your feet, and prepare to move again. If you can predict where your opponent will return the ball, move to this area instead and assume your ready stance. The objective of footwork is to reach the ball quickly so you can prepare to hit it with good form.

Form involves the position and use of the parts of your body as you hit the ball. By the time you have reached the place where you intend to hit the ball, you should have completed your backswing, cocking your racket back until it points behind you. A short backswing resulting from not bringing your racket back soon enough will almost always result in a mistake. On the other hand, by having your racket back, you still may be able to successfully return a ball hit beyond the physical range you can usually reach.

As you wait for the ball with your racket held back, plant your feet firmly, shoulder width apart. If you are using forehand, your left shoulder should be pointing approximately in the direction you wish to hit the ball. Concentrate on firmly gripping the racket handle because a loose grip can result in a wobbly shot. As the ball comes toward you, bend your knees and step with your lead foot toward the ball, the left foot when using forehand. The ball often goes in the net if you hit it standing stiffly. Keep your wrist and elbow rigid as you swing at the ball; using either of these joints for the force of your swing will cause inconsistency in your ground strokes and promote tennis elbow. Use your arm and shoulder as a unit and twist your torso, throwing the weight of your body onto your lead foot and into your swing. Make your swing quick, snappy, and parallel to the ground. If your stroke is not level, the ball will either be scooped up into the air by a rising swing or be hit directly into the net by a swing directed toward the ground. Stroke through the ball as if it were not there and then follow through with your swing bringing the racket up over your shoulder close to your ear. You will have good control over the ball if you hit it in the middle of your racket, the sweet spot, when it is slightly in front of you. Deviations from these basic coaching instructions may cause problems with your form and weaken your ground strokes. Try to concentrate on them while you practice until you develop an unconscious, smooth, consistent swing.

It requires conscious effort to pinpoint the flaws in your tennis game but often your repeated errors will indicate what you are doing incorrectly. Footwork and form, the basics of the game of tennis may be constantly improved with attention to a few coaching tips. Most important, however, remember to "keep your eye on the ball."

QUESTIONS

1. The essay addresses itself to a beginning player. How successful, for a beginner, would you expect these tips to be?

2. An earlier draft of the essay began with the following paragraph:

Playing tennis requires determined practice and hard work. There are many well-known coaching suggestions which can help improve the consistency of your ground strokes and thereby increase your confidence in your game. With practice, you can integrate these coaching prompts until you execute them automatically. Your concentration may then be focused on game strategy, such as how to capitalize on your opponent's weaknesses, and on more difficult strokes, such as the top spin.

Do you agree with the student's decision to drop the paragraph from her revised essay? Why, or why not?

EXPLAINING A PROCESS

Exposition is often used to explain how something works, or how to do something. The following brief example comes from a popular book by a physician.

How to Deal with the Crying
Leonard Cammer

If you are a soft, sentimental person you probably cannot stand to see your sick relative cry. It breaks you up. However, where tears serve as a necessary emotional outlet they can be encouraged. In a grief reaction especially, when the person has suffered a loss, crying comes easily and produces a healthy release for pent-up emotion. Momentarily, the tears wash away the depressed feelings.

However, when an exhausting bout of tearfulness continues on and on with extreme agitation, breast beating, and self-abuse, it is time for you to call a halt. Let me show you how to terminate almost any flood of tears by the correct use of a psychologic device.

First, sit directly in front of your relative and say, "Go on crying if you want to, but face me. Look into my eyes." It is a simple fact that no one can sustain crying while gazing straight into another's eyes. If the person does what you ask, his tears will stop. Not right away; he may continue to cry and avert his gaze. Take his hands in yours and again coax him to look at you. You may have to repeat the request several times, but at last he will turn and fix his eyes on you, almost hypnotically. The flow of tears then trickles to an end, and the person may begin to talk about the things that give him mental pain.

Every time you shorten such a spell of crying you stem the waste of energy and give the person a chance to preserve his or her stamina in fighting the depression.

Notice that in addition to describing a process, the essay begins by explaining the value of crying and ends by explaining the value of bringing crying to an end. Would the essay be equally good if the first paragraph came last? Notice, too, that although the essay is fairly impersonal, we do get some sense of a human being behind the words. Try, in a sentence or two, to characterize the author. (For more conspicuously personal expository essays, see the pieces by Pirsig, pages 113–14, and Kraemer, pages 130–32.) Cammer is explaining a process, not offering an argument, yet (like every other writer) he must somehow persuade his readers that he knows what he is talking about. How does he persuade us?

Here is another essay, this one a little longer, on a process.

How to Grow an Avocado

To grow an avocado tree indoors, begin with a ripe Florida avocado. (The varieties grown in California, Puerto Rico, and the West Indies can be used, but for some reason they often do not flourish.) The fruit is ripe if the stemmed end yields to the pressure of your thumb. Remove the pit and place it in warm water for about three hours (during the interval you may eat the fruit) and then gently rub off any remaining traces of the fruit and also as much of the paper-thin brown coating as comes easily off the pit. Dry the pit and set it aside for a moment.

Fill a glass almost to the top with warm water. (Remember, the avocado is a tropical tree; cold water harms it.) Next, notice where the base of the pit is (an avocado has a relatively flat base and a relatively tapered top) and insert four toothpicks to half of their length about one-third the way up from the base. If you look down on the avocado from the top, toothpicks are sticking out at what on a clock would be 12:00, 3:00, 6:00, and 9:00. Next, place the avocado in the glass; the base will be in about half an inch of water, but the toothpicks will prevent the pit — or seed, for that is what it is — from sinking to the bottom of the glass. Put the glass in a warm dark place, such as a kitchen closet.

A root may appear at the base within a week, but it is quite usual for nothing to happen for several weeks. Be patient; unless the water turns cloudy, which is a sign that the seed has rotted and must be tossed out, sooner or later the seed will germinate. During this waiting period, all you can do is keep the water at the proper level. (Reminder: make sure the added water is warm.) In time the root will appear at the base and some time later a pale green shoot will appear at the top. Possibly several shoots will appear, but one will establish itself as the main shoot; ignore the others, which may or may not survive. When the main shoot or stem is about eight inches tall, with a scissors cut off the top four inches so that the top growth will not outstrip the root development. Failure to cut the stem will result in a spindly plant with a few leaves. By cutting, you force the stem to send out a new shoot which will grow slowly but which will hold its leaves longer.

When the glass is fairly full of roots (this may be about two weeks after cutting the stem, or as many as six weeks after you prepared the pit), it is time to take it out of the dark and to pot the plant. Use a clay pot about eight and a half inches in diameter. Cover the drainage hole with some pieces of broken pot, and fill the pot to about two-thirds of its height with a mixture of equal parts of good garden soil and sand, mixed with a teaspoon of bonemeal or a couple of tablespoons of dried manure for fertilizer. Remove the toothpicks from the seed, place it on the soil, and then add more of the mixture, until the seed is covered to half of its height. Pour the glass of water over the seed, and then pour an additional glassful of warm water over it. The soil will probably settle; if so, add enough soil to cover the lower half of the seed. Under the pot put a saucer with warm water, and place the saucer and pot in the sunniest place you have.

Water the plant with warm water when the soil appears dry, probably once a day, and be patient. When you cut the main stem you interrupted the plant's growth, and weeks may pass before another stem grows out of the first. But if you water it and give it light, and add plant food about once a month, you are doing all that you can. The main stem — really the trunk of a tree — will in time produce branches that will produce leaves. When leaves develop, you need do nothing except insert a dowel in the pot and loosely tie up any sagging branches. In time you may wish to prune at the top, in order to encourage the lower branches, so that your tree will be bushy rather than spindly. With luck, the tree will flourish; when it is about six feet tall, transplant it to a larger clay pot simply by smashing with a hammer the first pot and then by placing the tree with its ball of roots and earth in a pot prepared just as the first one was. Aside from daily watering (but don't fret if you sometimes miss a day) and occasional fertilizing and pruning, you need do nothing to your tree but enjoy it. But do not spoil your enjoyment by hoping for flowers or fruit; they will never appear.

A good expository essay tries to anticipate any questions the reader might have (how? who? what? why? when? where?). Reread the essay on growing an avocado and notice how the writer answers questions almost before the reader forms them. For example, in the first paragraph, the writer does not simply assert that a Florida avocado should be used; he answers our question, "why?" (we will have a greater chance for success).

ORGANIZING AN EXPOSITORY ESSAY

The organization of the preceding essay is simple but adequate: because it describes a *process* (from the Latin *pro* = "forward" and *cessus* = "movement, step") the essay begins at the beginning and takes the reader through a sequence of steps. This chronological organization is almost inevitable in describing a process, although it is possible to vary the beginning — you needn't begin with step one of the process. The commonest variation uses the opening paragraph to set forth the goal (here, it might be a description of a flourishing avocado, or a gently persuasive paragraph on the pleasure of growing things) — but the process itself would still be described chronologically.

Other patterns of organization common in expository essays are:

1. movement from cause to effect, or from effect to cause (see, for example, Chuck Kraemer's "Indecent Exposure," pages 130–32)
2. comparison (see pages 39–45)
3. classification into subgroups (see pages 30–38)

WRITING SUMMARIES

Another common form of exposition is the summary, a compressed version of a piece of writing. It gives the gist of the original, stripped of details, examples, dialogue, or extensive quotations. A summary is usually said to be less than one-fourth the length of the original. The rule is arbitrary, but useful; anything longer can probably be further condensed. But there are times when a shorter summary suits your purpose. In writing a letter to the editor, you may summarize the view you're opposing in a sentence or two; in reviewing a book, you may summarize its contents in one or two paragraphs.

In summaries of about one-fourth the length of the original, one usually follows the organization of the original. Sometimes, though, a reorganization allows for greater condensation or clarity. If, for example, the writer begins by setting forth the evidence, and states the essay's thesis only in its conclusion, it may be economical to reverse the order: first a summary of the thesis, then a summary of the evidence. Summaries may also use the key terms and expressions of the original. But, since it should be clear from your work that you are summarizing someone else's, there is little need for quotation marks or such expressions as "she says," "she then goes on to prove," and so forth. Transitions, though, are still useful. Remember that a summary of someone else's writing is a sample of your own writing; it should be clear and coherent. Remember, too, that it's customary in writing summaries of literary works to use the present tense, though that rule too can be altered to suit your purpose.

The following example is a student's summary of Chuck Kraemer's "Indecent Exposure," an essay you'll find at the end of this chapter.

> Chuck Kraemer believes that sunbathing is "demented." Exposure to the sun's rays is harmful to the body: a day in the sun will upset the molecular structure of the skin's layers, destroy skin cells, and wound tissues; long-term exposure may promote skin cancer, wrinkling, spotting, freckling, yellowing, and coarsening of the skin. Today, suntans are believed to be a sign of health and social status, but this belief is only a "long-running fad." Before the nineteenth century, a pallid complexion was the sign of wealth and leisure; bronzed arms and faces belonged to the inferior working class.
>
> For those who insist on sunbathing, summer issues of almost any women's magazine offer instructions on tanning without burning; the best burn-preventing sun lotions are those that contain para-

aminobenzoic acid. Those who enjoy the outdoors, but are not concerned with skin color, should stay in the shade.

After you have read "Indecent Exposure," reread this summary of it. Did the student who wrote it follow Kraemer's organization? If not, what departures do you find? Are they justified? Did she present the key points of the original? Did she omit any material you feel ought to be included? Was her summary well written? These are the chief questions to keep in mind when you write summaries, either as parts of longer essays, or as exercises in reading and writing.

In most of your writing, a summary will appear as part of a longer essay in which your purpose might be to analyze an argument, or to compare two interpretations of a text or a problem, or to persuade. But in studying composition, in learning how to improve your own writing, practice in writing summaries alone is useful because it requires of you a more thorough understanding of someone else's writing than you would have had from merely reading it. In organizing a summary you are studying not only what the passage says but how the writer thinks. If his organization is clear, you learn by imitating it; if unclear, you learn by improving it. In condensing the material you get practice in the precise use of key terms, and of course, in writing concisely.

Finally, though a summary of someone else's thoughts must be faithful to those thoughts and will probably imitate or reflect the style of the original, a summary may also have a style of its own. Notice how in the newspaper article, "It's the Portly Penguin That Gets the Girl" (pages 132–34), chiefly a summary of a lecture, the journalist's own style and the lecturer's happily coexist.

EXERCISES

(Reminder: A good expository essay anticipates questions a reader may have about *how, who, what, why, when,* and *where.*)

1. In 300–500 words explain a process, for example, how to do one of the following: perform a card trick; tell a joke; apply to college; refinish a table; develop a photograph. (A reminder: as pages 123–24 imply, readable expository essays not only let

the reader understand something; they also let the reader hear a human voice. If you choose a topic you are strongly interested in, you will probably find that an interesting voice will emerge.)

2. Reread the essay on pingoes (page 119), and then write an expository essay of similar length (about 250 words) on something that is likely to be unfamiliar to your classmates. Examples: a little-known group of musicians; a little-known kind of cooking; a natural phenomenon you have closely observed.

3. Choose a current editorial and summarize it in about one-fourth its number of words. Include a copy of the editorial with your summary.

4. Using the outline of "Columbo Knows the Butler Didn't Do It" (pages 66–67) and the essay itself (pages 57–59), write a summary of the essay, in about 250 words.

5. Read "It's the Portly Penguin That Gets the Girl" (pages 132–34) and then attend a lecture in your community on a topic that interests you. Go prepared to take notes and, if possible, meet the speaker. Then write a two to three page summary of the lecture, including some of your sense of the speaker and perhaps of the occasion.

6. Write an expository essay objectively setting forth someone else's views on a topic or limited range of topics. Suggested length: 500 words. Your source for these views should be a published interview. If possible, submit a copy of the interview with your essay. Suggested sources: Dick Cavett and Christopher Porterfield, *Cavett* (New York: Harcourt Brace Jovanovich, 1974); *Rolling Stone Interviews* (New York: Paperback Library, 1971); *The Playboy Interviews With John Lennon and Yoko Ono*, ed. G. Barry Golson (New York: Playboy Press, 1981); Charles Thomas Samuels, *Encountering Directors* (New York: G. P. Putnam's Sons, 1972); *Particular Passions: Intimate Talks With Women Who Have Shaped Our Times*, ed. Lynn Gilbert and Gaylen Moore (New York: Clarkson N. Potter, 1981); *Writers at Work: The Paris Review Interviews*, ed. Malcolm Cowley (New York: Viking Press, 1958–1968); and the *Paris Review*, a quarterly publication, which usually includes an interview with an author. If you found Philip Roth's essay (pages 7–9) interesting, you may want to summarize an

interview with Roth. He prints several of them in his *Reading Myself and Others* (New York: Farrar, Straus & Giroux, 1975).

EXPOSITION AT WORK

Indecent Exposure

Chuck Kraemer

I spotted my first one of the season on a warm day in mid-March, beside the Charles River near No. Harvard St., lying on his back with his shirt off, arms spread, palms up, chin high, letting the UV photons in the 3500–4000 angstrom range severely agitate the molecular structure of his keratin layer.

Actually, he was just sunbathing, but it was, biologically, a strange, masochistic bath indeed. Ultraviolet radiation was attacking his epidermis, sending its molecules into reactive states, producing dangerous reaction products. Deeper down, the dark pigment called melanin was being manufactured as a shield against the attack, but the process was slow, and if my sun worshipper was as unwary as most on this, his first exposure of the season, he probably killed off a few billion skin cells within fifteen minutes — long before his biological defenses could muster. It was truly a bloodbath — the blood being rushed through swollen vessels to the surface of the skin to begin repairing wounded tissue, producing the lobster-red color we call a sunburn.

The harmful effects of his worship were not as transient or superficial as this supplicant probably assumed, especially if he paid regular spring-through-September homage. The adverse vascular effects of a moderately severe burn may last for a year or more. Skin cancer is a distinct possibility. Twenty-three percent of all cancers in men and 13 percent in women are cancers of the skin, and of all those, 90 percent are sun-related. Most are cured, but often only by surgery.

Perhaps no less dire to the average narcissistic sunbather, the cosmetic toll can be very high. Prolonged exposure to the sun can cause long-lasting and permanent yellowing, wrinkling, spotting, freckling, and coarsening of the skin, such as that seen on the necks of sailors, farmers, and cowboys. It usually takes years, but it can start very early. Loss of skin elasticity has been found in solarphiles as young as 20 years — a condition interestingly omitted from the luscious body of the 20-year-old model in those Coppertone ads.

If only these war wounds were incurred for a just cause, maybe it would all make sense. But as far as I can see, sun worship is just plain demented — stranger than even its sister, star worship (astrology), which is bizarre enough but has no adverse physical effects, as far as I know. Getting a tan is, literally, self-abuse. As dermatologist John Knox of Baylor has said, "A suntan is a response to an injury." For anybody with an adequate diet, direct sunshine is medically useless at best, dangerous at worst.

Of course we justify our masochism on cosmetic grounds. Bronze is beautiful. Strident advertising by the suntan lotion companies, airlines, and Florida real estate outfits assures us of that, and fervently, by the peeling beachfuls, we believe. (One ad for a Bahamas vacation implores, "Get out of the kitchen and bake.")

But history shows that the tan body as a sign of health and status is only a rather long-running fad, rooted in ignorance and elitism. Before the nineteenth century a *pallid* complexion was considered fashionable and wholesome. The working classes toiled mostly outdoors, where they acquired the dark skins that marked them as socially inferior. The rich sensibly avoided the sun, preferring an iced tea in the shade, or a stroll in the filtered aura of an expensive parasol. Hence the poetic necks and bosoms "as white as alabaster," and upon them the consequently prominent blue veins — giving rise to the term "blue bloods."

Then came the Industrial Revolution, reversing the code of snobbery. Workers now spent their daylight hours in factories in coal-smoke-polluted cities, so sun became fashionable for those who could afford it. Sunshine was even seriously prescribed as a panacea for tuberculosis — a quaint over-reaction to the plague of tuberculosis and rickets among the vitamin-D-deficient working classes.

Today, the summer tan is less a status symbol than an imagined necessity. (The status-conscious must now graduate to the *year-round* tan, which implies sufficient wealth to vacation in the South Seas.) There may not be a mass leisure class yet, but the masses manage to cram plenty of leisure into their summer outings at the Cape or Nantucket or Nahant, where they bask 10,000 per acre for hours on end, sizzling away like Cornish hens in a pit at the Kiwanis Memorial Day barbecue.

I have no sympathy for these folks, but I am obliged — this being a practical column — to advise them how to protect themselves from the sun, even as they so indecently expose themselves to it. Truth to tell, my secret desire is that if they're all going to abuse themselves this way they should fry to a crisp and get washed out to sea like bits of burned bacon, but I'll set prejudice aside for the moment and grudgingly offer the following three tips:

(1). For the specific instructions on the absurdly complicated art of getting a tan without getting burned, see the May, June, or July issue of almost any women's magazine, where "Good Sense in the Sun" articles are a regular seasonal item. These are usually written by the in-house doc or a consulting dermatologist, and appear to be authoritative.

(2). For the dullards among us who enjoy the outdoors and don't want to burn, but don't give a squint about skin color either, the solution is simple: stay in the shade.

(3). The magazine pieces often go into greater detail on this, but, very briefly, the best sun lotions for preventing burns are those containing para-aminobenzoic acid, or PABA. Check the label — any product claiming to prevent sunburn must list the key ingredient.

See you at the beach. I'll be the one in long sleeves and work boots.

QUESTIONS

1. How is this essay organized?
2. Kraemer might have begun his essay thus: "I saw my first sunbather of the season. . . ." What does he gain by beginning the way he does? How does the technical language in the first paragraph contribute to the effect?
3. Drawing on the entire essay, in two or three sentences characterize the writer.

It's the Portly Penguin That Gets the Girl, French Biologist Claims

Anne Hebald Mandelbaum

The penguin is a feathered and flippered bird who looks as if he's on his way to a formal banquet. With his stiff, kneeless strut and natural dinner jacket, he moves like Charlie Chaplin in his heyday dressed like Cary Grant in his.

But beneath the surface of his tuxedo is a gallant bird indeed. Not only does he fast for 65 days at a time, sleep standing up, and forsake all others in a lifetime of monogamy, but the male penguin also guards, watches over, and even hatches the egg.

We owe much of our current knowledge of the life and loves of the king and emperor penguins to — *bien sûr* — a Frenchman. Twenty-eight-year-old Yvon Le Maho is a biophysiologist from Lyons who visited the University last week to discuss his discoveries and to praise the penguin. He had just returned from 14 months in Antarctica, where he went to measure, to photograph, to weigh, to take blood and urine samples of, to perform autopsies on — in short, to study the penguin.

Although his original intent had been to investigate the penguin's long fasts, Monsieur Le Maho was soon fascinated by the amatory aspect of the penguin. Copulating in April, the female produces the egg in May and then heads out to sea, leaving her mate behind to incubate the egg. The males huddle together, standing upright and protecting the 500-gram (or 1.1-pound) egg with their feet for 65 days. During this time, they neither eat nor stray: each steadfastly stands guard over his egg, protecting it from the temperatures which dip as low as −40 degrees and from the winds which whip the Antarctic wilds with gusts of 200 miles an hour.

For 65 days and 65 nights, the males patiently huddle over the eggs, never lying down, never letting up. Then, every year on July 14th — Bastille Day, the national holiday of France — the eggs hatch and thousands of penguin chicks are born, M. Le Maho told his amused and enthusiastic audience at the Biological Laboratories.

The very day the chicks are born — or, at the latest, the following day — the female penguins return to land from their two-and-a-half month fishing expedition. They clamber out of the water and toboggan along the snow-covered beaches toward the rookery and their mates. At this moment, the males begin to emit the penguin equivalent of wild, welcoming cheers — *"comme le cri de trompette,"* M. Le Maho later told the *Gazette* in an interview — "like the clarion call of the trumpet."

And, amid the clamorous thundering of 12,000 penguins, the female recognizes the individual cry of her mate. When she does, she begins to cry to him. The male then recognizes *her* song, lifts the newborn chick into his feathered arms, and makes a beeline for the female. Each singing, each crying, the males and females rush toward each other, slipping and sliding on the ice as they go, guided all the while by the single voice each instinctively knows.

The excitement soon wears thin for the male, however, who hasn't had a bite to eat in more than two months. He has done his duty and done it unflaggingly, but even penguins cannot live by duty alone. He must have food, and quickly.

Having presented his mate with their newborn, the male abruptly departs, heading out to sea in search of fish. The female, who has just returned from her sea-going sabbatical, has swallowed vast quantities of fish for herself and her chick. Much of what she has eaten she has not digested. Instead, this undigested food becomes penguin baby food. She regurgitates it, all soft and paplike, from her storage throat right into her chick's mouth. The chicks feed in this manner until December, when they first learn to find food on their own.

The penguins' reproductive life begins at age five, and the birds live about 25 years. Their fasting interests M. Le Maho because of its close similarities with fasting in human beings. And although many migratory birds also fast, their small size and indeed their flight make it almost impossible to study them closely. With the less-mobile and non-flying penguin, however, the scientist has a relatively accessible population to study. With no damage to the health of the penguin, M. Le Maho told the *Gazette*, a physiobiologist can extract blood from the flipper and sample the urine.

"All fasting problems are the same between man and the penguin," M. Le Maho said, "The penguin uses glucose in the brain, experiences ketosis as does man, and accomplishes gluconeogenesis, too." Ketosis is the build-up of partially burned fatty acids in the blood, usually as a result of starvation; gluconeogenesis is the making of sugar from non-sugar chemicals, such as amino acids. "The penguin can tell us a great deal about how our own bodies react to fasting conditions," M. Le Maho said.

He will return to Antarctica, M. Le Maho said, with the French government-sponsored *Expéditions Polaires Françaises* next December. There he will study the growth of the penguin chick, both inside the egg and after birth; will continue to study their mating, and to examine the penguin's blood sugar during fasting.

During the question-and-answer period following his talk, M. Le Maho was asked what the female penguin looks for in a mate. Responding, M. Le Maho drew himself up to his full five-foot-nine and said, *"La grandeur."*

QUESTIONS

1. Outline the essay, and then describe the organization.
2. Pick out three or four sentences that strike you as especially interesting, not just because they contain odd facts but because of the ways the sentences are written.

7
Persuasion

To persuade is to win over, or to convince. These two are not the same thing; if we win people over by, say, an appeal to their emotions, we have not convinced them, only conquered them. To convince them we must persuade them by presenting evidence and reasonable arguments for our opinions. But first we must present ourselves as writers worth reading.

In any kind of persuasive writing, whether it is emotional or logical or both, you must gain and then keep the audience's confidence. Unfortunately, confidence is easily lost: for instance, readers are not likely to trust (and therefore not likely to accept the argument of) a writer who spells the word "arguement." The writer's arguments may be sound, but the readers — reluctant to change their views in any case, and certainly unwilling to ally themselves with someone who can't even spell — seize on this irrelevant error and smugly put the essay aside, confident that they have nothing to learn. Convey your competence and your respect for your reader by getting the right word, defining crucial terms, and providing interesting examples. No writing can persuade if it is imprecise and dull.

PRESENTING EVIDENCE

A good essay not only presents a thesis but also supports it with evidence, just as a paragraph supports with evidence its topic sentence or idea. The evidence may be a series of reasons or, especially in essays on literature, of facts, details, examples, references to the text. The critic William Gass, for example, in a paragraph about William Faulkner, offers two generalizations in the first sentence — the second generalization being the reason ("because") for the first. The rest of the paragraph then offers supporting details.

> Nothing was too mean for his imagination because he did not believe there was any insignificance on earth. A dirt road was worthy of the most elevated consciousness. An old woman or an old mule: he found in them the forms and forces of History itself. To build a house, found a family, lay rails across a state: these were acts an Alexander might have engaged in. The Civil War was War, high water along the river was The Flood, the death of a dog was Sorrow. He managed to give even the mute heart speech, and invest a humble, private, oft-times red-necked life with those epic rhythms and rich sounds which were formerly the hired pomp and commissioned music of emperors and kings.

The details that follow Gass's first sentence are, in effect, pieces of evidence offered to persuade the reader to accept Gass's point of view.

ARGUMENT

Persuasive writing that, in addition to other evidence, relies chiefly on reasoning (rather than on appeals to the emotions) is usually called *argument*. An argument here is not a wrangle but a reasoned analysis. What distinguishes argument from exposition is this: whereas both consist of statements, in argument some statements are offered as reasons for other statements. Another way of characterizing the difference is to say that exposition assumes there is no substantial disagreement between informed persons, but argument assumes there is or may be substantial disagreement. To overcome this disagreement, the writer tries to offer reasons that convince by their validity. Here, for example, is C. S. Lewis arguing against vivisection (experimentation on live animals for scientific research):

> A rational discussion of this subject begins by inquiring whether pain is, or is not, an evil. If it is not, then the case against vivisection falls. But then so does the case for vivisection. If it is not defended

on the ground that it reduces human suffering, on what ground can it be defended? And if pain is not an evil, why should human suffering be reduced? We must therefore assume as a basis for the whole discussion that pain is an evil, otherwise there is nothing to be discussed.

Now if pain is an evil then the infliction of pain, considered in itself, must clearly be an evil act. But there are such things as necessary evils. Some acts which would be bad, simply in themselves, may be excusable and even laudable when they are necessary means to a greater good. In saying that the infliction of pain, simply in itself, is bad, we are not saying that pain ought never to be inflicted. Most of us think that it can rightly be inflicted for a good purpose — as in dentistry or just and reformatory punishment. The point is that it always requires justification. On the man whom we find inflicting pain rests the burden of showing why an act which in itself would be simply bad is, in those particular circumstances, good. If we find a man giving pleasure it is for us to prove (if we criticize him) that his action is wrong. But if we find a man inflicting pain it is for him to prove that his action is right. If he cannot, he is a wicked man.

And here is Supreme Court Justice Louis Brandeis, concluding his justly famous argument that government may not use evidence illegally obtained by wiretapping:

> Decency, security and liberty alike demand that government officials shall be subjected to the same rules of conduct that are commands to the citizen. In a government of laws, existence of the government will be imperilled if it fails to observe the law scrupulously. Our Government is the potent, the omnipresent teacher. For good or for ill, it teaches the whole people by its example. Crime is contagious. If the Government becomes a lawbreaker, it breeds contempt for law; it invites every man to become a law unto himself; it invites anarchy. To declare that in the administration of the criminal law the end justifies the means — to declare that the Government may commit crimes in order to secure the conviction of a private criminal — would bring terrible retribution. Against that pernicious doctrine this Court should resolutely set its face.

Notice here that, as in most arguments that attain celebrity, Brandeis's reasoning is highlighted by his forceful style, by his resonant use of parallel constructions, by the artful management of long and short sentences, and by the wit in his comparisons: government is a teacher, and crime is a disease.

WIT

In addition, then, to argument and other evidence, writers often use wit to persuade. Wit — which may include intelligent use of understatement, overstatement, metaphor, and allusion — can challenge the reader's beliefs, and intelligence, while still engaging the reader's sympathies. Let's look briefly at the first pages of Thoreau's *Walden*:

> When I wrote the following pages, or rather the bulk of them, I lived alone, in the woods, a mile from any neighbor, in a house which I had built myself, on the shore of Walden Pond, in Concord, Massachusetts, and earned my living by the labor of my hands only. I lived there two years and two months. At present I am a sojourner in civilized life again.
>
> I should not obtrude my affairs so much on the notice of my readers if very particular inquiries had not been made by my townsmen concerning my mode of life, which some would call impertinent, though they do not appear to me at all impertinent, but, considering the circumstances, very natural and pertinent. Some have asked what I got to eat; if I did not feel lonesome; if I was not afraid; and the like. Others have been curious to learn what portion of my income I devoted to charitable purposes; and some, who have large families, how many poor children I maintained. I will therefore ask those of my readers who feel no particular interest in me to pardon me if I undertake to answer some of these questions in this book. In most books, the *I*, or first person, is omitted; in this it will be retained; that, in respect to egotism, is the main difference. We commonly do not remember that it is, after all, always the first person that is speaking. I should not talk so much about myself if there were anybody else whom I knew as well. Unfortunately, I am confined to this theme by the narrowness of my experience. Moreover, I, on my side, require of every writer, first or last, a simple and sincere account of his own life, and not merely what he has heard of other men's lives; some such account as he would send to his kindred from a distant land; for if he has lived sincerely, it must have been in a distant land to me. Perhaps these pages are more particularly addressed to poor students. As for the rest of my readers, they will accept such portions as apply to them. I trust that none will stretch the seams in putting on the coat, for it may do good service to him whom it fits.
>
> I would fain say something, not so much concerning the Chinese and Sandwich Islanders as you who read these pages, who

are said to live in New England; something about your condition, especially your outward condition or circumstances in this world, in this town, what it is, whether it is necessary that it be as bad as it is, whether it cannot be improved as well as not. I have traveled a good deal in Concord; and everywhere, in shops, and offices, and fields, the inhabitants have appeared to me to be doing penance in a thousand remarkable ways. What I have heard of Bramins sitting exposed to four fires and looking in the face of the sun; or hanging suspended, with their heads downward, over flames; or looking at the heavens over their shoulders "until it becomes impossible for them to resume their natural position, while from the twist of the neck nothing but liquids can pass into the stomach"; or dwelling, chained for life, at the foot of a tree; or measuring with their bodies, like caterpillars, the breadth of vast empires; or standing on one leg on the tops of pillars — even these forms of conscious penance are hardly more incredible and astonishing than the scenes which I daily witness. The twelve labors of Hercules were trifling in comparison with those which my neighbors have undertaken; for they were only twelve, and had an end; but I could never see that these men slew or captured any monster or finished any labor. They have no friend Iolaus to burn with a hot iron the root of the hydra's head, but as soon as one head is crushed, two spring up.

I see young men, my townsmen, whose misfortune it is to have inherited farms, houses, barns, cattle, and farming tools; for these are more easily acquired than got rid of. Better if they had been born in the open pasture and suckled by a wolf, that they might have seen with clearer eyes what field they were called to labor in. Who made them serfs of the soil? Why should they eat their sixty acres, when man is condemned to eat only his peck of dirt? Why should they begin digging their graves as soon as they are born? They have got to live a man's life, pushing all these things before them, and get on as well as they can. How many a poor immortal soul have I met well nigh crushed and smothered under its load, creeping down the road of life, pushing before it a barn seventy-five feet by forty, its Augean stables never cleansed, and one hundred acres of land, tillage, mowing, pasture, and wood-lot! The portionless, who struggle with no such unnecessary inherited encumbrances, find it labor enough to subdue and cultivate a few cubic feet of flesh.

Now try to answer these questions.

1. In the first paragraph, how does Thoreau gain our respect?
2. In the middle of the second paragraph, Thoreau says "I should

not talk so much about myself if there were anybody else whom I knew as well. Unfortunately, I am confined to this theme by the narrowness of my experience." If "unfortunately" were changed to "but," what would be lost? What would be lost if the last sentence of this paragraph were omitted?

3. Why doesn't Thoreau omit the first two paragraphs and simply begin with the first sentence of the third? And in the third paragraph, why does he refer to Bramins and to the twelve labors of Hercules, instead of simply talking about the people he sees in New England?

4. In the fourth paragraph, what is gained by adding, within commas that serve as parentheses, "my townsmen"? What does Thoreau mean when he says some men "eat their sixty acres," and what does he mean when he says "man is condemned to eat only his peck of dirt"? Explain his statement that some men on the road of life push a barn and one hundred acres of land. In fact, why does he at this point not speak merely of a man but of an "immortal soul . . . pushing before it a barn seventy-five feet by forty"? Why the statistics?

Your answers to some of these questions will help you to see how persuasive wit can be. Thoreau offers scarcely anything that in the strict sense can be called an argument, yet attracted by his shrewdness we feel compelled to share his opinions.

Finally, then, almost every sentence in every piece of good writing in one way or another persuades, either by offering evidence or by keeping the reader's sympathy and attention so that the reader will stay with the writer until the end. The whole of this book, even the comments on spelling and punctuation, seeks to help you to write so that your readers are persuaded it is worth their time to listen to you.

Avoiding Sarcasm

Because writers must, among other things, persuade readers that they are humane, sarcasm has little place in persuasive writing. Although desk dictionaries usually define sarcasm as "bitter, caustic irony" or "a kind of satiric wit," if you think of a sarcastic comment that you have heard you will probably agree that "a crude, sneering remark" is a better definition. Lacking the ingenuity or wit of good satire and the wryness or carefully controlled mockery of irony, sarcasm usually relies on gross overstatement and intends simply to humiliate. *Sarcasm* is derived from a Greek word meaning "to tear flesh" or "to bite the lips in rage," altogether an unattractive business. Sarcasm is unfair, for it dismisses an opponent's arguments with ridicule rather than with reason; it is also unwise, for it turns the reader against you. Readers hesitate to ally themselves with a writer who apparently enjoys humiliating the opposition. A sarcastic remark can turn the hearers against the speaker and arouse sympathy for the victim. In short, sarcasm usually doesn't work.

AVOIDING FALLACIES

Let's briefly examine the reasoning process by considering some obvious errors in reasoning; in logic they are called *fallacies* (from a Latin verb meaning "to deceive"). As Tweedledee says in *Through the Looking-Glass,* "if it were so, it would be; but as it isn't, it ain't. That's logic." You cannot persuade readers unless they think you are reliable; if your argument includes fallacies, thoughtful readers will not take you seriously.

1. *False authority.* Don't try to borrow the prestige of authorities who are not authorities on the topic in question — for example, a heart surgeon speaking on politics. You will only discredit yourself if you think that a surgeon's opinions on redistricting or a politician's opinions on whaling have any special weight. Similarly, some former authorities are no longer authorities, because the problems have changed or because later knowledge has superseded their views. Adam Smith, Jefferson, and Einstein remain men of genius, but an attempt to use their opinions when you are examining modern issues — even in their fields — may be questioned. In short, before you rely on an authority, ask yourself if the person in question *is* an authority on the topic. And don't let stereotypes influence your idea of who is an authority. Don't assume that every black is an authority on ghetto life; many have never been in a ghetto. Remember the Yiddish proverb: "A goat has a beard, but that doesn't make him a rabbi."

2. *False quotation.* If you do quote from an authority, don't misquote. One can argue that the Bible itself says "commit adul-

tery" — the words do occur in it — but of course the quotation is taken out of context — the Bible says "Thou shalt not commit adultery." Few writers would misquote so outrageously, but it is easy to slip into taking from an authority the passages that suit us and neglecting the rest. For example, you may find someone who grants that "there are strong arguments in favor of abolishing the death penalty"; but if she goes on to argue that, on balance, the arguments in favor of retaining it seem stronger to her, it is dishonest to quote her words so as to imply that she favors abolishing it.

3. *Suppression of evidence.* Don't neglect evidence that is contrary to your own argument. To neglect evidence is unfair — and disastrous. You will be found out and your argument will be dismissed, even if it has some merit. You owe it to yourself and your reader to present all the relevant evidence. Be especially careful not to assume that every question is simply a matter of *either/or*. There may be some truth on both sides. Take the following thesis: "Grades encourage unwholesome competition, and should therefore be abolished." Even if the statement about the evil effect of grading is true, it may not be the whole truth, and therefore it may not follow that grades should be abolished. One might point out that grades do other things too: they may stimulate learning, and they may assist students by telling them how far they have progressed. One might nevertheless conclude, on balance, that the fault outweighs the benefits, but one can scarcely hope to be taken seriously if one does not recognize all the facts, or all the supposed facts. Concede to the opposition what is due it, and then outscore the opposition. Any failure to confront the opposing evidence will be noticed; your readers will keep wondering how you can be so foolish as not to see this or that, and soon they will dismiss your argument. Moreover, if you confront the opposition you will almost surely strengthen your own argument. As Edmund Burke said two hundred years ago, "He that wrestles with us strengthens our nerves, and sharpens our skill. Our antagonist is our helper."

4. *Generalization from insufficient evidence.* The process of generalizing (inferring a general principle from particular facts) is called *induction*; we study particular cases and then form a generalization. But the accuracy of the generalization may vary with the size and

representativeness of the sampled particulars. If, for example, my first two meals in Tucson are delicious, I may find myself talking about the excellent food there, and I may even slip into saying that all of the restaurants in Tucson serve great food — but if I do say such things I am offering a generalization based on insufficient evidence. This is a gross example, to be sure, but the error can be insidious. Take, for instance, an assertion about student opinion on intercollegiate athletics, based on a careful survey of the opinions of students living in the fraternity houses and dormitories. Such a survey leaves out those students who commute, a group that may be different (economically, religiously, and socially) from the surveyed group. Because the surveyed sample is not fully representative of student opinion, the generalizations drawn from the data may be false. The generalizations may, of course, happen to be true; they may indeed correspond to the views of the commuting students also. But that would be only a lucky accident. In short, when you offer a generalization based on induction, stand back, take another look at your evidence, and decide whether the generalization can be presented as a fact; maybe it's only a probability — or maybe only an opinion.

   5. *The genetic fallacy*. Don't assume that something can necessarily be explained in terms of its birth or origin. "He wrote the novel to make money, so it can't be any good" is palpable nonsense. The value of the novel need not depend on the initial pressure that motivated the author. If you think the novel is bad, you'll have to offer better evidence. Another example: "Capital punishment arose in days when men sought revenge, so now it ought to be abolished." Again an unconvincing argument: capital punishment may have some current value; for example, it may serve as a deterrent to crime. But that's another argument, and it needs evidence if it is to be believed. Be on guard, too, against the thoughtless tendency to judge people by their origins: Mr. X has a foreign accent, so he is probably untrustworthy or stupid or industrious.

   6. *Begging the question* and *circular reasoning*. Don't assume the truth of the point that you should prove. The term "begging the question" is a trifle odd. It means, in effect, "You, like a beggar, are asking me to grant you something at the outset." Examples:

"The barbaric death penalty should be abolished" (you should prove, not assert, that it is barbaric); "This senseless language requirement should be dropped," or "The foreign language requirement, a valuable thing, should be retained" (both of these opposed views assume what they should prove).

Circular reasoning is usually an extended form of begging the question. What ought to be proved is covertly assumed. Example: "T. S. Eliot is the best twentieth-century poet, because the best critics say so." Who are the best critics? Those who recognize Eliot's supremacy. Circular reasoning, then, normally includes intermediate steps absent from begging the question, but the two fallacies are so closely related that they can be considered one. Another example: "I feel sympathy for him because I identify with him." Despite the "because," no reason is really offered. What follows "because" is merely a restatement, in slightly different words, of what precedes; the shift of words, from "feel sympathy" to "identify with" has misled the writer into thinking he is giving a reason. Other examples: "Students are interested in courses when the subject matter and the method of presentation are interesting"; "There cannot be peace in the Middle East because the Jews and the Arabs will always fight." In each case, an assertion that ought to be proved is reasserted as a reason in support of the assertion.

7. *Post hoc ergo propter hoc.* Latin: "after this, therefore because of this." Don't assume that because X precedes Y, X must cause Y. Example: "He went to college and came back a pothead; college corrupted him." He might have taken up pot even if he had not gone to college. (The error, like the generalizations from insufficient evidence discussed on pages 143–44, is an error in induction.) Another example: "When a fifty-five-mile-per-hour limit was imposed, after the Arab embargo on oil, the number of auto fatalities decreased, so it is evident that a fifty-five-mile-per-hour limit saves lives." Not quite. Because gasoline was expensive after the embargo, the number of miles traveled decreased. The number of fatalities *per mile* remained constant. The price of gas, not the speed limit, seems responsible for the decreased number of fatalities.

8. *Argumentum ad hominem.* Here the argument is directed "toward the man," rather than toward the issue. Don't shift from your topic to your opponent. A speaker argues against legalizing

abortions and his opponent, instead of facing the merits of the argument, attacks the character or the associations of the opponent: "You're a Catholic, aren't you?"

9. *Argument from analogy.* Don't confuse an analogy with proof. An analogy is an extended comparison between two things; it can be useful in exposition, for it explains the unfamiliar by means of the familiar: "A government is like a ship, and just as a ship has a captain and a crew, so a government has . . ."; "Writing an essay is like building a house; just as an architect must begin with a plan, so the writer must. . . ." Such comparisons can be useful, helping to clarify what otherwise might be obscure, but their usefulness goes only so far. Everything is what it is, and not another thing. A government is not a ship, and what is true of a captain's power need not be true of a president's power; and a writer is not an architect. Some of what is true about ships may be (roughly) true of governments, and some of what is true about architects may be (again, roughly) true of writers, but there are differences too. Consider the following analogy between a lighthouse and the death penalty:

> The death penalty is a warning, just like a lighthouse throwing its beams out to sea. We hear about shipwrecks, but we do not hear about the ships the lighthouse guides safely on their way. We do not have proof of the number of ships it saves, but we do not tear the lighthouse down.
>
> — J. Edgar Hoover

How convincing is it as an argument, that is, as a reason for retaining the death penalty?

10. *False assumption.* Consider the Scot who argued that Shakespeare must have been a Scot. Asked for his evidence, he replied, "The ability of the man warrants the assumption." Or take such a statement as "She goes to Yale, so she must be rich." Possibly the statement is based on faulty induction (the writer knows four Yale students, and all four are rich) but more likely he is just passing on a cliché. The Yale student in question may be on a scholarship, may be struggling to earn the money, or may be backed by parents of modest means who for eighteen years have saved money for her college education. Other examples: "I haven't heard him complain about French 10, so he must be satisfied";

"She's a writer, so she must be well read." A little thought will show how weak such assertions are; they *may* be true, but they may not.

The errors we have discussed are common, and are unforgivable if they are consciously used. You have a point to make, and you should make it fairly. If it can only be made unfairly, you do an injustice not only to your reader but to yourself; you should try to change your view of the topic. Alas, as George Santayana said, "Nothing requires a rarer intellectual heroism than willingness to see one's equation written out." Difficult, yes; still, you don't want to be like the politician whose speech had a marginal reminder: "Argument weak; shout here."

Making Reasonable Assumptions

Probably the chief faults in most persuasive writing are not so much faults of reasoning as they are faults of initial assumptions. We may argue with faultless logic from faulty premises which are rooted in our tendency to be intolerant of views and prejudices other than our own. We begin with certain cherished ideas, and then we argue from them, seeing only part of a problem or seeing a generality where there is really only an instance. Take, for example, a passage on page 63 in Caroline Bird's *The Case Against College* (New York: David McKay, 1975). Ms. Bird argues that "in strictly financial terms, college is the dumbest investment a young man can make." She supports her claim thus: a high school graduate of 1972 will find that it costs about $34,181 to go to Princeton for four years (total costs and "foregone income"); the high school graduate who invests this amount in a savings bank at 7.5 percent interest will, despite the greater earning power of the college graduate, at age 64 be richer than the one who spends the money to go to college. But Ms. Bird overlooks the fact that few people (including those who go to Princeton) have $34,181 to invest at the time they graduate from high school; and so for most people the argument is irrelevant. Like Ms. Bird, we all sometimes reason in a vacuum. We reason — we have a maddening habit of saying "it stands to reason" — but we won't listen to reason. When it comes to listening, we are like the character in Elizabeth Gaskell's

"Spain — overrated. France — overrated. Switzerland! Germany! Belgium! England! Italy! All overrated!"

Drawing by Koren; © 1978 The New Yorker Magazine, Inc.

Cranford who said, "I'll not listen to reason. Reason always means what someone else has got to say."

Deduction

Deduction is the process of reasoning from assumptions (called premises) to a logical conclusion. Here is the classic example:

> *All men are mortal* (the major premise)
> *Socrates is a man* (the minor premise)
> *therefore Socrates is mortal* (the conclusion)

Such an argument, which takes two truths and joins them to produce a third truth, is called a *syllogism* (from Greek for "a reckoning together"). Deduction (from Latin "lead down from") moves from a general statement to a specific application; it is, therefore, the opposite of induction, which moves from specific instances to a general conclusion. *In*duction would note, for example, that Socrates was mortal and that all other observed people were also mortal, and it would thus arrive at the generalization that all people are mortal.

Deduction does not inevitably lead to truth. If a premise of a syllogism is not true, one can reason logically but come to a false conclusion. Example: "All teachers are members of a union"; "Jones is a teacher"; "therefore Jones is a member of a union." Although the process of reasoning is correct, the major premise is false and so the conclusion is worthless — Jones may or may not be a member of a union. Another trap to avoid is an argument that appears logical but is not. Let's take this attempt at a syllogism: "All teachers of Spanish know that in Spanish *hoy* means *today*" (major premise); "John knows that in Spanish *hoy* means *today*" (minor premise); "therefore John is a teacher of Spanish" (conclusion). Both premises are correct, but the conclusion does not follow. After all, John may be a student taking his first term of Spanish. What's wrong with the reasoning? For a deduction to be valid, the subject or condition of the major premise (in this case, teachers of Spanish) must appear also in the minor premise, but here it does not. The minor premise should be "John is a teacher of Spanish"; then the conclusion, that "therefore John knows that *hoy* means *today*," would be valid.

One other point. On most questions, say on the value of bilingual education or on the need for rehabilitation programs in prisons, it's not possible to make a strictly logical case, in the sense of an absolutely airtight proof. Don't assume that it is your job to make an absolute proof. What you are expected to do is to offer a reasonable argument.

ORGANIZING AN ARGUMENT

The word *logic* is from *logos,* Greek for "pattern" or "plan"; and though today logic means the science of correct reasoning, one cannot neglect the pattern or plan. As a rough principle, begin with the simplest argument and work up to the most complex. Such an arrangement will keep your reader with you, step by step.

A second method of organization, which with luck may coincide with the one just suggested, is to arrange arguments in order of increasing strength. Now, the danger in following this plan is that you may lose the reader from the start, because you begin with a weak argument. Avoid the danger by telling your reader that indeed the first argument is relatively weak (if it is terribly weak, it isn't an argument at all, so scrap it), but that you offer it for the sake of completeness or because it is often given, and that you will soon give the reader far stronger arguments. Face the opposition to this initial argument, grant that opposition as much as it deserves, and salvage what is left of the argument. Then proceed to the increasingly strong arguments, devoting at least one paragraph to each. As you treat each argument, it is usually advisable to introduce it with an appropriate transition ("another reason," "even more important," "most convincing of all"), to state it briefly, to summarize the opposing view, and then to demolish this opposition. With this organization, your discussion of each of your own arguments ends affirmatively.

A third method of organizing an argument is, after stating what you wish to prove in an introductory paragraph, to mass all the opposing arguments, and then to demolish them one by one.

In short, remember that when you have done your thinking and your rethinking, you are not done. You still must turn your thinking into writing — courteous, clear, and concrete. Find the right order, get the right words and provide the right transitions, avoid sarcasm and logical fallacies, and enrich your argument with specific examples and perhaps even some narrative — an appropriate anecdote, for instance, or a bit of history. Guide your readers through your analysis of the opposition and bring them to your position.

A Checklist for Persuasive Essays

1. Are the terms clearly defined?
2. Is the thesis stated promptly and clearly?
3. Are the assumptions likely to be shared by your readers? If not, are they argued rather than merely stated?
4. Are the facts verifiable?
5. Is the reasoning sound?

6. Are the authorities really authorities?
7. Are all of the substantial counterarguments recognized and effectively responded to?
8. Does the essay make use, where appropriate, of concrete examples?
9. Is the organization effective? Does the essay begin interestingly, keep the thesis in view, and end interestingly?
10. Is the tone appropriate?

EXERCISES

1. Read the following passage (by Susan Brownmiller, reviewing a book called *With the Weathermen*) and then try to answer the questions.

> Once upon a time, six years ago, a fistful of the most impatient members of this country's white student left broke away from their contemporaries and issued a call to revolutionary arms. Enraged beyond endurance by the peace movement's inability to put a dent in America's war machine and end the madness in Vietnam, they took the madness upon themselves. Unable to erase their upper-middle-class white-skin privilege, they proposed to follow to the death the "vanguard" actions of their Black Panther "brothers." They would be Viet-cong cadre in the United States, exemplary terrorist urban guerrillas, street-fighting men and women. They would smash the state with their iron pipes and homemade bombs, fight the racism they saw all around them by building a new collective life-style based on a celebration of youth, rock 'n' roll, dope, acid and sex. The vision of the role they had ordained themselves to play was not humble. They were The Way, they announced. Those among their friends who refused to follow their leadership were wimpy Running-Dog pigs, among other descriptive phrases.

A summary of this paragraph — the gist of the explicit idea — might go thus: "Six years ago some of the most radical students, exasperated by the failure of the peace movement, arrogantly called for violence and a new life-style, and denounced all who did not follow them."

a. What is the effect of "Once upon a time, six years ago"? Of "a fistful"? (Why not "a small number" instead of "a fistful"?)

b. What is the effect of the repetition in "They would be" and "They would smash"?

c. What is the effect of capitalizing "The Way"?

d. At the end of the passage, "among other descriptive phrases" is vague and might be considered anticlimactic. How can it be justified?

e. What is the difference between the summary of the paragraph and the paragraph? Which is more persuasive, and why?

2. Analyze and evaluate each of the following arguments. If any of the arguments contain fallacies, name the fallacies.

a. To the Editor:

The recent senseless murder of a 15-year-old seminary student again emphasizes the insanity of our gun laws. No matter how guilty the 13-year-old boy who shot into the head of the victim, it seems that our Congressmen are even more guilty by not enacting stricter gun-control laws. They are supposedly sane, rational men; and the kindest thing that can be said about them is that they are merely motivated by greed.

b. To the Editor:

Your editorial last Wednesday arguing against censorship as an infringement on freedom is full of clever arguments but it overlooks an obvious fact. We have Pure Food and Drug laws to protect us against poison, and no one believes that such laws interfere with the freedom of those who produce food and drugs. The public is entitled, then, to laws that will similarly protect us from the poison that some movie-makers produce.

c. To the Editor:

On Dec. 5 *The Times* published a story saying that Harvard has come under pressure to improve the "quality of its teaching." Unfortunately nobody knows what good teaching is, let alone how to evaluate it.

Unlike scholarship, which has a visible product, namely published reports, the results of teaching are locked in the heads of students and are usually not apparent, even to the students themselves, for a very long period.

One device which is frequently used is a poll of students, the so-called "student evaluation of teachers." This type of measurement has been studied by Rodin & Rodin, who correlated it with how much the students learned, as demonstrated on tests. The correlation was highly negative ($-.75$). As the Rodins put it, "Students rate most highly instructors from whom they learn least."

What invariably happens is that attempts to reward "good teaching" turn out to reward good public relations.

d. [Written shortly after the United States entered the Second World War] The Pacific Coast is in imminent danger of a combined attack from within and from without. . . . It is [true] . . . that since the outbreak of the Japanese war there has been no important sabotage on the Pacific Coast. From what we know about the fifth column in Europe, this is not, as some have liked to think, a sign that there is nothing to be feared. It is a sign that the blow is well-organized and that it is held back until it can be struck with maximum effect. . . . I am sure I understand fully and appreciate thoroughly the unwillingness of Washington to adopt a policy of mass evacuation and internment of all those who are technically enemy aliens. But I submit that Washington is not defining the problem on the coast correctly. . . . The Pacific Coast is officially a combat zone: some part of it may at any moment be a battlefield. Nobody's constitutional rights include the right to reside and do business on a battlefield. And nobody ought to be on a battlefield who has no good reason for being there.

— Walter Lippmann

3. In the following poem, "The Flea," by John Donne (1572–1631), a man is urging a woman to go to bed with him. Between the second and the third stanzas (that is, between lines 18 and 19) the woman kills the flea. Summarize the man's argument, step by step, and evaluate it as a piece of persuasion.

Mark but this flea, and mark in this
How little that which thou deny'st me is;
It sucked me first, and now sucks thee,
And in this flea our two bloods mingled be;
Thou know'st that this cannot be said   5
A sin, nor shame, nor loss of maidenhead;
    Yet this enjoys before it woo,
        And pampered swells with one blood made of two,
        And this, alas, is more than we would do.

Oh stay, three lives in one flea spare,   10
Where we almost, yea, more than married are.
This flea is you and I, and this
Our marriage bed and marriage temple is;
Though parents grudge, and you, we are met
And cloistered in these living walls of jet.   15

Though use[1] make you apt to kill me,
Let not to that, self-murder added be,
And sacrilege, three sins in killing three.

Cruel and sudden, hast thou since
Purpled thy nail in blood of innocence?   20
Wherein could this flea guilty be,
Except in that drop which it sucked from thee?
Yet thou triumph'st and say'st that thou
Find'st not thyself, nor me the weaker now.
  'Tis true. Then learn how false fears be:
  Just so much honor, when thou yield'st to me,   25
  Will waste, as this flea's death took life from thee.

PERSUASION AT WORK

Four Letter Words Can Hurt You

Barbara Lawrence

Why should any words be called obscene? Don't they all describe natural human functions? Am I trying to tell them, my students demand, that the "strong, earthy, gut-honest" — or, if they are fans of Norman Mailer, the "rich, liberating, existential" — language they use to describe sexual activity isn't preferable to "phony-sounding, middle-class words like 'intercourse' and 'copulate'?" "Cop You Late!" they say with fancy inflections and gagging grimaces. "Now, what is *that* supposed to mean?"

Well, what is it supposed to mean? And why indeed should one group of words describing human functions and human organs be acceptable in ordinary conversation and another, describing presumably the same organs and functions, be tabooed — so much so, in fact, that some of these words still cannot appear in print in many parts of the English-speaking world?

The argument that these taboos exist only because of "sexual hangups" (middle-class, middle-age, feminist), or even that they are a result of class oppression (the contempt of the Norman conquerors for the language of their Anglo-Saxon serfs), ignores a much more

[1] custom.

likely explanation, it seems to me, and that is the sources and functions of the words themselves.

The best known of the tabooed sexual verbs, for example, comes from the German *ficken*, meaning "to strike"; combined, according to Partridge's etymological dictionary *Origins*, with the Latin sexual verb *futuere*; associated in turn with the Latin *fustis*, "a staff or cudgel"; the Celtic *buc*, "a point, hence to pierce"; the Irish *bot*, "the male member"; the Latin *battuere*, "to beat"; the Gaelic *batair*, "a cudgeller"; the Early Irish *bualaim*, "I strike"; and so forth. It is one of what etymologists sometimes call "the sadistic group of words for the man's part in copulation."

The brutality of this word, then, and its equivalents ("screw," "bang," etc.), is not an illusion of the middle class or a crotchet of Women's Liberation. In their origins and imagery these words carry undeniably painful, if not sadistic, implications, the object of which is almost always female. Consider, for example, what a "screw" actually does to the wood it penetrates; what a painful, even mutilating, activity this kind of analogy suggests. "Screw" is particularly interesting in this context, since the noun, according to Partridge, comes from words meaning "groove," "nut," "ditch," "breeding sow," "scrofula" and "swelling," while the verb, besides its explicit imagery, has antecedent associations to "write on," "scratch," "scarify," and so forth — a revealing fusion of a mechanical or painful action with an obviously denigrated object.

Not all obscene words, of course, are as implicitly sadistic or denigrating to women as these, but all that I know seem to serve a similar purpose: to reduce the human organism (especially the female organism) and human functions (especially sexual and procreative) to their least organic, most mechanical dimension; to substitute a trivializing or deforming resemblance for the complex human reality of what is being described.

Tabooed male descriptives, when they are not openly denigrating to women, often serve to divorce a male organ or function from any significant interaction with the female. Take the word "testes," for example, suggesting "witnesses" (from the Latin *testis*) to the sexual and procreative strengths of the male organ; and the obscene counterpart of this word, which suggests little more than a mechanical shape. Or compare almost any of the "rich," "liberating" sexual verbs, so fashionable today among male writers, with that much-derided Latin word "copulate" ("to bind or join together") or even that Anglo-Saxon phrase (which seems to have had no trouble surviving the Norman Conquest) "make love."

How arrogantly self-involved the tabooed words seem in comparison to either of the other terms, and how contemptuous of the female partner. Understandably so, of course, if she is only a "skirt," a "broad," a "chick," a "pussycat" or a "piece." If she is, in other words, no more than her skirt, or what her skirt conceals; no more than a breeder, or the broadest part of her; no more than a piece of a human being or a "piece of tail."

The most severely tabooed of all the female descriptives, incidentally, are those like a "piece of tail," which suggest (either explicitly or through antecedents) that there is no significant difference between the female channel through which we are all conceived and born and the anal outlet common to both sexes — a distinction that pornographers have always enjoyed obscuring.

This effort to deny women their biological identity, their individuality, their humanness, is such an important aspect of obscene language that one can only marvel at how seldom, in an era preoccupied with definitions of obscenity, this fact is brought to our attention. One problem, of course, is that many of the people in the best position to do this (critics, teachers, writers) are so reluctant today to admit that they are angered or shocked by obscenity. Bored, maybe, unimpressed, aesthetically displeased, but — no matter how brutal or denigrating the material — never angered, never shocked.

And yet how eloquently angered, how piously shocked many of these same people become if denigrating language is used about any minority group other than women; if the obscenities are racial or ethnic, that is, rather than sexual. Words like "coon," "kike," "spic," "wop," after all, deform identity, deny individuality and humanness in almost exactly the same way that sexual vulgarisms and obscenities do.

No one that I know, least of all my students, would fail to question the values of a society whose literature and entertainment rested heavily on racial or ethnic pejoratives. Are the values of a society whose literature and entertainment rest as heavily as ours on sexual pejoratives any less questionable?

QUESTION

In addition to giving evidence to support her view, what persuasive devices (for example, irony, analogy) does Lawrence use?

Here Is Why You Lost Your Job

Barbara R. Bergman

Dear Joe:

I was sorry to hear that you had lost your job. If it is any comfort, you may think of yourself as a foot soldier, wounded in our country's battle against inflation.

The Administration and the Federal Reserve, whose tight money policy helped to put you where you are, are counting on your plight to serve as a scary example to business and to labor so that they will go easy in raising wages and prices. Furthermore, the Fed knows that in your present situation you are going to spend less in the stores, and that will also put the screws to the business community. It may also increase the number of people laid off.

I am afraid that I cannot refrain from reminding you that you were pretty loud in your complaints against inflation in the last few years. In fact, it was loud complaints like yours that nerved up the Fed to reduce the money supply growth and bring on the recession.

Of course, everybody was complaining against inflation, you may well say. Well, I am sure that it has struck you by now that the solution to the inflation problem we have backed into does not spread the misery at all evenly. You are suffering for the benefit of the rest of us.

The Reagan Administration is taking credit for the reduction in the rate of inflation. On the other hand, the President's State of the Union address had remarkably little about you unemployed people, and he certainly didn't mention that your sacrifices are bringing inflation down for all of us. To add insult to injury, the President has even implied that much of the unemployment is caused by your bad behavior and low qualifications.

Exhibit A in this regard is the want ad section of the daily newspaper, which the President brought up in his last news conference. This section of the paper appears every day, even in Detroit, so it is always available as a good prop. The existence of this section is supposed to show first of all that there are plenty of jobs, and second, that the unemployed are too lazy or too unskilled or too demanding to take advantage of all those vacant jobs.

Brandishing the want ad section to show that there are plenty of jobs amounts to confusing the total number of jobs in the country with the flow into and out of jobs, which is called labor turnover. Even in periods when the number of jobs is low and falling, people are hired to replace employees who quit or retire or die or have been fired for unsatisfactory performance. It is these jobs that evidence themselves in the ever-present want ads.

The data on labor turnover for manufacturing industries show that new hires run about 2 percent of total employment per month. If turnover in manufacturing is at all typical of turnover in the rest of American industry, it means that in a typical year there are about 25 million new hires. You may take some comfort from that figure, but not too much. A 2 percent monthly turnover rate combined with a 9 percent unemployment rate works out to an average of four and a half months out of work for the people who lose their jobs.

Incidentally, Joe, information on turnover will no longer be available. You guessed it: The Bureau of Labor Statistics has had its budget cut.

Taking the fact that some businesses are hiring as evidence of the existence of an adequate number of jobs is the same thing as confusing the flow of water in and out of a swimming pool with the level of the water in the pool. We may see the water coming into the pool at a brisk rate, but if the flow in is matched by a flow out, and the level stays knee-deep, the swimming is not going to be very good.

After the President had brandished the want ads he proceeded on schedule to the denigration of the employability of the unemployed, particularly the black unemployed, who now amount to 17 percent of the black labor force. The simple fact is, of course, that the majority of these people were actually employed a few weeks ago.

Moreover, the black unemployment rate always recedes more rapidly than the white unemployment rate whenever the economic climate improves. Certainly some of the unemployed could benefit from job training. However, running down their qualifications is done with poor grace by a President who has just slashed job training programs to the bone.

Let me close by assuring you that what has happened to you was by no means inevitable. We could have chosen to live with the inflation somewhat longer, and wind it down more slowly, at a much lower cost in lost jobs and lost output. Or else we could have chosen to fight inflation by means that shared the burden more widely, by imposing wage controls, for example.

If the recession deepens significantly or lasts beyond next summer, the country may force the Administration to turn in that direction. In the meantime, you can expect to spend a lot of time in your local unemployment office. The lines will be longer and the service worse than usual because the staff has been cut. But there is a cheerful side. You'll meet some great people down there, just like yourself.

Very truly yours.

QUESTIONS

1. "Here Is Why You Lost Your Job," originally a column in the Business Section of *The New York Times*, pretends to be a letter to "Dear Joe." What do we know from the "letter" about Joe? What else can we surmise? Characterize the persona Bergman assumes as the letter writer, and characterize the persona's attitude toward Joe. What can we guess about the audience for Bergman's column? (On "persona," see page 322.)

2. Is Bergman's tone consistent throughout the essay? If not, where does it shift?

3. Notice the metaphor Bergman uses in her first paragraph. Do you find it original and illuminating, or is it trite? Later in her article Bergman uses an extended metaphor, or analogy. Locate and evaluate it, comparing it to the first metaphor.

4. About halfway through the article, Bergman says that "a 2 percent monthly turnover rate combined with a 9 percent unemployment rate works out to an average of four and a half months out of work for the people who lose their jobs." Explain how she arrived at this figure.

5. In her third from last paragraph Bergman says that "the black unemployment rate always recedes more rapidly than the white unemployment rate whenever the economic climate improves." Why do you suppose this is true? And why does Bergman mention this fact? That is, what point does she support by citing it?

6. Evaluate Bergman's article as a piece of persuasive writing.

8
Description

DESCRIPTION AS PERSUASION

Description represents in words our sensory impressions caught in a moment of time. In much descriptive writing visual imagery dominates. Look at the following example, part of a letter Vincent Van Gogh wrote to his brother, Theo.

> Twilight is falling, and the view of the yard from my window is simply wonderful, with that little avenue of poplars — their slender forms and thin branches stand out so delicately against the gray evening sky; and then the old arsenal building in the water — quiet as the "waters of the old pool" in the book of Isaiah — down by the waterside the walls of that arsenal are quite green and weather-beaten. Farther down is the little garden and the fence around it with the rosebushes, and everywhere in the yard the black figures of the workmen, and also the little dog. Just now Uncle Jan with his long black hair is probably making his rounds. In the distance the masts of the ships in the dock can be seen, in front the Atjeh, quite black, and the gray and red monitors — and just now here and there the lamps are being lit. At this moment the bell is ringing and the whole stream of workmen is pouring towards the gate; at the same time the lamplighter is coming to light the lamp in the yard behind the house.

First, notice that Van Gogh does not attempt to describe the view from the window at all times of day, but only now, when "twilight is falling." Thus, the figures of the workmen, the little dog, the masts in the distance, appear black; the evening sky is gray, and "just now here and there the lamps are being lit." Second, notice that Vincent tells Theo that he sees not "a row of trees" but a "little avenue of poplars — their slender forms and thin branches stand out so delicately against the gray evening sky." These details, the result of close observation, help the reader to see what Van Gogh saw, and to feel as he felt. Third, notice that while Van Gogh describes primarily what he *sees* (not surprising in a painter) he also notices and tells Theo what he *hears*: "At this moment the bell is ringing." And through every detail he communicates what he feels about the scene he describes: "the view of the yard from my window is simply wonderful."

Description is often a kind of persuasion. The writer wishes to persuade us to share his judgment that what he describes is beautiful or ugly, noble or ignoble, valuable or worthless. If we are persuaded, it is as a result less of the writer's telling us what to feel (often the judgment is not stated, but implied) than of his skill in representing to us what he sees, or experiences through other senses.

ORGANIZING A DESCRIPTION

Patient observation of details, and finding exactly the right words with which to communicate our impressions, are both part of the secret of good descriptive writing, but another part is organization, the translation of our disorderly, even chaotic, impressions into orderly structures. Limiting the description to what is sensed at a particular moment in time in itself imposes some order. But in addition, our descriptions must have some discernible pattern, such as from left to right, from bottom to top, from general to particular, or, as in Van Gogh's description, from near to far. Notice this structure, from near to far, as Walt Whitman uses it in his poem, "A Farm Picture."

> Through the ample open door of the peaceful country barn,
> A sunlit pasture field with cattle and horses feeding,
> And haze and vista, and the far horizon fading away.

Although the poem is only three lines long, the view is leisurely, beginning where the observer stands, inside the "ample open door," and then stretching slowly out to the "sunlit pasture field," still distinct, because still close up, then to the slightly more general "cattle and horses," and last to the indistinct "far horizon fading away." The leisurely pace persuades us that the scene is indeed "peaceful"; the orderly structure of the poem allows us to feel that it is.

Now look, by contrast, at a description not of a place, but of a phenomenon, a phenomenon not seen but felt, not peaceful, but "uneasy."

> There is something uneasy in the Los Angeles air this afternoon, some unnatural stillness, some tension. What it means is that tonight a Santa Ana will begin to blow, a hot wind from the northeast whining down through the Cajon and San Gorgonio Passes, blowing up sandstorms out along Route 66, drying the hills and the nerves to the flash point. For a few days now we will see smoke back in the canyons, and hear sirens in the night. I have neither heard nor read that a Santa Ana is due, but I know it, and almost everyone I have seen today knows it too. We know it because we feel it. The baby frets. The maid sulks. I rekindle a waning argument with the telephone company, then cut my losses and lie down, given over to whatever it is in the air. To live with the Santa Ana is to accept, consciously or unconsciously, a deeply mechanistic view of human behavior.
>
> — Joan Didion

Here the governing pattern of the description is more complex — from the general to the specific, and back to the general. Didion begins with the relatively general statement "There is something uneasy in the Los Angeles air this afternoon," and then moves to the specific details that support the generalization: the visible effects of the unseen wind first on the landscape and then on people (the baby, the maid, Didion herself). In the final sentence, again a relatively general one, she summarizes a further effect of what it is "to live with the Santa Ana." The organization is complex, but the passage is not disorderly. Or, we might say, it is just disorderly enough to make us feel, with the writer, "something uneasy in the Los Angeles air."

Specific details and concrete language help us to imagine what the writer has observed; a suitable organization further assists us in following the writer's representation of impressions and feelings.

ESTABLISHING A POINT OF VIEW

In addition to observing closely, finding the right word, and organizing the material, there is yet another technique that helps persuade the reader to accept the writer's observations as true, and his or her judgment as sound. This technique can be discovered by comparing two descriptions of a building on fire. The first is by a student, trying her hand at description in a composition class.

> The thick, heavy smoke, that could be seen for miles, filled the blue July sky. Firemen frantically battled the blaze that engulfed Hempstead High School, while a crowd of people sadly looked on. Eyes slowly filled up with tears as the reality of having no school to go to started to sink in. Students that had once downed everything that the high school stood for and did, began to realize how much they cared for their school. But it was too late, it was going up in smoke.

The second is by a professional writer, a practiced hand.

> We were on the porch only a short time when I heard a lot of hollering coming from toward the field. The hollering and crying got louder and louder. I could hear Mama's voice over all the rest. It seemed like all the people in the field were running to our house. I ran to the edge of the porch to watch them top the hill. Daddy was leading the running crowd and Mama was right behind him.
>
> "Lord have mercy, my children is in that house!" Mama was screaming. "Hurry, Diddly!" she cried to Daddy. I turned around and saw big clouds of smoke booming out of the front door and shooting out of cracks everywhere. "There, Essie Mae is on the porch," Mama said. "Hurry, Diddly! Get Adline outta that house!" I looked back at Adline. I couldn't hardly see her for the smoke.
>
> George Lee was standing in the yard like he didn't know what to do. As Mama got closer, he ran into the house. My first thought was that he would be burned up. I'd often hoped he would get killed, but I guess I didn't really want him to die after all. I ran inside after him but he came running out again, knocking me down as he passed and leaving me lying face down in the burning room. I jumped up quickly and scrambled out after him. He had the water bucket in his hands. I thought he was going to try to put out the fire. Instead he placed the bucket on the edge of the porch and picked up Adline in his arms.

Moments later Daddy was on the porch. He ran straight into the burning house with three other men right behind him. They opened the large wooden windows to let some of the smoke out and began ripping the paper from the walls before the wood caught on fire. Mama and two other women raked it into the fireplace with sticks, broom handles, and anything else available. Everyone was coughing because of all the smoke.

— Anne Moody

What can we learn from the professional writer? First notice her patience with detail, the concreteness of the passage. Where the student is content with "Firemen frantically battled the blaze that engulfed Hempstead High School," Anne Moody shows us individuals and exactly what each does. Where the student generalizes the reaction of the observers — "Eyes slowly filled up with tears" and "Students . . . began to realize how much they cared for their school" — in Moody's passage Mama screams, "Lord have mercy, my children is in that house!"

But equally important, the professional writer captures the reader's attention, and secures the reader's identification with the observer or narrator, by establishing the observer's physical position. At the beginning she is on the porch, looking toward the field. It is only when she hears her mother scream that she turns around and sees the smoke. And notice that she *does have to turn,* and the writer has the patience to tell us "I turned around and saw. . . ." We could, if we wished to, place the position of the observer, exactly, throughout the action, as if we were blocking a scene in a play. By contrast, notice that there is no real observer in the student's description. If there were, she would first have to be miles away from the scene and looking up into the sky to see the smoke. Then, in the second sentence she would be across the street, watching the firemen. By the third sentence she'd be closer still — not close to the fire, but close to the other observers. In fact, she'd have to be inside their heads to know what they were thinking. As readers we sense this lack of focus; we have no one to identify with. Though we may find the passage moderately interesting, it will not engage us and we will soon forget it.

In addition to the observer's physical location, a good description also provides a consistent psychological position, or *point of view,* with which we can identify ourselves. In the following passage from *Black Elk Speaks,* Black Elk, an Oglala Sioux holy man, is describing the Battle of Little Bighorn (1876).

> The valley went darker with dust and smoke, and there were only shadows and a big noise of many cries and hoofs and guns. On the left side of where I was I could hear the shod hoofs of the soldiers' horses going back into the brush and there was shooting everywhere. Then the hoofs came out of the brush, and I came out and was in among men and horses weaving in and out and going upstream, and everybody was yelling, "Hurry! Hurry!" The soldiers were running upstream and we were all mixed there in the twilight and the great noise. I did not see much; but once I saw a Lakota charge at a soldier who stayed behind and fought and was a very brave man. The Lakota took the soldier's horse by the bridle, but the soldier killed him with a six-shooter. I was small and could not crowd in to where the soldiers were, so I did not kill anybody. There were so many ahead of me, and it was all dark and mixed up.

Black Elk was an old man when he told this story. How old would you guess he was at the time it happened? How do you know?

DESCRIPTION AND NARRATION

At the beginning of this chapter we defined description as a representation, in words, of sensory impressions caught in a moment of time. Strictly speaking, description is static. The passage from Van Gogh's letter, and Whitman's poem, most nearly conform to this definition: they each describe a scene caught in a single moment, like a snapshot. Didion's paragraph about the Santa Ana is less static; it implies the passage of time. That time passes is, however, somewhat masked because Didion represents almost everything as happening simultaneously: "The baby frets. The maid sulks. I rekindle a waning argument with the telephone company." By contrast, in Moody's description of a house on fire, we not only hear (with Essie Mae) "a lot of hollering," and see "big clouds of smoke booming out of the front door and shooting out of cracks everywhere," we also know that moments have passed between the first sensory impression and the second, and that several more have passed before the passage ends with all the adults raking the burning wallpaper into the fireplace. The description is thoroughly interwoven with narration. Black Elk's account of the Battle of Little Bighorn is similarly a blend of description and narration.

Pure descriptive writing is relatively rare; long passages of pure description are even more rare. The reason is simple. A description of a place will be much more interesting if the writer shows us something happening there. Similarly descriptions of people are seldom, except briefly, static. In real life we seldom observe people at dead rest; we see them in action; we form our impressions of them from how they move, what they do. Good descriptions, then, frequently show us a person performing some action, a particularly revealing action, or a characteristic one. If, for example, you want to suggest a person's height and weight, it's much more interesting to show him maneuvering through a subway turnstile, perhaps laden with packages, than to say, "He was only five feet four but weighed 185 pounds" or "he was short and stocky." Here is Maya Angelou describing Mr. Freeman, a man who lived for a while with her mother.

> Mr. Freeman moved gracefully, like a big brown bear, and seldom spoke to us. He simply waited for Mother and put his whole self into the waiting. He never read the paper or patted his foot to the radio. He waited. That was all.
>
> If she came home before we went to bed, we saw the man come alive. He would start out of the big chair, like a man coming out of sleep, smiling. I would remember then that a few seconds before, I had heard a car door slam; then Mother's footsteps would signal from the concrete walk. When her key rattled the door, Mr. Freeman would have already asked his habitual question, "Hey, Bibbi, have a good time?"
>
> His query would hang in the air while she sprang over to peck him on the lips. Then she turned to Bailey and me with the lipstick kisses. "Haven't you finished your homework?" If we had and were just reading — "O.K., say your prayers and go to bed." If we hadn't — "Then go to your room and finish . . . then say your prayers and go to bed."
>
> Mr. Freeman's smile never grew, it stayed at the same intensity. Sometimes Mother would go over and sit on his lap and the grin on his face looked as if it would stay there forever.

Notice how animated this description is, how filled not only with Mr. Freeman's physical presence but also with his mysterious inner life. We have a portrait of Mother, too, reflected in Mr. Freeman's waiting, his concentration on the slam of her car door, her footsteps, her key rattling, and, most of all, in his smile. More subtly and more pervasively, the description is animated by our identification with the observer, the small child watching the man who waits so intently for the woman who is her mother.

DESCRIPTION AND ANALYSIS

Descriptive passages are also commonly used in essays to support analysis. In the following brief essay, for example, a writer asks and answers the question "What are the functions of cemeteries for the living?" The essay is primarily analytical; reading it, we share the writer's thoughts, but these thoughts are not the random and fleeting notions of reverie. The thoughts have been organized for us; the effects of cemeteries on the living have been classified and presented to us in an orderly and coherent account made vivid by passages of description. Through them we share at least imaginatively in the experiences that gave rise to the thinking. And through them, if the communication between writer and reader has been successful, we are persuaded to share the writer's opinions.

How Cemeteries Bring Us Back to Earth
Jim Doherty

A while ago, we said goodbye to a beloved aunt in a rural Wisconsin cemetery pulsing with birdsong. It was a splendid morning, gusty and bright. Puffy white clouds went sailing across the deep blue sky and calves were bawling in the distance. Later, we would sing hymns in a pretty church that smelled of coffee and candle wax, but first we stood blinking in the sunlight while a choir of robins, red-winged blackbirds and meadowlarks lustily serenaded the casket.

Curiously enough, graveyards often seem more alive than the places where many of us live. To soften the harshness of tombstones and obelisks, we plant trees and bushes, create ponds and manicure vast lawns. Even as developers transform old marshlands and forests into shopping centers and subdivisions, our forebears moulder away in lush new groves that nourish raccoons, woodchucks, rabbits and birds.

Cemeteries are good places for living people, too. My oldest daughter attends a Connecticut college where she spends many pleasant afternoons studying in a 17th-century boneyard. I remember a shady marble orchard in Mamaroneck, N.Y., where couples could usually find enough privacy for petting. Out here in southeastern Wisconsin, rabbit hunters patrol secluded country cemeteries that are bounded by overgrown fence rows and cornfields.

Tombstones can teach us a little about history but the overall ambience of a cemetery tells us much more.

One snowy spring morning near a ghost town in Idaho, my wife and I happened across a cluster of faded wooden markers surrounded by a rusting wrought-iron fence. The wind blew mournfully through the tall evergreens, and off in the distance the peaks of the Rockies glowed like The Promised Land. As we meandered among the graves, we tried to imagine what kind of lives those pioneers led and gradually we seemed to absorb an impression of it — the loneliness, the uncertainty, the overpowering presence of the mountains.

Hiking in Vermont one day, we found a century-old family plot on a hillside where two generations lived and died. Most of those who perished were children — eight of them were buried side-by-side — and there were also a number of small unmarked stones. It was impossible to romanticize the past at the gravesite of a patriarch preceded in death by two wives and so many sons and daughters. We wondered: Was he ready to go when his time came?

Cemeteries bring us back to earth in more ways than one.

By their very presence, they remind us that the meter is running. In so doing, they admonish us not to love winter less but to appreciate summer more. They reassure us, too, for if the dead can reside in such benign surroundings, then death itself somehow seems less formidable.

A man I know works as a caretaker up north. Whenever an old grave caves in, he spades off the sod and throws in enough dirt to fill the hole. Now and then he turns up a bone and simply tamps it down into the soil before replacing the sod. It bothers him not at all.

Recently, I took a 90-year-old woman to a hilltop cemetery in Johnson Creek, the small town where she grew up. It was a hot summer day and the air was sweet with the perfume of cedar trees and cut hay. Somewhere, a meadowlark was calling. My companion was looking for the headstone of a distant relative, which she did not find, but she came across many other familiar names: a neighbor, the man who ran the creamery, the banker, several childhood friends, some students from her teaching days. She stopped at each one to remember a story or two and then moved on until she grew tired, and we left.

I retain a vivid image of that windblown lady tottering gamely between the rows of mossy tombstones, full of anticipation and absolutely unafraid. It is a brave picture. I shall cherish it until the day I die.

QUESTIONS

1. Descriptive writing often falls into sentimentality, or triteness, or both. If you agree with us that Doherty avoids sentimentality (on a subject that would seem to invite it) try to explain how he avoids it. If the concluding sentence is not trite, what keeps it from being trite?
2. What were your feelings about cemeteries before you read this essay? Did the essay change your thinking in any way, or reinforce feelings and thoughts arising from your own experience? Explain.

EXERCISES

1. In one paragraph, describe what you see from your window. Choose a particular time of day and describe only what you see (or might see) or otherwise sense within a moment or two.
2. In one paragraph, describe something that cannot be seen, or cannot be seen except by the effects it creates. (Something hot, or smelly, or loud?)

3. In one paragraph, describe something from the point of view of a child, or an old person, or someone of the opposite sex. (Note *person*. The point of view of a dog, or stone, or carrot is *out*.)
4. In one paragraph, describe a room by showing something happening in it. Your description should reveal (without explicitly stating) your attitude toward it. The reader should be able to sense that the room is, for example, comfortable or sterile or pretentious or cozy or menacing, though no such words are used in the description.
5. First read the following two paragraphs from Saul Bellow's novel *The Victim*. Then answer the questions that follow the paragraphs.

> Leventhal's apartment was spacious. In a better neighborhood, or three stories lower, it would have rented for twice the amount he paid. But the staircase was narrow and stifling and full of turns. Though he went up slowly, he was out of breath when he reached the fourth floor, and his heart beat thickly. He rested before unlocking the door. Entering, he threw down his raincoat and flung himself on the tapestry-covered low bed in the front room. Mary had moved some of the chairs into the corners and covered them with sheets. She could not depend on him to keep the windows shut and the shades and curtains drawn during the day. This afternoon the cleaning woman had been in and there was a pervasive odor of soap powder. He got up and opened a window. The curtains waved once and then were as motionless as before. There was a movie house strung with lights across the street; on its roof a water tank sat heavily uneven on its timbers; the cowls of the chimneys, which rattled in the slightest stir of air, were still.
>
> The motor of the refrigerator began to run. The ice trays were empty and rattled. Wilma, the cleaning woman, had defrosted the machine and forgotten to refill them. He looked for a bottle of beer he had noticed yesterday; it was gone. There was nothing inside except a few lemons and some milk. He drank a glass of milk and it refreshed him. He had already taken off his shirt and was sitting on the bed unlacing his shoes when there was a short ring of the bell. Eagerly he pulled open the door and shouted, "Who is it?" The flat was unbearably empty. He hoped someone had remembered that Mary was away and had come to keep him company. There was no response below. He called out again, impatiently. It was very prob-

able that someone had pushed the wrong button, but he heard no other doors opening. Could it be a prank? This was not the season for it. Nothing moved in the stair well, and it only added to his depression to discover how he longed for a visitor. He stretched out on the bed, pulling a pillow from beneath the spread and doubling it up. He thought he would doze off. But a little later he found himself standing at the window, holding the curtains with both hands. He was under the impression that he had slept. It was only eight-thirty by the whirring electric clock on the night table, however. Only five minutes had passed.

Questions: How old, approximately, is Leventhal? Of what social or economic class is he? Who is Mary? What do you know of her relationship to Leventhal? What is the weather like? What is Leventhal's mood? How did you know all these things?

6. In one or two paragraphs, describe a person by showing him or her performing some action that takes less than five minutes. From the description we should be able to infer some of the following: the time of day; the weather; and the person's height, weight, age, sex, occupation, economic or educational background, and mood.

7. Read the essay, "Adman's Atlanta" (pages 172–74). Then, describe and analyze an advertisement in about 500 words. To do this, you will need a thesis, such as "This advertisement appeals to male chauvinism," or "This advertisement plays on our fear that we may lack sex appeal." Include a copy of the advertisement with your essay.

8. Choose a recent political cartoon to describe and analyze. In your first paragraph identify the cartoon (cartoonist's name, place and date of publication) and describe the drawing (including any words in it) thoroughly enough so that someone who has not seen it can visualize or even draw it fairly accurately. In a second paragraph explain the political message. Don't inject your own opinion; present the cartoonist's point objectively. Submit a copy of the cartoon with your essay. Be sure to choose a cartoon of sufficient complexity to make the analysis worthwhile.

9. "At fifty," George Orwell wrote, "everyone gets the face he deserves." Using this sentence as your opening sentence, write

a paragraph — supporting or refuting the assertion — chiefly devoted to describing one face. (Your instructor may tell you to choose a widely known face [Lincoln, Churchill, Elizabeth Taylor] or, on the other hand, a face not known to the public.)

DESCRIPTION AT WORK

Adman's Atlanta[1]

Lynda Martin

Centered in the top third of the page is a three-line, deep black headline: "Atlanta's suburban style of urban living." The first A is the only capital letter, there is a period after living, and the letters are the Roman script of a regular typewriter. A round picture in black and white with a diameter the size of half the page is separated from the heading by three blocks of copy and a very small black and white rectangular picture. Each photo has a caption under it. In the round picture a beautifully gnarled tree casts its shadow over the driveway and cobblestone sidewalks that front two clean-lined, white apartment buildings at right angles to each other. In the break between the buildings a lamp of five white globes contrasts with dark trees behind it. A well-dressed businessman and business-woman walk in the sun in front of the building on the left; at the entrance of the other building another suited man climbs into a new-looking compact car. In the other photo Atlanta's skyline glows pale in a flawless afternoon sky behind a mass of trees that covers the bottom two-thirds of the shot. The copy tells of the joys of living in Atlanta, explaining that life there combines the best of the city with the best of the suburb.

In attempting to persuade the reader that "Atlanta's style of living" is worth finding out about (by writing to the Atlanta Chamber of Commerce), the creators of the ad have used several techniques to associate living in Atlanta with business and with luxury; in short, with the common idea of success.

First to catch the reader's eye is the dark solid heading. The

[1] This essay was written by a freshman in response to an assignment requiring students to describe and analyze an advertisement.

Atlanta's suburban style of urban living.

In Atlanta you can live close in and still be close to wooded green. This blending of the urban and suburban makes Atlanta one of the most attractive and convenient big cities you'll find. And you can live here in almost any manner you choose. Up in a high-rise. In a formal town house. In a garden apartment with pool and tennis courts. Or amidst a rolling lawn and garden of your own.

And no matter which you choose, you're never far from the necessities and pleasures: schools, shopping, churches, cultural activities, entertainment, and of course your office.

Find out about Atlanta's style of living. Contact: Paul Miller, Atlanta Chamber of Commerce, 1314 Commerce Building, Atlanta, Ga. 30303. 404—521-0845.

TREES IN ATLANTA REACH INTO THE HEART OF DOWNTOWN.

TREES SURROUND LUXURY APARTMENTS ON PEACHTREE ROAD, 10 MINUTES FROM DOWNTOWN.

forceful deep black print is softened by its curved, but simple, design. Compact but not crowded, these words add up to a plain positive statement with a modestly assertive period at the end.

This business-like handling shows also in the picture centered below. It depicts clean white modern buildings lived in by purposeful people who are apparently going about a normal day in their successful lives. The dominance of the foreground tree and other trees in the background complement the buildings, preventing any appearance of harshness. A sense of gentleness and luxury is augmented by the blurred round border that makes the pictures seem to be surrounded by sunlight. The sun is important in this picture, and also in the rectangular picture to the left. In both, the sun heightens the contrast between the clean brightness of the buildings and the luxurious darkness of the trees, producing an atmosphere of happy leisure.

Lest leisure seem to be merely idleness, any emptiness created by the word "suburban" is immediately filled by the word "urban." The copy emphasizes both the convenience of living "close in" — that is, being near "necessities and pleasures: schools, shopping, churches, cultural activities . . ." — and the flexibility of being able to live in the city "in almost any manner you choose," be it some kind of urban apartment or a home of your own. Life in Atlanta is urban but "close to the wooded green." This idea is not only brought out in the copy, but is also emphasized in the pictures by beginning both captions with the word "trees."

This advertisement creates a favorable impression of city living, counteracting many readers' associations of a city with dirt, smog, and crowds. It indirectly advertises the "good life" of a prosperous businessman, be it in "a formal town house" or with "a rolling lawn and garden of your own." It also advertises middle-class values, beginning with religion and ending with business: "churches, cultural activities, entertainment, and of course your office."

Los Angeles Notebook

Joan Didion

There is something uneasy in the Los Angeles air this afternoon, some unnatural stillness, some tension. What it means is that tonight a Santa Ana will begin to blow, a hot wind from the northeast whining down through the Cajon and San Gorgonio Passes, blowing up sandstorms out along Route 66, drying the hills and the nerves to the flash point. For a few days now we will see smoke back in the canyons, and hear sirens in the night. I have neither heard nor read that a Santa Ana is due, but I know it, and almost everyone I have seen today knows it too. We know it because we feel it. The baby frets. The maid sulks. I rekindle a waning argument with the telephone company, then cut my losses and lie down, given over to whatever it is in the air. To live with the Santa Ana is to accept, consciously or unconsciously, a deeply mechanistic view of human behavior.

I recall being told, when I first moved to Los Angeles and was living on an isolated beach, that the Indians would throw themselves into the sea when the bad wind blew. I could see why. The Pacific turned ominously glossy during a Santa Ana period, and one woke in the night troubled not only by·the peacocks screaming in the olive trees but by the eerie absence of surf. The heat was surreal. The sky had a yellow cast, the kind of light sometimes called "earthquake weather." My only neighbor would not come out of her house for days, and there were no lights at night, and her husband roamed the place with a machete. One day he would tell me that he had heard a trespasser, the next a rattlesnake.

"On nights like that," Raymond Chandler once wrote about the Santa Ana, "every booze party ends in a fight. Meek little wives feel the edge of the carving knife and study their husbands' necks. Anything can happen." That was the kind of wind it was. I did not know then that there was any basis for the effect it had on all of us, but it turns out to be another of these cases in which science bears out folk wisdom. The Santa Ana, which is named for one of the canyons it rushes through, is a *foehn* wind, like the *foehn* of Austria and Switzerland and the *hamsin* of Israel. There are a number of persistent malevolent winds, perhaps the best known of which are the mistral of France and the Mediterranean sirocco, but a *foehn* wind has distinct characteristics: it occurs on the leeward slope of a mountain range and, although the air begins as a cold mass, it is warmed as it comes down the mountain and appears finally as a hot dry wind. Whenever and wherever a *foehn* blows, doctors hear about headaches and nausea and allergies, about "nervousness," about "depression." In Los Angeles some teachers do not attempt to conduct formal classes during a Santa Ana, because the children become unmanageable. In Switzerland the suicide rate goes up during the *foehn*, and in the courts of some Swiss cantons the wind is considered a mitigating circumstance for crime. Surgeons are said to watch the wind, because blood does not clot normally during a *foehn*. A few years ago an Israeli physicist discovered that not only during such winds, but for the ten or twelve hours which precede them, the air carries an unusually high ratio of positive to negative ions. No one seems to know exactly why that should be; some talk about friction and others suggest solar disturbances. In any case the positive ions are there, and what an excess of positive ions does, in the simplest terms, is make people unhappy. One cannot get much more mechanistic than that.

Easterners commonly complain that there is no "weather" at all in Southern California, that the days and the seasons slip by relentlessly, numbingly bland. That is quite misleading. In fact the climate is characterized by infrequent but violent extremes: two periods of torrential subtropical rains which continue for weeks and wash out the hills and send subdivisions sliding toward the sea; about twenty scattered days a year of the Santa Ana, which, with its incendiary dryness, invariably means fire. At the first prediction of a Santa Ana, the Forest Service flies men and equipment from northern California into the southern forests, and the Los Angeles Fire Department cancels its ordinary non-firefighting routines. The Santa Ana caused Malibu to burn the way it did in 1956, and Bel Air in 1961, and Santa Barbara in 1964. In the winter of 1966–67 eleven men were killed fighting a Santa Ana fire that spread through the San Gabriel Mountains.

Just to watch the front-page news out of Los Angeles during a Santa Ana is to get very close to what it is about the place. The longest single Santa Ana period in recent years was in 1957, and it lasted not the usual three or four days but fourteen days, from November 21 until December 4. On the first day 25,000 acres of the San Gabriel Mountains were burning, with gusts reaching 100 miles an hour. In town, the wind reached Force 12, or hurricane force, on the Beaufort Scale; oil derricks were toppled and people ordered off the downtown streets to avoid injury from flying objects. On November 22 the fire in the San Gabriels was out of control. On November 24 six people were killed in automobile accidents, and by the end of the week the Los Angeles *Times* was keeping a box score of traffic deaths. On November 26 a prominent Pasadena attorney, depressed about money, shot and killed his wife, their two sons, and himself. On November 27 a South Gate divorcée, twenty-two, was murdered and thrown from a moving car. On November 30 the San Gabriel fire was still out of control, and the wind in town was blowing eighty miles an hour. On the first day of December four people died violently, and on the third the wind began to break.

It is hard for people who have not lived in Los Angeles to

realize how radically the Santa Ana figures in the local imagination. The city burning is Los Angeles's deepest image of itself: Nathanael West perceived that, in *The Day of the Locust*; and at the time of the 1965 Watts riots what struck the imagination most indelibly were the fires. For days one could drive the Harbor Freeway and see the city on fire, just as we had always known it would be in the end. Los Angeles weather is the weather of catastrophe, of apocalypse, and, just as the reliably long and bitter winters of New England determine the way life is lived there, so the violence and the unpredictability of the Santa Ana affect the entire quality of life in Los Angeles, accentuate its impermanence, its unreliability. The wind shows us how close to the edge we are.

QUESTIONS

1. Paraphrase or explain the last sentence of the first paragraph. What passages in the essay offer the most persuasive evidence supporting the point?
2. Beginning with the third paragraph, Didion defines the Santa Ana. Would the essay have been clearer or more effective if the definition had introduced the essay? Explain.
3. Explain the last sentence, and evaluate it as a conclusion.

9
Narration

THE USES OF NARRATIVE

Usually we think of narrative writing as the art of the novelist or short story writer, but narratives need not be fictional. Biography and autobiography, history and books of travel are all largely narrative. And of course narrative passages may appear in writings that as a whole are not themselves narratives. For instance, expository and persuasive essays may include narratives — perhaps anecdotes, or brief sketches of historical occurrences or of personal experiences — that serve to clarify the essayist's point. Suppose, for example, that you are writing a paper for a course in ethics, arguing that it is immoral for physicians to withhold the truth (supposedly for the patients' own good) from terminally ill patients. You might include a brief narrative recounting how such a patient, when told the truth, responded not by withdrawing, but by increasing her useful activities — which included helping the members of her family to adjust to her imminent death. In writing any essay you may find that a paragraph or two of narrative helps you first to engage your readers' attention and then to make an abstract point concretely and persuasively.

In the following passage, addressed to English teachers, Paul B. Diederich, a specialist in the teaching of writing, explains mostly through narrative the "effects of excessive correction" on students in writing classes.

I can judge one of the main effects of . . . grading by the attitudes of students who land in my remedial course in college. They hate and fear writing more than anything else they have had to do in school. If they see a blank sheet of paper on which they are expected to write something, they look as though they want to scream. Apparently they have never written anything that anyone thought was good. At least, no one ever *told* them that anything in their writing was good. All their teachers looked for were mistakes, and there are so many kinds of mistakes in writing that their students despair of ever learning to avoid them.

The attitude toward writing that these students have developed is well illustrated by a story told by the Russian writer Chekhov about a kitten that was given to his uncle. The uncle wanted to make the kitten a champion killer of mice, so while it was still very young, he showed it a live mouse in a cage. Since the kitten's hunting instinct had not yet developed, it examined the mouse curiously but without any hostility. The uncle wanted to teach it that such fraternizing with the enemy was wrong, so he slapped the kitten, scolded it, and sent it away in disgrace. The next day the same mouse was shown to the kitten again. This time the kitten regarded it rather fearfully but without any aggressive intent. Again the uncle slapped it, scolded it, and sent it away. This treatment went on day after day. After some time, as soon as the kitten saw or smelled that mouse, it screamed and tried to climb up the walls. At that point the uncle lost patience and gave the kitten away, saying that it was stupid and would never learn. Of course the kitten had learned perfectly, and had learned exactly what it had been taught, but unfortunately not what the uncle intended to teach. "I can sympathize with that kitten," says Chekhov, "because that same uncle tried to teach me Latin."

If everything written by our less gifted writers get slapped down for its mistakes, and if this treatment continues year after year, can we expect that their attitude toward writing will differ from the attitude of the kitten toward that mouse? I saw the result year after year in my remedial classes. If I asked them to write anything, they reacted as though I had asked them to walk a tight-rope sixty feet above the ground with no net to catch them if they fell. It took some time to build up their confidence, to convince them that writing is as simple and natural as talking, and that no reader would mind a few mistakes if he got interested in what was being written about. For some time I never commented adversely on anything they wrote but expressed appreciation of anything I found interesting, no matter how badly it was expressed. After students gained confidence I continued to express appreciation but offered one suggestion for improvement at the end of each paper. If poor writers learn one thing about writing per paper, that is far above the average.

Notice that in the brief passage, three paragraphs in all, there are two narratives. The first, a retelling of Chekhov's anecdote about a kitten, memorably illustrates Diederich's point that students subjected to excessive correction are not taught to write but taught to fear writing. The third paragraph, while mainly expository, recounts Diederich's own experiences — year after year — of restoring confidence in students in his remedial classes.

Often a short narrative provides an arresting opening to an essay. You may have noticed how often speakers rely on this device; writers, too, find it effective. Flannery O'Connor begins "The King of the Birds" (an essay on her passion for collecting and raising peacocks) with the following story:

> When I was five, I had an experience that marked me for life. Pathé News sent a photographer from New York to Savannah to take a picture of a chicken of mine. This chicken, a buff Cochin Bantam, had the distinction of being able to walk either forward or backward. Her fame had spread through the press, and by the time she reached the attention of Pathé News, I suppose there was nowhere left for her to go — forward or backward. Shortly after that she died, as now seems fitting.

What makes this anecdote arresting? First of all, we can hardly read that an experience marked a person for life without wanting to know what the experience was. We expect to learn something sensational; perhaps, human nature being what it is, we hope to learn something horrifying. But O'Connor cannily does not gratify our wish. Instead she treats us to something like a joke. The chicken, whose fame had "spread through the press," has her picture taken by Pathé News (one of the companies that made the newsreels shown regularly in movie theaters before television became popular) and then dies. If the joke is in part on us, O'Connor takes the sting out of it by turning it around on herself. In her second paragraph she explains:

> If I put this information in the beginning of an article on peacocks, it is because I am always being asked why I raise them, and I have no short or reasonable answer.

But of course her answer, contained in the first paragraph, *is* short, and about as reasonable an explanation as any of us can offer about our passion for collecting anything. If these opening paragraphs persuade us to keep reading, it is not because they deliver the melodrama they at first hinted at, but because O'Connor's irony persuades us that she is entertaining, and that she is honest about her experience. We want to learn more about her, and we may thereby be seduced into learning what she wants to teach us about peacocks. Moreover, O'Connor's explanation that she tells the story because "I have no short or reasonable answer," reveals a profound truth about the impulse to tell stories. When a writer, even the writer of an expository essay, tells a story, it is because that story happens to be the best way to make the particular point he or she wants to make.

NARRATIVE PACE

A narrative is concerned with action, and the pace is normally swift. The narrator tries to communicate the concreteness of the events as they occurred, or as they registered on him, at the speed at which they occurred, or seemed to occur. The good storyteller cuts any details or incidents that clog the action or blur the point of the story. The kitten in Chekhov's narrative is shown a live mouse "while [the kitten] was still very young," and again "the next day." Since the kitten's behavior doesn't change (nor, more significantly, does the uncle's) Chekhov swiftly summarizes what happened next: "This treatment went on day after day." We are then given only one sentence of description, directly relevant to the narrative, before we are told that the uncle lost patience and gave the kitten away. It is not important to Chekhov's point, or to Diederich's, whether the kitten was gray or calico, long haired or short, cuddly or scrawny, but only that it "screamed and tried to climb up the walls" when it saw or smelled the mouse. *These* details are the relevant ones, and so Chekhov gives them to us. Similarly, O'Connor describes her chicken only enough to convince us of its reality — it was a "buff Cochin Bantam." The point of the anecdote lies not in the unremarkable chicken (who achieves her fame and dies in three sentences) but in the effect on the writer of a brief moment of celebrity. On a deeper level, the point of the anecdote is the writer's wish to secure our attention and goodwill.

ORGANIZING A NARRATIVE

The organization of a narrative is normally chronological, though purposeful variations are welcome. For example, fairly often narratives begin at the end, for a dramatic opening, and then present the earlier parts of the story in chronological order. Such a structure deliberately dispels surprise about the outcome, but gains suspense; the reader enjoys the pleasure of anticipating how events will move toward the known ending. In the following essay (two paragraphs in all) you'll find the end of the story foreshadowed in the word "amiable" in the first sentence.

Out in Akron, Ohio, there is an underground church called Alice's Restaurant, which figures in the most amiable story of the season just past. This group, led by unfrocked priests and unchurched ministers, was doing a deal of earnest good work in a quiet way, all to dramatize and protest the commercialization of Christmas. At shopping centers, for instance, they passed out leaflets calling upon shoppers to limit individual gifts to two-fifty and to devote the overplus to the poor. Then it occurred to one underground churchman, David Bullock by name, to demonstrate the fate that would inevitably befall the Holy Family in a society of heartless abundance. "Joseph and Mary were poor people," Mr. Bullock observed, and he proceeded to devise a scheme that would reveal "what would happen when a poor young couple dressed like Joseph and Mary tried to get a room nearly two thousand years after the birth of Christ." And so it came to pass in those days that Mr. Bullock, in beard and robe, walked out of the cold and darkness of Akron into the lobby of the Downtown Holiday Inn, accompanied by a young woman and a donkey. "I need a room for the night," he told the manager. "My wife is heavy with child." He then filled out the registration form, identifying himself as Joseph of Nazareth, travelling with his wife from Judea. Then he waited. The night manager, Mr. Robert Nagel, affably observed that they had come a long way and handed over a key to Room 101.

We picture Mr. Bullock with the key in his hand, his rented donkey lurking behind him, and his faith in human nature crumbling to the ground. To crown his discomfiture, Mr. Nagel offered the wayfarers a free meal. But, alas, in an era of affluence, satiety, like the indiscriminate rain, is apt to descend upon the just and unjust alike. "We weren't very hungry," Mr. Bullock said later, "so I asked him if we could have some drinks." Then he added, "And you know what? He sent them around." For his own part, Mr. Nagel was under no illusions about the financial standing of his new guests. "I knew they couldn't pay," he said. "I mean, a donkey is not a normal form of transportation." One would like to shake him by the hand. We thank Mr. Nagel for adding immeasurably to the merriment of our Christmas, and for his exhibition of that unpredictable, shrewd, and sometimes highly inconvenient human generosity that makes sweeping moral judgments so risky — even for the most earnest of moralists — and makes life so richly interesting for the rest of us.

Notice that although the narrative within the essay is organized chronologically, it is framed — at the beginning by some background information, and at the end by the writer's response to the incident, his reason for sharing it. Note also that the writer interrupts the narrative briefly at the beginning of the second paragraph to speculate how Mr. Bullock looked and, more important, how he felt. Although the writer makes the point unobtrusively, it is clear that he was not an eyewitness to the story or an actor in it, but pieced it together from two interviews with the participants and perhaps from some additional research. Finally, notice that if you skim the essay you can easily spot the narrative portion by observing the appearance of verbs in the past tense ("walked," "told," "filled out," "waited," "observed," "handed") and by the frequency of the word "then." Narratives, however they are organized, are almost always told in the past tense; and good storytellers help us to follow the succession of events, the passage of time, by using such transitional words as *first, then, next, at last,* and *finally*.

Finally, we reprint a letter to the editor in which a college student, an assault victim, tells her experience. You may observe here too that the organization is for the most part chronological, made clear by transitions, and framed by the writer's analysis of her experience and of her reasons for revealing it. As readers, we may or may not notice these points; gripped by the story being told, we are largely unaware of the techniques of successful writers. As students of writing, however, we study these techniques.

To the Editor:
I write this letter out of concern for women of the college community. I am one of the two students who were assaulted during

the winter recess. I do not feel any shame or embarrassment over what happened. Instead, I want to share some of my experience because in doing so I may help other women to think about rape and rape prevention.

First I think it is important for the community to understand what happened to me. At my request, during the vacation a well-intentioned employee let me into my residence hall to collect some things from my room. It was after dark. I was alone in my room when a man appeared at the door with a stocking over his head and a knife in his hand. He said he was going to rape me. I had no intention of submitting, and I struggled with him for about five minutes. One of the reasons why I chose not to submit but to resist was that as a virgin I did not want my first sexual experience to be the horror of rape. While struggling I tried to get him to talk to me, saying such things as "Why do you want to rape me? Don't you understand I want no part of this? I am a woman, not an object. In God's name, please don't rape me." He finally overpowered me and attempted to rape me, but stopped when he realized I had a tampax in. Then at knife point he asked me a number of questions. He ended by threatening that if I reported and identified him he would kill me. As he was leaving he made me lie on my bed and count to five hundred, which I started to do. Then as I reached one hundred he returned and told me to start over. Thus it was good I did not get up right after he left.

It is impossible to say what should be done in all instances of assault. Each incident is different and requires a different response. I think what helped me most was my ability to remain calm, assess the situation, and then act firmly. I did struggle, I did talk, but I also did act in such a way as to ensure my own safety at knife point.

I believe there are some reasons why I was able to cope with the situation. One is that I had talked with other women about rape and self-defense. As a result I was more aware of the possibility of rape and had thought some about what I might do if confronted with an attacker. Also my active involvement in the women's movement has helped me develop confidence in myself, especially in my strength, both emotional and physical. I believe such confidence helped me not to panic. Another reason why I was able to cope was that I prayed.

I think it is important also to share with you the aftermath of the attack. The first thing I did after leaving my room was to report the incident to security and to the campus police. I did not hesitate to report the attack since I realized that reporting it was vital to protect the safety of the college community. The police were efficient and helpful in taking the report and starting search procedures. (The police also told me they did not think I was in further danger, despite the threats on my life. There seemed to be little reason for him to come back.) Also, two female members of the student services staff stayed with me most of the evening. Their presence and support were very helpful to me, especially while I talked to the police. Since the incident, I have also found support from professional staff and from friends. The residence office, the medical and psychiatric staff, the dean's office, and the chaplaincy staff have all been very helpful. All have protected my confidentiality.

At first I did not realize that I would want or need to seek out people's help, but now I am glad I did. The rape experience goes beyond the assault itself. I have come to understand the importance of dealing with the complex emotions that follow. Also I now know that there is no reason for women to feel ashamed, embarrassed, or scared about seeking help.

I hope you now have a greater concern for your own safety after reading about what happened to me. I think this is the most important point of my writing. It never occurred to me that entering an unoccupied residence hall was dangerous. We all have been too accustomed to doing things on and off this campus without considering our own safety or vulnerability to attacks. But we ourselves are our own best security, so please protect yourselves and each other.

I am aware I will be working through this experience for a long time to come. I am thankful that there are people in this community to help me do that. I in turn want to be helpful in any way I can. So I invite women who are genuinely concerned about rape and assault to join me in sharing experiences and thoughts next Tuesday, February 18 at 7 P.M. in the Women's Center.

Name withheld upon request.

EXERCISES

1. In one or two paragraphs tell a story that illustrates an abstraction, such as courage, endurance, a misunderstanding, a putdown, pride, the generation gap, embarrassment, loneliness. For an example, see "Conceit" (page 310) and the brief discussion following it.

2. In 750–1000 words survey your development as a writer and explain your current attitude toward writing. Focus your essay on one narrative or on two contrasting narratives to exemplify what you have learned and how you learned it. Whether your thesis is stated or implied, be sure that your essay makes a clear point. Your point might be, for example, that you learned more about writing from working on your school newspaper or from studying geometry than from most of your English classes, or that the different approaches of two teachers reinforced each other, or left you hopelessly confused about writing.

3. For an essay on any topic you choose, write an opening paragraph that includes an anecdote. Don't write the essay, but indicate from the anecdote and, if you wish, an additional sentence or two, the topic of your essay.

4. In 500–1000 words narrate an experience in such a way that you communicate not only the experience but the significance of it. For example, you might tell of an interview for a job which gave you some awareness of the attitude of people with jobs toward those without jobs. Or you might narrate an experience at school that seems to you to illuminate the virtues or defects or assumptions of the school. A variation: John Keats in a letter says, "Nothing ever becomes real till it is experienced — Even a proverb is no proverb to you till your life has illustrated it." Recount an experience that has made you feel the truth of a proverb.

NARRATION AT WORK

Shooting an Elephant
George Orwell

In Moulmein, in Lower Burma, I was hated by large numbers of people — the only time in my life that I have been important enough for this to happen to me. I was sub-divisional police officer of the town, and in an aimless, petty kind of way anti-European feeling was very bitter. No one had the guts to raise a riot, but if a European woman went through the bazaars alone somebody would probably spit betel juice over her dress. As a police officer I was an obvious target and was baited whenever it seemed safe to do so. When a nimble Burman tripped me up on the football field and the referee (another Burman) looked the other way, the crowd yelled with hideous laughter. This happened more than once. In the end the sneering yellow faces of young men that met me everywhere, the insults hooted after me when I was at a safe distance, got badly on my nerves. The young Buddhist priests were the worst of all. There were several thousands of them in the town and none of them seemed to have anything to do except stand on street corners and jeer at Europeans.

All this was perplexing and upsetting. For at that time I had already made up my mind that imperialism was an evil thing and the sooner I chucked up my job and got out of it the better. Theoretically — and secretly, of course — I was all for the Burmese and all against their oppressors, the British. As for the job I was doing, I hated it more bitterly than I can perhaps make clear. In a job like that you see the dirty work of Empire at close quarters. The wretched prisoners huddling in the stinking cages of the lock-ups, the grey, cowed faces of the long-term convicts, the scarred buttocks of the men who had been flogged with bamboos — all these oppressed me with an intolerable sense of guilt. But I could get nothing into perspective. I was young and ill-educated and I had had to think out my problems in the utter silence that is imposed on every Englishman in the East. I did not even know that the British Empire is dying, still less did I know that it is a great deal better than the younger empires that are going to supplant it. All I knew was that I was stuck between my hatred of the empire I served and my rage against the evil-spirited little beasts who tried to make my job impossible. With one part of my mind I thought of the British Raj as an unbreakable tyranny, as something clamped down, in *saecula saeculorum,*[1] upon the will of prostrate peoples; with another part I thought that the greatest joy in the world would be to drive a bayonet into a Buddhist priest's guts. Feelings like these are the normal by-products of imperialism; ask any Anglo-Indian official, if you can catch him off duty.

One day something happened which in a roundabout way was enlightening. It was a tiny incident in itself, but it gave me a better glimpse than I had had before of the real nature of imperialism —

[1] For world without end.

the real motives for which despotic governments act. Early one morning the sub-inspector at a police state the other end of the town rang me up on the 'phone and said that an elephant was ravaging the bazaar. Would I please come and do something about it? I did not know what I could do, but I wanted to see what was happening and I got on to a pony and started out. I took my rifle, an old .44 Winchester and much too small to kill an elephant, but I thought the noise might be useful *in terrorem.*[2] Various Burmans stopped me on the way and told me about the elephant's doings. It was not, of course, a wild elephant, but a tame one which had gone "must." It had been chained up, as tame elephants always are when their attack of "must" is due, but on the previous night it had broken its chain and escaped. Its mahout, the only person who could manage it when it was in that state, had set out in pursuit, but had taken the wrong direction and was now twelve hours' journey away, and in the morning the elephant had suddenly reappeared in the town. The Burmese population had no weapons and were quite helpless against it. It had already destroyed somebody's bamboo hut, killed a cow and raided some fruit-stalls and devoured the stock; also it had met the municipal rubbish van and, when the driver jumped out and took to his heels, had turned the van over and inflicted violences upon it.

The Burmese sub-inspector and some Indian constables were waiting for me in the quarter where the elephant had been seen. It was a very poor quarter, a labyrinth of squalid bamboo huts, thatched with palmleaf, winding all over a steep hillside. I remember that it was a cloudy, stuffy morning at the beginning of the rains. We began questioning the people as to where the elephant had gone and, as usual, failed to get any definite information. That is invariably the case in the East; a story always sounds clear enough at a distance, but the nearer you get to the scene of events the vaguer it becomes. Some of the people said that the elephant had gone in one direction, some said that he had gone in another, some professed not even to have heard of any elephant. I had almost made up my mind that the whole story was a pack of lies, when we heard yells a little distance away. There was a loud, scandalized cry of "Go away, child! Go away this instant!" and an old woman with a switch in her hand came round the corner of a hut, violently shooing away a crowd of naked children. Some more women followed, clicking their tongues and exclaiming; evidently there was something that the children ought not to have seen. I rounded the hut and saw a

[2] As a warning.

man's dead body sprawling in the mud. He was an Indian, a black Dravidian coolie, almost naked, and he could not have been dead many minutes. The people said that the elephant had come suddenly upon him round the corner of the hut, caught him with its trunk, put its foot on his back and ground him into the earth. This was the rainy season and the ground was soft, and his face had scored a trench a foot deep and a couple of yards long. He was lying on his belly with arms crucified and head sharply twisted to one side. His face was coated with mud, the eyes wide open, the teeth bared and grinning with an expression of unendurable agony. (Never tell me, by the way, that the dead look peaceful. Most of the corpses I have seen look devilish.) The friction of the great beast's foot had stripped the skin from his back as neatly as one skins a rabbit. As soon as I saw the dead man I sent an orderly to a friend's house nearby to borrow an elephant rifle. I had already sent back the pony, not wanting it to go mad with fright and throw me if it smelt the elephant.

The orderly came back in a few minutes with a rifle and five cartridges, and meanwhile some Burmans had arrived and told us that the elephant was in the paddy fields below, only a few hundred yards away. As I started forward practically the whole population of the quarter flocked out of the houses and followed me. They had seen the rifle and were all shouting excitedly that I was going to shoot the elephant. They had not shown much interest in the elephant when he was merely ravaging their homes, but it was different now that he was going to be shot. It was a bit of fun to them, as it would be to an English crowd; besides they wanted the meat. It made me vaguely uneasy. I had no intention of shooting the elephant — I had merely sent for the rifle to defend myself if necessary — and it is always unnerving to have a crowd following you. I marched down the hill, looking and feeling a fool, with the rifle over my shoulder and an ever-growing army of people jostling at my heels. At the bottom, when you got away from the huts, there was a metalled road and beyond that a miry waste of paddy fields a thousand yards across, not yet ploughed but soggy from the first rains and dotted with coarse grass. The elephant was standing eight yards from the road, his left side towards us. He took not the slightest notice of the crowd's approach. He was tearing up bunches of grass, beating them against his knees to clean them and stuffing them into his mouth.

I had halted on the road. As soon as I saw the elephant I knew with perfect certainty that I ought not to shoot him. It is a serious matter to shoot a working elephant — it is comparable to destroying a huge and costly piece of machinery — and obviously one ought not to do it if it can possibly be avoided. And at that distance, peacefully eating, the elephant looked no more dangerous than a cow. I thought then and I think now that his attack of "must" was already passing off; in which case he would merely wander harmlessly about until the mahout came back and caught him. Moreover, I did not in the least want to shoot him. I decided that I would watch him for a little while to make sure that he did not turn savage again, and then go home.

But at that moment I glanced round at the crowd that had followed me. It was an immense crowd, two thousand at the least and growing every minute. It blocked the road for a long distance on either side. I looked at the sea of yellow faces above the garish clothes — faces all happy and excited over this bit of fun, all certain that the elephant was going to be shot. They were watching me as they would watch a conjurer about to perform a trick. They did not like me, but with the magical rifle in my hands I was momentarily worth watching. And suddenly I realized that I should have to shoot the elephant after all. The people expected it of me and I had got to do it; I could feel their two thousand wills pressing me forward, irresistibly. And it was at this moment, as I stood there with the rifle in my hands, that I first grasped the hollowness, the futility of the white man's dominion in the East. Here was I, the white man with his gun, standing in front of the unarmed native crowd — seemingly the leading actor of the piece; but in reality I was only an absurd puppet pushed to and fro by the will of those yellow faces behind. I perceived in this moment that when the white man turns tyrant it is his own freedom that he destroys. He becomes a sort of hollow, posing dummy, the conventionalized figure of a sahib. For it is the condition of his rule that he shall spend his life in trying to impress the "natives," and so in every crisis he has got to do what the "natives" expect of him. He wears a mask, and his face grows to fit it. I had got to shoot the elephant. I had committed myself to doing it when I sent for the rifle. A sahib has got to act like a sahib; he has got to appear resolute, to know his own mind and do definite things. To come all that way, rifle in hand, with two thousand people marching at my heels, and then to trail feebly away, having done nothing — no, that was impossible. The crowd would laugh at me. And my whole life, every white man's life in the East, was one long struggle not to be laughed at.

But I did not want to shoot the elephant. I watched him beating his bunch of grass against his knees, with that preoccupied grandmotherly air that elephants have. It seemed to me that it would be murder to shoot him. At that age I was not squeamish about killing animals, but I had never shot an elephant and never wanted to. (Somehow it always seems worse to kill a *large* animal.) Besides, there was the beast's owner to be considered. Alive, the elephant was worth at least a hundred pounds; dead, he would only be worth the value of his tusks, five pounds, possibly. But I had got to act quickly. I turned to some experienced-looking Burmans who had been there when we arrived, and asked them how the elephant had been behaving. They all said the same thing: he took no notice of you if you left him alone, but he might charge if you went too close to him.

It was perfectly clear to me what I ought to do. I ought to walk up to within, say, twenty-five yards of the elephant and test his behavior. If he charged, I could shoot; if he took no notice of me, it would be safe to leave him until the mahout came back. But also I knew that I was going to do no such thing. I was a poor shot with a rifle and the ground was soft mud into which one would sink at every step. If the elephant charged and I missed him, I should have about as much chance as a toad under a steam-roller. But even then I was not thinking particularly of my own skin, only of the watchful yellow faces behind. For at that moment, with the crowd watching me, I was not afraid in the ordinary sense, as I would have been if I had been alone. A white man mustn't be frightened in front of "natives"; and so, in general, he isn't frightened. The sole thought in my mind was that if anything went wrong those two thousand Burmans would see me pursued, caught, trampled on and reduced to a grinning corpse like that Indian up the hill. And if that happened it was quite probable that some of them would laugh. That would never do. There was only one alternative. I shoved the cartridges into the magazine and lay down on the road to get a better aim.

The crowd grew very still, and a deep, low, happy sigh, as of people who see the theatre curtain go up at last, breathed from innumerable throats. They were going to have their bit of fun after all. The rifle was a beautiful German thing with cross-hair sights. I did not then know that in shooting an elephant one would shoot to cut an imaginary bar running from ear-hole to ear-hole. I ought, therefore, as the elephant was sideways on, to have aimed straight at his ear-hole; actually I aimed several inches in front of this, thinking the brain would be further forward.

When I pulled the trigger I did not hear the bang or feel the kick — one never does when a shot goes home — but I heard the devilish roar of glee that went up from the crowd. In that instant, in too short a time, one would have thought, even for the bullet to get there, a mysterious, terrible change had come over the elephant. He neither stirred nor fell, but every line of his body had altered. He looked suddenly stricken, shrunken, immensely old, as though the frightful impact of the bullet had paralysed him without knocking him down. At last, after what seemed a long time — it might have been five seconds, I dare say — he sagged flabbily to his knees. His mouth slobbered. An enormous senility seemed to have settled upon him. One could have imagined him thousands of years old. I fired again into the same spot. At the second shot he did not collapse but climbed with desperate slowness to his feet and stood weakly upright, with legs sagging and head drooping. I fired a third time. That was the shot that did for him. You could see the agony of it jolt his whole body and knock the last remnant of strength from his legs. But in falling he seemed for a moment to rise, for as his hind legs collapsed beneath him he seemed to tower upward like a huge rock toppling, his trunk reaching skywards like a tree. He trumpeted, for the first and only time. And then down he came, his belly towards me, with a crash that seemed to shake the ground even where I lay.

I got up. The Burmans were already racing past me across the mud. It was obvious that the elephant would never rise again, but he was not dead. He was breathing very rhythmically with long rattling gasps, his great mound of a side painfully rising and falling. His mouth was wide open. I could see far down into caverns of pale pink throat. I waited a long time for him to die, but his breathing did not weaken. Finally I fired my two remaining shots into the spot where I thought his heart must be. The thick blood welled out of him like red velvet, but still he did not die. His body did not even jerk when the shots hit him, the tortured breathing continued without a pause. He was dying, very slowly and in great agony, but in some world remote from me where not even a bullet could damage him further. I felt I had got to put an end to that dreadful noise. It seemed dreadful to see the great beast lying there, powerless to move and yet powerless to die, and not even to be able to finish him. I sent back for my small rifle and poured shot after shot into his heart and down his throat. They seemed to make no impression. The tortured gasps continued as steadily as the ticking of a clock.

In the end I could not stand it any longer and went away. I heard later that it took him half an hour to die. Burmans were bringing dahs and baskets even before I left, and I was told they had stripped his body almost to the bones by the afternoon.

Afterwards, of course, there were endless discussions about the shooting of the elephant. The owner was furious, but he was only an Indian and could do nothing. Besides, legally I had done the right thing, for a mad elephant has to be killed, like a mad dog, if its owner fails to control it. Among the Europeans opinion was divided. The older men said I was right, the younger men said it was a damn shame to shoot an elephant for killing a coolie, because an elephant was worth more than any damn Coringhee coolie. And afterwards I was very glad that the coolie had been killed; it put me legally in the right and it gave me a sufficient pretext for shooting the elephant. I often wondered whether any of the others grasped that I had done it solely to avoid looking a fool.

QUESTIONS

1. How does Orwell characterize himself at the time of the events he describes? What evidence in the essay suggests that he wrote it some years later?
2. Orwell says the incident was "enlightening." What does he mean? Picking up this clue, state in a sentence or two the thesis or main point of the essay.
3. Compare Orwell's description of the dead coolie (in the fourth paragraph) with his description of the elephant's death (in the eleventh and twelfth paragraphs). Why does Orwell devote more space to the death of the elephant?
4. How would you describe the tone of the last paragraph, particularly of the last two sentences? Do you find the paragraph an effective conclusion to the essay? Explain.

10

The Research Paper

WHAT RESEARCH IS

Because a research paper requires its writer to collect the available evidence — usually including the opinions of earlier investigators — one sometimes hears that a research paper, unlike a critical essay, is not the expression of personal opinion. But such a view is unjust both to criticism and to research. A critical essay is not a mere expression of personal opinion; to be any good it must offer evidence that supports the opinions, thus persuading the reader of their objective rightness. And a research paper is largely personal, because the author continuously uses his or her own judgment to evaluate the evidence, deciding what is relevant and convincing. A research paper is not merely an elaborate foot-noted presentation of what a dozen scholars have already said about a topic; it is a thoughtful evaluation of the available evidence, and so it is, finally, an expression of what the author thinks the evidence adds up to.[1]

Before we talk at some length about research papers, we should mention that you may want to do some research even for a paper that is primarily critical. Consider the difference between a paper on Bob Dylan's emergence as a popular singer, and a paper

[1] Because footnotes may be useful or necessary in a piece of writing that is *not* a research paper (such as this chapter), and because we wish to emphasize the fact that a thoughtful research paper requires more than footnotes, we have put our discussion of footnotes in another chapter, on pages 363–72.

on Bob Dylan's songs of social protest. The first of these, necessarily a research paper, will require you to dig into magazines and newspapers to find out about his reception in clubs in New York; but even if you are writing an analysis of his songs of social protest you may want to do a little research into Dylan's indebtedness to Woody Guthrie. You may, for example, study Dylan's record jackets and read some interviews in magazines and newspapers to find out if he has anything to say about his relation to Guthrie. Our point is that writers must learn to use source material thoughtfully, whether they expect to work with few sources or with many.

Research involving many sources can be a tedious and frustrating business; there are hours spent reading books and articles that prove to be irrelevant, there are contradictory pieces of evidence, and there is never enough time. Research, in short, is not a procedure that is attractive to everyone. The poet William Butler Yeats, though an indefatigable worker on projects that interested him, engagingly expressed an indifference to the obligation that confronts every researcher: to look carefully at all of the available evidence. Running over the possible reasons why Jonathan Swift did not marry (that he had syphilis, for instance, or that he feared he would transmit a hereditary madness), Yeats says, "Mr. Shane Leslie thinks that Swift's relation to Vanessa was not platonic, and that whenever his letters speak of a cup of coffee they mean the sexual act; whether the letters seem to bear him out I do not know, for those letters bore me."

Though research sometimes requires one to read boring works, those who engage in it feel, at least at times, an exhilaration, a sense of triumph at having studied a problem thoroughly and at having arrived at conclusions that at least for the moment seem objective and irrefutable. Later perhaps new evidence will turn up that will require a new conclusion, but until that time, one may reasonably feel that one knows *something*.

PRIMARY AND SECONDARY MATERIALS

The materials of most research can be conveniently divided into two sorts, primary and secondary. The primary materials or sources are the real subject of study, the secondary materials are critical and historical accounts already written about these primary materials. For example, if you want to know whether Shakespeare's attitude toward Julius Caesar was highly traditional or highly original, or a little of each, you would read *Julius Caesar,* other Elizabethan writings about Caesar, and Roman writings known to the Elizabethans; and in addition to these primary materials you would also read secondary material such as modern books on Shakespeare and on Elizabethan attitudes toward Rome and toward monarchs.

The line between these two kinds of sources, of course, is not always clear. For example, if you are concerned with the degree to which Joyce's *Portrait of the Artist as a Young Man* is autobiographical, primary materials include not only *A Portrait* and Joyce's letters, but perhaps also his brother Stanislaus' diary and autobiography. Although the diary and autobiography might be considered secondary sources — certainly a scholarly biography about Joyce or his brother would be a secondary source — because Stanislaus' books are more or less contemporary with your subject they can reasonably be called primary sources.

FROM SUBJECT TO THESIS

First, a subject. No subject is unsuited. Perhaps sports, war, art, dreams, food. As G. K. Chesterton said, "There is no such thing on earth as an uninteresting subject; the only thing that can exist is an uninterested person." Even a subject so apparently unpromising as the corset has been the material of research — and, what is more, of research that is fascinating, as readers of David Kunzle's *Fashion and Fetishism* know. By the way, Kunzle's thesis — the argument that holds together his wide-ranging findings — is this: the tightly-laced corset gave "positive and erotic pleasures" and thus was an image not of repression but of bodily freedom. Males who crusaded against tight-lacing spoke of freeing women from sexual tyranny but they were often, Kunzle suggests, really seeking to restrict sexuality and to enslave women to regular childbearing and to domestic labor.

Research, then, can be done on almost anything that interests you, though you should keep in mind two limitations. First, materials on current events may be extremely difficult to get hold of, since crucial documents may not yet be in print and you may not have access to the people involved. And, second, materials on some subjects may be unavailable to you because they are in languages you can't read or in publications that your library doesn't have. So you probably won't try to work on the stuff of today's headlines, and (because almost nothing in English has been written on it) you won't try to work on Japanese attitudes toward the hunting of whales. But no subject is too trivial for study: Newton, according to legend, wondered why an apple fell to the ground.

You cannot, however, write a research paper on subjects as broad as sports, war, art, dreams, or food. You have to focus on a much smaller area within such a subject. Let's talk about food. You might want to study the dietary laws of the Jews, the food of American Indians before the white man came, the consumption of whale meat, subsidies to hog farmers, or legislation governing the purity of food. Your own interests will guide you to the topic — the part of the broad subject — that you wish to explore.

But of course, though you have an interest in one of these narrower topics, you don't know a great deal about it; that's one of the reasons you are going to do research on it. Let's say that you happened to read or hear about Ralph Nader's stomach-turning essay on frankfurters (*New Republic,* 18 March 1972, pages 12–13), in which Nader reports that although today's frankfurters contain only 11.7 percent protein (the rest is water, salt, spices, and preservatives), they contain a substantial dose of sodium nitrate to inhibit the growth of bacteria and to keep the meat from turning gray.

Assuming that your appetite for research on food continues, you decide that you want to know something more about additives, that is, substances (such as sodium nitrate) added to preserve desirable properties — color, flavor, freshness — or to suppress undesirable properties. You want to do some reading, and you must now find the articles and books. Of course, as you do the reading, your focus may shift a little; you may stay with frankfurters, you may shift to the potentially dangerous effects, in various foods, of sodium nitrate, or to the controversy over the effects of saccharin (an artificial sweetener), or you may concentrate on so-called enriched bread, which is first robbed of many nutrients by refining and bleaching the flour and is then enriched by the addition of some of the nutrients in synthetic form. Exactly what you will focus on, and exactly what your *thesis* or point of view will be, you may not know until you do some more reading. But how do you find the relevant material?

FINDING THE MATERIAL

You may happen already to know of some relevant material that you have been intending to read, but if you are at a loss where to begin, consult the card catalog of your library and consult the appropriate guides to articles in journals.

The Card Catalog

The card catalog has cards arranged alphabetically not only by author and by title but also by subject. It probably won't have a subject heading for "frankfurter," but it will have one for "food," followed by cards listing books on this topic. And on the "food" card will be a note telling you of relevant subjects to consult. In fact, even before you look at the catalog you can know what subject headings it contains by checking one of two books: *Sears*

```
        FOOD

          see also

   COOKERY
   DIET
   DIETARIES
   FARM PRODUCE
   FRUIT
   GASTRONOMY
   GRAIN
   MARKETS
   MEAT
   NUTRITION
   POULTRY
                         see next card

                            ●
```

List of Subject Headings (for libraries that use the Dewey decimal system of arranging books) and *Subject Headings Used in the Dictionary Catalogs of the Library of Congress,* 7th edition. (Because most academic libraries use the Library of Congress system, the second of these is probably the book you'll use.) If you look for "food" in *Subject Headings,* you will find two pages of listings, including cross references such as "*sa* [= see also] Animal Food." Among the subject headings that sound relevant are Bacteriology, Food Contamination, and Preservation. Notice also the abbreviation "xx," referring to broader headings you may want to look at. If you make use of some of these subject headings you will probably find that the library has a fair amount of material on your topic.

Whether you went to *Subject Headings* or to the "food" card, you have now gathered a number of subject headings that seem relevant. With this information you can locate useful books — even though you began without knowing the author or title of even one book — simply by turning to the subject heading in the card file, and writing down the information on the books filed under that subject. For example, if you look up "Diet" or "Nutrition" or "Proteins in Human Nutrition" you will find cards for the books on each topic. On the next page is an example of a *subject card.* Notice the following about the subject card:

1. The subject is given at the top of the card.
2. The classification number at the left enables you to find the book in the library.
3. The card gives the author's name, title, and other information, such as the fact that this book includes a bibliography.
4. Near the bottom there is a list of other subject headings under which this card is filed. By checking these other subject headings (called *tracings* by librarians), you will be able to find additional books that probably are relevant to your research.

An *author card,* that is, a card filed alphabetically under the author's last name, is identical with a subject card except that the subject is not given at the top of the card. If you know the author's name, just look for it in the catalog.

Finally, a *title card* is identical with an author card, except that the title is added to the top of the card and the card is indexed

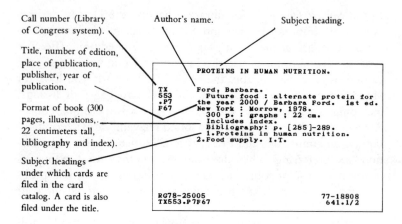

Call number (Library of Congress system).

Author's name.

Subject heading.

Title, number of edition, place of publication, publisher, year of publication.

Format of book (300 pages, illustrations, 22 centimeters tall, bibliography and index).

Subject headings under which cards are filed in the card catalog. A card is also filed under the title.

```
                    PROTEINS IN HUMAN NUTRITION.

TX          Ford, Barbara.
553            Future food : alternate protein for
.P7         the year 2000 / Barbara Ford.  1st ed.
F67         New York : Morrow, 1978.
               300 p. : graphs ; 22 cm.
               Includes index.
               Bibliography: p. [285]-289.
               1.Proteins in human nutrition.
            2.Food supply. I.T.


RG78-25005                                    77-18808
TX553.P7F67                                   641.1/2
```

under the first word of the title, or the second word if the first is *A, An,* or *The,* or a foreign equivalent.

Three Notes on the Alphabetic Arrangement of the Card Catalog

1. The catalog is arranged alphabetically from A to Z, of course, but the arrangement is word by word, not letter by letter. This means, for example, that "ion implantation" *precedes* "ionic crystals," because "i-o-n" precedes "i-o-n-i-c." (If the catalog were letter by letter instead of word by word, of course "i-o-n-i-c" would precede "i-o-n-i-m. . . .") Similarly, in the card catalog "folk tales" precedes "folklorists." Here is a short list of cards in the order they are in the catalog:

> Good, Emanual
> *Good Men and True*
> *Good Old Days*
> Goodall, Ann
> Goodman, Paul

2. Under the author's name, books are usually arranged alphabetically by title, but for highly prolific authors the cards listing the collected works may be grouped before those listing individual works. Cards for books *about* the author follow cards for books *by* the author. Note that authors whose surnames begin *Mc* or *Mac*

are all listed — in most libraries — as though spelled *Mac;* authors whose surnames begin with a prefix (for example, *De, Le, Van*) are listed as though the prefixes and surname formed a single word: De Lisle would come after Delano and before Delos.

3. Under the title, remember that books are alphabetized under the *second* word if the first word is *A, An,* or *The,* or a foreign equivalent. Note, too, that words normally abbreviated are spelled out in the catalog: *Doctor Zhivago, Mister Roberts, Saint Joan.*

Scanning Books, Book Reviews, and Encyclopedias

Having checked the card catalog and written down the relevant data (author, title, call number), you can begin to scan the books, or you can postpone looking at the books until you have found some relevant articles in periodicals. For the moment, let's postpone the periodicals.

Put a bunch of books in front of you, and choose one as an introduction. How do you choose one from half a dozen? Partly by its size — choose a thin one — and partly by its quality. Roughly speaking, it should be among the more recent publications, and it should strike you as fair. A pamphlet published by a meat-packers association is desirably thin but you have a hunch that it may be biased. Roger John Williams' *Nutrition in a Nutshell* is published by a well-known commercial press (Doubleday), and it is only 171 pages, but because it was published in 1962 it may not reflect current food chemistry. Though it is rather big (260 pages), Michael Jacobson's *Eater's Digest: The Consumer's Factbook of Food Additives* (New York: Doubleday, 1972) probably is about right.

When you have found the book that you think may serve as your introductory study, read the preface in order to get an idea of the author's purpose and outlook, scan the table of contents in order to get an idea of the organization and the coverage, and scan the final chapter or the last few pages, where you may be lucky enough to find a summary. The index, too, may let you know if the book will suit your purpose, by showing you what topics are covered and how much coverage they get. If the book still seems suitable, scan it.

At this stage it is acceptable to trust one's hunches — you are only going to scan the book, not buy it or even read it — but you may want to look up some book reviews to assure yourself that the book has merit. There are five especially useful indexes to book reviews:

> *Book Review Digest* (published from 1905 onward)
> *Book Review Index* (1965–)
> *Index to Book Reviews in the Humanities* (1960–)
> *Humanities Index* (1974–)
> *Social Sciences Index* (1974–)

The last two publications are chiefly indexes to articles, but at the rear of each issue you'll find indexes to book reviews, arranged alphabetically under the name of the author of the book.

Most reviews of books will come out in the same year as the book, or within the next two years, so if, for example, a book was published in 1979, look in the 1979 volume of the appropriate index and see what is there. If you want some more reviews, look in 1980 and 1981. Begin with *Book Review Digest,* because it includes excerpts from and synopses of the reviews; if it has your book, the excerpts and synopses may be enough, and you won't have to dig out the reviews themselves. But *Book Review Digest* does not have as broad coverage as the other indexes, and you may have to turn to them for citations, and then to the journals to which they refer you. Read the synopses in *Book Review Digest,* or some reviews in journals, and draw some conclusions about the merit of the book in question. Of course you cannot assume that every review is fair, but a book that on the whole gets good reviews is probably at least good enough for a start.

By quickly reading such a book (take few or no notes at this stage) you will probably get an overview of your topic, and you will see exactly what part of the topic you wish to pursue.

We should also mention that often you can get a quick general view of a subject from an encyclopedia. The chief encyclopedias are

> *Chambers's Encyclopaedia* (1973)
>
> *Collier's Encyclopedia* (1972; and the annual *Collier's Encyclopedia Year Book*)

Encyclopedia Americana (1974; and the annual yearbook, *The Americana Annual*) ·

Encyclopaedia Britannica (1974; and the annual *Encyclopaedia Britannica: Book of the Year*)

The first three of these encyclopedias simply use an alphabetic arrangement: *aardvark* is in the first volume, *zoo* in the last. But the organization of the *Encyclopaedia Britannica* is somewhat different and so we will briefly explain it here.

The fifteenth edition of the *Britannica* (1974) comprises thirty volumes. These are divided into three parts. (1) *Propaedia: Outline of Knowledge and Guide to the Britannica.* This is one volume. It divides all knowledge into ten categories, with many subdivisions. It is an outline or a table of contents to the remaining volumes. (2) *Micropaedia: Ready Reference and Index.* This is ten volumes, containing 102,214 short entries arranged alphabetically. No entry is longer than 750 words, which means that only the most essential points get mentioned. (3) *Macropaedia: Knowledge in Depth.* Nineteen volumes containing 4,207 articles averaging five pages each. All of the subjects treated in the *Macropaedia* were also treated, more briefly, in the *Micropaedia*.

Finding Bibliographies

Many researchers have published lists of the works they consulted, sometimes as articles in scholarly journals or as appendices to books, or even as entire books. All of these kinds of bibliographies are listed in *Bibliographic Index*, which is issued three times a year and cumulates in an annual volume. Begin, of course, with the most recent issue, check it for your subject, and then work back for a few years.

Indexes to Periodicals

An enormous amount is published in magazines and scholarly journals; you can start thumbing through them at random, but such a procedure is monstrously inefficient. Fortunately there are indexes to publications. We have already suggested that you can locate bibliographies listing articles and books on your topic, but it is possible that there is no relevant bibliography. You can still find material — books, of course, by consulting the card catalog, and articles by consulting indexes to periodicals. Among the most widely used indexes are

> *Readers' Guide to Periodical Literature* (1900–)
> *Humanities Index* (1974–)
> *Social Sciences Index* (1974–)
> *Social Sciences and Humanities Index* (1965–74)
> *International Index* (1907–64)

Readers' Guide indexes more than one hundred of the more familiar magazines — such as *Atlantic, Ebony, Nation, Scientific American, Sports Illustrated, Time*. The other indexes are guides to many of the less popular, more scholarly journals, for example journals published by learned societies. Notice that *Humanities Index* and *Social Sciences Index* are fairly new; for indexes to older articles in these two fields, look in *Social Sciences and Humanities Index* (1965–74), and for still older ones look in *International Index*.

The names of the periodicals indexed in these volumes are printed at the front of the volumes. All of these invaluable indexes include subject headings as well as entries alphabetically by author. If you know that you are looking for a piece by Ralph Nader, look it up under Nader. But if you don't know the author, look under the subject. For example, if you look up "additives" in the *Readers' Guide* you will find: "Additives, *See* Food additives," and so you next turn to "Food additives," where you will find a listing (by title) of the relevant articles. You will also find, under "Food," a note referring you to other subject headings that may be relevant, for example "Food, Organic," and "Food adulteration."

> FOOD additives
>   *See also*
>   Monosodium glutamate
>   Nitrites
>
> In science we trust (unless it involves sugarless soda) [survey by National Science Foundation] R. W. Miller. il FDA Consumer 15:27 My '81
> Yesterday's additives–generally safe [GRAS (generally recognized as safe) list] FDA Consumer 15:14–15 Mr '81
>   Laws and regulations
>   *See* Food laws and regulations

This material is not attractive reading, but it is useful. From the front of the *Readers' Guide* you will learn what the abbreviations mean. The first item here, for example, is an essay called "In Science We Trust (Unless It Involves Sugarless Soda)," by R. W. Miller. This essay, which has illustrations (note "il"), was published in *FDA Consumer*, volume 15, page 27, which is the May 1981 issue.

Another index that you are likely to use is *The New York Times Index* (covering from 1851 to the present). This index, enabling you to locate articles that were published in *The Times* newspaper, is especially useful if you are working on a recent public event.

The indexes just mentioned (along with the indexes to book reviews mentioned on page 202) are the ones you are most likely to use, but here are some others that may be valuable, depending on what your topic is:

Applied Science and Technology Index (1958–); formerly *Industrial Arts Index* (1913–57)

Art Index (1929–)

Biological and Agricultural Index (1964–); before 1964 it was known as *Agricultural Index* (1942–64)

Biography Index (1947–)

Business Periodicals Index (1958–)

Dramatic Index (1909–49)

Education Index (1929–)

International Index to Film Periodicals (1972–)

MLA International Bibliography (1921–); an annual listing of books and scholarly articles on linguistics and on literature in modern languages

Monthly Catalog of United States Government Publications (1895–)

Music Index (1949–)

Poole's Index for Periodical Literature (1802–1907)

Public Affairs Information Service Bulletin (1915–)

United Nations Documents Index (1950–)

Whichever indexes you use, begin with the most recent years and work your way back. If you collect the titles of articles published in the last five years you will probably have as much as you can read. These articles will probably incorporate the significant points of earlier writings. But of course it depends on the topic; you may have to — and want to — go back fifty or more years before you find a useful body of material.

Caution: Indexes drastically abbreviate the titles of periodicals. Before you put the indexes back on the shelf, be sure to check the key to the abbreviations, so that you know the full titles of the periodicals you are looking for.

Other Guides to Published Material

There are a great many reference books — not only general dictionaries and encyclopedias but dictionaries of technical words, and encyclopedias of special fields. For example, Leslie Halliwell, *The Filmgoer's Companion,* 6th edition (1977), has thousands of brief entries, listing films, directors, motifs, and so forth. Some of these entries conclude with references to books for further reading. There are also books chiefly devoted to telling you where to find material in special fields. Examples: Helen J. Poulton, *The Historian's Handbook: A Descriptive Guide to Reference Works* (1972); Elizabeth Miller and Mary Fisher, eds., *The Negro in America: A Bibliography,* revised edition (1970); Bernard Klein and Daniel Icolari, eds., *Reference Encyclopedia of the American Indian,* 2nd edition (1971); James Monaco, *Film: How and Where to Find Out What You Want to Know* (1976). The best guide to such guides — a book telling you about such books — is Eugene P. Sheehy, *Guide to Reference Books,* 9th edition (1976), with a *Supplement* (1980). There are also guides to all of these guides: reference librarians. If you don't know where to turn to find something, turn to the librarian.

TAKING BIBLIOGRAPHIC NOTES

Practice and theory differ. In theory, one should write down each citation (whether a book or an article) on a separate three-by-five index card, giving complete information. Our own practice at the start of any research is more shoddy. Instead of carefully recording all of this information from the card catalog (for a book that may be lost) or from an index to periodicals (for a periodical that may not be in the library) we usually jot down the citations of books on one sheet of paper, and of articles on another sheet. Then we see how much of this material is available. When we actually get hold of the material, we make out a card, as illustrated. True, we sometimes regret our attempted shortcut if we later find that on the sheet we forgot to write the year of the periodical and we must now hunt through indexes again to locate it. We recall the wisdom of the Chinese proverb, "It is foolish to go to bed early to save the candle if the result is twins," but we have never been able to resist economizing at the start.

Caution: Because it is easy to misspell names, turning unfamiliar forms into familiar ones (Barnet into Barnett, Stubbs into Stubbes, and even Christensen into Christianson), it is advisable to *print* the name in block letters, and, having done so, to check your version against the original.

READING AND TAKING NOTES

As you read, you will of course find references to other publications and you will jot these down so that you can look at them later. It may turn out, for example, that a major article was published twenty years ago, and that most commentary is a series of footnotes to this piece. You will have to look at it, of course, even though common sense had initially suggested (incorrectly, it seems) that the article would be out of date.

Our own practice in reading an article or a chapter of a book is to read it through, *not* taking notes. By the time you reach the end, you may find it isn't noteworthy. Or you may find a useful summary near the end that will contain most of what you can get from the piece. Or you will find that, having a sense of the whole, you can now quickly reread the piece and take notes on the chief points.

When you take notes use four-by-six-inch cards, and write on one side only; material on the back of a card is usually neglected when you come to write the paper. Use four-by-six cards because

TX
553. 83
J23

Jacobson, Michael F.
Eater's Digest New York: Doubleday 1972

Bibliographic card for a book

Zwerdling, Daniel "Death for
Dinner," The New York Review,
21, No. 1 (21 Feb. 1974), 22-24.

Bibliographic card for an article in a periodical

the smaller cards, suitable for bibliographic notes, do not provide enough space for your summaries of useful material. Here is a guide to note taking:

1. We suggest summaries rather than paraphrases (that is, abridgments rather than restatements which in fact may be as long as or longer than the original) because there is rarely any point to paraphrasing; generally speaking, either quote exactly (and put the passage in quotation marks, with a notation of the source, including the page number or numbers) or summarize, reducing a page or even an entire article or chapter of a book to a single four-by-six card. Even when you summarize, indicate your source (including the page numbers) on the card, so that you can give appropriate credit in your paper.

2. Of course in your summary you will sometimes quote a phrase or a sentence — putting it in quotation marks — but quote sparingly. You are not doing stenography; rather you are assimilating knowledge and you are thinking, and so for the most part your source should be digested rather than engorged whole. Thinking now, while taking notes, will also help you later to avoid plagiarism. If, on the other hand, when you take notes you mindlessly copy material at length, later when you are writing the paper you may be tempted to copy it yet again, perhaps without giving credit. Similarly, if you photocopy pages from articles or books, and then merely underline some passages, you probably will not be thinking; you will just be underlining. But if you make a terse summary on a note card you will be forced to think and to find your own words for the idea. Most of the direct quotations you copy should be effectively stated passages or crucial passages or both. In your finished paper these quotations will provide authority and emphasis.

3. If you quote but omit some material within the quotation, be sure to indicate the omission by three spaced periods, as explained on page 358.

4. *Never* copy a passage by changing an occasional word, under the impression that you are thereby putting it into your own words. Notes of this sort may find their way into your paper, your reader will sense a style other than your own, and suspicions of plagiarism may follow. (For a detailed discussion of plagiarism, see pages 360–63.)

5. Feel free to jot down your own responses to the note. For example, you may want to say "Gold seems to be generalizing

from insufficient evidence," or "Corsa made the same point five years earlier"; but make certain that later you will be able to distinguish between these comments and the notes summarizing or quoting your source. A suggestion: surround all comments recording your responses with double parentheses, thus: ((. . .))

6. In the upper corner of each note card, write a brief key — for example "effect on infants' blood" — so that later you can tell at a glance what is on the card. The sample card shown here summarizes a few pages; notice that it includes a short quotation and records the source. The source is not given in full bibliographic form because the full form is recorded on a bibliography card.

> Verrett, pp. 152-54   botulism argument
>   search for substitute
>
> p. 152 Industry and gov't approved nitrite as
> color fixer. Now shifting ground, saying it
> prevents botulism. Verrett points out "legal
> snag": new approval needed for new use.
> (Thus public hearing and unwanted attention.)
>
> p. 154 ". . . the industry - USDA-FDA coalition, seems
> firm in its position that there is no sub-
> stitute for nitrate, now or ever. Their
> posture is misdirected at defending nitrites,
> devising ways to keep it in food rather
> than ways to get it out."
>
>   Verrett and Carper, Eating May Be Hazardous

As you work, especially if you are working on a literary or historical topic, you'll of course find yourself returning again and again to the primary materials — and you'll probably find to your surprise that a good deal of the secondary material is unconvincing or even wrong, despite the fact that it is printed in a handsome book. One of the things we learn from research is that not everything in print is true; one of the pleasures we get from research results from this discovery.

WRITING THE PAPER

There remains the difficult job of writing up your findings, usually in 2000–3000 words (eight to twelve double-spaced typed pages). Beyond referring you to the rest of this book, we can offer only seven pieces of advice.

1. Begin by rereading your note cards and sorting them into packets by topic. Put together what belongs together. Don't hesitate to reject material that — however interesting — now seems irrelevant or redundant. In doing your research you quite properly took lots of notes (as William Blake said, "You never know what is enough unless you know what is more than enough"), but now, in looking over your material, you see that some of it is unnecessary, and so you reject it. Your finished paper should not sandbag the reader. After sorting, resorting, and rejecting, you will have a kind of first draft without writing a draft.

2. From your packets of cards you can make a first outline. (In arranging the packets into a sequence, and then in sketching an outline, of course you will be guided by your *thesis*. Without a thesis you will have only a lot of note cards, not an essay.) This outline will be a formal outline, indicating not only the major parts of the essay but also the subdivisions within these parts. (The formal outline is discussed on pages 65–67, and an example of an outline preceding a research paper is given on pages 214–15.) Do not, however, confuse this outline with a paragraph outline; when you come to write your essay, a single heading may require two or three or even more paragraphs.

3. When you write your first draft, leave lots of space at the top and bottom of each page so that you can add material, which will be circled and connected by arrows to the proper place. For example, as you are drafting page 6, from perhaps your tenth packet, you may find a note card that now seems more appropriate to a point you made back on page 2. Write it on page 2, and put the card in the appropriate earlier packet so that if for some reason you later have to check your notes you can find it easily.

4. Write or type your quotations, even in the first draft, exactly as you want them to appear in the final version. Short quotations (fewer than three lines of poetry or fewer than five lines

of prose) are enclosed within quotation marks but are not otherwise set off; longer quotations, however, are set off (triple space before them and after them), slightly indented, and are *not* enclosed in quotation marks.

5. Include, right in the body of the draft, all of the relevant citations (later these will become footnotes), so that when you come to revise you don't have to start hunting through your notes to find who said what, and where. You can, for the moment, enclose these citations within diagonal lines, or within double parentheses — anything at all to remind you that they will be your footnotes.

6. Beware of the compulsion to include every note card in your essay. You have taken all these notes, and there is a strong temptation to use them all. But, truth to tell, in hindsight many are useless. Conversely, you will probably find, as you write your draft, that here and there you need to do more research, to check a quotation or to collect additional examples. Probably it is best to continue writing your draft if possible, but remember to insert the necessary material after you get it.

7. As you revise your draft, make sure that you do not merely tell the reader "A says . . . B says . . . C says. . . ." When you write a research paper, you are not merely setting the table with other people's dinnerware; you are cooking the meal. You must have a point, an opinion, a thesis; you are working toward a conclusion, and your readers should always feel they are moving toward that conclusion (by means of your thoughtful evaluation of the evidence) rather than reading an anthology of commentary on the topic.

While you were doing your research you may have noticed that the more interesting writers persuade the reader of the validity of their opinions by (1) letting the reader see that they know what of significance has been written on the topic; (2) letting the reader hear the best representatives of the chief current opinions, whom they correct or confirm; and (3) advancing their opinions, by offering generalizations supported by concrete details. Adopt these techniques in your own writing. Thus, because you have a focus, we should get things like: "There are three common views on. . . . The first two are represented by A and B; the third, and by far the most reasonable, is C's view that . . ." or "A argues . . . but . . ." or "Although the third view, C's, is not conclusive, still . . ." or "Moreover, C's point can be strengthened when we consider a piece of evidence that he does not make use of." We have already mentioned that you cannot merely say "A says . . ., B says . . ., C says . . .," because your job is not to report what everyone says but to establish the truth of a thesis. When you introduce a quotation, then, try to let the reader see the use to which you are putting it. "A says" is of little help; giving the quotation and then following it with "thus says A" is even worse. You need a lead-in such as "A concisely states the common view," "B shrewdly calls attention to a fatal weakness," "Without offering any proof, C claims that. . . ." In short, it is usually advisable to let the reader know why you are quoting, or, to put it a little differently, how the quotation fits into your organization.

Your overall argument, then, is fleshed out with careful summaries and with effective quotations and with judicious analyses of your own, so that by the end of the paper the readers not only have read a neatly typed paper, but they also are persuaded that under your guidance they have seen the evidence, heard the arguments justly summarized, and reached a sound conclusion. They may not become better persons but they are better informed.

When you have finished your paper prepare a final copy that will be easy to read. Type the paper (see pages 353–54), putting the footnotes into the forms given on pages 363–72.

A bibliography or list of works consulted (see pages 373–75) is usually appended to the research paper, so that the reader may easily look further into the primary and secondary material if she wishes. But if you have done your job well, the reader will be content to leave things where you left them, grateful that you have set things straight.

SAMPLE RESEARCH PAPER

Here is a sample research paper. This essay is preceded by a thesis statement and an outline, helpful but not obligatory additions.

Nitrites: Cancer for Many, Money for Few

by

Jacob Alexander

English 1B

Mr. Cavitch

May 10, 1982

Thesis

Sodium nitrite and sodium nitrate, added to cured meats and smoked fish
as a color fixative, combine in meat and in the stomach to form a
powerful carcinogen (cancer-producing substance). This fact puts the
profit motive of the food industry and the health of the American
public squarely into opposition, and thus far the government regulatory
agencies are supporting the food industry.

Outline

   I. Sodium nitrite and nitrate can be poison.

      A. Nitrites combine with blood to form a pink pigment which does
         not carry oxygen.

      B. They have a number of other ominous side-effects.

  II. Nitrites combine with amines to form nitrosamines, among the most
     potent carcinogens known.

      A. Nitrites are likely to combine with amines in the human stomach
         to form nitrosamines.

      B. Animals of all kinds, fed nitrites and amines, develop cancer in
         various parts of their bodies.

      C. Nitrosamines are sometimes present in nitrited food even before
         we ingest it.

 III. Why are nitrites used in food?

      A. Nitrites are traditionally used as color fixers.

      B. Producers argue that they are also preservatives.

  IV. Why does the government allow nitrites?

      A. Nitrites and nitrates have a very long history of use.

      B. Government regulatory mechanisms are full of loopholes.

         1. Delaney Clause in Food Additive Amendment (1958) does not
            apply.

         2. FDA controls fish; USDA controls meats.

         3. Both depend on industry-oriented NAS.

C. The agencies defend themselves.

    1. They find fault with the experiments.

    2. They claim nitrites prevent botulism.

    3. They claim that there is a "no-effect" level of use for carcinogens, though doctors disagree.

V. American government is serving the food industry rather than the people.

    A. Food industry's enormous profits enable them to bring pressure to bear on regulatory agencies.

    B. Hazy patriotic optimism contributes to inaction.

VI. Stop eating nitrated fish and meat.

Americans eat between three thousand and ten thousand additives in their food today, most of them untested[1] and many of them known to be dangerous. Of these, nitrites are among the most hazardous of all. In this country, ham, bacon, corned beef, salami, bologna, lox, and other cold cuts and smoked fish almost invariably contain sodium nitrite (or sodium nitrate, which readily converts to nitrite in the human body). In fact, one-third of the federally inspected meat and fish we consume—more than seven billion pounds of it every year—contains this chemical.[2]

To begin with, nitrite is just plain poison in amounts only slightly greater than those allowed in cured meats. Jacqueline Verrett, who worked for the Food and Drug Administration (FDA) for fifteen years, and Jean Carper list in their book, Eating May Be Hazardous to Your Health, recent instances of people poisoned by accidental overdoses.

> In Buffalo, New York, six persons were hospitalized with "cardiovascular collapse" after they ate blood sausage which contained excessive amounts of nitrites. . . . In New Jersey, two persons died and many others were critically poisoned after eating fish illegally loaded with nitrites. In New Orleans, ten youngsters between the ages of one and a half and five became seriously ill . . . after eating wieners or bologna overnitrited by a local meat-processing firm; one wiener that was obtained later from the plant was found to contain a whopping 6,570 parts per million of nitrate, whereas the federal limitation is 200 parts per million. In Florida, a three-year-old boy died after eating hot dogs with three times greater nitrite concentration than the government allows.[3]

The chemical has the unusual and difficult-to-replace quality of keeping meat a fresh-looking pink throughout the cooking, curing, and

[1] Daniel Zwerdling, "Food Pollution," Ramparts, 9, No. 11 (June 1971), 34.

[2] Michael F. Jacobson, Eater's Digest (New York: Doubleday, 1972), p. 169.

[3] Eating May Be Hazardous to Your Health (New York: Simon and Schuster, 1974), pp. 138–39.

storage process. The nitrous acid from the nitrite combines with the hemoglobin in the blood of the meat, fixing its red color so that the meat does not turn the tired brown or gray natural to cured meats.

Unfortunately, it does much the same thing in humans. Although most of the nitrite passes through the body unchanged, a small amount is released into the bloodstream. This combines with the hemoglobin in the blood to form a pigment called methemoglobin, which cannot carry oxygen. If enough oxygen is incapacitated, a person dies. The allowable amount of nitrite in a quarter pound of meat can incapacitate between 1.4 and 5.7 percent of the hemoglobin in an average-sized adult.[4] When 10 to 20 percent is incapacitated, a victim discolors and has difficulty breathing.[5] One of the problems with nitrite poisoning is that infants under a year, because of the quantity and makeup of their blood, are especially susceptible to it.

If the consumer of nitrite is not acutely poisoned, his blood soon returns to normal and this particular danger passes; the chemical, however, has long-term effects. Nitrite can cause headaches in people who are especially sensitive to it, an upsetting symptom in light of the fact that in rats who ate it regularly for a period of time it has produced lasting "epileptic-like" changes in the brain—abnormalities which showed up when the rats were fed only a little more than an American fond of cured meats might eat.[6] Experiments with chickens, cattle, sheep, and rats have shown that nitrite, when administered for several days, inhibits the ability of the liver to store vitamin A and carotene.[7] And, finally, Nobel laureate Joshua Lederberg points out that,

[4] Verrett and Carper, pp. 138–39.

[5] Jacobson, p. 166.

[6] Harrison Wellford, Sowing the Wind (New York: Bantam, 1973), p. 173.

[7] Beatrice Trum Hunter, Fact/Book on Food Additives and Your Health (New Canaan, Conn.: Keats, 1972), p. 90.

in microorganisms, nitrite enters the DNA. "If it does the same thing in humans," he says, "it will cause mutant genes." Geneticist Bruce Ames adds, "If out of one million people, one person's genes are mutant, that's a serious problem. . . . If we're filling ourselves now with mutant genes, they're going to be around for generations."[8]

By far the most alarming characteristic of nitrite, however, is that in test tubes, in meats themselves, in animal stomachs, and in human stomachs—wherever a mildly acidic solution is present—it can and does combine with amines to form nitrosamines. And nitrosamines are carcinogens. They cause cancer. Even the food industry and the agencies responsible for allowing the use of nitrite in foods admit that nitrosamines cause cancer. Those people who have studied them feel, in fact, that they are among the surest and most deadly of all the carcinogens currently recognized.

Now it is important to note that nitrite alone, when fed to rats on an otherwise controlled diet, does not induce cancer. It must first combine with amines to form nitrosamines. Considering, however, that the human stomach has the kind of acidic solution in which amines and nitrites readily combine, and considering as well that amines are present in beer, wine, cereals, tea, fish, cigarette smoke, and a long list of drugs including antihistamines, tranquilizers, and even oral contraceptives, it is hardly surprising to find that nitrosamines have been found in human stomachs.

When animals are fed amines in combination with nitrite, they develop cancer with a statistical consistency that is frightening, even to scientists. Verrett and Carper report that William Lijinsky, a scientist at Oak Ridge National Laboratory who has been studying the effects

[8] Zwerdling, pp. 34–35.

of nitrite in food since 1961, after feeding animals 250 parts per million (ppm) of nitrites and amines—an amount comparable to what some Americans are taking in today—

> found malignant tumors in 100 percent of the test animals within six months, and he thinks they all will be dead in the next three months. "Unheard of," he says. . . . "You'd usually expect to find 50 percent at the most. And the cancers are all over the place—in the brain, lung, pancreas, stomach, liver, adrenals, intestines. We open up the animals and they are a bloody mess."[9]
>
> [He] believes that nitrosamines, because of their incredible versatility in inciting cancer, may be the key to an explanation of the mass production of cancer in seemingly dissimilar populations. In other words, nitrosamines may be a common factor in cancer that has been haunting us all these years.[10]

Lijinsky also claims that nitrites "seem to be most effective in eliciting tumors when they are applied in small doses over a long period, rather than as large single doses."[11]

Verrett and Carper list still more damning evidence. Nitrosamines have caused cancer in rats, hamsters, mice, guinea pigs, dogs, and monkeys. It has been proven that nitrosamines of over a hundred kinds cause cancer. Nitrosamines have been shown to pass through the placenta from the mother to cause cancer in the offspring. Even the lowest levels of nitrosamines ever tested have produced cancer in animals. When animals are fed nitrite and amines separately over a period of time, they develop cancers of the same kind and at the same frequency as animals fed the corresponding nitrosamines already formed. In a part of South Africa where the people drink a locally distilled liquor containing a high concentration of nitrosamines, there is an "extraordinarily

[9] P. 136.

[10] P. 142.

[11] Statement of Dr. William Lijinsky, Eppely Institute, Univ. of Nebraska, before the Intergovernmental Relations Subcommittee of the Committee on Government Operations, U.S. House of Representatives, 16 March 1971, quoted in Wellford, p. 172.

high incidence of human esophageal cancer." Finally, Verrett and Carper
quote Lijinsky again:

> We have evidence that while the amount of carcinogen might not
> build up, the effect in the animal body does build up. In other
> words, the more carcinogen you are exposed to, the more cells are
> damaged and the more likely you are to develop a tumor within your
> lifetime. So I feel no amount of a nitrosamine can be ignored.[12]

Nitrosamines even form _in_ food, before it reaches the table. According to Verrett and Carper,

> In February 1972 the Agriculture Department and the FDA detected
> nitrosamines in eight samples of processed meat taken from packing
> plants and retail stores. Nitrosamines at levels of eleven to
> forty-eight parts per billion were found in dried beef and cured
> pork, at five parts per billion in ham, and at eighty parts per
> billion in hot dogs. More alarmingly, four bacon samples—all dif-
> ferent brands—that when raw yielded no nitrosamines revealed up to
> 106 parts per billion of nitrosamines _after_ _cooking_. In November
> 1972 the FDA revealed that further experiments had found high lev-
> els of a cancer-causing nitrosamine—up to 108 parts per billion—
> in four other brands of bacon that had been pan-fried, proving that
> nitrosamines are widespread in cooked bacon. . . . The FDA also
> found nitrosamines in smoked chub and salmon at levels up to
> twenty-six parts per billion.[13]

As if this were not enough, Beatrice Trum Hunter claims that "some nitrosamines, in Cantonese dried fish, were capable of inducing cancer by
a single dose."[14]

The question, then, is why nitrite continues to be used in a third
of the meat Americans consume. Although nitrite adds a small amount to
flavor, it is used primarily for cosmetic purposes, and is, in fact, legally sanctioned _only_ as a color fixative. United States meat proces-
sors, however, are allowed to use up to twenty times as much nitrite as
is needed to fix color.

[12] Pp. 143–46.

[13] Pp. 146–47.

[14] P. 93.

Recently, as controversy over nitrite has accelerated, food producers are arguing that nitrite also prevents the growth of botulinum, an
argument to which the public is particularly susceptible because of a
number of recent botulism scares. Michael Jacobson explains the preser-
vative action of nitrite:

> Nitrite makes botulinum spores sensitive to heat. When foods are
> treated with nitrite and then heated, any botulinum spores that may
> be present are killed. In the absence of nitrite, spores can be
> inactivated only at temperatures that ruin the meat products. . . .
> Nitrite's preservative action is particularly important in foods
> that are not cooked after they leave the factory, such as ham, be-
> cause these offer an oxygen-free environment, the kind in which
> botulinum can grow. The toxin does not pose a danger in foods that
> are always well cooked, such as bacon, because the toxin would be
> destroyed in cooking. Laboratory studies demonstrate clearly that
> nitrite can kill botulinum, but whether it actually does in commer-
> cially processed meat is now being questioned. Frequently, the
> levels used may be too low to do anything but contribute to the
> color.[15]

It seems unlikely that sodium nitrite is really necessary as a pre-
servative. After extensive hearings in 1971, a congressional subcommittee concluded it was not, except possibly in a few cases like that of
canned ham.[16] Bratwurst and breakfast sausage are manufactured now
without nitrite because they don't need to be colored pink; bacon is always cooked thoroughly enough to kill off any botulinum spores present;
and the Maple Crest Sausage Company has been distributing frozen
nitrite-free hot dogs, salami, and bologna to health food stores since
1966 without poisoning anyone. Certainly there are other ways of dealing with botulism. High or low temperature prevents botulism. What
nitrite undoubtedly does lower, however, is the level of care and
sanitation necessary in handling meat.

The use of nitrite in smoked fish is particularly frivolous. If

[15] P. 165.

[16] Verrett and Carper, p. 138.

the fish is heated to 180° for thirty minutes, as it is supposed to be by law, and then distributed with adequate refrigeration, there should be no need for nitrite. The fish industry has appealed to the government with the argument that it should be allowed to use nitrite in more prod—ucts precisely because some plants do not possess the facilities to pro—cess fish at properly high temperatures. Furthermore, the government exercises little control over nitrite in fish. In 1969, three out of six food packaging firms surveyed were putting dangerously high levels of nitrite into their fish, yet only in the most extreme case did the FDA confiscate the fish.[17]

Clearly, the use of nitrite adds immeasurably to the profit—making potential of the meat industry, but why does the federal government al—low this health hazard in our food——that same government which stands firmly behind the message that "Americans . . . are blessed with better food at lower costs than anyone in any other country," a message William Robbins calls the "big lie"?[18]

In the first place, nitrite and nitrate have been used for so long that it is hard for lawmakers to get past their instinctive reaction, "But that's the way we've always done it." Indeed, the Romans used saltpeter, a nitrate, to keep meat and, as early as 1899, scientists discovered that the nitrate breaks down into nitrite and that it is the nitrite which actually preserves the red color in meats.[19] Thus, by the time the U.S. Department of Agriculture and the Food and Drug Adminis—tration got into the business of regulating food, they tended to accept nitrite and nitrate as givens. For example, the tolerance level of

[17] Verrett and Carper, pp. 149–50.

[18] William Robbins, The American Food Scandal (New York: Morrow, 1974), p. 2.

[19] Jacobson, pp. 164–65.

nitrite set by these agencies is based, not on experiment, but on the level found, in 1925, to be the maximum level usually found in cured ham. Following this government standard, a representative of the fish industry, petitioning to use nitrite, claimed that "no extensive reports of investigations to establish safety are required in view of the long history in common use and the previously accepted safety of these curing agents in the production of meat and fish products within the already established tolerances."[20]

A second reason for the inadequacy of regulation is that government mechanisms for protecting the consumer are full of curious loopholes. In 1958 Congress passed the Food Additive Amendment, including the Delaney Clause which clearly states that additives should be banned if they induce cancer in laboratory animals. Unfortunately, however, the amendment does not apply to additives that were in use before it was passed, so, since nitrite and nitrate had already been in use for a long time, they were automatically included on the list of chemicals "Generally Recognized as Safe." To complicate matters further, nitrite in meat is regulated by the USDA, while nitrite in fish is under the jurisdiction of the FDA. And these agencies generally leave it to industry—the profit-maker—to determine whether or not an additive is safe. The final irony in this long list of governmental errors is that the FDA depends heavily, for "independent" research and advice, on the food committees of the National Academy of Sciences, which Daniel Zwerdling claims are "like a Who's Who of the food and chemical industry."[21]

Nevertheless, as they have come under fire in recent years on the subject of nitrite and nitrate, the FDA and the USDA have found it necessary to give reasons for their continued sanction of these chemicals.

[20] Verrett and Carper, p. 148.

[21] P. 34.

First, they find fault with the experiments done to date. According to
the USDA, for example,

> The Department was aware that under certain conditions, nitrites do
> interact with secondary amines to form nitrosamines and that some
> nitrosamines are carcinogenic. However, knowledge in this area was
> limited and analytical methods available to study the possibility
> of nitrosamine formation in meat food products containing the per-
> missible amount of sodium nitrate lacked the necessary accuracy and
> reliability to give conclusive results.[22]

Despite the Delaney Clause, moreover, the FDA points out, "Man is
the most important experimental animal and nitrites have not been linked
to cancer in all the years that man has been eating the chemical."[23]
This is an almost foolproof argument, since cancer usually shows up only
after its inception, and it is extremely difficult to trace it to any
source. And certainly it is unlikely that any sizeable group will offer
to serve as guinea pigs for nitrite experiments. In evaluating this argument, it is significant that humans are generally _more_ susceptible to
chemical damage than animals—ten times more so than rats, for example.[24] Following through on its own logic, however, since nitrite has
indeed been proven to cause cancer in dogs, the FDA has dutifully and
responsibly banned its use in dog food.

The industry's second argument is that nitrite prevents botulism.
However, the USDA regulations approve the use of nitrite and nitrate
only as color fixers. If they are being used as preservatives, this is
a new use and comes squarely under the auspices of the Delaney Clause,
which would have them banned outright because they cause cancer in animals.

[22] Verrett and Carper, p. 152.

[23]_Regulation of Food Additives and Medicated Animal Feeds_, Hearings, Intergovernmental Relations Subcommittee, Committee on Government
Operations, U.S. House of Representatives (March 1971), pp. 215 ff.,
quoted in Wellford, p. 179.

[24] Verrett and Carper, p. 59.

The last argument is that small enough doses of carcinogens are not dangerous. Dr. Leo Friedman, director of the FDA's Division of Toxicology, puts it this way:

> . . . There is always a threshold level below which the substance does not exert any physiologically significant effect. . . . The design of a safety evaluation study is to determine a level at which there is no demonstrable effect. This level, when divided by a suitable safety factor, is then considered to be a safe level, in that there is a practical certainty that no harm will result from the use of the substance at that level.[25]

The medical community does not agree. The Surgeon General's committee stated in 1970, "The principle of a zero tolerance for carcinogenic exposures should be retained in all areas of legislation presently covered by it and should be extended to cover other exposures as well."[26] Hughes Ryser stated in the New England Journal of Medicine: ". . . weak carcinogenic exposures have irreversible and additive effects and cannot be dismissed lightly as standing 'below a threshold of action.'" He also commented that, until the carcinogens are removed from the environment, "efforts must continue to educate populations and government about their presence."[27] Even with this, the FDA Commissioner, Charles Edwards, strenuously disagrees: "We can't deluge the public with scare items based on our suspicions. . . . The pendulum swings too far in most cases, and consumers tend to boycott a product . . . even though we might feel that continued use within certain limits is entirely justified."[28]

Something has gone wrong. The issue is one of what we eat. It makes no sense at all to eat a substance until it is proven to be

[25] Memorandum from Dr. Leo Friedman to Dr. Virgil Wodicka, 17 Dec. 1971, quoted in Wellford, p. 180.

[26] Wellford, p. 181.

[27] "Chemical Carcinogenesis," 285, No. 13 (23 Sept. 1971), 721-34, quoted in Wellford, p. 181.

[28] Wellford, p. 18.

poison. Even a starving man is reluctant to eat mushrooms unless he knows what he's doing. Nitrite is banned altogether in Norway, and forbidden in fish in Canada. European allowances are generally lower than ours, and even the Germans make their "wursts" without nitrite.

One is forced to a radical conclusion. The American government is, in this instance, clearly serving the interests of the industry rather than the people. The fact is that the food industry is willing to spend millions every year to make sure the regulatory agencies act in ways that please them. Each time an additive is banned, the food industry finds itself in the spotlight. It feels an implicit threat to all its other additives, and ultimately to the immense profits Daniel Zwerdling describes:

> This marvelous chemical additive technology has earned $500 million a year for the drug companies . . . and it has given the food manufacturers enormous control over the mass market. Additives like preservatives enable food that might normally spoil in a few days or a week to endure unchanged for weeks, months, or even years. A few central manufacturers can saturate supermarket shelves across the country with their products because there's no chance the food will spoil. Companies can buy raw ingredients when they're cheap, produce and stockpile vast quantities of the processed result, then withhold the products from the market for months, hoping to manipulate prices upward and make a windfall.[29]

Under pressure from the food industry, and probably influenced as well by a sincere, if hazy, patriotic optimism, the FDA issued a fact sheet in May 1967, stating unequivocally that our soil is not being poisoned by fertilizers, that pesticide residues are entirely safe, that our soil is the "envy of every nation," and that food processing is a "modern marvel because the natural value of the food is not lost in the process." It concludes, "Today's scientific knowledge, working through good laws to protect consumers, assures the safety and wholesomeness of

[29] "Death for Dinner," The New York Review, 21, No. 1 (21 Feb. 1974), 22.

every component of our food supply."[30] The FDA's continuing support for nitrite allowances, despite increasing evidence that nitrite is lethal, indicates that the FDA has not removed its rose-colored glasses.

The most recent extended discussion, The Health Effects of Nitrate, Nitrite and N-Nitroso Compounds, issued in 1981 under the auspices of the National Academy of Sciences, offers no new information but by saying that nitrites in cured meats may be no more harmful than those in vegetables, baked goods, and cereals, it seems to suggest that cured meats may be less dangerous than has been thought. Still, as Marian Burros pointed out, many specialists feel that The Health Effects offers no new evidence.[31]

Until the FDA and other regulatory agencies begin to see clearly, then, the American consumer has little choice other than to give up eating the nitrited cured meats and smoked fish on the market today. If we do so, we will be following the practice of Dr. William Lijinsky, a biologist who has studied the problem for fifteen years. "I don't touch any of that stuff when I know nitrite has been added."[32]

[30] Regulation of Food Additives, pp. 215 ff., quoted in Wellford, p. 179.

[31] "The Nitrite Question: What Can You Eat?" New York Times, 23 December 1981, p. C 1.

[32] Quoted by Mimi Sheraton, in New York Times, 9 January 1976, p. 18.

Works Cited

Burros, Marian. "The Nitrite Question: What Can You Eat?" <u>New</u> <u>York</u>
<u>Times</u>, 23 December 1981, p. C 1.

Hunter, Beatrice Trum. <u>Fact/Book</u> <u>on</u> <u>Food</u> <u>Additives</u> <u>and</u> <u>Your</u> <u>Health</u>.
New Canaan, Conn.: Keats, 1972.

Jacobson, Michael F. <u>Eater's</u> <u>Digest</u>. New York: Doubleday, 1972.

Robbins, William. <u>The</u> <u>American</u> <u>Food</u> <u>Scandal</u>. New York: Morrow, 1974.

Sheraton, Mimi. "Take Away the Preservatives, and How Do Meats Taste?"
<u>New</u> <u>York</u> <u>Times</u>, 9 January 1976, p. 18.

Verrett, Jacqueline, and Jean Carper. <u>Eating</u> <u>May</u> <u>Be</u> <u>Hazardous</u> <u>to</u> <u>Your</u>
<u>Health</u>. New York: Simon and Schuster, 1974.

Wellford, Harrison. <u>Sowing</u> <u>the</u> <u>Wind</u>. New York: Bantam, 1973.

Zwerdling, Daniel. "Death for Dinner." <u>The</u> <u>New</u> <u>York</u> <u>Review</u>, 21, No. 1
(21 Feb. 1974), 22–24.

_____. "Food Pollution." <u>Ramparts</u>, 9, No. 11 (June 1971), 31–37,
53–54.

EXERCISES (Surviving in the Library)

If you have trouble finding material in the library, don't hesitate to ask a librarian for assistance. But you will soon learn to solve many of the commonest problems yourself. Here are a few.

1. You want to do some research for a paper on Mexican immigrants in the United States. You look in the card catalog and find only one card, reprinted below. How can you find other books on the subject?

```
              The Mexican immigrant.

JV           Gamio, Manuel, 1883-1960, comp.
6798             The Mexican immigrant.  New York,
.M6          Arno Press, 1969.
G28              xiii, 288 p. map. 22 cm.  (The
1969         American immigration collection)
                 Reprint of the 1931 ed.
                 1.United States--Emigration and
             immigration. 2.Mexico--Emigration and
             immigration. 3.Mexicans in the United
             States. I.T.



PG77-115225 r                       69-18778
JV6798.M6G28  1969                  301.453/72/
```

2. You want to do a paper on Richard Wright's short stories, and the catalog lists several relevant books, but when you check the stacks you find none of these books is on the shelf. What do you do, short of abandoning the topic or going to another library?

3. You are looking for a book by David McCord, called *Far and Few*. You look under the author's name, but find that a card for "Mbunda (Bantu tribe)" is followed not by a card for McCord but by a card for "Mchedishvili, Georgii." You next look for the book by its title; you find a card for an author named "Faral," and you assume that *Far and Few* should be the next card or so, but in fact the next card is for an author named "Fararo, T. J." Yet you know that the library has McCord's *Far and Few*. Where did you go wrong?

4. You need reviews of a film released a few months ago. There are no books on this film, and the *Readers' Guide* lists nothing under the film's title. What do you do?
5. You find references to *CQ Weekly Report,* the *Department of State Bulletin,* and the *Journal of the American Oriental Society,* but these journals don't seem to be listed alphabetically in the periodical file. Still, you have heard that the library does have them. How can that be?
6. You are looking for an issue of a journal published a few months ago. It is not on the shelf with the current issues, and it is not on the shelf with the bound volumes. Where is it?
7. You want to write a paper on bilingual education, or, more exactly, on bilingual education of Mexican Americans. What do you look for in the card catalog? And what periodical indexes do you consult?
8. You want to know if juvenile delinquency in the Soviet Union increased during the 1970's, but you can't find anything on the topic. What do you do?

A NOTE ON THE USE OF COMPUTERS IN RESEARCH AND WRITING

We've all become familiar in recent years with computers and their seemingly limitless uses: from guiding space vehicles to computing a day's business receipts. When you make an airline reservation, cash a check at a bank, or register as a student in college, the chances are that a computer has assisted (or impeded) you in reserving your air space, checking your balance, or electing your courses. Computers are also being used increasingly in research and writing.

Computers are used in research in at least two ways. First, computer services available at some libraries help scholars to generate bibliographies and refine research problems. If you are interested in food additives, for example, and your library subscribes to *Medline* (a computer-based system operated by the National Library of Medicine), a specially trained librarian can help you to retrieve a printed list of relevant articles published in some 1200 journals of biology, medicine, and related sciences within the last three years. If, after querying the computer and learning that there are some 1500 references, you decide your topic is too broad, you can, again with the assistance of the specialist and the computer, progressively narrow your search to a more compassable topic, perhaps the carcinogenic effects of nitrites in cured meat and fish. In about an hour and a half then — an hour with the computer specialist learning to translate your research problem into the language of the system, and half an hour at the terminal in conversation with the computer — you will not only have retrieved a comprehensive and up-to-date list of articles, you will have retrieved it far more quickly and with less tedium than you could have done by using catalogs, bound indexes, and note cards.

Second, computers are frequently used where research projects require statistical analyses, mathematical computations, or simulated experiments. With access to a computer and knowledge of its language you might, for example, use, modify, or devise a computer program to analyze election data, calculate the weight of a star, or simulate the air flow over an airplane wing.

When you come to write a report, a computer with a text-editing program can further assist you. You will again have to invest some time learning to use it, but if you are doing a substantial piece of work — a thesis, for example — you might find your time well spent. With a text-editing program — which functions something like a smart typewriter with a faultless memory — you can compose, revise, and edit your writing and then make copies of the finished essay, all on the same machine. You can, for example, start by typing a rough draft, then delete whole paragraphs or sections, and continue by adding new material. When you want to check your revisions, you can request a clean copy of any part of your text. If you discover that you have misspelled a word a dozen times, you can, with one command to the computer, correct the error every place it appears. When you have the final version of your essay stored in the computer's memory, you can request as many copies as you want; and, with a sophisticated program, your computer will present them to you correctly paged, footnotes in place, left and right margins adjusted, and all neatly typed.

Computer facilities vary greatly from place to place; those we describe here — automated bibliographic searches and mathematical, scientific, and text-editing programs — are only examples of some of the current uses of computers in research and writing. It's unlikely therefore that all of these particular facilities are available to you now. Even if they all are available, they may not prove useful for any work you are now doing, and even if they're useful, the chances are they'll cost more than you want to spend. (That hour and a half with *Medline* and the specialist, for example, would currently cost about $30.00.) Nevertheless, computers and their applications are proliferating, as computers become not only more powerful and more versatile, but also smaller and cheaper; and we expect them to be more commonly available within the next few years. If any facilities are available to you now, then, we suggest you find out about them and acquire some computer literacy, even if you must take a course, invent a project, or apply for a grant to do it. Look in your college catalog to see what opportunities exist, and ask your instructors and the reference librarian. Sometimes even where computer facilities exist, it takes some persistence to find out about them.

11

Special Assignments

WRITING AN EXPLICATION

An explication (literally, unfolding or spreading out) is a commentary, usually line by line, on what is going on in a poem or in a short passage of prose. An explication is not concerned with the writer's life or times, nor is it a paraphrase, a rewording — though it may include paraphrase; it is a commentary revealing your sense of the meaning of the work. To this end it calls attention, as it proceeds, to the implications of words, the function of rhymes, the shifts in point of view, the development of contrasts, and any other contributions to the meaning.

Take, for example, the short poem by William Butler Yeats that opens this book, "The Balloon of the Mind":

> Hands, do what you're bid:
> Bring the balloon of the mind
> That bellies and drags in the wind
> Into its narrow shed.

Now, if we have done research on the work of Yeats we may remember that in an autobiography, *Reveries over Childhood and Youth,* Yeats already had used the figure of a balloon (dirigible) to represent mental activity: "My thoughts were a great excitement, but when I tried to do anything with them, it was like trying to pack a balloon into a shed in a high wind." But because explication usually confronts the work itself, without relating it to biography, we can pass over this interesting anticipation and confine ourselves to the poem's four lines. Here is the final version of an explication that went through several drafts after many readings (some aloud) of the poem. After reading this explication do not chastise yourself for not seeing all the subtleties when you read the poem. The writer herself did not see them all during the first, or even the fifth, reading. Notice that among the topics discussed are the tone (of the first line), the lengths of the lines, and the effect of patterns of sound, including rhythm, rhyme, and alliteration.

> Yeats's "Balloon of the Mind" is about poetry, specifically about the difficulty of getting one's floating thoughts down into lines on the page. The first line, a short, stern, heavily stressed command to the speaker's hands, implies by its impatient tone that these hands will be disobedient or inept or careless if not watched closely: the poor bumbling body so often fails to achieve the goals of the mind. The bluntness of the command in the first line ("Hands, do what you're bid") is emphasized by the fact that it has fewer syllables than each of the subsequent lines. Furthermore, the first line is a grammatically complete sentence, whereas the thought of line 2 spills over into the subsequent lines, implying the difficulty of fitting ideas into confining spaces. Lines 2 and 3 amplify the metaphor already stated in the title (a thought is an airy but unwieldy balloon) and they also contain a second command, "Bring." Alliteration ties this command, "*B*ring," to the earlier "*b*id"; it also ties both of these verbs to their object, "*b*alloon," and to the verb that most effectively describes the balloon, "*b*ellies." In comparison with the peremptory first line of the poem, lines 2 and 3 themselves seem almost swollen, bellying and dragging, an effect aided by using adjacent unstressed syllables ("of the," "[bell]ies and," "in the") and by using an eye rhyme ("mind" and "wind") rather than an exact rhyme. And then comes the short last line: almost before we could expect it, the cumbersome balloon — here, the idea that is to be packed into the stanza — is successfully lodged in its "narrow shed." Aside from the relatively colorless "into," the only words of more than one syllable in the poem are "narrow," "balloon," and "bellies," and all three of them emphasize the difficulty of the task. But after "narrow" (the word itself almost looks long and narrow, in this context like a hangar) we get the simplicity of the monosyllable "shed," and the difficult job is done, the thought is safely packed away, the poem is completed — but again with an off rhyme ("bid" and "shed"), for neatness can go only so far when hands and the mind and a balloon are involved.

Because the language of a literary work is denser (richer in associations or connotations) than the language of discursive prose, such as this paragraph, explication is concerned with bringing to the surface the meanings that are in the words but may not be immediately apparent. Explication, in short, seeks to make explicit the implicit.

The reader of an explication needs to see the text. Since the explicated text is usually short, it is advisable to quote the entire text. You can quote it, complete, at the outset, or you can quote the first unit (for example, a stanza) and then explicate the unit, and then quote the next unit and explicate it, and so on. If the poem or passage of prose is longer than, say, six lines, it is advisable to number each line at the right for easy reference.

WRITING A BOOK REVIEW

Because book reviews in newspapers or magazines are usually about a newly published work, reviewers normally assume that their readers will be unfamiliar with the book. Reviewers take it as their job to acquaint readers with the book, its contents and its value, and to help them decide whether or not they wish to read it. Since most reviews are brief (500–1500 words) they cannot, like explications, comment on everything. On the other hand they cannot, like analyses, focus on one aspect of the writing; they usually attempt in some way to cover the book. Reviews, then, usually contain more summary and more evaluation than explications or analyses. Nevertheless, reviewers must approach the task analytically if they are to accomplish it in the relatively small space allotted. And if they are to be convincing, they must support their opinion by quotations (usually indispensable), examples, and specific references to the text so that readers may think and feel the way the reviewer thinks and feels.

A review commonly has a structure something like this:

1. an opening paragraph that names the author and the title, gives the reader some idea of the nature and scope of the work (a children's book; a book for the general reader; a book for specialists), and establishes the tone of the review (more about tone in a moment)

2. a paragraph or two of plot summary if the book is a novel; some summary of the contents if it is not
3. a paragraph on the theme, purpose, idea, or vision embodied in the book, perhaps within the context of related works
4. a paragraph or two on the strengths, if any (for instance, the book fulfills its purpose)
5. a paragraph or two on the weaknesses, if any
6. a concluding paragraph in which the reviewer delivers his or her point — but the point in some degree has probably been implied from the beginning, because the concluding paragraph is a culmination rather than a surprise.

Tone, as we suggest elsewhere in this book (see pages 323–25), usually refers to the writer's attitude toward the subject, the readers, and the writer's self. The tone of a review is therefore somewhat dependent on the publication in which it will appear. A review in *Scientific American* will have a different tone from one in *Ms*. Since you have not been commissioned to write your review and are essentially playing a game, you must *imagine* your reader. It's a reasonable idea to imagine that your classmates are your readers, forgetting of course that they may be reviewing the same book you are. (It's a very bad idea to imagine that your teacher is your reader.) And it's always productive to treat both your reader and your subject with respect. This does not mean you need to be solemn or boring; on the contrary, the best way to show your respect for your reader is to write something you would be interested in reading yourself.

Here is a published book review. Although some reviews are untitled, this one has a title; unless your instructor tells you otherwise, give your review a title. (Finding your title will help you, in revising your review, to see if you have focused your essay.)

*Family Man (Wampeters, Foma, & Granfalloons:
Opinions by Kurt Vonnegut, Jr.)*

W. T. Lhamon, Jr.

Readers of Vonnegut's novels will like these essays, speeches, reviews and an interview. But those who think his fiction thin, unformed and full of cheap tickles will find these essays just that.

Vonnegut seems an honest man, which is admirable enough these days. Yet honesty leaves him confessing many sad things. When he was confronted with a list of his publications, for instance, he "felt like a person who was creepily alive, still, and justly accused of petty crime." He says he has tried to "tell the truth plonkingly." That is, the writing trades "allow mediocre people who are patient and industrious to revise their stupidity, to edit themselves into something like intelligence." He goes on: "my career astonishes me. How could anybody have come this far with so little information, with such garbled ideas of what other writers have said?" He was the 98-pound weakling to whom a high school coach once awarded a Charles Atlas course. He remembers his family's maid reading to him from a book called *More Heart Throbs* — and he thinks that she contributed to the "almost intolerable sentimentality about everything" he's written.

There have of course been other contributions to that sentimentality. His mother committed suicide. As a POW he survived the fire-bombing of Dresden. The University of Chicago gave him his happiest day when they accepted him as a graduate student in anthropology — but then they rejected his thesis. To his own three children, his sister's early death from cancer added three more lives for him to father. And so he had a large family there on Cape Cod in his struggling days of what he calls "sleazo" paperbacks and short stories, when no one was reviewing him and, it seemed, not very many were reading him either.

Now, when people are reading him by the millions, he still has a feel for families, and especially for the fathering of families. He admires the Biafran extended families who obviated government welfare programs during much of that land's short life. And he yearns for a return to the 19th-century family structure as a sort of not-so-voluntary group. His next novel will even propose assigned families: the government will provide the same middle name — Chromium or Daffodil — to random groups of 20,000 persons, and these people will all rely on each other, just like cousins supposedly used to do. If he's thinking a lot about families these days, the father-family axis is still all the more telling as the sustenance of his style. Which is to say that his writing has a modern paternalism to it — that of a father who would like also to be a buddy. Or, of a buddy who would also like to be a father.

That is, Vonnegut is a sneaky moralist. He admires the simplicity and untextured responses of the young, just as they admire his reductiveness and his untextured precepts. He speaks to an audience which has not been compromised by the corruptions and conventions of getting on. And he hankers for an age that has not suffered the same fate. His analogies, therefore, are to the 19th century. Since the 19th century will not return, his plots are into the vague future. And so on.

The phrases *and so on* and *so it goes* are so essential to Vonnegut that even though his critics have complained that such expressions are irking, he's not about to excise them. He can't. The world is full of binary and-so-ons for him: people whose lives are compromised and those whose lives are not; bad officers and nice enlisted men; innocent scientists who cause harm, and cynical scientists who hate the destruction to which they inevitably contribute; smart people and dumb people; happy people and lonely people; and so it goes. People who are caught in this world, and those with the liberated perspective of having lived in space, and so on. People who are substantial and those who are not: the somebodies and the nothings; those who are the "merest wisp of an implication" and those who slip back into Nothing, and so it goes. He's not trying to be vague. Rather he's emphasizing how eternally the world is a simple place which we overcome or in which we are overcome. And so on.

The world is not that sort of place: not so clean nor well-lighted. It is messy, in fact, and most of us keep on going during and after being overcome by the dirt and the dark. Vonnegut knows that, and his life shows it if his writing does not. His taste shows it too. That he admires George Orwell and raves over Hunter Thompson tells us much about his own work. Orwell punctured duplicity with angry clarity and had the presence to keep it up all alone. Thompson overwhelms duplicity with manic rage. But Vonnegut has neither the clarity nor the rage of the authors he respects. Instead he has the professional's ability to send back a cable. He says, "I come to work every morning and I see what words come out of the typewriter. I feel like a copyboy whose job is to tear off stories from the teletype machine and deliver them to an editor." Creepily, plonkingly, he's still alive. This is the feeling of an honest man who is hoping at best for the merest wisp of an implication, for a whisper rebuking his silence and the silence around him: Billy Pilgrim wandering in snowdrifts, muttering. Still it would surely be great fun to drive across country with him, or share a bottle with him, or have him for a father. And, because he believes in all the right things even if loosely and only tepidly, he already is a brother.

QUESTIONS

1. Characterize or describe the tone of Lhamon's review.
2. Write a one-sentence summary of each paragraph. Your list of sentences should resemble an outline. (See the paragraph outline on page 65.)
3. How well does your outline correspond with the structure we say reviews commonly have? (See pages 236–37.)
4. If there are discrepancies between what we have said about reviews and the review by Lhamon, can you offer a reasonable explanation for these discrepancies? Or would you argue that we revise our discussion, or that we choose a different review as an example?
5. Write a brief argument (two or three paragraphs) defending your answer to question 4.

WRITING OTHER REVIEWS

Our suggestions for writing a book review, with obvious modifications, can serve as guidelines for other reviews you may be assigned or choose to write: of a play, a movie, a concert, or other performance. Again, it is the reviewer's job to acquaint readers, real or imagined, with a performance they are assumed to be unfamiliar with (although in fact reviews are often read by readers who want to see their own judgments confirmed, or their small talk improved). And again, you must adopt an appropriate tone, suggesting both your own expert knowledge of your topic and your respect for your readers' intelligence and taste. Your best preparation for writing a review is to read reviews in publications you trust, consciously noting what you find informative, interesting, and persuasive. Then, if you are covering a live event, you'll find it useful to ask to see in advance the promotional material usually in the hands of the organization sponsoring the event. You'll want to be skeptical of some of the rave reviews you'll find quoted (and of course you mustn't use them in your own review without acknowledging their sources), but you may well find biographical and other background information that will prepare you for the performance and make notetaking easier. And you must go prepared to take notes — often in the dark — and allow yourself sufficient time immediately after the event to type or rewrite them legibly.

Reviewing a record or tape obviously has some advantages. You can listen to it many times, you may have access to the score or lyrics and previous recordings, and you can choose your own time and place for listening. Or perhaps the relaxed and witty style of the review we print below just makes it seem easier. The review was written by a student for a college newspaper.

Jimmy Buffett Is Going Coconuts?!

Pat Bellanca

This is what Jimmy Buffett used to do: sail around the Caribbean with his friends, smoke a lot of pot, drink a lot of tequila, write some songs — and every year or so return (rather unwillingly, he would have had us believe) to the mainland to record an album, tour the country and make some money so that he could afford to keep his sailboat running and himself pleasantly numbed to the realities of humdrum, everyday American existence.

Romantically melancholy escapism is the theme that Buffett has consistently examined, espoused and re-examined in all of the albums he has released since he first achieved a kind of pop stardom with "Margaritaville," the single from his 1977 album *Changes in Latitudes, Changes in Attitudes*. In that album he developed a formula that worked commercially.

In his most recent effort, *Coconut Telegraph*, released several weeks ago, he reworks an extremely watered-down version of the formula into yet another of his silly celebrations of sailing, smoking and drinking with fellow "expatriated Americans." But now, in keeping with his absorption into the mainstream of pop music, he writes noticeably less about smoking, drinking and wandering than he did before. It sounds like he's raising a family.

Coconut Telegraph is a cleanly produced country-rock-pop album which, despite Buffett's latest change in attitude, almost entirely consists of musical and thematic clones of songs he has previously recorded.

There is the song about the escapades of the businessman in the islands: "The Weather is Here, Wish You Were Beautiful," which was recycled from "American Friend," a track from *Son of a Son of a Sailor,* Buffett's seventh album. There's the gee-I-kinda-wish-I-could-go-home song, "Incommunicado," this year's model of "Miss You So Badly" from *Changes.* And there's the campy crooner song, "Stars Fell on Alabama" (a 1934 Parish Perkins song, actually one of the brighter moments on the album), reminiscent of "Pencil Thin Moustache" which Buffett wrote for his 1974 album. *Living and Dying in 3/4 Time.*

With *Coconut Telegraph,* Buffett has completed his transformation from a cult songwriter of nutty hippie anthems (check out "God's Own Drunk" and "The Great Filling Station Hold-up" on two of his earlier albums) to an unambitious, unfunny middle of the middle of the road pop craftsman. In the year which Christopher Cross walked away with multiple Grammy Awards, it's hardly surprising.

In "Growing Older But Not Up" Buffett tells us, "My metabolic rate is pleasantly stuck/So let the winds of change blow over my head . . ." And that's probably the best summation of the attitude behind the album. It's entirely pleasant.

The combined effect of the ever-present congas, steel drums, acoustic guitars, unobstrusive strings and effortlessly wailing harmonica is pleasantly mellow. The song about Buffett's daughter, "Little Miss Magic," is pleasantly sentimental without being overly gooey. The hooks are pleasantly "catchy," particularly in "The Weather is Here, Wish You Were Beautiful," a single from the album which seems to be getting a fair amount of airplay on WEEI-FM. Even the photo of the star on the cover of the album is pleasantly unassuming — he is wearing topsiders, chinos and an off-white crew-neck.

Of course, all of this is about as relevant and meaningful as sitting in a wad of bubblegum, but if one could prevent oneself from becoming bored and irritated by the unrelieved "pleasantness" of *Coconut Telegraph,* one might find it — a-hem — enjoyable.

QUESTIONS

1. Characterize the writer's tone. It is appropriate to her material and her audience? Explain.
2. On the basis of this review, would you buy *Coconut Telegraph*? If you didn't have to pay for the record, would you be interested, because of the review, in listening to it? Explain why, or why not.

3. If you saw this writer's byline in your newspaper would you read the article? Explain.

TAKING ESSAY EXAMINATIONS

What Examinations Are

An examination not only measures learning and thinking but stimulates them. Even so humble an examination as a short-answer quiz — chiefly a device to coerce the student to do the assigned reading — is a sort of push designed to move the student forward. Of course internal motivation is far superior to external, but even such crude external motivation as a quiz can have a beneficial effect. Students know this; indeed they often seek external compulsion, choosing a course "because I want to know something about it, and I know that I won't do the reading on my own." (Teachers often teach a new course for the same reason; we want to become knowledgeable about, say, the theater of the absurd, and we know that despite our lofty intentions we may not seriously confront the subject unless we are under the pressure of facing a class.) In short, however ignoble it sounds, examinations force the student to acquire learning and then to convert learning into thinking.

Sometimes it is not until preparing for the final examination that the student — rereading the chief texts and classroom notes — sees what the course was really about; until this late stage, the trees obscured the forest, but now, as the student reviews and sorts things out, a pattern emerges. The experience of reviewing and then of writing an examination, though fretful, can be highly exciting as connections are made and ideas take on life. Such discoveries about the whole subject matter of a course can almost never be made by writing critical essays on topics of one's own construction, for such topics rarely require a view of the whole. Furthermore, most of us are more likely to make imaginative leaps when trying to answer questions that other people pose to us, than when we are trying to answer questions we pose to ourselves. And although questions posed by others cause anxiety, when they have been confronted and responded to on an examination students often make yet another discovery — a self-discovery, a sudden and satisfying awareness of powers they didn't know they had.

Writing Essay Answers

We assume that before the examination you have read the assigned material, made notes in the margins of your books, made summaries of the reading and of the classroom comments, reviewed all of this material, and had a decent night's sleep. Now you are facing the examination sheet.

Here are eight obvious but important practical suggestions.

1. Take a moment to jot down, as a kind of outline or source of further inspiration, a few ideas that strike you after you have thought a little about the question. You may at the outset realize there are three points you want to make: unless you jot these down — three key words will do — you may spend all the allotted time on only one.

2. Don't bother to copy the question in the examination booklet, but if you have been given a choice of questions do indicate the question number, or write a word or two that will serve as a cue to the reader.

3. Answer the question. Consider this question: "Fromm and Lorenz try to explain aggression. Compare their theories, and discuss the extent to which they assist us in understanding the Arab-Israeli conflict." Notice that you must compare — not just summarize — two theories, and that you must also evaluate their relevance to a particular conflict. In short, take seriously such words as *compare, define, evaluate,* and *summarize.* And don't waste time generalizing about aggression; again, answer the question.

4. You can often get a good start merely by turning the question into an affirmation, for example by turning "In what ways is the poetry of Ginsberg influenced by Whitman?" into "The poetry of Ginsberg is influenced by Whitman in at least . . . ways."

5. Don't waste time summarizing at length what you have read, unless asked to do so — but of course occasionally you may have to give a brief summary in order to support a point. The instructor wants to see that you can *use* your reading, not merely that you have done the reading.

6. Budget your time. Do not spend more time on a question than the allotted time.

7. Be concrete. Illustrate your arguments with facts — names, dates, and quotations if possible.

8. Leave space for last minute additions. Either skip a page between essays, or write only on the right-hand pages so that on rereading you can add material at the appropriate place on the left-hand pages.

Beyond these general suggestions, we can best talk about essay examinations by looking at specific types of questions.

Questions on Literature

The five most common sorts of questions encountered in literature examinations are

1. a passage to explicate
2. a historical question, such as "Trace T. S. Eliot's religious development," "Trace the development of Shakespeare's conception of the tragic hero," or "How is Frost's nature poetry indebted to Emerson's thinking?"
3. a critical quotation to be evaluated
4. a comparison, such as "Compare the dramatic monologues of Browning with those of T. S. Eliot"
5. a wild question, such as "What would Dickens think of Vonnegut's *Cat's Cradle*?" or "What would Macbeth do if he were in Hamlet's position?"

A few remarks on each of these types may be helpful:

1. For a discussion of how to write an explication, see pages 234–36. As a short rule, look carefully at the tone (speaker's attitude toward self, subject, and audience) and at the implications of the words (the connotations or associations), and see if there is a pattern of imagery. For example, religious language ("adore," "saint") in a secular love poem may define the nature of the lover and of the beloved. Remember, *an explication is not a paraphrase* (a putting into other words) but an attempt to show the relations of the parts, especially by calling attention to implications. Organization of such an essay is rarely a problem, since most explications begin with the first line and go on to the last.

2. A good essay on a historical question will offer a nice combination of argument and evidence; the thesis will be supported by concrete details (names, dates, perhaps even brief quotations). A discussion of Eliot's movement toward the Church of England cannot be convincing if it does not specify certain works as representative of Eliot in certain years. If you are asked to relate a writer or a body of work to an earlier writer or period, list the chief characteristics of the earlier writer or the period and then show *specifically* how the material you are discussing is related to these characteristics. And if you can quote some relevant lines from the works, your reader will feel that you know not only titles and stock phrases but also the works themselves.

3. If you are asked to evaluate a critical quotation, read it carefully and in your answer take account of *all* of the quotation. If the critic has said, "Eliot in his plays always . . . but in his poems rarely . . ." you will have to write about both the plays and the poems; it will not be enough to talk only about the plays (unless, of course, the instructions on the examination ask you to take only as much of the quotation as you wish). Watch especially for words like "always," "for the most part," "never"; although the passage may on the whole approach the truth, you may feel that some important qualifications are needed. This is not being picky; true thinking involves making subtle distinctions, yielding assent only so far and no further. And, again, be sure to give concrete details, supporting your argument with evidence.

4. Comparisons are discussed on pages 39–45. Because comparisons are especially difficult to write, be sure to take a few moments to jot down a sort of outline so that you can know where you will be going. A comparison of Browning's and Eliot's monologues might treat three poems by each, devoting alternate paragraphs to one author; or it might first treat one author's poems and then turn to the other. But if it adopts this second strategy, the essay may break into two parts. You can guard against this weakness by announcing at the outset that you will treat the authors separately, then by reminding your reader during your treatment of the first author that certain points will be picked up when you get to the second author, and again by briefly reminding your reader during the second part of the essay of certain points already made.

5. Curiously, a wild question such as "What would Dickens think of *Cat's Cradle?*" or "What would Macbeth do in Hamlet's position?" usually produces tame answers: a half dozen ideas about Dickens or Macbeth are neatly applied to Vonnegut or Hamlet, and the gross incompatibilities are thus revealed. But, as the previous paragraph suggests, it may be necessary to do more than to set up bold and obvious oppositions. The interest in such a question and in the answer to it may largely be in the degree to which superficially different figures *resemble* each other in some important ways. And remember that the wildness of the question does not mean that all answers are equally acceptable; as usual, a good answer will be supported by concrete details.

Questions on the Social Sciences

First, an obvious statement: courses in the social sciences almost always require lots of reading. Do the reading when it is assigned, rather than try to do it the night before the examination. Second, when confronted with long reading assignments, you probably will read more efficiently if you scan the table of contents of a book to see the layout of the material, and then read the first and last chapters, where the authors usually summarize their theses. Books and articles on history, psychology, and sociology are not whodunits; there is nothing improper about knowing at the start how it will all turn out. Indeed, if at the start you have a clear grasp of the author's thesis, you may have the pleasure of catching the author perpetrating the crime of arguing from insufficient evidence. The beginning and the end of an article in a journal also may offer summaries that will assist you to read the article with relative ease. But only a reading of the entire work (perhaps with a little skimming) will offer you all of the facts and — no less important — the fully developed view or approach that the instructor believes is essential to an understanding of the course.

The techniques students develop in answering questions on literature may be transferred to examinations in the social sciences. A political science student, for example, can describe through explication the implicit tone or attitude in some of the landmark decisions of the Supreme Court. Similarly, the student of history who has learned to write an essay with a good combination of argument and evidence will not simply offer generalizations or present a list of facts unconnected by some central thesis, but will use relevant facts to support a thesis. The student who is able to evaluate a critical quotation or to compare literary works can also evaluate and compare documents in all the social sciences. Answers to wild questions can be as effective or as trite in the social sciences as in literature. "You are the British ambassador in Petrograd in November 1918. Write a report to your government about the Bolshevik revolution of that month" is to some instructors and students an absurd question but to others it is an interesting and effective way of ascertaining whether a student has not only absorbed the facts of an event but has also learned how to interpret them.

Questions on the Physical Sciences and Mathematics

Although the answer to an examination question in the physical sciences usually requires a mathematical computation, a few sentences may be useful in explaining the general plan of the computation, the assumptions involved, and sometimes the results.

It is particularly valuable to set down at the outset in a brief statement, probably a single sentence, your plan for solving the problem posed by the examination question. The statement is equivalent to the topic sentence of a paragraph. For instance, if the examination question is "What is the time required for an object to fall from the orbit of the moon to the earth?" the statement of your plan might be: "The time required for an object to fall from the orbit of the moon to the earth can be obtained by integration from Newton's law of motion, taking account of the increasing gravitational force as the object approaches the earth." Explicitly setting down your plan in words is useful first in clarifying your thought: is the plan a complete one leading to the desired answer? Do I know what I need to know to implement the plan? If your plan doesn't make sense you can junk it right away before wasting more time on it.

The statement of plan is useful also in communicating with the instructor. Your plan of solution, although valid, may be a surprise to the instructor. (She may have expected a solution to the problem posed above starting from Kepler's laws without any integration.) When this is so, the instructor will need your explanation to become oriented to your plan, and to properly assess its merits. Then if you botch the subsequent computation or can't remember how the gravitational force varies with the distance you will still have demonstrated that you have some comprehension of the problem. If on the other hand you present an erroneous computation without any explanation, the instructor will see nothing but chaos in your effort.

Further opportunities to use words will occur when you make assumptions or simplifications: "I assume the body is released with zero velocity and accordingly set $b = 0$," or "The third term is negligible and I drop it."

Finally, the results of your computation should be summarized or interpreted in words to answer the question asked. "The object will fall to the earth in five days." (The correct answer, for those who are curious.) Or, if you arrive at the end of your computation and of the examination hour and find you have a preposterous result, you can still exit gracefully (and increase your partial credit) with an explanation: "The answer of 53 days is clearly erroneous since the fall time of an object from the moon's orbit must be less than the 7 days required for the moon to travel a quarter orbit."

PART TWO
Revising

The friends that have it I do wrong
When ever I remake a song,
Should know what issue is at stake:
It is myself that I remake.
— WILLIAM BUTLER YEATS

12

Revising for Conciseness

Excess is the common substitute for energy.
— MARIANNE MOORE

All writers who want to keep the attention and confidence of their readers revise for conciseness. The general rule is to say everything relevant in as few words as possible. The conclusion of the Supreme Court's decision in *Brown* v. *The Board of Education of Topeka*, for example — "Separate educational facilities are inherently unequal" — says it all in six words.

The writers of the following sentences talk too much; they bore us because they don't make every word count.

> There are two pine trees which grow behind this house.
>
> On his left shoulder is a small figure standing. He is about the size of the doctor's head.
>
> The judge is seated behind the bench and he is wearing a judicial robe.

Compare those three sentences with these revisions:

> Two pine trees grow behind this house.
>
> On his left shoulder stands a small figure, about the size of the doctor's head.
>
> The judge, wearing a robe, sits behind the bench.

We will soon discuss in some detail the chief patterns of wordiness, but here it is enough to say that if you prefer the revisions you already have a commendable taste for conciseness. What does your taste tell you to do with the following sentences?

> A black streak covers the bottom half. It appears to have been painted with a single stroke of a large brush.

The time to begin revising for conciseness is when you have an acceptable first draft in hand — something that pretty much covers your topic and comes reasonably close to saying what you believe about it. As you go over it, study each sentence to see what, without loss of meaning or emphasis, can be deleted. (Delete by crossing out, not erasing; this saves time, and keeps a record of something you may want to reintroduce.) Read each paragraph, preferably aloud, to see if each sentence supports the topic sentence or idea and clarifies the point you are making. Leave in the concrete and specific details and examples that support your ideas (you may in fact be adding more) but cut out all the deadwood that chokes them: extra words, empty or pretentious phrases, weak qualifiers, redundancies, negative constructions, wordy uses of the verb *to be*, and other extra verbs and verb phrases. We'll discuss these problems in the next pages, but first we offer some examples of sentences that cannot be improved upon; they're so awful there's nothing to do but cross them out and start over. Zonker, in Garry Trudeau's cartoon, is a master of what we call Instant Prose (stuff that sounds like the real thing, but isn't).

INSTANT PROSE (ZONKERS)

Here are some examples of Instant Prose from students' essays:

> Frequently a chapter title in a book reveals to the reader the main point that the author desires to bring out during the course of the chapter.

We could try revising this, cutting the twenty-seven words down to seven:

> A chapter's title often reveals its thesis.

DOONESBURY **by Garry Trudeau**

But why bother? Unless the title is an exception, is the point worth making?

The two poems are basically similar in many ways, yet they have their significant differences.

True; all poems are both similar to and different from other poems. Start over with your next sentence, perhaps something like: "The two poems, superficially similar in rough paraphrase, are strikingly different in diction and theme."

> Although the essay is simple in plot, the theme encompasses many vital concepts of emotional makeup.
>
> Following a transcendental vein, the nostalgia in the poem takes on a spiritual quality.
>
> Cassell only presents a particular situation concerning the issue, and with clear descriptions and a certain style sets up an interesting article.

Pure zonkers. Not even the writers of these sentences now know what they mean.

Writing Instant Prose is an acquired habit, like smoking cigarettes or watching soap operas; fortunately it's easier to kick. It often begins in high school, sometimes earlier, when the victim is assigned a ten-page paper, or is told that a paragraph *must* contain at least three sentences, or that a thesis is stated in the introduction to an essay, elaborated in the body, and repeated in the conclusion. If the instructions appear arbitrary, and the student is bored or intimidated by them, his response is likely to be, like Zonker's, meaningless and mechanical. He forgets, or never learns, the true purpose of writing — the discovery and communication of ideas, attitudes, and judgments — and concentrates instead on the word count: stuffing sentences, padding paragraphs, stretching and repeating points, and adding flourishes. Rewarded by a satisfactory grade, he repeats the performance, and in time, through practice, develops some fluency in spilling out words without thought or commitment, and almost without effort. Such a student enters, as Zonker would say, the college of his choice, feeling somehow inauthentic, perhaps even aware that he doesn't really mean what he writes: symptoms of habitual use of, or addiction to, Instant Prose.

How to Avoid Instant Prose

1. Trust yourself. Writing Instant Prose is not only a habit; it's a form of alienation. If you habitually write zonkers you probably don't think of what you write as your own but as something you produce on demand for someone else. (Clearly Zonker is

writing for that unreasonable authority, the teacher, whose mysterious whims and insatiable appetite for words he must somehow satisfy.) Breaking the habit begins with recognizing it, and then acknowledging the possibility that you can take yourself and your work seriously. It means learning to respect your ideas and experiences (unlearning the passive habits that got you through childhood) and determining that when you write you'll write what you mean — nothing more, nothing less. This involves taking some risks, of course; habits offer some security or they would have no grip on us. Moreover, we all have moments when we doubt that our ideas are worth taking seriously. Keep writing honestly anyway. The self-doubts will pass; accomplishing something — writing one clear sentence — can help make them pass.

2. Distrust your first draft. Learn to recognize Instant Prose Additives when they crop up in your writing, and in what you read. And you *will* find them in what you read — in textbooks and in academic journals, notoriously.

Here's an example from a recent book on contemporary theater:

> One of the principal and most persistent sources of error that tends to bedevil a considerable proportion of contemporary literary analysis is the assumption that the writer's creative process is a wholly conscious and purposive type of activity.

Notice all the extra stuff in the sentence: "principal and most persistent," "tends to bedevil," "considerable proportion," "type of activity." Cleared of deadwood the sentence might read: "The assumption that the writer's creative process is wholly conscious bedevils much contemporary criticism."

3. Acquire two things: a new habit, Revising for Conciseness; and what Isaac Singer calls "the writer's best friend," a wastebasket.

REVISING FOR CONCISENESS

Extra Words and Empty Words

Extra words should, by definition, be eliminated; vague, empty, or pretentious words and phrases may be replaced by specific and direct language.

Wordy

However, it must be remembered that Ruth's marriage could have positive effects on Naomi's situation.

Concise

Ruth's marriage, however, will also provide security for Naomi.

In the second version, the unnecessary "it must be remembered that" has been eliminated; for the vague "positive effects" and "situation," specific words communicating a precise point have been substituted. The revision, though briefer, says more.

Wordy

In high school, where I had the opportunity for three years of working with the student government, I realized how significantly a person's enthusiasm could be destroyed merely by the attitudes of his superiors.

Concise

In high school, during three years on the student council, I saw students' enthusiasm destroyed by insecure teachers and cynical administrators.

Again, the revised sentence gives more information in fewer words. How?

Wordy

The economic situation of Miss Moody was also a crucial factor in the formation of her character.

Concise

Anne Moody's poverty also helped to form her character.

"Economic situation" is evasive for poverty; "crucial factor" is pretentious. Both are Instant Prose.

Wordy

It creates a better motivation of learning when students can design their own programs involving education. This way students' interests can be focused on.

Concise

Motivation improves when students design their own programs, focused on their own interests.

Now revise the following wordy sentences:

1. Perhaps they basically distrusted our capacity to judge correctly.
2. The use of setting is also a major factor in conveying a terrifying type atmosphere.

Notice how, in the examples provided, the following words crop up: "basically," "significant," "situation," "factor," "involving," "effect," "type." These words have legitimate uses, but are often no more than Instant Prose Additives. Cross them out whenever you can. Similar words to watch out for: *aspect, facet, fundamental, manner, nature, ultimate, utilization, viable, virtually, vital.* If they make your writing sound good don't hesitate — cross them out at once.

Weak Intensifiers and Qualifiers

Words like *very, quite, rather, completely, definitely,* and *so* can usually be struck from a sentence without loss. Paradoxically, sentences are often more emphatic without intensifiers. Try reading the following sentences both with and without the bracketed words:

At that time I was [very] idealistic.
We found the proposal [quite] feasible.
The remark, though unkind, was [entirely] accurate.
It was a [rather] fatuous statement.
The scene was [extremely] typical.
Both films deal with disasters [virtually] beyond our control.
The death scene is [truly] grotesque.
What she did next was [completely] inexcusable.
The first line [definitely] establishes that the father had been drinking.

Always avoid using intensifiers with *unique*. Either something is unique — the only one of its kind — or it is not. It can't be very, quite, so, pretty, or fairly unique.

Circumlocutions

Roundabout ways of saying things enervate your prose and tire your reader. Notice how each circumlocution in the first column is matched by a concise expression in the second.

I came to the realization that	I realized that
She is of the opinion that	She thinks that
The quotation is supportive of	The quotation supports
Concerning the matter of	About
During the course of	During
For the period of a week	For a week
In the event that	If
In the process of	During, while
Regardless of the fact that	Although
Due to the fact that	Because
For the simple reason that	Because
The fact that	That
Inasmuch as	Since
If the case was such that	If
It is often the case that	Often
In all cases	Always
I made contact with	I called, saw, phoned, wrote
At that point in time	Then
At this point in time	Now

Now revise this sentence:

> These movies have a large degree of popularity for the simple reason that they give the viewers insight in many cases.

Wordy Beginnings

Vague, empty words and phrases clog the beginnings of some sentences. They're like elaborate windups before the pitch.

1. *Wordy*

By analyzing carefully the last lines in this stanza, you find the connections between the loose ends of the poem.

Concise

The last lines of the stanza connect the loose ends of the poem.

2. *Wordy*

What the cartoonist is illustrating and trying to get across is the greed of the oil producers.

Concise

The cartoon illustrates the greed of the oil producers.

3. *Wordy*

Dealing with the crucial issue of the year, the editorial is expressing ironical disbelief in any possible solution to the Middle East crisis.

Concise

The editorial ironically expresses disbelief in the proposed solutions to the Middle East crisis.

4. *Wordy*

In the last stanza is the conclusion (as usual) and it tells of the termination of the dance.

Concise

The last stanza concludes with the end of the dance.

5. *Wordy*

In opposition to the situation of the younger son is that of the elder who remained in his father's house, working hard and handling his inheritance wisely.

Concise

The elder son, by contrast, remained in his father's house, worked hard, and handled his inheritance wisely.

Notice in the above examples that when the deadwood is cleared from the beginning of the sentence, the subject appears early, and the main verb appears close to it:

1. The last lines . . . connect . . .
2. The cartoon illustrates . . .
3. The editorial . . . expresses . . .
4. The last stanza concludes . . .
5. The elder son . . . remained . . .

Locating the right noun for the subject, and the right verb for the predicate, is the key to revising sentences with wordy beginnings. Try revising the following sentences:

1. The way that Mabel reacts toward her brother is a fine representation of her nature.
2. In Langston Hughes's case he was "saved from sin" when he was going on thirteen.

Empty Conclusions

Often a sentence that begins well has an empty conclusion. The words go on but the sentence seems to stand still; if it's not revised, it requires another sentence to explain it. A short sentence is not necessarily concise.

1. *Empty*

"Those Winter Sundays" is composed so that a reader can feel what the poet was saying. (How is it composed? What is he saying?)

Concise

"Those Winter Sundays" describes the speaker's anger as a child, and his remorse as an adult.

2. *Empty*

In both Orwell's and Baldwin's essays the feeling of white supremacy is very important. (Why is white supremacy important?)

Concise

Both Orwell and Baldwin trace the insidious consequences of white supremacy.

3. *Empty*

Being the only white girl among about ten black girls was quite a learning experience. (What did she learn?)

Concise

As the only white girl among about ten black girls, I began to understand the experiences of isolation, helplessness, and rage regularly reported by minority students.

Wordy Uses of the Verbs "To Be," "To Have," and "To Make"

Notice that in the preceding unrevised sentences a form of the verb *to be* introduces the empty conclusion: "*was* saying," "*is* very important," "*was* quite a learning experience." In each revision, the right verb added and generated substance. In the following sentences, substitutions for the verb *to be* both invigorate and shorten otherwise substantial sentences.

1. *Wordy*

The scene is taking place at night, in front of the capitol building.

Concise

The scene takes place at night, in front of the capitol building.

2. *Wordy*

In this shoeshining and early rising there are indications of church attendance.

Concise

The early rising and shoeshining indicate church attendance.

3. *Wordy*

The words "flashing," "rushing," "plunging," and "tossing" are suggestive of excitement.

Concise

The words "flashing," "rushing," "plunging," and "tossing" suggest excitement.

The rule is, whenever you can, replace a form of the verb *to be* with a stronger verb.

To Be	*Strong Verb*
1. and a participle ("is taking")	1. takes
2. and a noun ("are indications")	2. indicate
3. and an adjective ("are suggestive")	3. suggest

Try revising the following sentence:

> The rising price of sugar is representative of the spiraling cost of all goods.

Sentences with the verbs *to have* and *to make* can similarly be reduced:

1. *Wordy*

The Friar has knowledge that Juliet is alive.

Concise

The Friar knows that Juliet is alive.

2. *Wordy*

The stanzas make a vivid contrast between Heaven and Hell.

Concise

The stanzas vividly contrast Heaven and Hell.

Like all rules, this one has exceptions. We don't list them here; you'll discover them by listening to your sentences.

Redundancy

This term, derived from a Latin word meaning "overflowing, overlapping," refers to unnecessary repetition in the expression of ideas. Unlike repetition, which often provides emphasis or coherence (for example, "government of the people, by the people, for the people"), redundancy can always be eliminated.

1. *Redundant*

Any student could randomly sit anywhere. (If the students could sit anywhere, the seating was random.)

Concise

Students could sit anywhere.
Students chose their seats at random.

2. *Redundant*

I have no justification with which to excuse myself.

Concise

I have no justification for my action.
I can't justify my action.
I have no excuse for my action.
I can't excuse my action.

3. *Redundant*

In the orthodox Cuban culture, the surface of the female role seemed degrading. (Perhaps this sentence means what it says. More probably "surface" and "seemed" are redundant.)

Concise

In the orthodox Cuban culture, the female role seemed degrading.
In the orthodox Cuban culture, the female role was superficially degrading.

4. *Redundant*

In "Araby" the boy feels alienated emotionally from his family.

Concise

In "Araby" the boy feels alienated from his family.

Try eliminating redundancy from the following sentences:

1. The reason why she hesitates is because she is afraid.
2. Marriage in some form has long existed since prehistoric times.

What words can be crossed out of the following phrases?

1. throughout the entire article
2. her attitude of indifference
3. a conservative type suit
4. all the different tasks besides teaching
5. his own personal opinion
6. elements common to both of them
7. emotions and feelings
8. shared together
9. falsely padded expense accounts
10. alleged suspect

Many phrases in common use are redundant. Watch for phrases like these when you revise:

round in shape	resulting effect
purple in color	close proximity
poetic in nature	connected together
tall in stature	prove conclusively
autobiography of her life	must necessarily
basic fundamentals	very unique
true fact	very universal
free gift	the reason why is because

Negative Constructions

Negative constructions are often wordy and sometimes pretentious.

1. *Wordy*

Housing for married students is not unworthy of consideration.

Concise

Housing for married students is worthy of consideration.

Better

The trustees should earmark funds for married students' housing. (Probably what the author meant)

2. *Wordy*

After reading the second paragraph you aren't left with an immediate reaction as to how the story will end.

Concise

The first two paragraphs create suspense.

The following example from a syndicated column is not untypical:

> Although it is not reasonably to be expected that someone who fought his way up to the Presidency is less than a largely political animal and sometimes a beast, it is better not to know — really — exactly what his private conversations were composed of.

The Golden Rule of writing is "Write for others as you would have them write to you," not "Write for others in a manner not unreasonably dissimilar to the manner in which you would have them write for you." (But see the discussion of *not . . . un-* on page 427 for effective use of the negative.)

Extra Sentences, Extra Clauses: Subordination

Sentences are sometimes wordy because ideas are given more elaborate grammatical constructions than they need. In revising, these constructions can be grammatically subordinated, or reduced. Two sentences, for example, may be reduced to one, or a clause may be reduced to a phrase.

"See what I mean? You're never sure just where you stand with them."
Drawing by Ross; © 1971 The New Yorker Magazine, Inc.

1. *Wordy*

The Book of Ruth was probably written in the fifth century B.C. It was a time when women were considered the property of men.

Concise

The book of Ruth was probably written in the fifth century B.C., when women were considered the property of men.

2. *Wordy*

The first group was the largest. This group was seated in the center of the dining hall.

Concise

The first group, the largest, was seated in the center of the dining hall.

3. *Wordy*

The colonists were upset over the tax on tea and they took action against it.

Concise

The colonists, upset over the tax on tea, took action against it.

Watch particularly for clauses beginning with *who, which,* and *that.* Often they can be shortened.

1. *Wordy*

George Orwell is the pen name of Eric Blair who was an English writer.

Concise

George Orwell is the pen name of Eric Blair, an English writer.

2. *Wordy*

They are seated at a table which is covered with a patched and tattered cloth.

Concise

They are seated at a table covered with a patched and tattered cloth.

3. *Wordy*

There is one feature that is grossly out of proportion.

Concise

One feature is grossly out of proportion.

Also watch for sentences and clauses beginning with *it is, this is, there are.* (Again, wordy uses of the verb *to be.*) These expressions often lead to a *which,* but even when they don't they may be wordy.

1. *Wordy*

The trail brings us to the timberline. This is the point where the trees become stunted from lack of oxygen.

Concise

The trail brings us to the timberline, the point where the trees become stunted from lack of oxygen.

2. *Wordy*

This is a quotation from Black Elk's autobiography which discloses his prophetic powers.

Concise

This quotation from Black Elk's autobiography discloses his prophetic powers.

3. *Wordy*

It is frequently considered that *Hamlet* is Shakespeare's most puzzling play.

Concise

Hamlet is frequently considered Shakespeare's most puzzling play.

4. *Wordy*

In Notman's photograph of Buffalo Bill and Sitting Bull there are definite contrasts between the two figures.

Concise

Notman's photograph of Buffalo Bill and Sitting Bull contrasts the two figures.

Try revising the following sentences:

1. There are many writers who believe that writing can't be taught.
2. Always take more clothes than you think you will need. This ensures that you will be prepared for the weather no matter what it is.
3. This is an indication that the child has a relationship with his teacher which is very respectful.

(For further discussion of subordination see pages 315–17. On *which* clauses, see also pages 434–35.)

SOME CONCLUDING REMARKS

We spoke earlier about how students learn to write Instant Prose and acquire other wordy habits — by writing what they think the teacher has asked for. We haven't forgotten that teachers assign papers of a certain length in college too. But the length given is not an arbitrary limit that must be reached — the teacher who asks for a five-page or twenty-page paper is probably trying to tell you the degree of elaboration expected on the assignment. Such, apparently, was the intention of William Randolph Hearst, the newspaper publisher, who cabled an astronomer, "Is there life on Mars? Cable reply 1000 words." The astronomer's reply was, "Nobody knows," repeated five hundred times.

What do you do when you've been asked to produce a ten-page paper and after diligent writing and revising you find you've said everything relevant to your topic in seven and a half pages? Our advice is, hand it in. We can't remember ever counting the words or pages of a substantial, interesting essay; we assume that our colleagues elsewhere are equally reasonable and equally over-worked. If we're wrong, tell us about it — in writing, and in the fewest possible words.

EXERCISE

First identify the fault or faults that make the following sentences wordy, and then revise them for conciseness.

1. There were quite a number of contrasts that White made between the city school and the country school which was of a casual nature all throughout.
2. The study of political topics involves a careful researching of the many components of the particular field.

3. Virtually the most significant feature of any field involving science is the vital nature of the technical facilities, the fundamental factor of all research.

4. Like a large majority of American people, I, too, have seen the popular disaster films.

5. Something which makes this type of film popular (disaster) is the kind of subconscious aspect of "Can man overcome this problem?" Horror films, on the other hand, produce the aspects of whether or not man can make amends for his mistakes.

6. The average American becomes disappointed and downtrodden due to the fact that he can't help himself and is at the mercy of inflation and unemployment.

7. Some relationships have split up because of the simple fear of having an abnormal child, while perhaps there might have been other alternatives for these couples.

8. Reading has always been a fascinating and exciting pastime for me for as long as I can remember.

9. This cartoon appeared in the 17 September 1979 issue of *Newsweek*. This political cartoon was originally taken from the *Tulsa Tribune*. The cartoonist is Simpson.

10. Only once in the first two sentences does the author make reference to the first person.

11. The length of the sentences are similar in moderation and in structural clarity.

12. The magnitude of student satisfaction with the program ranged from total hatred to enthusiastic approval.

13. Taking a look at the facial expressions of the man and the woman in both pictures one can see a difference in mood.

14. One drawing is done in watercolor and the other is done in chalk which is a revision of the watercolor.

15. The dialogue places the role of the two gods on a believable basis.

16. Senseless crimes such as murder and muggings are committed on a daily basis.

17. One must specify that the current disco craze which is so very popular today is not considered to be black music.

18. The two major aspects behind the development of a performer are technique and musicianship.

19. I remember my first desire to smoke cigarettes as I watched my father smoke. My father often sat in his favorite easy chair idly smoking cigarettes.

20. Christopher Stone's article "Putting the Outside Inside the Fence of Law" is concerning the legal rights of the environment. He comments on the legal rights of other inanimate entities which seem to be acceptable. Just as these entities are represented, so should the environment be represented.

13
Revising
for Clarity

CLARITY

We have seen new realities created by the advance of physics. But this chain of creation can be traced back far beyond the starting point of physics. One of the most primitive concepts is that of an object. The concepts of a tree, a horse, any material body, are creations gained on the basis of experience, though the impressions from which they arise are primitive in comparison with the world of physical phenomena. A cat teasing a mouse also creates, by thought, its own primitive reality. The fact that the cat reacts in a similar way toward any mouse it meets shows that it forms concepts and theories which are its guide through its own world of sense impressions.

— Albert Einstein and Leopold Infeld

Skills constitute the manipulative techniques of human goal attainment and control in relation to the physical world, so far as artifacts or machines especially designed as tools do not yet supplement them. Truly human skills are guided by organized and codified *knowledge* of both the things to be manipulated and the human capacities that are used to manipulate them. Such knowledge is an aspect of cultural-level symbolic processes, and, like other aspects to be discussed presently, requires the capacities of the human central nervous system, particularly the brain. This organic system is clearly essential to all of the symbolic processes; as we well know, the human brain is far superior to the brain of any other species.

— Talcott Parsons

Why is the first passage easier to understand than the second?

Both passages discuss the relationship between the brain and the physical world it attempts to understand. The first passage, by Einstein and Infeld, is, if anything, more complex both in what it asserts and in what it suggests than the second, by Parsons. Both passages explain that the brain organizes sense impressions. But Einstein and Infeld further explain that the history of physics can be understood as an extension of the simplest sort of organization, such as we all make in distinguishing a tree from a horse, or such as even a cat makes in teasing a mouse. Parsons only promises that "other aspects" will "be discussed presently." How many of us are eager for those next pages?

Good writing is clear, not because it presents simple ideas, but because it presents ideas in the simplest form the subject permits. A clear analysis doesn't reduce a complex problem to a simple one; it breaks it down into its simple, comprehensible parts and discusses them, one by one, in a logical order. A clear paragraph explains one of these parts coherently, thoroughly, and in language as simple and as particular as the reader's understanding requires and the context allows. Where Parsons writes of "organized and codified *knowledge* of . . . the things to be manipulated," Einstein and Infeld write simply of the concept of an object. And even "object," a simple but general word, is further clarified by the specific, familiar examples, "tree" and "horse." Parsons writes of "the manipulative techniques of . . . goal attainment and control in relation to the physical world, so far as artifacts or machines especially designed as tools do not yet supplement them." Einstein and Infeld show us a cat teasing a mouse.

Notice also the clear organization of Einstein and Infeld's paragraph. The first sentence, clearly transitional, refers to the advance of physics traced in the preceding pages. The next sentence, introduced by "But," reverses our direction: we are now going to look not at an advance, but at primitive beginnings. And the following sentences, to the end of the paragraph, fulfill that promise. We move back to primitive human concepts, clarified by examples, and finally to the still more primitive example of the cat. Parsons' paragraph is also organized, but the route is much more difficult to follow.

Why do people write obscurely? Walter Kaufmann, in an introduction to Martin Buber's *I and Thou*, says "Men love jargon. It is so palpable, tangible, visible, audible; it makes so obvious what one has learned; it satisfies the craving for results. It is impressive for the uninitiated. It makes one feel that one belongs. Jargon divides men into Us and Them."

Maybe. (For our definition of jargon, see pages 281–84.) Surely some students learn to write obscurely by trying to imitate the style of their teachers or textbooks. The imitation may spring from genuine admiration for these authorities, mixed perhaps with an understandable wish to be one of Us (the authorities) not one of Them (the dolts). Or students may feel that a string of technical-sounding words is what the teacher expects. If this thought has crossed your mind, we can't say you're entirely wrong. Learning a new discipline often involves acquiring a specialized vocabulary. But we add the following cautions:

1. What teachers expect is that your writing show thought and make sense. They are likely to be puzzled by the question, "Do you want me to use technical terms in this paper?"
2. If you try to use technical terms appropriate to one field when you write about another, you are likely to write nonsense. Don't write "the machine was viable" if you mean only that it worked.
3. When you do write for specialists in a particular field use technical terms precisely. Don't write in an art history paper, "This print of Van Gogh's *Sunflowers*" if you mean "This reproduction of Van Gogh's *Sunflowers*."
4. No matter what you are writing, don't become so enamored of technical words that you can't write a sentence without peppering it with *input, interface, death-symbol, parameter, feedback,* and so on.

But to return to the question, "Why do people write obscurely?" — we'd like to offer a second answer to Kaufmann's "Men love jargon." It's difficult to write clearly.[1] Authorities may be unintelligible not because they want to tax you with unnecessary difficulties, but because they don't know how to avoid them. In

---

[1] Our first draft of this sentence read "Writing clearly is difficult." Can you see why we changed it?

our era, when we sometimes seem to be drowning in a flood of print, few persons who write know how to write well. If you have ever tried to assemble a mechanical toy or to thread an unfamiliar sewing machine by following the "easy instructions," you know that the simplest kind of expository writing, giving instructions, can foil the writers most eager for your goodwill (that is, those who want you to use their products). Few instructions, unfortunately, are as unambiguous as "Go to jail. Go directly to jail. Do not pass Go. Do not collect $200."

You can, though, learn to write clearly, by learning to recognize common sources of obscurity in writing and by consciously revising your own work. We offer, to begin with, three general rules:

1. Use the simplest, most exact, most specific language your subject allows.
2. Put together what belongs together, in the essay, in the paragraph, and in the sentence.
3. Keep your reader in mind, particularly when you revise.

Now for more specific advice, and examples — the cats and mice of revising for clarity.

CLARITY AND EXACTNESS: USING THE RIGHT WORD

Denotation

Be sure the word you choose has the right *denotation* (explicit meaning). Did you mean sarcastic or ironic? Fatalistic or pessimistic? Disinterested or uninterested? Biannual or semiannual? Enforce or reinforce? Use or usage? If you're not sure, check the dictionary. You'll find some of the most commonly misused words discussed in Chapter 20. Here are examples of a few others.

1. Daru faces a dilemma between his humane feelings and his conceptions of justice. (Strictly speaking, a dilemma requires a choice between two equally unattractive alternatives. "Conflict" would be a better word here.)
2. However, as time dragged on, exercising seemed to lose its charisma. (What is charisma? Why is it inexact here?)

3. Ms. Wu's research contains many symptoms of depression which became evident during the reading period. (Was Ms. Wu depressed by her research? We hope not. Probably she described or listed the symptoms.)
4. When I run I don't allow myself to stop until I have reached my destiny. (Which word is inexact?)

A related error is the use of one part of speech for another part. Politicians and sociologists seem especially fond of using, for instance, "impact" as a verb, but few have equalled former Secretary of State Alexander Haig, who regularly began his answers with "Let me context that for you." Such talk sounds silly; hearers don't quite know if the speaker is being pretentious or is just ignorant, but they do know that they are confused. A journalist nicely spoofed Haig's unnerving way of talking, and although Haig is gone, the way of talking, and writing, persists:

> Haig, in congressional hearings before his confirmatory, paradoxed his auditioners by abnormalling his responds so that verbs were nouned, nouns verbed and adjectives adverbised. He techniqued a new way to vocabulary his thoughts so as to informationally uncertain anybody listening about what he had actually implicated.

This is good fun, but avoid nouning verbs and verbing nouns unless you want to evoke smiles.

Connotation

Be sure the word you choose has the right *connotation* (association, implication). As Mark Twain said, the difference between the right word and the almost right word is the difference between lightning and the lightning bug.

1. Boston politics has always upheld the reputation of being especially crooked. ("Upheld" inappropriately suggests that Boston has proudly maintained its reputation. "Has always had" would be appropriate here, but pale. "Deserved" would, in this context, be ironic, implying — accurately — the writer's scorn.)
2. This book, unlike many other novels, lacks tedious descriptive passages. ("Lacks" implies a deficiency. How would you revise the sentence?)

3. New Orleans, notorious for its good jazz and good food. . . . (Is "notorious" the word here? or "famous"?)
4. Sunday, Feb. 9. Another lingering day at Wellesley. (In this entry from a student's journal, "lingering" strikes us as right. What does "lingering" imply about Sundays at Wellesley that "long" would not?)

Because words have connotations, most writing — even when it pretends to be objective — conveys attitudes as well as facts. Consider, for example, this passage by Jessica Mitford, describing part of the procedure used today for embalming:

> A long, hollow needle attached to a tube . . . is jabbed into the abdomen, poked around the entrails and chest cavity, the contents of which are pumped out. . . .

In a way this passage accurately describes part of the procedure, but it also, of course, records Mitford's contempt for the procedure. Suppose she wanted to be more respectful — suppose, for example, she were an undertaker writing an explanatory pamphlet. Instead of the needle being "jabbed" it would be "inserted," and instead of being "poked around the entrails" it would be "guided around the viscera," and the contents would not be "pumped out" but would be "drained." Mitford's words would be the wrong words for an undertaker explaining embalming to apprentices or to the general public, but, given her purpose, they are exactly the right ones because they convey her attitude with great clarity.

Note too that many words have social, political, or sexist overtones. We read for example of the *children* of the rich, but the *offspring* of the poor. What is implied by the distinction? Consider the differences in connotation in each of the following series:

1. friend, boyfriend, young man, lover (What age is the speaker?)
2. dine, eat (What was on the menu? Who set the table?)
3. spinster, bachelor (Which term is likely to be considered an insult?)
4. underdeveloped nations, developing nations, emerging nations
5. preference, bias, prejudice
6. upbringing, conditioning, brainwashing
7. message from our sponsor, commercial, ad, plug
8. intelligence gathering, espionage, spying
9. emigrate, defect, seek asylum
10. anti-abortion, pro-life; pro-abortion, pro-choice

Quotation Marks as Apologies

When you have used words with exact meanings (denotations) and appropriate associations (connotations) for your purpose, don't apologize for them by putting quotation marks around them. If the words *copped a plea, ripped off,* or *kids* suit you better than *plea-bargained, stolen,* or *children,* use them. If they are inappropriate, don't put them in quotation marks; find the right words.

Being Specific

In writing descriptions, catch the richness, complexity, and uniqueness of things. Suppose, for example, you are describing a scene from your childhood, a setting you loved. There was, in particular, a certain tree . . . and you write: "Near the water there was a big tree that was rather impressive." Most of us would produce something like that sentence. Here is the sentence Ernesto Galarza wrote in *Barrio Boy*:

> On the edge of the pond, at the far side, there was an enormous walnut tree, standing like an open umbrella whose ribs extended halfway across the still water of the pool.

We probably could not have come up with the metaphor of the umbrella because we wouldn't have seen the similarity. (As Aristotle observed, the gift for making metaphors distinguishes the poet from the rest of us.) But we can all train ourselves to be accurate observers and reporters. For "the water" (general) we can *specify* "pond"; for "near" we can say how near, "on the edge of the pond," and add the specific location, "at the far side"; for "tree" we can give the *species,* "walnut tree"; and for "big" we can provide a picture, its branches "extended halfway across" the pond: it was, in fact, "enormous."

Galarza does not need to add limply, as we did, that the tree "was rather impressive." The tree he describes *is* impressive. That he accurately remembered it persuades us that he was impressed, without his having to tell us he was. For writing descriptions, a good general rule is: show, don't tell.

Be as specific as you can be in all forms of exposition too. Take the time, when you revise, to find the exact word to replace vague, woolly phrases or clichés. (In the following examples we have had to guess or invent what the writer meant.)

1. *Vague*

The clown's part in *Othello* is very small.

Specific

The clown appears in only two scenes in *Othello*.
The clown in *Othello* speaks only thirty lines.
(Notice the substitution of the verb "appears" or "speaks" for the frequently debilitating "is." And in place of the weak intensifier "very" we have specific details to tell us how small the role is.)

2. *Vague*

He feels uncomfortable at the whole situation. (Many feelings are uncomfortable. Which one does he feel? What's the situation?)

Specific

He feels guilty for having distrusted his father.

3. *Vague*

The passage reveals a somewhat calculating aspect behind Antigone's noble motives. ("A somewhat calculating aspect" is vague — and wordy — for "calculation." Or did the writer mean "shrewdness"? What differences in connotation are there between "shrewd" and "calculating"?)

4. *Vague*

She uses simplicity in her style of writing. (Do we know, exactly, what simplicity in style means?)

Specific

She uses familiar words, normal word order, and conversational phrasing.

5. *Vague Cliché*

Then she criticized students for living in an ivory tower. (Did she criticize them for being detached or secluded? For social irresponsibility or studiousness?)

Specific

Then she criticized students for being socially irresponsible.

Using Examples

In addition to exact words and specific details, illustrative examples make for clear writing. Einstein and Infeld, in the passage quoted on page 272, use as an example of a primitive concept a cat teasing not only its first mouse, but "any mouse it meets." Here are two paragraphs which clarify their topic sentences through examples; the first is again from *Barrio Boy*.

> In Jalco people spoke in two languages — Spanish and with gestures. These signs were made with the face or hands or a combination of both. If you bent one arm and tapped the elbow with the other hand, it meant "He is stingy." When you sawed one arm across the other you were saying that someone you knew played the fiddle terribly. To say that a man was a tippler you made a set of cow's horns with the little finger and the thumb of one hand, bending the three middle fingers to the palm and pointing the thumb at your mouth. And if you wanted to indicate, without saying so for the sake of politeness, that a mutual acquaintance was daffy, you tapped three times on your forehead with your middle finger.
>
> — Ernesto Galarza

In the next paragraph, Northrop Frye, writing about the perception of rhythm, illustrates his point:

> Ideally, our literary education should begin, not with prose, but with such things as "this little pig went to market" — with verse rhythm reinforced by physical assault. The infant who gets bounced on somebody's knee to the rhythm of "Ride a cock horse" does not need a footnote telling him that Banbury Cross is twenty miles northeast of Oxford. He does not need the information that "cross" and "horse" make (at least in the pronunciation he is most likely to hear) not a rhyme but an assonance. . . . All he needs is to get bounced.

Frye does not say our literary education should begin with "simple rhymes" or with "verse popular with children." He says "with such things as 'this little pig went to market,'" and then he goes on to add "Ride a cock horse." We know exactly what he means. Notice, too, that we do not need a third example. Be detailed, but know when to stop.

Your reader is likely to be brighter and more demanding than Lady Pliant, who in a seventeenth-century play says to a would-be seducer, "You are very alluring — and say so many fine Things, and nothing is so moving to me as a fine Thing." "Fine Things," of course, are what is wanted, but only exact words and apt illustrations will convince intelligent readers that they are hearing fine things.

Now look at a paragraph from a student's essay whose thesis is that rage can be a useful mechanism for effecting change. Then compare the left hand paragraph with the same paragraph, revised, at the right. Note the specific ways, sentence by sentence, the student revised for clarity.

In my high school we had little say in the learning processes that were used. The subjects that we were required to take were irrelevant. One had to take them to earn enough points to graduate. Some of the teachers were sympathetic to our problem. They would tell us about when they were young, how they tried to oppose their school system. But when they were young it was a long time ago, for most of them. The principal would call assemblies to speak on the subject. They were entitled, "The Value of an Education" or "Get a Good Education to Have a Bright Future." The titles were not inviting. They had nothing to do with our plight. Most students never came to any agreements with the principal because most of his thoughts and views seemed old and outdated.

In my high school we had little say about our curriculum. We were required, for example, to choose either American or European History to earn enough points for graduation. We wanted, but were at first refused, the option of Black History. Some of our teachers were sympathetic with us; one told me about her fight opposing the penmanship course required in her school. Nor was the principal totally indifferent — he called assemblies. I remember one talk he gave called "The Value of an Education in Today's World," and another, "Get a Good Education to Have a Bright Future." I don't recall hearing about a Black History course in either talk. Once, he invited a group of us to meet with him in his office, but we didn't reach any agreement. He solemnly showed us an American History text (not the one we used) that had a whole chapter devoted to Black History.

Jargon and Technical Language

Jargon is the unnecessary, inappropriate, or inexact use of technical or specialized language. Look at this passage:

Dodgers Keep Perfect Record in Knocking Out Southpaws

NEW YORK (AP) — The Brooklyn Dodgers didn't win the first World Series game yesterday, but they got a measure of comfort in that they maintained one of their season records.

No left-hander went the distance in beating them the past season. Six lefties got the decision but none was around at the end.

New York hurler Whitey Ford made No. 7, but he, too, went the way of the other southpaws . . . empty consolation, to be sure, in view of the Yanks' 6–5 victory in the World Series opener.

Consider the diction of this sports story: "went the distance," "lefties," "got the decision," "around at the end," "hurler," "southpaws," "opener," "made No. 7." Do you understand the individual words? Most of them, probably. Do you know what the item is about? Some of us do, some don't. Is it written in technical language, or jargon?

The answer depends, as we define jargon, on where the story appeared, and for whom it was intended. Because it appeared on the sports page of a newspaper, we would classify the diction as technical language, not jargon. Properly used, technical language communicates information concisely and clearly, and can, as it does here, create a comfortable bond between reader and writer. Both are having fun. If the same story appeared on the front page of the newspaper, we would classify the language as jargon because it would baffle the general reader.

If the baseball story makes perfect sense to you, as an exercise, try to explain it in nontechnical language to someone who does not understand it. And while you're at it, can you explain why baseball fans are particularly interested in left-handed pitchers — in other words, what makes the statistic here a statistic? Why are baseball fans so interested in statistics anyway — more interested, say, than football or hockey fans? Is it because baseball is intrinsically boring?

Let's move quickly to another example:

For many years Boston parents have tried to improve the public schools. But any input the parents might have desired has been stifled by the Boston School Committee.

"With you, I think I've found a maximization of experience."
Drawing by Donald Reilly; © 1978 The New Yorker Magazine, Inc.

What does "input" mean in this sentence? Is the term used as technical language here, or jargon? (And by the way, how would you go about stifling an input?)

A student wrote the passage just quoted. But recently in Dallas, parents of children in kindergarten through third grade received a twenty-eight page manual written by a professional educator to help them decipher their children's report cards. The title of the manual: *Terminal Behavioral Objectives for Continuous Progression Modules in Early Childhood Education.* Terminal objectives, it seems, means goals. What does the rest mean? If you were one of the parents, would you expect much help from the manual?

Here's a film critic discussing the movie *Last Tango in Paris*:

> The failure of the relationship between Paul and Jeanne is a function of the demands placed on the psyche by bourgeoise society, and it is the family as mediator of psychological and social repression which provides the dialectic of Bertolucci's film.

Perhaps some film criticism should be x-rated?

And finally, a deliberate parody. A. P. Herbert in his book *What a Word!* tells us how a social scientist might write a familiar Biblical command:

> In connection with my co-citizens, a general standard of mutual good will and reciprocal non-aggression is obviously incumbent upon me.

What is the command? (See Leviticus xix. 18.)

In general, when you write for nonspecialists, avoid technical terms; if you must use them, define them. If you use a technical term when writing for specialists, be sure you know its precise meaning. But whenever you can, even among specialists, use plain English.

Clichés

Clichés (literally, in French, molds from which type is cast) are trite expressions, mechanically — that is, mindlessly — produced. Since they are available without thought they are great Instant Prose Additives (see pages 254–59). Writers who use them are usually surprised to be criticized: they find the phrases attractive, and may even think them exact. (Phrases become clichés precisely because they have wide appeal and therefore wide use.) But clichés, by their very nature, cannot communicate the uniqueness of your thoughts. Furthermore, because they come instantly to mind, they tend to block the specific detail or exact expression that will let the reader know what precisely is in your mind. When, in revising, you strike out a cliché, you force yourself to do the work of writing clearly. The following examples are full of clichés:

> Finally, the long awaited day arrived. Up bright and early. . . .
>
> She peered at me with suspicion; then a faint smile crossed her face.

Other examples:

first and foremost	time honored
the acid test	bustled to and fro
fatal flaw	short but sweet
budding genius	few and far between
slowly but surely	D-day arrived
little did I know	sigh of relief
the big moment	last but not least

"You're right as rain. It's the dawn of history,
and there are no clichés as yet. I'll drink to that!"

Drawing by Handelsman; © 1972 The New Yorker Magazine, Inc.

In attempting to avoid clichés, however, don't go to the other extreme of wildly original, super-vivid writing — "'well then, say something to her,' he roared, his whole countenance gnarled in rage." It's often better to simply say, "he said." (Anyone who intends to write dialogue should memorize Ring Lardner's intentionally funny line, "'Shut up!' he explained.") Note also that such common expressions as "How are you?" "Please pass the salt," and "So long" are not clichés; they make no claim to be colorful.

Mixed Metaphors

Ordinary speech abounds with metaphors (implied comparisons). We speak or write of the foot of a mountain, the germ (seed) of an idea, the root of a problem. Metaphors so deeply embedded in the language that they no longer evoke pictures in our minds are called *dead metaphors*. Ordinarily, they offer us, as writers, no problems: we need neither seek them nor avoid them; they are simply there. (Notice, for example, "embedded" two sentences back.) Such metaphors become problems, however, when we unwittingly call them back to life. Howard Nemerov observes: "That these metaphors may be not dead but only sleeping, or that they may arise from the grave and walk in our sentences, is something that has troubled everyone who has ever tried to write plain expository prose. . . ."

Dead metaphors are most likely to haunt us when they are embodied in clichés. Since we use clichés without attention to what they literally say or point to, we are unlikely to be aware of the dead metaphors buried in them. But when we attach one cliché to another, we may raise the metaphors from the grave. The result is likely to be a mixed metaphor; the effect is almost always absurd.

> Water seeks its own level whichever way you want to slice it.
>
> Traditional liberal education has run out of gas and educational soup kitchens are moving into the vacuum.
>
> The low ebb has been reached and hopefully it's turned the corner.
>
> Her energy, drained through a stream of red tape, led only to closed doors.
>
> We no longer ask for whom the bell tolls but simply chalk it up as one less mouth to feed.

As Joe E. Lewis observed, "Show me a man who builds castles in the air and I'll show you a crazy architect." Unless you're sure that you've hit on an original and accurate comparison leave metaphor making to poets and comedians.

Euphemisms

Euphemisms are words substituted for other words thought to be offensive. In deodorant advertisements there are no armpits, only *underarms*, which may *perspire*, but not sweat, and even then they don't smell. A parent reading a report card is likely to learn not that his child got an F in conduct, but that she "experiences difficulty exercising self-control: (a) verbally (b) physically." And where do old people go? To Sun City, "a retirement community for senior citizens."

Euphemisms are used for two reasons: to avoid giving offense, and, sometimes unconsciously, to disguise fear and animosity. We do not advise you to write or speak discourteously; we do advise you, though, to use euphemisms consciously and sparingly, when tact recommends them. It's customary in a condolence letter to avoid the word "*death*," and, depending both on your own feelings and those of the bereaved, you may wish to follow that custom. But there's no reason on earth to write "Hamlet passes on." You should be aware, moreover, that some people find euphemisms themselves offensive. There may be more comfort for your friend in "I'm sorry about his death" or even in "too bad about your old lady," than in "I regret to hear of your loss." And speaking of old ladies, there is one in Philadelphia, Margaret Kuhn, who would probably prefer to be called a woman than a lady, and certainly prefers "old" to "senior" — because "Old," she says, "is the right word. . . . I think we should wear our gray hair, wrinkles, and crumbling joints as badges of distinction. After all, we worked damn hard to get them." She has organized a militant group called the Gray Panthers to fight agism.

In revising, replace needless euphemisms with plain words. Your writing will be sharper, and you might, in examining and confronting them, free yourself of a mindless habit, an unconscious prejudice, or an irrational fear.

A Digression on Public Lying

Mr. Wilson: How do you know that, Mr. Chairman?
Senator Ervin: Because I can understand the English language. It is my mother tongue.

— From the Senate hearings on Watergate

There is a kind of lying which, in the words of Walker Gibson, we may call *public lying*. Its rules are to avoid substance, direct answers, and plain words. Its tendency is to subvert the English language. It employs and invents euphemisms, but the public liar intends to protect not his listeners, but himself and his friends, and he misleads and deceives consciously. Public lying was not invented during the Vietnam War or the Watergate hearings.

(In 1946 George Orwell had already written the definitive essay on it, "Politics and the English Language.") Nor did it cease with the return of American prisoners, or with the resignation of our thirty-seventh president. But the war and the hearings produced some classic examples, from which we select a few.

The war, of course, was not a war, but a "conflict" or an "era." "Our side" never attacked "the other side," we made "protective reaction raids"; we didn't invade, we "incursed." We didn't bomb villages, we "pacified" them; peasants were not herded into concentration camps, but "relocated." We didn't spray the countryside with poisons, destroying forests, endangering or killing plant, animal, and human life, we "practiced vegetation control."

"In the interests of national security," some buildings and rooms ("the White House," "the Oval Office") hired not burglars but "electronic surveillance experts" who didn't bug, spy, break and enter, or steal, but "performed intelligence-gathering operations" — all of this according to "a game plan" designed to ensure "deniability."

More recently, it was disclosed that the CIA experimented with brainwashing under cover of "The Society for Investigation of Human Ecology." The Pentagon now refers to the neutron bomb (which kills all living creatures but leaves valuable buildings intact) as a "radiation enhancement weapon." And when approx-

Feiffer

imately a million people in four counties surrounding the Three Mile Island nuclear power plant in Pennsylvania were threatened with "radiation enhancement" following a series of accidents, an officer of the Nuclear Regulatory Commission arrived to "dispel some of the multi-directional reports or facts." When asked by a reporter whether a menacing hydrogen bubble that had formed in the reactor could be removed, another official explained: "We are in a situation not comparable to previous conditions."

There is a Gresham's law in rhetoric as there is in economics: bad language drives out good. Bad language is contagious; learn to detect the symptoms: use of vague words for clear words; use of sentences or phrases where words suffice; evasive use of the passive voice; and outright lying.

Passive or Active Voice?

1. I baked the bread. (Active voice)
2. The bread was baked by me. (Passive voice)
3. The bread will be baked. (Passive voice)

Although it is the verb that is in the active or the passive voice, notice that the words *active* and *passive* describe the subjects of the sentences. That is, in the first sentence the verb "baked" is in the active voice; the subject "I" acts. In the second and third sentences the verbs "was baked" and "will be baked" are in the passive voice; the subject "bread" is acted upon. Notice also the following points:

1. The *voice* of the verb is distinct from its *tense*. Don't confuse the passive voice with the past tense. (Sentence 2 happens to be in the past tense, but 3 is not; both 2 and 3 are in the passive voice.)
2. The passive voice uses more words than the active voice. (Compare sentences 1 and 2.)
3. A sentence with a verb in the passive voice may leave the doer of the action unidentified. (See sentence 3.)
4. Finally, notice that in each of the three sentences the emphasis is different.

In revising, take a good look at each sentence in which you have used the passive voice. If the passive clarifies your meaning, retain it; if it obscures your meaning, change it. More often than not, the passive voice obscures meaning.

1. *Obscure*

The revolver given Daru by the gendarme is left in the desk drawer. (Left by whom? The passive voice here obscures the point.)

Clear

Daru leaves the gendarme's revolver in the desk drawer.

2. *Obscure*

Daru serves tea and the Arab is offered some. (Confusing shift from the active voice "serves" to the passive voice "is offered.")

Clear

Daru serves tea and offers the Arab some.

3. *Appropriate*

For over fifty years *Moby-Dick* was neglected. ("Was neglected" suggests that the novel was neglected by almost everyone. The passive voice catches the passivity of the response. Changing the sentence to "For over fifty years few readers read *Moby-Dick*" would make "readers" the subject of the sentence, but the true subject is — as in the original — *Moby-Dick*.)

Finally, avoid what has been called the Academic Passive: "In this essay it has been shown that. . . ." This cumbersome form used to be common in academic writing (to convey scientific objectivity) but *I* is usually preferable to such stuffiness.

The Writer's "I"

It is seldom necessary in writing an essay (even on a personal experience) to repeat "I think that" or "in my opinion." Your reader knows that what you write is your opinion. Nor is it necessary, if you've done your job well, to apologize. "After reading the story over several times I'm not really sure what it is about, but. . . ." Write about something you are reasonably sure of. Occasionally, though, when there is a real problem in the text, for example the probable date of the Book of Ruth, it is not only permissible to disclose doubts and to reveal tentative conclusions; it may be necessary to do so.

Note also that there is no reason to avoid the pronoun *I* when you are in fact writing about yourself. Attempts to avoid *I* ("this writer," "we," expressions in the passive voice such as "it has been said above" and "it was seen") are noticeably awkward and distracting. And sometimes you may want to focus on your subjective response to a topic in order to clarify a point. The following opening paragraph of a movie review provides an example:

> I take the chance of writing about Bergman's *Persona* so long after its showing because this seems to me a movie there's no hurry about. It will be with us a long time, just as it has been on my mind for a long time. Right now, when I am perhaps still under its spell, it seems to me Bergman's masterpiece, but I can't imagine ever thinking it less than one of the great movies. This of course is opinion; what I know for certain is that *Persona* is also one of the most difficult movies I will ever see; and I am afraid that in this case there is a direct connection between difficulty and value. It isn't only that *Persona* is no harder than it has to be; its peculiar haunting power, its spell, and its value come directly from the fact that it's so hard to get a firm grasp on.
>
> — Robert Garis

Students who have been taught not to begin sentences with *I* often produce sentences that are eerily passive even when the verbs are in the active voice. For example:

1. Two reasons are important to my active participation in dance.
2. The name of the program that I was in is the Health Careers Summer Program.
3. An eager curiosity overcame my previous feeling of fear to make me feel better.

But doesn't it make more sense to say:

1. I dance for two reasons.
2. I was enrolled in the Health Careers Summer Program.
3. My curiosity aroused, I was no longer afraid.

A good rule: make the agent of the action the subject of the sentence. A practical suggestion: to avoid a boring series of sentences all beginning with *I*, subordinate for conciseness and emphasis. (See pages 266–69 and 315–17.)

CLARITY AND COHERENCE

Writing a coherent essay is hard work; it requires mastery of a subject and skill in presenting it; it always takes a lot of time. Writing a coherent paragraph often takes more fussing and patching than you expect, but once you have the hang of it, it's relatively easy and pleasant. Writing a coherent sentence requires only that you stay awake until you get to the end of it. We all do nod sometimes, even over our own prose. But if you make it a practice to read your work over several times, at least once aloud, you give yourself a chance to spot the incoherent sentence before your reader does, and to revise it. Once you see that a sentence is incoherent, it's usually easy to recast it.

Cats Are Dogs

In some sentences a form of the verb *to be* asserts that one thing is in a class with another. Passover is a Jewish holiday. Dartmouth is a college. But would anyone not talking in his sleep say "Dartmouth is a Jewish Holiday"? Are cats dogs? Students did write the following sentences:

1. *Incoherent*

X. J. Kennedy's poem "Nothing in Heaven Functions as It Ought" is a contrast between Heaven and Hell. (As soon as you ask yourself the question "Is a poem a contrast?" you have, by bringing the two words close together, isolated the problem. A poem may be a sonnet, an epic, an ode — but not a contrast. The writer was trying to say what the poem does, not what it is.)

Coherent

X. J. Kennedy's poem "Nothing in Heaven Functions as It Ought" contrasts Heaven and Hell.

2. *Incoherent*

Besides, he tells himself, a matchmaker is an old Jewish custom. (Is a matchmaker a custom?)

Coherent

Besides, he tells himself, consulting a matchmaker is an old Jewish custom.

Try revising the following:

> The essay is also an insight into imperialism.

In a related problem, one part of the sentence doesn't know what the other is doing:

1. *Incoherent*

Ruth's devotion to Naomi is rewarded by marrying Boaz. (Does devotion marry Boaz?)

Coherent

Ruth's marriage to Boaz rewards her devotion to Naomi.

2. *Incoherent*

He demonstrates many human frailties, such as the influence of others' opinions upon one's actions. (Is influence a frailty? How might this sentence be revised?)

False Series

If you were given a shopping list that mentioned apples, fruit, and pears, you would be puzzled and possibly irritated by the inclusion of "fruit." Don't puzzle or irritate your reader. Analyze sentences containing items in a series to be sure that the items are of the same order of generality. For example:

False Series

His job exposed him to the "dirty work" of the British and to the evils of imperialism. ("The 'dirty work' of the British" is a *specific* example of the more *general* "evils of imperialism." The false series makes the sentence incoherent.)

Revised

His job, by exposing him to the "dirty work" of the British, brought him to understand the evils of imperialism.

In the following sentence, which item in the series makes the sentence incoherent?

> Why should one man, no matter how important, be exempt from investigation, arrest, trial, and law enforcing tactics?

Modifiers

A modifier should appear close to the word it modifies (that is, describes or qualifies). Three kinds of faulty modifiers are common: misplaced, squinting, and dangling.

MISPLACED MODIFIERS

If the modifier seems to modify the wrong word, it is called *misplaced*. Misplaced modifiers are often unintentionally funny. The judo parlor that advertised "For $20 learn basic methods of protecting yourself from an experienced instructor" probably attracted more amused readers than paying customers.

1. *Misplaced*

Orwell shot the elephant under pressured circumstances. (Orwell was under pressure, not the elephant. Put the modifier near what it modifies.)

Revised

Orwell, under pressure, shot the elephant.

2. *Misplaced*

Orwell lost his individual right to protect the elephant as part of the imperialistic system. (The elephant was not part of the system; Orwell was.)

Revised

As part of the imperialistic system, Orwell lost his right to protect the elephant.

3. *Misplaced*

Amos Wilder has been called back to teach at Harvard Divinity School after ten years retirement due to a colleague's illness. (Did Wilder retire for ten years because a colleague was ill? Revise the sentence.)

Revise the following:

1. Sitting Bull and William Cody stand side by side, each supporting a rifle placed between them with one hand.
2. Complete with footnotes the author has provided her readers with some background information.

Sometimes other parts of sentences are misplaced:

1. *Misplaced*

We learn from the examples of our parents who we are. (The sentence appears to say we are our parents.)

Revised

We learn who we are from the examples of our parents.

2. *Misplaced*

It is up to the students to revise the scheme, not the administrators. (We all know you can't revise administrators. Revise the sentence.)

SQUINTING MODIFIERS

If the modifier is ambiguous, that is, if it can be applied equally to more than one term, it is sometimes called a *squinting modifier*: it seems to look forward, and it seems to look backward.

1. *Squinting*

Being with Jennifer more and more enrages me. (Is the writer spending more time with Jennifer, or is he more enraged? Probably more enraged.)

Revised

Being with Jennifer enrages me more and more.

2. *Squinting*

Writing clearly is difficult. (The sentence may be talking about writing — it's clearly difficult to write — or about writing clearly — it's difficult to write clearly.)

3. *Squinting*

Students only may use this elevator. (Does "only" modify students? If so, no one else may use the elevator. Or does it modify elevator? If so, students may use no other elevator.)

Revised

Only students may use this elevator.
Students may use only this elevator.

Note: the word *only* often squints. In general, put *only* immediately before the word or phrase it modifies. Often it appears too early in the sentence. (See page 428.)

DANGLING MODIFIERS

If the term it should modify appears nowhere in the sentence, the modifier is called *dangling*.

1. *Dangling*

Being small, his ear scraped against the belt when his father stumbled. (The writer meant that the boy was small, not the ear. But the boy is not in the sentence.)

Revised

Because the boy was small his ear scraped against the belt when his father stumbled.

Being small, the boy scraped his ear against the belt when his father stumbled.

2. *Dangling*

A meticulously organized person, his suitcase could be tucked under an airplane seat. (How would you revise the sentence?)

The general rule: *when you revise sentences, put together what belongs together*.

Reference of Pronouns

A pronoun is used in place of a noun. Because the noun usually precedes the pronoun, the noun to which the pronoun refers is called the antecedent (Latin: "going before"). For example: in "When Sheriff Johnson was on a horse, he was a big man" the noun, "Sheriff Johnson," precedes the pronoun, "he." But the noun can also follow the pronoun, as in "When he was on a horse, Sheriff Johnson was a big man."

Be sure that whenever possible a pronoun has a clear reference. Sometimes it isn't possible: *it* is commonly used with an unspecified reference, as in "It's hot today," and "Hurry up please, it's time"; and there can be no reference for interrogative pronouns: "What's bothering you?" and "Who's on first?" But otherwise always be sure that you've made clear what noun the pronoun is standing for.

VAGUE REFERENCES

1. *Vague*

Apparently, they fight physically and it can become rather brutal. ("It" doubtless refers to "fight," but "fight" in this sentence is the verb, not an antecedent noun.)

Clear

Their fights are apparently physical, and sometimes brutal.

2. *Vague*

I was born in Colon, the second largest city in the Republic of Panama. Despite this, Colon is still an undeveloped town. ("This" has no specific antecedent. It appears to refer to the writer's having been born in Colon.)

Clear

Although Colon, where I was born, is the second largest city in Panama, it remains undeveloped.
(On *this,* see also page 433.)

Revise the following sentence:

They're applying to medical school because it's a well-paid profession.

SHIFT IN PRONOUNS

This common error is easily corrected.

1. In many instances the child was expected to follow the profession of your father. (Expected to follow the profession of whose father, "yours" or "his or hers"?)
2. Having a tutor, you can get constant personal encouragement and advice that will help me budget my time. (If "you" have a tutor will that help "me"?)
3. If one smokes, you should at least ask permission before you light up. (If "one" smokes, why should "you" ask permission? But here the change to "If one smokes, one should at least ask permission before one lights up," though correct, sounds inappropriately formal. Omit a "one": "If one smokes, one should at least ask permission before lighting up." Or forget about "one" and use "you" throughout the sentence.)

Revise the following sentences:

1. Schools bring people of the same age together and teach you how to get along with each other.
2. If asked why you went to a mixer, one might say they were simply curious.

AMBIGUOUS REFERENCE OF PRONOUNS

A pronoun normally refers to the first appropriate noun or pronoun preceding it. Same-sex pronouns and nouns, like dogs, often get into scraps.

1. *Ambiguous*

Her mother died when she was eighteen. (Who was eighteen, the mother or the daughter?)

Clear

Her mother died when Mabel was eighteen.
Her mother died at the age of eighteen. (Note the absence of ambiguity in "His mother died when he was eighteen.")

2. *Ambiguous*

Daru learns that he must take an Arab to jail against his will. (Both Daru and the Arab are male. The writer of the sentence meant that Daru learns he must act against his will.)

Clear

Daru learns that he must, against his will, take an Arab to jail.

The general rule: *put together what belongs together.*

Agreement

NOUN AND PRONOUN

Everyone knows that a singular noun requires a singular pronoun, and a plural noun requires a plural pronoun, but writers sometimes slip.

1. *Faulty*

A dog can easily tell if people are afraid of them.

Correct

A dog can easily tell if people are afraid of it.

2. *Faulty*

Every student feels that Wellesley expects them to do their best.

Correct

Every student feels that Wellesley expects her to do her best.

Each, everybody, nobody, no one, and *none* are especially troublesome. See the entries on these words in the chapter on usage.

SUBJECT AND VERB

A singular subject requires a singular verb, a plural subject a plural verb.

Faulty

Horror films bring to light a subconscious fear and shows a character who succeeds in coping with it.

Correct

Horror films bring to light a subconscious fear and show a character who succeeds in coping with it.

The student who wrote "shows" instead of "show" thought that the subject of the verb was "fear," but the subject really is "Horror films," a plural.

Faulty

The manager, as well as the pitcher and the catcher, were fined.

Correct

The manager, as well as the pitcher and the catcher, was fined.

If the sentence had been "The manager and the pitcher . . . ," the subject would have been plural and the required verb would be "were," but in the sentence as it is given, "as well as" (like *in addition to, with,* and *together with*) does *not* add a subject to a subject and thereby make a plural subject. "As well as" merely indicates that what is said about the manager applies to the pitcher and the catcher.

Revise the following:

About mid-morning during Spanish class the sound of jeeps were heard.

Sometimes a sentence that is grammatically correct may nevertheless sound awkward:

> One of its most noticeable features is the lounges.

Because the subject is "one," the verb must be singular, "is," but "is" sounds odd when it precedes the plural "lounges." The solution: revise the sentence.

> Among the most noticeable features are the lounges.

Repetition and Variation

1. Don't be afraid to repeat a word if it is the best word. The following paragraph repeats "interesting," "paradox," "Salinger," "What makes," and "book"; notice also "feel" and "feeling." Repetition, a device necessary for continuity and clarity, holds the paragraph together.

> The reception given to *Franny and Zooey* in America has illustrated again the interesting paradox of Salinger's reputation there; great public enthusiasm, of the *Time* magazine and Best Seller List kind, accompanied by a repressive coolness in the critical journals. What makes this a paradox is that the book's themes are among the most ambitiously highbrow, and its craftsmanship most uncompromisingly virtuoso. What makes it an interesting one is that those who are most patronising about the book are those who most resemble its characters; people whose ideas and language in their best moments resemble Zooey's. But they feel they ought not to enjoy the book. There is a very strong feeling in American literary circles that Salinger and love of Salinger must be discouraged.
>
> — Martin Green

2. Use pronouns, when their reference is clear, as substitutes for nouns. Notice Green's use of pronouns; notice also his substitution of "the book," for *"Franny and Zooey,"* and then "its" for "the book's." Substitutions that neither confuse nor distract keep a paragraph from sounding like a broken phonograph record.

3. Do not, however, confuse the substitutions we have just spoken of with the fault called Elegant Variation. A groundless fear of repetition sometimes leads students to write first, for example, of "Salinger," then of "the writer," then of "our author."

Such variations strike the reader as silly. They can, moreover, be confusing. Does "the writer" mean "Salinger," or the person writing about him? Substitute "he" for "Salinger" if "he" is clear and sounds better. Otherwise, repeat "Salinger."

4. But don't repeat a word if it is being used in two different senses.

1. *Confusing*

Green's theme focuses on the theme of the book. (The first "theme" means "essay"; the second means "underlying idea" or "motif.")

Clear

Green's essay focuses on the theme of the book.

2. *Confusing*

Caesar's character is complex. The comic characters, however, are simple. (The first "character" means "personality"; the second means "persons" or "figures in the play.")

Clear

Caesar is complex; the comic characters, however, are simple.

5. Finally, eliminate words repeated unnecessarily. Use of words like *surely, in all probability, it is noteworthy* may become habitual. If they don't help your reader to follow your thoughts, they are Instant Prose Additives. Cross them out.

In general, when you revise, decide if a word should be repeated, varied, or eliminated, by testing sentences and paragraphs for both sound and sense.

Euphony

The word is from the Greek, "sweet voice," and though you need not aim at sweetness, try to avoid cacophony, or "harsh voice." Avoid distracting repetitions of sound, as in "The story is marked by a remarkable mystery," and "This is seen in the scene in which. . . ." Such echoes call attention to themselves, getting in the way of the points you are making. When you revise, tune out irrelevant sound effects.

Not all sound effects are irrelevant; some contribute meaning. James Baldwin, in his essay "Stranger in the Village," argues that the American racial experience has permanently altered black and white relationships throughout the world. His concluding sentence is, "This world is white no longer, and it will never be white again." As the sentence opens, the repetition of sounds in "*w*orld is *w*hite," binds the two words together, but the idea that they are permanently bound is swiftly denied by the most emphatic repetition of sounds in "*no*," "*never*," "*again*," as the sentence closes. Or take another example: America, Love It or Leave It. If it read America, Love It or Emigrate, would the bumper sticker still imply, as clearly and menacingly, that there are only two choices, and for the patriot only one?

Transitions

Repetition holds a paragraph together by providing continuity and clarity. Transitions such as *next, on the other hand*, and *therefore* also provide continuity and clarity. Because we discuss transitions at length on pages 80–82, in our chapter on paragraphs, we here only remind you to make certain that the relation between one sentence and the next, and one paragraph and the next, is clear. Often it will be clear without an explicit transition: "She was desperately unhappy. She quit school." But do not take too much for granted; relationships between sentences may not be as clear to your readers as they are to you. You know what you are talking about; they don't. After reading the passage readers may see, in retrospect, that you have just given an example, or a piece of contrary evidence, or an amplification, but readers like to know in advance where they are going; brief transitions such as *for example, but, finally* (readers are keenly interested in knowing when they are getting near the end) are enormously helpful.

CLARITY AND SENTENCE STRUCTURE: PARALLELISM

Make the structure of your sentence reflect the structure of your thought. This is not as formidable as it sounds. If you keep your reader in mind, remembering that you are explaining something to someone who understands it less well than you, you will almost automatically not only say what you think but show how you think.

Almost automatically. In revising, read your work as if you were not the writer of it, but your intended reader. If you reach a bump or snag, where the shape of your thought, or the direction of it, isn't clear, revise your sentence structure. Three general rules help:

1. Put main ideas in main (independent) clauses.
2. Subordinate the less important elements in the sentence to the more important.
3. Put parallel ideas and details in parallel constructions.

The time to consult these rules consciously is not while you write, but while you revise. (The first two rules are amplified in the next chapter, "Revising for Emphasis." Clarity and emphasis are closely related, as the following discussion of parallel construction makes evident.)

Consider the following sentence and the revision:

Awkward
He liked eating and to sleep.

Parallel
He liked to eat and to sleep.

In the first version, "eating" and "to sleep" are not grammatically parallel; the difference in grammatical form blurs the writer's point that there is a similarity. Use parallel constructions to clarify relationships — for instance to emphasize similarities or to define differences.

> I divorce myself from my feelings and immerse myself in my obligations.
> > — From a student journal

> She drew a line between respect, which we were expected to show, and fear, which we were not.
> > — Ernesto Galarza

> I will not accept if nominated and will not serve if elected.
> > — William Tecumseh Sherman

> Fascist art glorifies surrender; it exalts mindlessness; it glamorizes death.
> > — Susan Sontag

In the following examples, the parallel construction is printed in italic type.

1. *Awkward*

The dormitory rules needed revision, a smoking area was a necessity, and a generally more active role for the school in social affairs were all significant to her.

Parallel

She recommended that the school *revise* its dormitory rules, *provide* a smoking area, and *organize* more social activities.

2. *Awkward*

Most Chinese parents disapprove of interracial dating or they just do not permit it.

Parallel

Most Chinese parents *disapprove* of interracial dating, and many *forbid* it.

Revise the following sentence:

The rogallo glider is recommended for beginners because it is easy to assemble, to maintain, and it is portable.

In parallel constructions, be sure to check the consistency of articles, prepositions, and conjunctions. For example, "He wrote papers on a play by Shakespeare, a novel by Dickens, and a story by Oates," *not* "He wrote papers on a play by Shakespeare, a novel of Dickens, and a story by Oates." The shift from "by" to "of" and back to "by" serves no purpose and is merely distracting.

Let's study this matter a little more, using a short poem as our text.

Love Poem

Robert Bly

When we are in love, we love the grass,
And the barns, and the lightpoles,
And the small mainstreets abandoned all night.

Suppose we change "Love Poem" by omitting a conjunction or an article here and there:

> When we are in love, we love the grass,
> Barns, and lightpoles,
> And the small mainstreets abandoned all night.

We've changed the rhythm, of course, but we still get the point: the lover loves all the world. In the original poem, however, the syntax of the sentence, the consistent repetition of "and the . . ." "and the . . ." makes us feel, without our thinking about it, that when we are in love we love the world, everything in it, equally. The list could extend infinitely, and everything in it would give us identical pleasure. In our altered version, we sacrifice this unspoken assurance. We bump a little, and stumble. As readers, without consciously being aware of it, we wonder if there's some distinction being made, some qualification we've missed. We still get the point of the poem, but we don't feel it the same way.

To sum up:

> A pupil once asked Arthur Schnabel [the noted pianist] whether it was better to play in time or to play as one feels; his characteristic mordant reply was another question: "Why not feel in time?"
>
> — David Hamilton

EXERCISES

1. Identify the specific faults that make the following sentences unclear, then revise each sentence for clarity. (Note that you will often have to invent what the writer thought he or she had said.)

   a. Actually, she was aging, and quite average in other respects.
   b. If technology cannot sort out its plusses and minuses, and work to improve them, man must.
   c. Brooks stresses the farm workers' strenuous way of life and the fact that they have the bare necessities of life.
   d. Instead of movable furniture, built-in ledges extend into the center of the room to be used as tables or to sit on.
   e. The issue has been saved for my final argument because it is controversial.
   f. I am neither indifferent nor fond of children.

g. When the students heard that their proposal was rejected a meeting was called.

h. A viable library is the cornerstone of any college campus.

i. Her main fault was that she was somewhat lacking in decision-making capabilities.

j. After industrialization a swarm of immigrants came bantering to our shores.

k. Each group felt there was very personal rapport and thus very candid feedback resulted.

l. He can tolerate crowding and pollution and seems disinterested or ignorant of these dangers.

m. The wooden door occupies the majority of the stone wall.

n. In *A History of the English Church and People* Bede uses examples from the past to enforce his own position.

o. One must strive hard to reach their goal.

p. Yale students frequently write to Ann Landers telling her fictional stories of their so-called troubles as a childish prank.

q. At my grandmother's house vegetables were only served because meat was forbidden.

r. My firm stand seemed to melt a little.

s. The conclusion leaves the conflict neatly tied in smooth knots.

t. The paragraph reeks of blandness.

2. The following sentences, published in *AIDE*, a magazine put out by an insurance company, were written to the company by various policyholders. The trouble is that the writers mean one thing but their sentences say another. Make each sentence clearly say what the writer means.

a. The other car collided with mine without giving warning of its intentions.

b. I collided with a stationary truck coming the other way.

c. The guy was all over the road; I had to swerve a number of times before I hit him.

d. I pulled away from the side of the road, glanced at my mother-in-law, and headed over the embankment.

e. In my attempt to kill a fly, I drove into a telephone pole.

f. I had been driving for forty years when I fell asleep at the wheel and had the accident.

g. To avoid hitting the bumper of the car in front, I struck the pedestrian.

h. The pedestrian had no idea which direction to run, so I ran over him.

i. The indirect cause of this accident was a little guy in a small car with a big mouth.

14
*Revising
for
Emphasis*

In revising for conciseness and clarity we begin to discover what we may have been largely unaware of in the early stages of writing: what in our topic most concerns us and precisely why it interests us. That moment of discovery (or those several discrete moments) yields more pleasure than any other in writing. From there on we work, sometimes as if inspired, to make our special angle of vision seem as inevitable to our readers as it is to us. Now as we tighten sentences or expand them, as we shift the position of a word or a paragraph, or as we subordinate a less important idea to a more important one, we are assigning relative value and weight to each of our statements. The expression of value and weight is what is meant by emphasis.

Inexperienced writers may *try* to achieve emphasis as Queen Victoria did, by a style consisting *almost entirely* of italics and exclamation marks!!! Or they may spice their prose with clichés ("little did I realize," "believe it or not") or with a liberal sprinkling of intensifiers ("really beautiful," "definitely significant," and so on). But experienced writers abandon these unconvincing devices. Emphasis is more securely achieved by exploiting the possibilities of position, of brevity and length, of repetition, and of subordination.

EMPHASIS BY POSITION

First, let's see how a word or phrase may be emphasized. If it appears in an unusual position it gains emphasis, as in "This course he liked." Because in English the object of the verb usually comes after the verb (as in "He liked this course"), the object is emphasized if it appears first. But this device is tricky; words in an unusual position often seem ludicrous, the writer fatuous: "A mounted Indian toward the forest raced."

Let's now consider a less strained sort of emphasis by position. The beginning and the end of a sentence or a paragraph are emphatic positions; of these two positions, the end is usually the more emphatic. What comes last is what stays most in the mind. Compare these two sentences:

> The essay is brief but informative.
> The essay is informative but brief.

The first sentence leaves the reader with the impression that the essay, despite its brevity, is worth looking at. The second, however, ends more negatively, leaving the reader with the impression that the essay is so brief that its value is fairly slight. Because the emphasis in each sentence is different, the two sentences say different things.

It usually makes sense, then, to put the important point near the end, lest the sentence become anticlimactic. Here is a sentence that properly moves to an emphatic end:

> Although I could not read its six hundred pages in one sitting, I never willingly put it down.

If the halves are reversed the sentence trails off:

> I never willingly put it down, although I could not read its six hundred pages in one sitting.

This second version straggles away from the real point — that the book was interesting.

Anticlimactic
Besides not owning themselves women also could not own property.

Emphatic

Women could not own property; in fact, they did not own themselves.

The commonest anticlimaxes are caused by weak qualifiers (*in my opinion, it seems to me, in general, etc.*) tacked on to interesting statements. Weak qualifiers usually can be omitted. Even useful ones rarely deserve an emphatic position.

Anticlimactic

Poodles are smart but they are no smarter than pigs, I have read.

Emphatic

Poodles are smart, but I have read that they are not smarter than pigs.

The rule: try to bury dull but necessary qualifiers in the middle of the sentence.

EMPHASIS BY BREVITY AND LENGTH: SHORT AND LONG SENTENCES

How long should a sentence be? One recalls Lincoln's remark to a heckler who asked him how long a man's legs should be: "Long enough to reach the ground." No rules about length can be given, but careful not to bore your reader with a succession of short sentences (say, under ten words) and be careful not to tax your reader with a monstrously long sentence. Victor Hugo's sentence in *Les Misérables* containing 823 words punctuated by ninety-three commas, fifty-one semicolons, and four dashes, is not a good model for beginners.

Consider this succession of short sentences:

The purpose of the refrain is twofold. First, it divides the song into stanzas. Second, it reinforces the theme of the song.

These sentences are clear, but since the points are simple the reader feels he is addressed as though he were a kindergarten child. There is too much emphasis (too many heavy pauses) on too little. The reader can take all three sentences at once:

The purpose of the refrain is twofold: it divides the song into stanzas and it reinforces the theme.

The three simple sentences have been turned into one compound sentence, allowing the reader to keep going for a while.

Now compare another group of sentences with a revision.

> Hockey is by far the fastest moving team sport in America. The skaters are constantly on the go. They move at high speeds. The action rarely stops.

These four sentences, instead of suggesting motion, needlessly stop us. Here is a revision:

> Hockey is by far the fastest moving team sport in America. The skaters, constantly on the go, move at high speeds, and the action rarely stops.

By combining the second, third, and fourth sentences, the reader, like the players, is kept on the go.

Next, a longer example that would be thoroughly delightful if parts of it were less choppy.

Conceit

At my high school graduation we had two speakers. One was a member of our class, and the other was a faculty member. The student speaker's name was Alva Reed. The faculty speaker's name was Mr. Williams. The following conversation took place after the graduation ceremony. Parents, relatives, faculty, and friends were all outside the gymnasium congratulating the class of 1979. Alva was surrounded by her friends, her parents, and some faculty members who were congratulating her on her speech. Not standing far from her was Mr. Williams with somewhat the same crowd.

"Alva dear, you were wonderful!"

"Thanks Mom. I sure was scared though; I'm glad it's over."

At that moment, walking towards Alva were her grandparents. They both were wearing big smiles on their faces. Her grandfather said rather loudly, "That was a good speech dear. Nicely done, nicely done." Walking past them at that moment was Mr. Williams. He stuck his head into their circle and replied, "Thank you," and walked away.

The first four sentences seem to be written in spurts. They can easily be combined and improved thus:

> At my high school graduation we had two speakers. One was a member of our class, Alva Reed, and the other was a faculty member, Mr. Williams.

If we think that even this version, two sentences instead of four, is a little choppy, we can rewrite it into a single sentence:

> At my high school graduation we had two speakers, Alva Reed, a member of our class, and Mr. Williams, a faculty member.

Or:

> The two speakers at my high school graduation were Alva Reed, a member of our class, and Mr. Williams, a faculty member.

The rest of the piece is less choppy, but reread it and see if you don't discover some other sentences that should be combined. Revise them.

Sometimes, however, the choppiness of a succession of short sentences is effective. Look at this description of the methods by which George Jackson, in prison, resisted efforts to destroy his spirit:

> He trains himself to sleep only three hours a night. He studies Swahili, Chinese, Arabic and Spanish. He does pushups to control his sexual urge and to train his body. Sometimes he does a thousand a day. He eats only one meal a day. And, always, he is reading and thinking.
>
> — Julius Lester

That the author is capable of writing longer, more complicated sentences is evident in the next paragraph:

> Yet, when his contact with the outside world is extended beyond his family to include Angela Davis, Joan, a woman who works with the Soledad defense committee, and his attorney, he is able to find within himself feelings of love and tenderness.

Can we account for the success of the passage describing Jackson's prison routine? First, the short sentences, with their repeated commonplace form (subject, verb, object) in some degree imitate Jackson's experience: they are almost monotonously disciplined, almost as regular as the pushups the confined Jackson does. Later, when Jackson makes contact with Angela Davis and others, the long sentence helps to suggest the expansion of his world. Second, the brevity of the sentences suggests their enormous importance, certainly to Jackson and to Julius Lester and, Lester hopes, to the reader.

Keep in mind this principle: *any one sentence in your essay is roughly equal to any other sentence.* If a sentence is short, it must be relatively weighty. A lot is packed into a little. Less is more. (The chief exceptions are transitional sentences such as, "Now for the second point.") Consider the following passage:

> It happened that in September of 1933 Lord Rutherford, at the British Association meeting, made some remark about atomic energy never becoming real. Leo Szilard was the kind of scientist, perhaps just the kind of good-humored, cranky man, who disliked any statement that contained the word "never," particularly when made by a distinguished colleague. So he set his mind to think about the problem.
>
> — Jacob Bronowski

The first two sentences are relatively long (twenty-three words and thirty-one words); the third is relatively short (ten words), and its brevity — its weight or density — emphasizes Szilard's nonsense attitude.

EMPHASIS BY REPETITION

Don't be afraid to repeat a word if it is important. The repetition will add emphasis. Notice in these lucid sentences by Helen Gardner the effective repetition of "end" and "beginning."

> *Othello* has this in common with the tragedy of fortune, that the end in no way blots out from the imagination the glory of the beginning. But the end here does not merely by its darkness throw up into relief the brightness that was. On the contrary, beginning and end chime against each other. In both the value of life and love is affirmed.

The substitution of "conclusion" or "last scene" for the second "end" would be worse than pointless; it would destroy Miss Gardner's point that there is *identity* or correspondence between beginning and end.

EMPHASIS BY SUBORDINATION

Five Kinds of Sentences

Before we can discuss the use of subordination for emphasis, we must first talk about what a sentence is, and about five kinds of sentences.

If there is an adequate definition of a sentence, we haven't found it. Perhaps the best definition is not the old one, "a complete thought," but "a word or group of words that the reader takes to be complete." This definition includes such utterances as "Who?" and "Help!" and "Never!" and "Maybe." Now, in speaking, "While he was walking down the street" may be taken as a complete thought, if it answers the question "When did the car hit him?" In writing, however, it would be a sentence fragment that probably should be altered to, say, "While he was walking down the street he was hit by a car." We will discuss intentional fragments on pages 314–15 and ways to correct unintentional fragments on pages 380–82. But first we should take a closer look at complete sentences.

Usually a sentence names someone or something (this is the subject) and it tells us something about the subject (this is the predicate); that is, it "predicates" something about the subject. Let us look at five kinds of sentences: simple, compound, complex, compound-complex, and sentence fragments.

1. A *simple sentence* has one predicate, here italicized:

Shakespeare *died.*
Shakespeare and Jonson *were contemporaries.*

The subject can be elaborated ("Shakespeare and Jonson, England's chief Renaissance dramatists, were contemporaries"), or the predicate can be elaborated ("Shakespeare and Jonson were contemporaries in the Renaissance England of Queen Elizabeth"); but the sentence remains technically a simple sentence, consisting of only one main (independent) clause with no dependent (subordinate) clause.

2. A *compound sentence* has two or more main clauses, each containing a subject and a predicate. It is, then, two or more simple sentences connected by a coordinating conjunction (*and, but, for, nor, or, yet*) or by *not only . . . but also*, or by a semicolon or colon or, rarely, by a comma.

> Shakespeare died in 1616, and Jonson died in 1637.
> Shakespeare not only wrote plays, but he also acted in them.
> Shakespeare died in 1616; Jonson died twenty-one years later.

3. A *complex sentence* has one main (independent) clause and one or more subordinate (dependent) clauses. Here the main clause is italicized.

> Although Shakespeare died, *England survived.*
> *Jonson did not write a commemorative poem* when Shakespeare died.

The parts not italicized are subordinate or dependent because they cannot stand as sentences by themselves.

4. A *compound-complex sentence* has two or more main clauses (here italicized) and one or more subordinate clauses.

> *In 1616 Shakespeare died* and *his wife inherited the second-best bed* because he willed it to her.

Each of the two italicized passages could stand by itself as a sentence, but "because he willed it to her" could not (except as the answer to a question). Each italicized passage, then, is a main (independent) clause, and "because he willed it to her" is a subordinate (dependent) clause.

We will return to subordination, but let us first look at the fifth kind of sentence, the sentence fragment.

5. A *sentence fragment* does not fit the usual definition of a sentence, but when the fragment is intended the thought is often clear and complete enough. Intentional fragments are common in advertisements:

> Made of imported walnut. For your pleasure. At finer stores.
> More native than the Limbo. More exciting than the beat of a steel drum. Tia Maria. Jamaica's haunting liqueur.

And yet another example, this one not from an advertisement but from an essay on firewood:

> Piles of it. Right off the sidewalk. Split from small logs of oak or ash or maple. Split. Split again.
>
> — John McPhee

All these examples strike us as pretentious in their obviously studied efforts at understatement. Words are hoarded, as though there is much in little, and as though to talk more fully would demean the speaker and would desecrate the subject. A few words, and then a profound silence. Here less is not more; it is too much. The trouble with these fragmentary sentences is not that they don't convey complete thoughts but that they attract too much attention to themselves; they turn our minds too emphatically to their writers, and conjure up images of unpleasantly self-satisfied oracles.

Here, however, is a passage from a student's essay, where the fragmentary sentences seem satisfactory to us. The passage begins with a simple sentence, and then gives three fragmentary sentences.

> The film has been playing to sellout audiences. Even though the acting is inept. Even though the sound is poorly synchronized. Even though the plot is incoherent.

If this passage is successful, it is because the emphasis is controlled. The author is dissatisfied, and by means of parallel fragments (each beginning with the same words) she conveys a moderately engaging weariness and a gentle exasperation.

Then, too, we see that if the first three periods were changed to commas we would have an orthodox complex sentence. In short, because the fragments are effective we find them acceptable.

For ways to correct ineffective or unacceptable fragments, see pages 380–82.

Subordination

Having surveyed the kinds of sentences, we can at last talk about using subordination to give appropriate emphasis.

Make sure that the less important element is subordinate to the more important. In the following example the first clause, summarizing the writer's previous sentences, is a subordinate or dependent clause; the new material is made emphatic by being put into two independent clauses, italicized here:

> As soon as the Irish Literary Theatre was assured of a nationalist backing, *it started to dissociate itself from any political aim,* and *the long struggle with the public began.*

The second and third clauses in this sentence, linked by "and," are coordinate — that is, of equal importance.

Probably most of the sentences that you read and write are complex sentences: an independent clause and one or more subordinate clauses. Whatever is outside of the independent clause is subordinate, less important. Consider this sentence:

> When Miss Horniman provided money, Yeats dreamed of a poetic drama.

The writer puts Yeats's dream in the independent clause, subordinating the relatively unimportant Miss Horniman. Miss Horniman and her money are of some importance, of course, or they would not have been mentioned, but they are *less* important than Yeats's dream. (Notice, by the way, that emphasis by subordination often works along with emphasis by position. Here the independent clause comes *after* the subordinate clause; the writer appropriately put the more important material in the more emphatic position.) Had the writer wished to give Miss Horniman more prominence, the passage might have run:

> Yeats dreamed of a poetic drama, and Miss Horniman subsidized that dream.

Here Miss Horniman at least stands in an independent clause, linked to the previous independent clause by "and." The two clauses, and the two people, are now of approximately equal importance. If the writer had wanted to emphasize Miss Horniman and to deemphasize Yeats, she might have written:

> While Yeats dreamed of a poetic drama, Miss Horniman provided the money.

Here Yeats is reduced to the subordinate clause, and Miss Horniman is given the dignity of the only independent clause. (And again notice that the important point is also in the emphatic position, near the end of the sentence. A sentence is likely to sprawl if an independent clause comes first, followed by a long subordinate clause of lesser importance, such as the sentence you are now reading. See the discussion of emphasis by position on pages 308–09.)

In short, though simple sentences and compound sentences have their place, they make everything of equal importance. Since everything is not of equal importance, you must often write complex and compound-complex sentences, subordinating some things to other things. Look again at the first four sentences of "Conceit" (page 310), and at the suggested revisions.

Having made the point that subordination reduces monotony and conveys appropriate emphasis, we must again say that there are times when a succession of simple or compound sentences is effective, as in the passage on page 311 describing George Jackson. As a rough rule, however, don't write more than two consecutive simple sentences unless you know what you are doing.

EXERCISES

1. Here is one way to test your grasp of the relationship of independent and subordinate elements in a sentence. This *haiku* (a Japanese poetic form) consists of one sentence that can be written as prose: "After weeks of watching the roof leak, I fixed it tonight by moving a single board."

Hitch Haiku

Gary Snyder

After weeks of watching the roof leak
   I fixed it tonight
by moving a single board.

---

   a. Identify the independent clause and the subordinate elements in the poem.
   b. The "I" in the poem's sentence does or has done three things. Write three simple sentences, each expressing one of the actions.

    c. Write one sentence in which all three of the poem's actions are expressed, but put in the independent clause one of the two actions that appear in a subordinate element in the poem.

    d. Compare your sentence with the poem's. Both sentences should be clear. How do they vary in emphasis?

    e. Optional: Compare the original sentence written as poetry and written as prose.

2. First identify the fault or faults that make the following sentences unemphatic, and then revise them for emphasis.

    a. He lists some of the rights given to humans and things and both admits and accounts for the oddity of his proposal well by citing examples.

    b. Rights for women, blacks and the insane were granted though many couldn't see the value in it and so now our environment should be granted rights even though it takes some getting used to the idea.

    c. Thus Creon's pride forces Antigone's death which drives his son to suicide and then his wife.

    d. Stock breeding will give the same result as population evolution, defenders of positive eugenics claim.

    e. The family today lacks the close relationship it had before the industrial age, for example.

    f. The woman's face is distraught, her hair is unkempt, and her dress is rumpled.

    g. There is probably no human being who would enjoy being eaten by a shark.

3. Analyze the ways of achieving emphasis in the following passage by Theodore Roosevelt on Grand Canyon.

> In Grand Canyon Arizona has a natural wonder which, so far as I know, is in kind absolutely unparalleled throughout the rest of the world. . . . Leave it as it is. You cannot improve upon it. The ages have been at work on it, and man can only mar it. What you can do is to keep it for your children, your children's children, and for all those who come after you as one of the great sights which every American, if he can travel at all, should see.

PART THREE
Acquiring Style and Fluency

Two monks were arguing about a flag.
One said: "The flag is moving."
The other said: "The wind is moving."
The sixth patriarch happened to be
passing by. He told them: "Not the wind,
not the flag: mind is moving."

— ZEN ANECDOTE

15
Defining Style

The style is the man.
    — BUFFON
(or the woman)
    — BARNET AND STUBBS

Style is not simply a flower here and some gilding there; it pervades the whole work. Van Gogh's style, or Walt Disney's, let us say, consists in part of features recurring throughout a single work and from one work to the next: angular or curved lines, hard or soft edges, strong or gentle contrasts, and so on. Pictures of a seated woman by each of the two artists are utterly different, and if we have seen a few works by each, we can readily identify who did which one. Artists leave their fingerprints, so to speak, all over their work; writers leave their voiceprints.

The word *style* comes from the Latin *stilus,* a Roman writing instrument. Even in Roman times *stilus* had acquired a figurative sense, referring not only to the instrument but also to the writer's choice of words and arrangement of words into sentences. But is it simply the choice and arrangement of words we comment on when we speak of a writer's style, or are we also commenting on the writer's mind? Don't we feel that a piece of writing, whether it's on Civil War photographs or on genetics and intelligence, is also about the writer? The writing, after all, sets forth the writer's views of his or her topic. It sets forth perceptions and responses to something the writer has thought about. The writer has, from the start, from the choice of a topic, revealed that he or she found it worth thinking about. The essay, in attempting to persuade us to think as the writer does, reveals not only how and what the writer thinks, but what he or she values.

When we write about things "out there," our writing always reveals the form and likeness of our minds, just as every work of art reveals the creator as well as the ostensible subject. A portrait painting, for example, is not only about the sitter; it is about the artist's perceptions of the sitter, hence the saying that every portrait is a self-portrait. Even photographs are as much about the photographer as they are about the subject. Richard Avedon said of his portraits of famous people, "They are all pictures of me, of the way I feel about the people I photograph." A student's essay similarly, if it is truly written, is not exclusively about "*La Causa* and the New Chicana"; it is also about her perceptions and responses to both racism and sexism.

Still, a useful distinction can be made between the author and the speaker of an essay. The flesh-and-blood author creates, through words, a particular speaker or voice or (to use the term common in literary criticism) persona. The persona is the author in a role adopted for a specific audience. When Abraham Lincoln wrote, he sometimes did so in the persona of the commander in chief of the Union Army, but he sometimes did so in the very different persona of the simple man from Springfield, Illinois. The persona is a mask put on for a performance (*persona* is the Latin word for mask). If mask suggests insincerity, we should remember that whenever we speak or write we do so in a specific role — as friend, or parent, or teacher, or applicant for a job, or whatever. Although Lincoln was a husband, a father, a politician, a president, and many other things, when he wrote a letter to his son, the persona (or, we might say, personality) is that of the father, not that of the commander in chief. The distinction between the writer (who necessarily fills many roles) and the persona who writes or speaks a given work is especially useful in talking about satire, because the satirist often invents a mouthpiece very different from himself or herself. The satirist — say Jonathan Swift — may be strongly opposed to a view, but the persona (the invented essayist) may favor the view; the reader must perceive that the real writer is ridiculing the invented essayist.

STYLE AND TONE

The style is the man. Rather say the
style is the way the man takes himself.
— ROBERT FROST

Suppose we take a page of handwriting, or even a signature.
We need not believe that graphology is an exact science to believe
that the shape of the ink-lines on paper (apart from the meaning
of the words) often tells us something about the writer. We look
at a large, ornate signature, and we sense that the writer is confident; we look at a tiny signature written with the finest of pens,
and we wonder why anyone is so self-effacing.

More surely than handwriting, the writer's style reveals,
among other things, his attitude toward himself (as Frost's addition
to Buffon's epigram suggests), toward his reader, and toward his
subject. The writer's attitudes are reflected in what is usually called
tone. It is difficult to distinguish between style and tone, but we
can try. Most discussions of style concentrate on what might be
thought of as ornament: figurative language ("a sea of troubles"),
inversion ("A leader he is not"), repetition and parallelism ("government of the people, by the people, for the people"), balance
and antithesis ("It was the best of times, it was the worst of times").
Indeed, for centuries style has been called "the dress of thought,"
implying that the thought is something separate from the expression; the thought, in this view, is dressed up in stylistic devices.
But in most of the writing that we read with interest and pleasure
the stylistic devices are not ornamental and occasional but integral
and pervasive. When we talk about wit, sincerity, tentativeness,
self-assurance, aggressiveness, objectivity, and so forth, we can
say we are talking about style, but we should recognize that style
now is not a matter of ornamental devices that dress up some idea,
but part of the idea itself. And "the idea itself" includes the writer's
unified yet appropriately varied tone of voice. To take a brief
example: the famous English translation of Caesar's report of a
victory, "I came, I saw, I conquered," might be paraphrased thus:
"After getting to the scene of the battle I studied the situation.
Then I devised a strategy that won the battle." But this paraphrase
loses much of Caesar's message; the brevity and the parallelism of

the famous version, as well as the alliteration (*c*ame, *c*onquered), convey tight-lipped self-assurance — convey, that is, the tone that reveals Caesar to us. And this tone is a large part of Caesar's message. Caesar is really telling us not only about what he did, but about what sort of person he is. He is perceptive, decisive, and effective. The three actions, Caesar in effect tells us, are (for a man like Caesar) one. (The Latin original is even more tight-lipped and more unified by alliteration: *veni, vidi, vici*.)

Here is a short paragraph from John Szarkowski's *Looking at Photographs*. Szarkowski is writing about one of Alexander Gardner's photographs of a dead Confederate sharpshooter.

> Among the pictures that Gardner made himself is the one reproduced here. Like many Civil War photographs, it showed that the dead of both sides looked very much the same. The pictures of earlier wars had not made this clear.

Try, in a word or two, to characterize the tone (the attitude, as we sense it in the inflection of the voice) of the first sentence. Next, the tone of the second, and then of the third. Suppose the second and third sentences had been written thus:

> It showed that the dead of both sides looked very much the same. This is made clear in Civil War photographs, but not in pictures of earlier wars.

How has the tone changed? What word can you find to characterize the tone of the whole, as Szarkowski wrote it?

Now another passage from Szarkowski's book:

> Jacob A. Riis was a newspaper reporter by occupation and a social reformer by inclination. He was a photographer rather briefly and apparently rather casually; it seems beyond doubt that he considered photography a useful but subservient tool for his work as reporter and reformer. It is clear that he had no interest in "artistic" photography, and equally clear that the artistic photographers of his time had no interest in him.

Do you find traces of Szarkowski's voiceprint here?

Finally, a longer passage by the same writer. After you read it, try to verbalize the resemblances between this and the other passages — the qualities that allow us to speak of the writer's tone.

> There are several possible explanations for the fact that women have been more important to photography than their numbers alone

would warrant. One explanation might be the fact that photography has never had licensing laws or trade unions, by means of which women might have been effectively discriminated against. A second reason might be the fact that the specialized technical preparation for photography need not be enormously demanding, so that the medium has been open to those unable to spend long years in formal study.

A third possible reason could be that women have a greater natural talent for photography than men do. Discretion (or cowardice) suggests that this hypothesis is best not pursued, since a freely speculative exploration of it might take unpredictable and indefensible lines. One might for example consider the idea that the art of photography is in its nature receptive, or passive, thus suggesting that women are also.

STYLE AND LEVELS OF USAGE

Although the dividing lines between levels of usage cannot always be drawn easily, tradition recognizes three: *formal, informal,* and *popular* or *vulgar.* Sometimes *popular* is used to designate a level between informal and vulgar. (*Vulgar* here doesn't mean dirty words; rather, it refers to the speech characteristic of uneducated people, speech that uses such expressions as *ain't, nohow,* and *he don't.*) In textbooks, the most obvious purpose of discussions of these levels has been to dislodge older, more rigid ideas about "good" and "bad" or "correct" and "incorrect" English, and to replace them with the more flexible and more accurate standard of appropriateness. The labels *formal* and *informal* (we can for the moment drop *vulgar,* since few essays are written in it) attempt to describe the choices a writer makes under particular circumstances, rather than to prescribe those he ought to make under all circumstances. The choices, often unconscious, include those of vocabulary, sentence structure, and tone.

Formal writing, found mostly in scholarly articles, textbooks, ceremonial speeches, and scientific reports, assumes an audience not only generally well educated but also with special knowledge of or interest in the writer's subject. The writer can therefore use a wide vocabulary (including words and references that in another context would be pretentious or obscure) and sentence patterns that demand close attention. A noted figure, say a

respected literary critic, examining an influential book and addressing the world of thoughtful readers, may use a formal style, as
Lionel Trilling does here in a criticism of V. L. Parrington's *Main
Currents in American Literature*. Trilling assumes an attentive reader,
capable of holding in mind a long sentence.

> To throw out Poe because he cannot be conveniently fitted into
> a theory of American culture, to speak of him as a biological sport
> and as a mind apart from the main current, to find his gloom to be
> merely personal and eccentric, "only the atrabilious wretchedness
> of a dipsomaniac," as Hawthorne's was "no more than the skeptical
> questioning of life by a nature that knew no fierce storms," to judge
> Melville's response to American life to be less noble than that of
> Bryant or of Greeley, to speak of Henry James as an escapist, as an
> artist similar to Whistler, a man characteristically afraid of stress —
> this is not merely to be mistaken in aesthetic judgment; rather it is
> to examine without attention and from the point of view of a limited
> and essentially arrogant conception of reality the documents which
> are in some respects the most suggestive testimony to what America
> was and is, and of course to get no answer from them.
>
> — Lionel Trilling

Now, although "to throw out" is fairly informal, as opposed to,
say, "to dismiss," the sentence as a whole is formal. Notice the
structure: "To throw . . . to speak . . . to find . . . to judge . . .
to speak," and we still do not have an independent clause. Two-
thirds of the way through, with "this is not merely to be mistaken," the previous words come into focus, but the meaning is
still incomplete. To do such-and-such "is not merely to be mistaken," but what *is* it to be? At last we are told: "it is to examine
without attention . . . and . . . to get no answer. . . ."

A formal sentence need not be long. Here is a fairly short
formal sentence by W. H. Auden:

> Owing to its superior power as a mnemonic, verse is superior to
> prose as a medium for didactic instruction.

In another frame of mind Auden might have written something
less formal, along these lines:

> Because it stays more easily in the memory, verse is better than
> prose for teaching.

This revision of Auden's sentence can be called informal, but it is high on the scale, the language of an educated man writing courteously to an audience he conceives of as his peers. It is the level of almost all serious writing about literature. A low informal version might be:

> Poetry sticks in the mind better than prose; so if you want to teach something, poetry is better.

This is the language any of us might use in conversation; it is almost never the language used in writing to our peers.

Finding the Appropriate Level

What is appropriate in writing, as in dress, is subject to change, and the change recently has been to greater informality in both. Students who attend classes, concerts, and even their own weddings in blue jeans might experiment with similar freedom in writing college essays, and work toward a style that feels comfortable and natural to them. Developing a natural style, writing at an appropriate level, does take work. Consider, for example, the following opening paragraph from a student's theme:

> The college experience is traumatic, often because one must adjust not only to new academic horizons and new friends but also to the new physical environment constituted by the college and by the community surrounding it. One might think that, coming from a city only sixty miles from Wellesley, I would be exempt from this aspect of adaptation. However, this assumption has proven to be false.

"Traumatic"? "Academic horizons"? "Constituted"? "Exempt from this aspect of adaptation"? "Assumption . . . proven to be false"? There's nothing wrong with the language here, that is, nothing ungrammatical. But the paragraph has a hollow ring, a tone of insincerity, because the diction and syntax — the writer's level of usage — so ill suit the theme: a personal and spirited defense of the writer's lower-middle-class industrial home town, whose liveliness, friendliness, and above all, informality, she emphatically prefers to the aloofness of suburban Wellesley.

By contrast, in a review of *Soledad Brother — The Prison Letters of George Jackson,* another student described Jackson's style

"Robert? Oh, he's out somewhere chasing a buck."

Drawing by Whitney Darrow, Jr.; © 1978 The New Yorker Magazine, Inc.

as "clear, simple, expressive, and together." The word "together," though technically incorrect (an adverb, here used as an adjective), strikes us, in context, as exactly right. And, when later in the essay we read "Surviving on glasses of water, crumbs of bread, deep concentration, daily push-ups, and cigarettes, Jackson shouts to the black world to wake up: get off your knees and start kicking asses," we feel that the deliberately inconsistent use of the formal series of parallels with the colloquial or vulgar "kicking asses" exactly expresses both Jackson's discipline and rage, and the writer's empathy with them.

In most of your college writing you are addressing people like yourself; use a language that you would like to read, neither stuffy nor aggressively colloquial. Probably it will stand somewhere in between the levels of "aspects of adaptation" and "kicking asses."

Tone: Four Examples

The first two excerpts are the opening paragraphs of two speeches. The third, though not an opening paragraph, is also from a speech. The fourth, by Pauline Kael, is the beginning of an essay on the tedium of most modern films.

1. It is indeed both an honor and a challenge to be invited to participate in this most significant occasion, the observance of the one hundredth anniversary of the birth of Max Weber. It is also a great pleasure to revisit the University of Heidelberg, though not quite for the first time, just short of forty years after my enrollment here as a student in 1925. This was too late to know Max Weber in person, but of course his intellectual influence was all-pervasive in the Heidelberg of that time, constituting the one primary point of reference about which all theoretical and much empirical discussion in the social and cultural fields revolved. I was also privileged to know his gracious and highly intelligent widow, Marianne Weber, in particular to attend a number of her famous "sociological teas" on Sunday afternoons. It was an extraordinarily stimulating intellectual environment, participation in which was one of the most important factors in determining my whole intellectual and professional career.

   — Talcott Parsons

2. It has been suggested that I discuss what it is like to be a poet these days (the only days in which my opinion could possibly be useful), or, if that is immodest, what it is like to write poetry, what one thinks about the art, what its relation is to the life we supposedly live these days, and so on. This is a fascinatingly large range in which to wander, and I shall be interested to find out what I do think. I hope you will be interested, too. But I must advise you that this will not be a

coherently organized essay running in a smooth and logical progression from question to conclusion. Nor will the views expressed necessarily be consistent. I have consulted with my selves, and come up, as usual, with a number of fragmentary notions, many of them aphoristic in expression, and I believe I will do best simply to put these before you without much in the way of explanation or connective tissue.

— Howard Nemerov

3. Style, in its finest sense, is the last acquirement of the educated mind; it is also the most useful. It pervades the whole being. The administrator with a sense for style hates waste; the engineer with a sense for style economizes his material; the artisan with a sense for style prefers good work. Style is the ultimate morality of mind. . . . With style the end is attained without side issues, without raising undesirable inflammations. With style you attain your end and nothing but your end. With style the effect of your activity is calculable, and foresight is the last gift of gods to men. With style your power is increased, for your mind is not distracted with irrelevancies, and you are more likely to attain your object.

— Alfred North Whitehead

4. Early this year, the most successful of the large-circulation magazines for teen-age girls took a two-page spread in the *Times* for an "interview" with its editor-in-chief, and after the now ritual bulling (Question: "You work with young people — what is your view of today's generation?" Answer: "My faith in them is enormous. They make a sincere attempt at being totally honest, at sharing. They're happily frank about their experiences. They're the most idealistic generation in history. . . . When you consider the vast problems confronting us, their optimism and activism is truly inspirational"), and after the obeisance to the new myths ("They are the best-educated and most aware generation in history"), the ad finally got to the come-on. Question: "Is it true that your readers don't differentiate between your ads and your editorials?" Answer: "Yes, that's true. Our readers are very impressionable, not yet cynical about advertising . . . eager to learn . . . to believe." The frightening thing is, it probably is true that the teen-agers don't differentiate between the ads and the editorials, and true in a much more complex sense than the delicately calculated Madison Avenue-ese of the editor's pitch to advertisers indicates. Television is blurring the distinction for all of

us; we don't know what we're reacting to anymore, and, beyond that, it's becoming just about impossible to sort out the con from the truth because a successful con makes its lies come true.

— Pauline Kael

EXERCISES

1. What is Parsons' attitude toward himself? Exactly how do you know?
2. What is Nemerov's attitude toward himself, and how do you know?
3. Suppose that the first sentence of Whitehead's passage began thus: "I want to point out to you today that style may be regarded not only as the last acquirement of what I consider the mind that has been well educated, but it is also the most useful, I definitely believe." What is lost?
4. Do you think that Pauline Kael knows what she is talking about? Why?
5. Read a political speech (you can find lots of examples in a periodical called *Vital Speeches*), and in a paragraph analyze the speaker's attitude toward himself or herself. In another paragraph analyze his or her attitude toward the audience.

16

Acquiring Style

Draw lines, young man,
draw many lines
— OLD INGRES TO
THE YOUNG DEGAS

In the preceding pages on style we said that your writing reveals not only where you stand (your topic) and how you think (the structure of your argument), but also who you are and how you take yourself (your tone). To follow our argument to its limit, we might say that everything in this book — including rules on the comma (where you breathe) — is about style. We do. What more is there to say?

CLARITY AND TEXTURE

First, a distinction Aristotle makes between two parts of style: that which gives *clarity,* and that which gives *texture.* Exact words, concrete illustrations of abstractions, conventional punctuation, and so forth — matters we treat in some detail in the sections on revising and editing — make for clarity. On the whole, this part of style is inconspicuous when present; when absent the effect ranges from mildly distracting to ruinous. Clarity is the foundation of style. It can be achieved by anyone willing to make the effort.

Among the things that give texture, or individuality, are effective repetition, variety in sentence structure, wordplay, and so forth. This second group of devices, on the whole more noticeable, makes the reader aware of the writer's particular voice. These devices can be learned too, but seldom by effort alone. In fact playfulness helps here more than doggedness. Students who work at this part of style usually enjoy hanging around words. At the same time, they're likely to feel that when they put words on paper, even in a casual letter to a friend, they're putting themselves on the line. Serious, as most people are about games they really care about, but not solemn, they'll come to recognize the rules of play in John Holmes's advice to young poets: "You must believe that your feelings and your words for your feelings are important. . . . That they are unique is a fact; that you believe they are unique is necessary."

A REPERTORY OF STYLES

We make a second distinction: between style as the reader perceives it from the written word, and style as the writer experiences it. The first is static: it's fixed in writing or print; we can point to it, discuss it, analyze it. The second, the writer's experience of his or her own style, changes as the writer changes. In his essay "Why I Write" George Orwell said, "I find that by the time you have perfected any style of writing, you have always outgrown it." An exaggeration that deposits a truth. The essay concludes, however, "Looking back through my work, I see that it is invariably where I lacked a *political* purpose that I wrote lifeless books and was betrayed into purple passages, sentences without meaning, decorative adjectives and humbug generally." A suggestion surely, that through trial and error, and with maturity, a writer comes to a sense of self, a true style, not static and not constantly changing, but achieved.

Undergraduates seldom know what purpose, in Orwell's sense, they will have. You may be inclined toward some subjects and against others, you may have decided on a career — many times. But if your education is worth anything like the money and time invested in it, your ideas and feelings will change more rapidly in the next few years than ever before in your memory, and perhaps more than they ever will again. Make use of the confusion you're in. Reach out for new experiences to assimilate; make whatever connections you can from your reading to your inner life, reaching back into your past and forward into your future. And keep writing: "Draw lines . . . draw many lines."

To keep pace with your changing ideas — and here is our main point — you'll need to acquire not one style, but a repertory of styles, a store of writing habits on which you can draw as the need arises.

ORIGINALITY AND IMITATION

Finally, a paradox: one starts to acquire an individual style by studying and imitating the style of others. The paradox isn't limited to writing. Stylists in all fields begin as apprentices. The young ball player imitates the movements of Reggie Jackson, the potter joins a workshop in California to study under Marguerite Wildenhain, the chess player hangs around the park or club watching the old pros, then finds a book that probably recommends beginning with Ruy Lopez' opening. When Michelangelo was an apprentice he copied works by his predecessors; when Millet was young he copied works by Michelangelo; when Van Gogh was young he copied works by Millet. The would-be writer may be lucky enough to have a teacher, one he can imitate; more likely he will, in W. H. Auden's words, "serve his apprenticeship in the library."

PRACTICE IN ACQUIRING STYLE

Benjamin Franklin's Exercise

Benjamin Franklin says in his *Autobiography*, "Prose writing has been of great use to me in the course of my life, and was a principal means of my advancement," and he reveals how he acquired his ability in it. (He had just abandoned, at about the age of eleven, his ambition to be a great poet — after his father told him that "verse-makers were generally beggars.")

> About this time I met with an odd volume of the *Spectator*. It was the third. I had never before seen any of them. I bought it, read it over and over, and was much delighted with it. I thought the writing excellent, and wished, if possible, to imitate it. With that view I took some of the papers, and making short hints of the sentiment in each sentence, laid them by a few days, and then, without looking at the book, tried to complete the papers again by expressing each sentiment at length, and as fully as it had been expressed before, in any suitable words that should come to hand. Then I compared my *Spectator* with the original, discovered some of my faults, and corrected them.

A few pages later Franklin confides, with characteristic understatement (which he learned, he thought, by imitating Socrates), "I sometimes had the pleasure of fancying that in certain particulars of small import I had been lucky enough to improve the method or the language."

EXERCISES

1. Outline, in a list of brief notes, Franklin's exercise.
2. Choose a passage of current prose writing whose style you admire and follow Franklin's method. (Don't forget the last step: where you've improved on your model, congratulate yourself with becoming modesty.)

Paraphrasing

Do not confuse a paraphrase with a summary.

A summary is always much shorter than the original; a paraphrase is often a bit longer. To paraphrase a sentence, replace each word or phrase in it with one of your own. (Articles, pronouns, and conjunctions need not be replaced.) Your sentence should say substantially what the original says, but in your own words, and in a fluent, natural style. Consider the following sentence by W. H. Auden, and the paraphrase that follows it:

> Owing to its superior power as a mnemonic, verse is superior to prose as a medium for didactic instruction.
>
> — W. H. Auden

> Because it is more easily memorized and can be retained in the mind for a longer time, poetry is better than prose for teaching moral lessons.

Paraphrasing is useful for several reasons. First, paraphrasing helps you to increase your vocabulary. (Many students say that a limited vocabulary is their chief source of difficulty in writing.) You may know, for example, that "didactic" means "intended for instruction, or instructive." But why then does Auden say "didactic instruction"? Are the words redundant, or is Auden stipulating a kind of instruction? Your dictionary, which may list "tending to teach a moral lesson" as one of three or four meanings of didactic, will help you understand Auden's sentence. But notice, first, that you'll have to choose the appropriate definition, and second, that you won't be able to insert that definition as is into your sentence. To paraphrase "didactic instruction" you'll have to put "didactic" in your own words. (If you look up "mnemonic" you'll find an even more complex puzzle resolved in our paraphrase.) Paraphrasing, then, expands your vocabulary because to paraphrase accurately and gracefully you must actively understand the use of an unfamiliar word, not simply memorize a synonym for it.

Paraphrasing also helps you to focus your attention on what you read. If you want, for example, to become a better reader of poetry, the best way is to *pay attention,* and the best way of paying attention is to try paraphrasing a line whose meaning escapes you. So too with understanding art history or economics or any specialized study. If you come across a difficult passage, don't just stare at it, paraphrase it. (If you don't have time to stop and puzzle through a sentence that is not entirely clear to you, you can always make time to jot it down on a three-by-five card. As Stanislav Andreski says, "Paper is patient.")

Finally, in paraphrasing, you are observing closely and actively the way another mind works. You are, in effect, serving as an apprentice stylist. (Some masters, of course, are not worth serving or emulating. Be discriminating.)

EXERCISE

Try paraphrasing the following sentences:

Generally speaking and to a varying extent, scientists follow their temperaments in their choice of problems.

— Charles Hermite

To commit violent and unjust acts, it is not enough for a government to have the will or even the power; the habits, ideas, and passions of the time must lend themselves to their committal.

— Alexis de Tocqueville

The most intolerable people are provincial celebrities.

— Anton Chekhov

A distinction must be made between my uncle's capricious brutality and my aunt's punishments and repressions, which seem to have been dictated to her by her conscience.

— Mary McCarthy

Consciousness reigns but doesn't govern.

— Paul Valéry

The more extensive your acquaintance is with the works of those who have excelled, the more extensive will be your powers of invention, and what may appear still more like a paradox, the more original will be your composition.

— Sir Joshua Reynolds

The fashion wears out more apparel than the man.

— William Shakespeare

What is expressed is impressed.

— Aristotle

All the road to heaven is heaven.

— Saint Teresa of Avila

When the shoe fits, the foot is forgotten.

— Chuang Tzu

Imitating the Cumulative Sentence

When you write, you make a point, not by subtracting as though you sharpened a pencil, but by adding. When you put one word after another, your statement should be more precise the more you

add. If the result is otherwise, you have added the wrong thing, or
you have added more than was needed.

— John Erskine

In *Notes Toward a New Rhetoric* Francis Christensen cites
"Erskine's principle" and argues that "the cumulative sentence"
best fulfills it. The cumulative sentence makes a statement in the
main clause; the rest of the sentence consists of modifiers *added* to
make the meaning of the statement more precise. The cumulative
sentence adds *texture* to writing because as the writer adds modifiers
he is examining his impressions, summarized in the main clause.
At the same time he reveals to the reader how those impressions
impinged on his mind. Here are some of Christensen's examples:

He dipped his hands in the bichloride solution and shook them,
a quick shake, fingers down, like the fingers of a pianist above the
keys.

— Sinclair Lewis

The jockeys sat bowed and relaxed, moving a little at the waist
with the movement of their horses.

— Katherine Anne Porter

The Texan turned to the nearest gatepost and climbed to the
top of it, his alternate thighs thick and bulging in the tight trousers,
the butt of the pistol catching and losing the sun in pearly gleams.

— William Faulkner

George was coming down in the telemark position, kneeling,
one leg forward and bent, the other trailing, his sticks hanging like
some insect's thin legs, kicking up puffs of snow, and finally the
whole kneeling, trailing figure coming around in a beautiful right
curve like points of light, all in a wild cloud of snow.

— Ernest Hemingway

EXERCISE

Try writing a cumulative sentence. First, reread Christensen's
sample sentences out loud. Then, during a second reading, try to
sense the similarities in structure. For the next few days train
yourself to observe people closely, the way they walk, move, gesture, smile, speak. Take notes when you can. Then, after reading
the sentences again, try writing one. Either imitate one of the

sentences closely, word by word (substituting your own words) or start with your subject, imitating the structure you have detected or have simply absorbed.

Transformations

If you take a proverb, an epigram, or any interesting, suggestive sentence and change it enough to make it say something else, something on *your* mind, you have a transformation. To cite a famous example, G. K. Chesterton transformed

If a thing is worth doing it is worth doing well

to

If a thing is worth doing it is worth doing badly.

Professor Marion Levy transformed Leo Durocher's

Nice guys finish last

to

Last guys don't finish nice.

A student transformed Marianne Moore's

We must be as clear as our natural reticence allows us to be

to

We must be as outspoken as our adversaries would forbid us to be.

EXERCISE

How can you transform one or more of the following?

When a poor man eats a chicken, one of them is sick.
— Yiddish proverb
The Battle of Waterloo was won on the playing fields of Eton.
— Attributed to the Duke of Wellington
You can't step into the same river twice.
— Heraclitus

Mañana es otro día.
— Proverb

Finding Poems

Finding poems is a variation of the language game called acquiring style. It amuses the student who enjoys hanging around words but who is tired of writing, tired of pulling words out of his mind and making them shape up — weary too, very weary, of reading "fine things." Still, he hungers for print, consuming the words on the cereal box along with the cereal, reading last week's classified ads when he has nothing to sell, no money to buy. What can be made of such an affliction? A poem.

Here are X. J. Kennedy's directions for finding a poem.

> In a newspaper, magazine, catalogue, textbook, or advertising throwaway, find a sentence or passage that (with a little artistic manipulation on your part) shows promise of becoming a poem. Copy it into lines like poetry, being careful to place what seem to be the most interesting words at the ends of lines to give them greatest emphasis. According to the rules of found poetry you may excerpt, delete, repeat, and rearrange elements but not add anything.

Here are some examples of "found poems." The first, "And All Those Others," was found by Jack S. Margolis in the Watergate transcripts; he published it in *The Poetry of Richard Milhous Nixon*.

> I'm the President
> Of the country —
> And I'm going
> To get on with it
>   And meet
>   Italians
>   and
>   Germans,
> And all those others.

Here is a passage from a textbook, followed by the poem, "Symbolism," a student found in it:

> A symbol, then, is an image so loaded with significance that it is not simply literal, and it does not simply stand for something else; it is both itself *and* something else that it richly suggests, a kind of manifestation of something too complex or too elusive to be otherwise revealed.

An image
so loaded with
  significance
that it is not
  simply literal,
and it does not
  simply stand
for
  something else;
it is both
  itself
and
  something else
that it
  richly suggests,
a kind of
  manifestation
of
  something
  too complex
or
  too elusive
to be
  otherwise revealed,
is a
  symbol.

Finally, a poem found by a student in an advertisement in *Newsweek:*

Winchester model 101
made for hands
that know the difference
There's more
than meets the eye
to any fine
shotgun

EXERCISES

1. Find a poem.
2. Explain in one sentence (a) how finding poems might help you acquire style or (b) why such an exercise is a waste of time.

17

Acquiring Fluency

Nulla dies sine linea.
No day without a line.

KEEPING A JOURNAL

Sometimes our efforts to improve our writing make us too conscious of what we say, or too self-critical to say anything. To guard against hyperconsciousness, or as an antidote to it, practice writing daily: keep a journal. The word *journal* derives from the Latin *dies* ("day") and *diurnalis* ("daily"), which became *journal* ("daily") in medieval French. Keep a journal: *nulla dies sine linea.*

Writing in a journal keeps your writing loose, fluent. It helps you to overcome the fear of writing most people have, and it gives you a chance to practice skills you are acquiring. As we said at the start, writing is a physical act, and to keep in trim, you should practice daily. (Or, to be honest, as close to daily as you can manage.) Keeping a journal then is practical; for many students it is, from the start, enjoyable.

If keeping a journal is an assignment in your composition course, your instructor may ask you to write in a loose-leaf notebook — so that pages may be turned in occasionally, and the instructor won't have to stagger home with twenty or thirty notebooks. If you're keeping a journal strictly for your own use, write with, and on, whatever materials feel comfortable: pen, pencil, typewriter; loose sheets, bound notebook, or whatever. (Dr. William Carlos Williams often wrote poems on prescription blanks.)

When to write? Any time; ten to fifteen minutes a day. Some people find it helpful to establish a regular time of day for writing, just before they go to sleep, for example. Habits can be helpful; but not all of us can or should lead well-regulated lives. Suit yourself.

How long is an entry? An entry may be a few words, a line or two, a few pages. There's no special length, but keep writing for at least the minimum recommended time.

Write freely. Don't correct or revise, don't worry about spelling, vocabulary, punctuation. Use whatever language, idiom, voice you wish. If you have a "home language" — black or Puerto Rican, for example — write entries in it. It's a good way to keep in touch with yourself, and the friends and family you've temporarily left. You *can* go home again; you can, that is, if you don't leave college an educated zombie.

As for content, write about anything that comes to mind. But don't confuse a journal with a diary. A diary mentions things that have happened ("Concert at 8, with J. and R."); a journal reflects on the happenings. A diary lists appointments; a journal records events, but gives some sense of why they were meaningful. Think of your journal as a record of your life now, which you might read with pleasure some years from now when many of the rich details of your daily experience would otherwise be buried in your memory. Still, it's probably better to write "Had a peanut butter sandwich for lunch" than to write nothing.

Write down your thoughts, feelings, impressions, responses, dreams, memories. May Sarton once said, "The senses are the keys to the past." If you have a strong sensory memory of something — the mixed smell of saltwater, sand, and machinery oil, for example — try to describe it in words, and then to track it down. You may find a buried scene from your childhood that you can rescue from your memory by a train of associations. If you keep tracking, and writing, you may discover why that scene is important to you still. But don't be afraid to embroider the truth a little, or to understate it. As Santayana observed, "Sometimes we have to change the truth in order to remember it."

Jot down reactions, ideas, feelings about something you are reading, something you may want to use later, in an essay. Did you stop reading and start daydreaming? What is the link between the text and your daydream? If you write it down, you may be able to cut down on the daydreaming, or, better still, make something out of it.

Practice writing descriptions; short, medium, long; of persons, places, things; literal, figurative, or impressionistic. Try cross-cutting from one description of a scene or an experience to another that might illuminate it. (When writing about real people observe one caution: use fictitious names.)

When you have nothing to say, write anyway. Practice writing paraphrases and transformations (see pages 335–37 and 339). Or copy out a passage of someone else's writing. If you can, explain why you find it attractive, why you want to remember it.

If you're too preoccupied to write because there's a decision you must make, and can't make, start writing. List all the reasons for following a course of action; then all the reasons against it.

Here, to prime the pump, are some examples of journal entries. Some are by professional writers, others by students. You'll find nothing remarkable in many of these entries (except honesty) and perhaps you'll discover in yourself the assurance that you can do as well or better.

SOME JOURNAL ENTRIES
BY PUBLISHED WRITERS

You hear a lot of jazz about Soul Food. Take chitterlings: the ghetto blacks eat them from necessity while the black bourgeoisie has turned it into a mocking slogan. Eating chitterlings is like going slumming to them. Now that they have the price of a steak here they come prattling about Soul Food. The people in the ghetto want steaks. *Beef Steaks.* I wish I had the power to see to it that the bourgeoisie really *did* have to make it on Soul Food.

— Eldridge Cleaver

August A sudden idea of the relationship between "lovers." We are neither male nor female. We are a compound of both. I choose the male who will develop and expand the male in me; he chooses me to expand the female in him. Being made whole. . . . And why I choose *one* man for this rather than many is for safety. We bind ourselves within a ring and that ring is as it were a wall against the outside world. It is our refuge, our shelter. Here the tricks of life will not be played. Here is *safety* for us to *grow. Why, I talk like a child.*

— Katherine Mansfield

Wanted: a dog that neither barks nor bites, eats broken glass and shits diamonds.

— Goethe

The difficulty about all this dying is that you can't tell a fellow anything about it, so where does the fun come in?

— Alice James

With Brett to a nearby "movie," perhaps a little worse than the usual average of mediocrity. Yet why is it that I can be emotionally moved at the most vapid climax, the while I intellectually deride the whole false and mushy mess? It is of course but the awakening of memories by some act or gesture related to the past, — some unrealized hope is returned, a lost thread is for the moment woven into reality. However, the absurdity of my Jekyll and Hyde situation, with my mouth in a grin and my throat choked, and this from viewing some quite preposterous melodrama, ridiculously conceived, acted by imbeciles, presented for bovine clodhoppers, brings the question am I infantile? senile? maudlin? or also beef-witted? With a superlative stretch of the neck I answer these questions, "No!" — yet feeling uneasy over the sureness of my self-estimation. Better to wink at my weakness than to discover it a truth!

— Edward Weston

The man who would be stupid enough to defend the present economic order would be ass enough to do nothing for it.

Disorderly thinking should be as unwelcome in polite society as disorderly conduct. In fact, it *is* disorderly conduct.

On the sands of Ogunquit I saw a sandpiper, one of whose legs was lamed, rest on its wings as a man would on a pair of crutches.

— Lewis Mumford

It is so many years before one can believe enough in what one feels even to know what the feeling is.

For some months now I have lived with my own youth and childhood, not always writing indeed but thinking of it almost every day, and I am sorrowful and disturbed. It is not that I have accomplished too few of my plans, for I am not ambitious; but when I think of all the books I have read, and of the wise words I have heard spoken, and of the anxiety I have given to parents and grand-parents, and of the hopes that I have had, all life weighed in the scales of my own life seems to me a preparation for something that never happens.

— William Butler Yeats

The Pillow Book
of Sei Shōnagon[1]

Hateful Things

One is in a hurry to leave, but one's visitor keeps chattering away. If it is someone of no importance, one can get rid of him by saying, "You must tell me all about it next time"; but, should it be the sort of visitor whose presence commands one's best behavior, the situation is hateful indeed.

One finds that a hair has got caught in the stone on which one is rubbing one's inkstick, or again that gravel is lodged in the inkstick, making a nasty, grating sound.

One is just about to be told some interesting piece of news when a baby starts crying.

A flight of crows circle about with loud caws.

An admirer has come on a clandestine visit, but a dog catches sight of him and starts barking. One feels like killing the beast.

One has gone to bed and is about to doze off when a mosquito appears, announcing himself in a reedy voice. One can actually feel the wind made by his wings and, slight though it is, one finds it hateful in the extreme.

One is telling a story about old times when someone breaks in with a little detail that he happens to know, implying that one's own version is inaccurate — disgusting behavior!

Very hateful is a mouse that scurries all over the place.

Some children have called at one's house. One makes a great fuss of them and gives them toys to play with. The children become

[1] Perhaps the most marvelous of all journals is the one kept about a thousand years ago by Sei Shōnagon, a Japanese woman who served for some ten years as lady-in-waiting to an empress. Presumably she wrote most of these entries before going to bed, hence the title: *The Pillow Book of Sei Shōnagon.* We give a few selections, translated by Ivan Morris.

accustomed to this treatment and start to come regularly, forcing their way into one's inner rooms and scattering one's furnishings and possessions. Hateful!

A man with whom one is having an affair keeps singing the praises of some woman he used to know. Even if it is a thing of the past, this can be very annoying. How much more so if he is still seeing the woman! (Yet sometimes I find that it is not as unpleasant as all that.)

A lover who is leaving at dawn announces that he has to find his fan and his paper. "I know I put them somewhere last night," he says. Since it is pitch dark, he gropes about the room, bumping into the furniture and muttering, "Strange! Where on earth can they be?" Finally he discovers the objects. He thrusts the paper into the breast of his robe with a great rustling sound; then he snaps open his fan and busily fans away with it. Only now is he ready to take his leave. What charmless behavior! "Hateful" is an understatement.

Equally disagreeable is the man who, when leaving in the middle of the night, takes care to fasten the cord of his headdress. This is quite unnecessary; he could perfectly well put it gently on his head without tying the cord. And why must he spend time adjusting his cloak or hunting costume? Does he really think someone may see him at this time of night and criticize him for not being impeccably dressed?

A good lover will behave as elegantly at dawn as at any other time. He drags himself out of bed with a look of dismay on his face. The lady urges him on: "Come, my friend, it's getting light. You don't want anyone to find you here." He gives a deep sigh, as if to say that the night has not been nearly long enough and that it is agony to leave. Once up, he does not instantly pull on his trousers. Instead he comes close to the lady and whispers whatever was left unsaid during the night. Even when he is dressed, he still lingers, vaguely pretending to be fastening his sash.

Presently he raises the lattice, and the two lovers stand together by the side door while he tells her how he dreads the coming day, which will keep them apart; then he slips away. The lady watches him go, and this moment of parting will remain among her most charming memories.

Indeed, one's attachment to a man depends largely on the elegance of his leave-taking. When he jumps out of bed, scurries about the room, tightly fastens his trouser-sash, rolls up the sleeves of his Court cloak, overrobe, or hunting costume, stuffs his belongings into the breast of his robe and then briskly secures the outer sash — one really begins to hate him.

Rare Things

People who live together and still manage to behave with reserve towards each other. However much these people may try to hide their weaknesses, they usually fail.

To avoid getting ink stains on the notebook into which one is copying stories, poems, or the like. If it is a very fine notebook, one takes the greatest care not to make a blot; yet somehow one never seems to succeed.

One has given some silk to the fuller and, when he sends it back, it is so beautiful that one cries out in admiration.

Enviable People

One has been learning a sacred text by heart; but, though one has gone over the same passage again and again, one still recites it haltingly and keeps on forgetting words. Meanwhile one hears other people, not only clerics (for whom it is natural) but ordinary men and women, reciting such passages without the slightest effort, and one wonders when one will ever be able to come up to their standard.

When one is ill in bed and hears people walking about, laughing loudly and chatting away as if they did not have a care in the world, how enviable they seem!

SOME JOURNAL ENTRIES BY STUDENTS

Helpless! I remember when I used to stand on a kitchen chair with both my arms raised in the air so that my grandmother could dress me for school. I was so spoiled that the only muscles I moved were in my mouth. Those were the days when breakfast tasted good.

The Rat: "You gap-legged, sky-scraping, knock-kneed, pot-bellied, flat-chested, slack-behind, wooly-headed hollow sculpture of a man!" . . . I died laughing!

I divorce myself from my feelings and immerse myself in my obligations.

It is difficult to believe that not understanding a physics problem isn't the worst problem in the world.

The rain can be heard on the roof and I feel a steady sprinkling through the open window. Trucks are loading and unloading down in the courtyard. Cars beeping as they turn the blind corner. Distraction . . .

The trees swish outside, the curtains inside. . . .

Anticipating something is like falling off a cliff and never reaching the bottom.

63rd Street Rap: What's happening? Ain't nothing to it. What's going on at the Woods? Everything is Everything. Been to any sets lately? Yeah it was on 64th street last night. We partied back. Wish I could have made it. Well times will get better they can't get no worse. Right On! Right On!

Translation: Hello. How are you. I am fine. What activities are taking place at your high school named Englewood? There are many exciting activities taking place at my high school. Have you attended any parties recently? Yes I attended a party on 64th street last night. We had a very nice time. I wish I could have attended the party also. Well you will probably be fortunate enough to attend the next party, there is no logical reason for you not to. That is correct, that is correct.

School begins at 8:40 and ends at 2:00 the next morning. What did you say about revising for conciseness?

It seems that much of my daily writing consists of unresolved questions to which I am still seeking answers. Every answer that I do find serves to ask more questions. Finding answers to my questions creates such a feeling of accomplishment within me that I feel as though I could burst with happiness. However questions that remain unresolved for any length of time begin to puzzle me more and more. I find myself thinking about them at the oddest and most inconvenient times . . . sitting in French class. . . .

PART FOUR
Editing

No iron can stab the heart
with such force as a period
put just at the right place.
— ISAAC BABEL

18

Manuscript Form

To edit a manuscript is to refine it for others to read. When your essay at last says what you want to say, you are ready to get it into good physical shape, into an edited manuscript.

BASIC MANUSCRIPT FORM

Much of what follows is nothing more than common sense. Unless your instructor specifies something different, you can adopt these principles as a guide.

1. Use 8½-by-11-inch paper of good weight. Keep as lightweight a carbon copy as you wish — or make a photocopy — but hand in a sturdy original. Do not use paper torn out of a spiral notebook; the ragged edges will distract a reader.

2. Write on one side of the page only. If you typewrite, double-space, typing with a reasonably fresh ribbon. If you submit a handwritten copy, use lined paper and write, in ink, on every other line if the lines are closely spaced.

3. Put your name and class or course number in the upper right-hand corner of the first page. It is a good idea to put your name in the upper right corner of each page, so the instructor can easily reassemble your essay if somehow a page gets detached and mixed with other papers.

4. Center the title of your essay about two inches from the top of the first page. Capitalize the first letter of the first and last words of your title, the first word after a semicolon or colon if you use either one, and the first letter of all the other words except articles, conjunctions, and prepositions, thus:

```
The Diabolic and Celestial Images in The Scarlet Letter
```

Notice that your title is neither underlined nor enclosed in quotation marks (though of course if, as here, it includes material that would normally be italicized or in quotation marks, that material continues to be so written).

5. Begin the essay an inch or two below the title. If your instructor prefers a title page, begin the essay on the next page.

6. Leave an adequate margin — an inch or an inch and a half — at top, bottom, and sides.

7. Number the pages consecutively, using arabic numerals in the upper right-hand corner. If you give the title on a separate page, do not number that page; the page that follows it is page 1.

8. Indent the first word of each paragraph five spaces from the left margin.

9. Fasten the pages of your paper with a paper clip in the upper left-hand corner. Stiff binders are unnecessary; indeed, they are a nuisance to the instructor, adding bulk and making it awkward to write annotations.

CORRECTIONS IN THE FINAL COPY

Your extensive revisions should have been made in your drafts, but minor last-minute revisions may be made on the finished copy. Proofreading may catch some typographical errors, and you may notice some small weaknesses. For example, you may notice in the final copy an error in agreement between subject and verb, as in "The insistent demands for drastic reform has disappeared from most of the nation's campuses." The subject is "demands" and so the verb should be plural, "have" rather than "has." You need not retype the page, or even erase. You can make corrections with the following proofreader's symbols.

Changes in wording may be made by crossing through words and rewriting just above them, either on the typewriter or by hand in pen:

```
The insistent demands for drastic reform has disappeared from most of

the nation's campuses.
```

Additions should be made above the line, with a caret (∧) below the line at the appropriate place:

```
The insistent demands for drastic reform have disappeared most of the

nation's campuses.
```

Transpositions of letters may be made thus:

```
The insistent demands for drastic reform have disappeared from most of

the nation's campuses.
```

Deletions are indicated by a horizontal line through the word or words to be deleted. Delete a single letter by drawing a vertical or diagonal line through it.

```
The insistent demands for drastic reform reform have disappeared from

most of the nation's campuses.
```

Separation of words accidentally run together is indicated by a vertical line, *closure* by a curved line connecting the things to be closed up.

```
The insistent demands for drastic reform have disappeared from most of

the nation's campuses.
```

Paragraphing may be indicated by the symbol ⁋ before the word that is to begin the new paragraph.

```
The insistent demands for drastic reform have disappeared from most of

the nation's campuses. ⁋Another sign that the country's mood has
```

QUOTATIONS AND QUOTATION MARKS

Quotations from the material you are writing about are indispensable. They not only let your readers know what you are talking about; they give your readers the material you are responding to, thus letting them share your responses. But quote sparingly and quote briefly. Use quotations as evidence, not as padding. If the exact wording of the original is crucial, or especially effective, quote it directly, but if it is not, don't bore the reader with material that can be effectively reduced either by summarizing or by cutting. And make sure, by a comment before or after a quotation, that your reader understands why you find the quotation relevant. Don't count on a quotation to make your point for you.

Here are some mechanical matters:

1. Distinguish between short and long quotations, and treat each appropriately. Short quotations (usually defined as fewer than three lines of poetry or five lines of prose) are enclosed within quotation marks and run into the text (rather than set off, without quotation marks).

LeRoi Jones's "Preface to a Twenty Volume Suicide Note" ends with a glimpse of the speaker's daughter peeking into her "clasped hands," either playfully or madly.

Pope's Essay on Criticism begins informally with a contraction, but the couplets nevertheless have an authoritative ring: "'Tis hard to say, if greater want of skill / Appear in writing or in judging ill."

Notice that in the second example a slash (diagonal line, virgule) is used to indicate the end of a line of verse other than the last line quoted. The slash is, of course, not used if the poetry is set off, indented, and printed as verse, thus:

Pope's Essay on Criticism begins informally with a contraction, but the couplets nevertheless have an authoritative ring:

```
'Tis hard to say, if greater want of skill
Appear in writing or in judging ill;
But of the two less dangerous is the offense
To tire our patience than mislead our sense.
```

Material that is set off (usually three or more lines of verse, five or more lines of prose) is *not* enclosed within quotation marks. To set it off, triple-space before and after the quotation and single-space the quotation, indenting prose quotations five spaces (ten spaces for the first line, if the quotation begins with the opening of a paragraph) and centering quotations of poetry. (Note: our suggestion that you single-space longer quotations seems reasonable to us but is at odds with various manuals that tell how to prepare a manuscript for publication. Such manuals usually say that material that is set off should be indented and double-spaced. Find out if your instructor has a preference.)

2. An embedded quotation (that is, a quotation embedded into a sentence of your own) must fit grammatically into the sentence of which it is a part. For example, suppose you want to use Othello's line, "I have done the state some service."

Incorrect

Near the end of the play Othello says that he "have done the state some service."

Correct

Near the end of the play Othello says that he has "done the state some service."

Correct

Near the end of the play, Othello says, "I have done the state some service."

Don't try to introduce a long quotation (say, more than a complete sentence) into the middle of one of your own sentences. It is almost impossible for the reader to come out of the quotation and to pick up the thread of your own sentence. It is better to lead into the long quotation with "Jones says . . ." and then, after the quotation, to begin a new sentence of your own.

3. The quotation must be exact. Any material that you add must be in square brackets (not parentheses), thus:

```
When Pope says that Belinda is "the rival of his [i.e., the sun's]
beams," he uses comic hyperbole.
```

```
Stephen Dedalus sees the ball as a "greasy leather orb [that] flew like
a heavy bird through the grey light."
```

If you wish to omit material from within a quotation, indicate the ellipsis by three spaced periods. If a sentence ends in an omission, add a regular period and then three spaced periods to indicate the omission. The following example is based on a quotation from the sentences immediately above this one:

```
The manual says that "if you . . . omit material from within a quota-
tion, [you must] indicate the ellipsis. . . . If a sentence ends in an
omission, add a regular period and then three spaced periods. . . ."
```

Notice that if you begin the quotation with the beginning of a sentence (in the example we have just given, "If you" is the beginning of a quoted sentence) you do *not* indicate that material preceded the words you are quoting. Similarly, if you end your quotation with the end of the quoted sentence, you give only a single period, not four periods, although of course the material from which you are quoting may have gone on for many more sentences. But if you begin quoting from the middle of a sentence, or end quoting before you reach the end of a sentence in your source, it is customary to indicate the omissions. But even such omissions need not be indicated when the quoted material is obviously incomplete — when, for instance, it is a word or phrase. (See the first example in this section, which quotes Pope's phrase "the rival of his beams.") Notice, too, that although quotations must be given word for word, the initial capitalization can be adapted, as here where "If" is reduced to "if."

When a line or more of verse is omitted from a passage that is set off, the three spaced periods are printed on a separate line.

4. Identify the speaker or writer of the quotation, so that readers are not left with a sense of uncertainty. Usually this identification precedes the quoted material (e.g., "Smith says . . .") in accordance with the principle of letting readers know where they

are going, but occasionally it may follow the quotation, especially if it will provide something of a pleasant surprise. For example, in a discussion of T. S. Eliot's poetry, you might quote a hostile comment on one of the poems and then reveal that Eliot himself was the speaker.

5. Commas and periods go inside the quotation marks; semi-colons and colons go outside. Question marks, exclamation points, and dashes go inside if they are part of the quotation, outside if they are your own.

```
Amanda ironically says to her daughter, "How old are you, Laura?" Is it
possible to fail to hear Laura's weariness in her reply, "Mother, you
know my age"?
```

6. Use *single* quotation marks for material contained within a quotation that itself is within quotation marks, thus:

```
T. S. Eliot says, "Mr. Richards observes that 'poetry is capable of sav-
ing us.'"
```

7. Use quotation marks around titles of short works, that is, for titles of chapters in books and for stories, essays, short poems, songs, lectures, and speeches. Titles of unpublished works, even book-length dissertations, are also enclosed in quotation marks. But underline — to indicate *italics* — titles of pamphlets and of books, that is, novels, periodicals, collections of essays, and long poems, such as *The Rime of the Ancient Mariner* and *Paradise Lost*. Underline also titles of films, radio and television programs, ballets and operas, works of art, and the names of planes, ships, and trains.

Exception: titles of sacred works (for example, the Old Testament, the Bible, Genesis, Acts, the Gospels, the Koran) are neither underlined nor enclosed within quotation marks. To cite a book of the Bible with chapter and verse, give the name of the book, then a space, then a small roman numeral for the chapter, a period, and an arabic numeral (*not* preceded by a space) for the verse, thus: Exodus xx.14–15. Standard abbreviations for the books of the Bible (for example, Chron.) are permissible in footnotes and in parenthetic citations within the text.

ACKNOWLEDGING SOURCES

Borrowing without Plagiarizing

Honesty requires that you acknowledge your indebtedness for material when (1) you quote directly from a work, or (2) you paraphrase or summarize someone's words (the words of your paraphrase or summary are your own, but the points are not), or (3) you appropriate an idea that is not common knowledge.

Let's suppose you are going to make use of Ralph Linton's comment on definitions of primitive art:

> The term "primitive art" has come to be used with at least three distinct meanings. First and most legitimate is its use with reference to the early stages in the development of a particular art, as when one speaks of the Italian primitives. Second is its use to designate works of art executed by persons who have not had formal training in our own art techniques and aesthetic canons. Third is its application to the art works of all but a small group of societies which we have chosen to call civilized. The present discussion will deal only with the last.
>
> — Ralph Linton, Preface to Eliot Elisofon,
> *The Sculpture of Africa*
> (New York: Frederick A. Praeger, 1958), p. 9.

1. *Acknowledging a direct quotation.* You may want to use some or all of Linton's words, in which case you will write something like this:

```
As Ralph Linton says, "The term 'primitive art' has come to be used
with at least three distinct meanings. First and most legitimate is its
use with reference to the early stages in the development of a particu-
lar art, as when one speaks of the Italian primitives."[1]
```

Notice that the digit, indicating a footnote, is raised, and that it follows the period and the quotation marks. (The form of footnotes is specified on pages 366–72.) And, of course, in a relatively informal paper it may be enough merely to mention, in the body of the paper, the author and title, without using a footnote specifying place of publication, publisher, and date. Our point here is not that you must use detailed footnotes, but that you must give credit.

2. *Acknowledging a paraphrase or summary.* We have already suggested (page 209) that summaries (abridgments) are usually superior to paraphrases (rewordings, of approximately the same length as the original) because summaries are briefer; but occasionally you may find that you cannot greatly abridge a passage in your source and yet don't want to quote it word for word — perhaps because it is too technical or poorly written. Even though you are changing some or all of the words, you must give credit to the source because the idea is not yours. Here is an example of a summary:

> Ralph Linton, in his Preface to Eliot Elisofon's The Sculpture of Africa, suggests that there are at least three common but distinct meanings of the term "primitive art": the early stages of a particular art; the art of untrained artists; and the art of societies that we consider uncivilized.

Not to give credit to Linton is to plagiarize, even though the words are yours. And of course if you say something like this, and do not give credit, you are also plagiarizing:

> "Primitive art" is used in three different senses. First and most reasonable is the use of the word to refer to the early years of a certain art. . . .

It is pointless to offer this sort of rewording; if there is a point, it is to conceal the source and to take credit for thinking that is not your own.

3. *Acknowledging an idea.* Let us say that you have read an essay in which Irving Kristol argues that journalists who pride themselves on being tireless critics of national policy are in fact irresponsible critics because they have no policy they prefer. If this strikes you as a new idea and you adopt it in an essay — even though you set it forth entirely in your own words and with examples not offered by Kristol — you should acknowledge your debt to Kristol. Not to acknowledge such borrowing is plagiarism.

Your readers will not think the less of you for naming your source; rather, they will be grateful to you for telling them about an interesting writer.

In short, acknowledge your source (1) if you quote directly, and put the quoted words in quotation marks, (2) if you summarize or paraphrase someone's material, even though not one word of your source is retained, and (3) if you borrow a distinctive idea, even though the words and the concrete application are your own.

Fair Use of Common Knowledge

If in doubt as to whether or not to give credit (either in a footnote or merely in an introductory phrase such as "Ralph Linton says . . ."), give credit. But as you begin to read widely in your field or subject, you will develop a sense of what is considered common knowledge. Unsurprising definitions in a dictionary can be considered common knowledge, and so there is no need to say "According to Webster, a novel is a long narrative in prose." (That's weak in three ways: it's unnecessary, it's uninteresting, and it's unclear, since "Webster" appears in the titles of several dictionaries, some good and some bad.) Similarly, the date of Freud's death can be considered common knowledge. Few can give it when asked, but it can be found out from innumerable sources, and no one need get the credit for providing you with the date. Again, if you simply *know*, from your reading of Freud, that Freud was interested in literature, you need not cite a specific source for an assertion to that effect, but if you know only because some commentator on Freud said so, and you have no idea whether the fact is well known or not, you should give credit to the source that gave you the information. Not to give credit — for ideas as well as for quoted words — is to plagiarize.

"But How Else Can I Put It?"

If you have just learned — say from an encyclopedia — something that you sense is common knowledge, you may wonder, How can I change into my own words the simple, clear words that this source uses in setting forth this simple fact? For example, if before writing about the photograph of Buffalo Bill and Sitting

Bull (page 51), you look up these names in the *Encyclopaedia Britannica*, you will find this statement about Buffalo Bill (William F. Cody): "In 1883 Cody organized his first Wild West exhibition." You cannot use this statement as your own, word for word, without feeling uneasy. But to put in quotation marks such a routine statement of what can be considered common knowledge, and to cite a source for it, seems pretentious. After all, the *Encyclopedia Americana* says much the same thing in the same routine way: "In 1883, . . . Cody organized Buffalo Bill's Wild West." It may be that the word "organized" is simply the most obvious and the best word, and perhaps you will end up using it. Certainly to change "Cody organized" into "Cody presided over the organization of" or "Cody assembled" or some such thing, in an effort to avoid plagiarizing, would be to make a change for the worse and still to be guilty of plagiarism. But you won't get yourself into this mess of wondering whether to change clear, simple wording into awkward wording if in the first place, when you take notes, you summarize your sources, thus: "1883: organized Wild West," or "first Wild West: 1883." Later (even if only thirty minutes later), when drafting your paper, if you turn this nugget — probably combined with others — into the best sentence you can, you will not be in danger of plagiarizing, even if the word "organized" turns up in your sentence.

Of course, even when dealing with material that can be considered common knowledge — and even when you have put it into your own words — you probably *will* cite your source if you are drawing more than just an occasional fact from a source. If, for instance, your paragraph on Buffalo Bill uses half a dozen facts from a source, cite the source. You do this both to avoid charges of plagiarism and to protect yourself in case your source contains errors of fact.

FOOTNOTES AND ENDNOTES

Kinds of Notes

When we speak of kinds of notes we are not distinguishing between footnotes, which appear at the bottom of the page, and endnotes, which appear at the end of the essay; for simplicity, we will use *footnote* to cover both of these types. Rather, we are distinguishing between (1) notes that give the sources of quotations, facts, and opinions used, and (2) those that give additional comment that would interrupt the flow of the argument in the body of the paper. This second type perhaps requires a comment. You may wish to indicate that you are familiar with an opinion contrary to the one you are offering, but you may not wish to digress upon it during the course of the argument. A footnote lets you refer to it and indicate why you are not considering it. Or a footnote may contain full statistical data that support your point but that would seem unnecessarily detailed and even tedious in the body of the paper.

But this kind of footnote, which gives additional commentary, should be used sparingly. There are times when supporting details may be appropriately relegated to a footnote, but if the thing is worth saying, it is usually worth saying in the body of the paper. A writer should not get into the habit of affixing either trivia or miniature essays to the bottom of each page of an essay.

Reducing the Number of Footnotes

Similarly, the number of footnotes citing sources should be reduced — kept down to an honest minimum, partly by including the documentation within the body of the paper where reasonable and partly by not cluttering up the bottoms of the pages with reference to material that is common knowledge. If you give frequent quotations from one book — for example, *Black Elk Speaks* or a play by Shakespeare — you can, in the footnote to the first quotation, specify which edition you are using, and then mention that all subsequent quotations from the work are from that edition. After each subsequent quotation, then, you need only put parentheses including the page number or — a more useful procedure when you are quoting from plays — act, scene, and line numbers (III.ii.178); if you are quoting from various plays, be sure to include the title of the play in the parentheses. If the quotation is run into the text, close the quotation, give the parenthetic material, and then add the final period.

Let's assume that you have already quoted from *Black Elk Speaks*, and have cited the edition. When you next quote from the book you do not need another footnote, for you may cite the page immediately after the quotation marks, thus:

Artists have painted pretty pictures of Custer just before his death, standing gorgeous against the sun, but we have Black Elk's word that "it was all dark and mixed up" (p. 113).

Another example, this time quoting from a play:

The idea that a tragic hero has exhausted all of his life's possibilities is revealed in <u>Macbeth</u>, when Malcolm says, "Macbeth / Is ripe for shaking" (IV.iii.237–38).

If the quotation is set off, end the quotation with a period (unless what follows in your essay is a continuation of a sentence, of which the quotation is a part), and then, after allowing two spaces to follow the period, put the page number within parentheses. This parenthetic identification in the body of the paper does everything that a footnote would do.

Here is part of a student's essay that includes a set-off quotation followed by a page reference:

Huckleberry Finn, whether he consciously knows it or not, identifies his own flight with Nigger Jim's attempt to escape from slavery. When Huck learns that the Duke and the King have sold Jim, Mark Twain gives these words to Huck:

> I went to the raft and set down in the wigwam to think. But I couldn't come to nothing. I thought till I wore my head sore, but I couldn't see no way out of the trouble. After all this long journey, and after all we'd done for them scoundrels, here it was all come to nothing, everything all busted up and ruined, because they could have the heart to serve Jim such a trick as that, and make him a slave again for all his life, and amongst strangers, too, for forty dirty dollars. (P. 105)

Of course Huck does not explicitly equate himself with Jim, but the reader understands that Jim's freedom has become part of Huck's own goal.

Footnote Numbers and Position

Number the notes consecutively throughout the essay or chapter. Although some instructors allow students to group all of the notes at the rear of the essay, most instructors — and surely all readers — believe that the best place for a footnote is at the foot of the appropriate page. If in your draft you type all your footnotes, when typing your final copy you can easily gauge how much space the footnotes for any given page will require. Micrometric carbon paper (carbon paper with a protruding margin that bears the line numbers from 64, at the top, down to 1, at the bottom) is a great help.

Footnote Style

The principles discussed here are derived from the *MLA Handbook for Writers of Research Papers, Theses, and Dissertations,* issued by the Modern Language Association. The *MLA Handbook* is based on the *MLA Style Sheet,* a guide used by those who write about the humanities for scholarly journals and university presses. But some of the sciences and social sciences follow different principles; it is therefore advisable to ask your instructors in other courses if they have strong ideas about the form of references. On pages 376–77 we list some manuals of style concerned with the preparation of scholarly manuscripts in disciplines other than the humanities.

To indicate that there is a footnote, put a raised arabic numeral (without a period and without parentheses) after the final punctuation of the sentence, unless clarity requires it earlier. At the bottom of the page skip three lines (double-space twice) before giving the first footnote. Then indent five spaces, raise the typewriter carriage half a line, and type the arabic numeral (without a period). Lower the carriage to the regular position, skip one space, and type the footnote, single-spacing it. (Some manuals suggest double-spacing footnotes that run more than one line. Ask your instructors if they have a preference.) If the note runs more than one line, the subsequent lines are flush with the left margin, but each new note begins with an indentation of five spaces. Each note begins with an indented, raised numeral, then a capital letter, and ends with a period or other terminal punctuation. Double-space between footnotes.

FIRST REFERENCE TO A BOOK
Here is a typical first reference to a book:

[1] Curtis F. Brown, <u>Ingrid Bergman</u> (New York: Pyramid, 1973), p. 55.

Notice that you give the author's name as it appears on the title page, *first name first.* You need not give the subtitle, but if you do give it, put a colon between the title and the subtitle and underline the subtitle. The name of the city (without the state or country) is usually enough; but if the city is not well known, or may be confused with another city of the same name (Cambridge, England, and Cambridge, Massachusetts), the state or country is added. The name of the publisher (here, Pyramid Publications) may be shortened. The conventional abbreviation for page is "p." and for pages is "pp." (*not* "pg." and "pgs."). If you give the author's name in the body of the page — for example, in such a sentence as "Curtis F. Brown says that Bergman . . ." — do not repeat the name in the footnote. Merely begin with the title.

[1] <u>Ingrid Bergman</u> (New York: Pyramid, 1973), p. 55.

But do not get carried away by the principle of not repeating in the note any material already given in the body of the paper. If the author and the title are given, convention nevertheless requires you to repeat the title — though not the author's name — in the first note citing the source.

For a book in one volume, by one author, revised edition:

[2] X. J. Kennedy, <u>An Introduction to Poetry</u>, 3d ed. (Boston: Little, Brown, 1974), p. 41.

For a book in one volume, by one author, later reprint:

[3] D. H. Lawrence, <u>Studies in Classic American Literature</u> (1923; rpt. Garden City, N.Y.: Doubleday, 1953), pp. 87–88.

For a book in more than one volume (notice that the volume number is given in roman numerals, the page number in arabic numerals, and abbreviations such as "vol." and "p." are *not* used):

[4] Frank Freidel, <u>Franklin</u> <u>D.</u> <u>Roosevelt</u>: <u>Launching</u> <u>the</u> <u>New</u> <u>Deal</u> (Boston: Little, Brown, 1973), IV, 197–201.

For a book by more than one author (if there are more than three authors, give the full name of the first author and add *et al.*, the Latin abbreviation for "and others"):

[5] Carl Bernstein and Bob Woodward, <u>All</u> <u>the</u> <u>President's</u> <u>Men</u> (New York: Simon and Schuster, 1974), pp. 163–72.

For an edited or translated book:

[6] <u>The</u> <u>Letters</u> <u>of</u> <u>John</u> <u>Keats,</u> <u>1814–1821</u>, ed. Hyder Edward Rollins (Cambridge, Mass.: Harvard Univ. Press, 1958), II, 129.

[7] Paul Ginestier, <u>The</u> <u>Poet</u> <u>and</u> <u>the</u> <u>Machine</u>, trans. Martin B. Friedman (Chapel Hill: Univ. of North Carolina Press, 1961), p. 28.

[8] Albert Gilman and Roger Brown, "Personality and Style in Concord," in <u>Transcendentalism</u> <u>and</u> <u>Its</u> <u>Legacy</u>, eds. Myron Simon and Thornton H. Parsons (Ann Arbor: Univ. of Michigan Press, 1966), pp. 103–104.

As note 8 indicates, when you are quoting from an essay in an edited book, you begin with the essayist(s) and the essay, then go on to give the title of the book and the name of the editor(s). If there is one editor, as in note 6, the abbreviation is "ed.," but if there are two or more, the abbreviation (as in note 8) is "eds."

For an *encyclopedia*, publisher and place of publication need not be given. If the article is signed, begin with the author's name (first name first); if it is unsigned, simply begin with the title of the article, in quotation marks. The first example is for a signed article on William F. Cody, known as Buffalo Bill:

[9] Don Russell, "Cody, William Frederick," <u>Encyclopedia</u> <u>Americana</u>, 1973, VII, 177.

Some manuals say that references to alphabetically arranged articles (signed or unsigned) need not include the volume and page number, but if you do include them, as we just did, use roman numerals for the volume (but do not write "vol.") and arabic numerals for the page (but do not write "p.").

The most recent edition of the *Encyclopaedia Britannica*, as we explain on page 203, comprises three groups of books, called *Propaedia, Micropaedia,* and *Macropaedia,* so you must specify which of the three you are referring to. The following example cites an unsigned article on Sitting Bull:

[10] "Sitting Bull," Encyclopaedia Britannica: Micropaedia, 1974, IX, 243–44.

FIRST REFERENCE TO A JOURNAL

Footnote 11 is for a journal (here, volume 43) paginated consecutively throughout the year; footnote 12 is for a journal that paginates each issue separately. A journal paginated separately requires you to list the issue number or month or week or day as well as the year because if it is, for example, a monthly, there will be twelve page 10's in any given year. Current practice favors omitting the volume number for popular weeklies (see footnote 13) and for newspapers, in which case the full date is given without parentheses.

[11] John Demos, "The American Family in Past Time," American Scholar, 43 (1974), 423–24.

[12] Hortense J. Spillers, "Martin Luther King and the Style of the Black Sermon," The Black Scholar, 3, No. 1 (1971), 15.

[13] Bernard McCabe, "Taking Dickens Seriously," Commonweal, 14 May 1965, p. 245.

Notice that footnote 11 identifies volume 43 as having been issued in 1974. If a journal begins a new volume with each new calendar year, the season or month need not be specified; but if the volume number straddles two calendar years, say from Summer 1978 through Spring 1979, the season or month is specified inside the parentheses, before the year.

The author's name and the title of the article are given as they appear in the journal (first name first), the title of the article in quotation marks and the title of the journal underlined (to indicate italics). Until recently the volume number, before the date, was given with capital roman numerals, the page or pages with arabic numerals, but current practice uses arabic numerals for both the volume and the page or pages. Notice that when a volume number is given, as in notes 11 and 12, the page number is *not* preceded by *p.* or *pp.*

If a *book review* has a title, the review may be treated as an article. If, however, the title is merely that of the book reviewed, or even if the review has a title but for clarity you wish to indicate that it is a review, the following form is commonly used:

[14] N. R. McWilliams, review of Kate Millett, <u>Sexual Politics</u> (Garden City, N.Y.: Doubleday, 1970), <u>Commonweal</u>, 2 October 1970, p. 25.

FIRST REFERENCE TO A NEWSPAPER

The first example is for a *signed article*, the second is for an *unsigned one*.

[15] Bertha Brody, "Illegal Immigrant Allowed to Stay," <u>New York Times</u>, 8 March 1979, Sec. B, p. 12, col. 2.

[16] "Fossils Stolen Again," <u>Washington Post</u>, 28 February 1979, p. 7, col. 3.

SUBSEQUENT REFERENCES

If you quote a second or third or fourth time from a work and you do not wish to incorporate the reference within your text, use a short form in your footnote. The most versatile short form is simply the author's last name and the page number, thus:

[17] Lawrence, p. 34.

You can even dispense with the author's name if you have mentioned it in the sentence to which the footnote is keyed. That is, if you have said "Lawrence goes on to say . . .," the footnote need only be:

[18] P. 34.

If, however, you have made reference to more than one work by the author, you must indicate by a short title which work you are referring to, thus:

[19] Lawrence, <u>Studies</u>, p. 34.

Or, if your sentence mentions that you are quoting Lawrence, the footnote may be:

[20] <u>Studies</u>, p. 34.

If you have said something like "Lawrence, in *Studies in Classic American Literature*, argues . . .," the reference may be merely:

[21] P. 34.

In short, a subsequent reference should be as brief as clarity allows. The form "ibid." (for *ibidem*, in the same place), indicating that the material being footnoted comes from the same place as the material of the previous footnote, is no longer preferred for second references. "Op. cit." (for *opere citato*, in the work cited) and "loc. cit." (for *loco citato*, in the place cited) have almost disappeared. Identification by author, or by author and short title if necessary, is preferable.

A reminder: as pages 364–65 suggest, if you are going to quote frequently from one source, it will be best to say in your first reference to this source that sources of subsequent quotations from this work will be cited in parentheses within the body of the paper.

*REFERENCES
TO INTRODUCTIONS AND TO
REPRINTED ESSAYS*

You may want to footnote some material that is printed along with a reprint of a work of literature. If, for example, you use Robert B. Heilman's edition of Shakespeare's *The Taming of the Shrew*, and you say "Robert B. Heilman points out . . . ," your footnote will look like this:

[22] Introd. to William Shakespeare, <u>The Taming of the Shrew</u> (New York: New American Library, 1966), p. xxv.

Heilman's edition of the play includes, as a sort of appendix, several previously published commentaries. If you want to quote from one of them, the monstrous, but accurate, footnote to the quotation might run:

[23] Maynard Mack, "Engagement and Detachment in Shakespeare's Plays," in <u>Essays on Shakespeare and Elizabethan Drama in Honor of Hardin Craig</u>, ed. Richard Hosley (Columbia: Univ. of Missouri Press, 1962), rpt. in William Shakespeare, <u>The Taming of the Shrew</u>, ed. Robert B. Heilman (New York: New American Library, 1966), p. 213.

(You learned from Heilman's credit-note the title, editor, etc., of the book in which Mack's essay originally appeared.)

SECONDHAND REFERENCES

If you are quoting, say, Sir Arthur Pickard-Cambridge, but have derived the quotation not from his book, *Dithyramb, Tragedy and Comedy,* but from a book or article that quotes from his book, your footnote should indicate both the place where you found it and (if possible) the place where the original passage appears.

> [24] Sir Arthur Pickard-Cambridge, <u>Dithyramb, Tragedy and Comedy</u> (Oxford: 1927), p. 243, quoted in Katherine Lever, <u>The Art of Greek Comedy</u> (London: Methuen, 1956), p. 57.

In this example, Lever's book is what you read. If her book had mentioned the publisher of Pickard-Cambridge's book, you would have included that too. Another example, this one from a journal that quoted from Charles Reich's *The Greening of America*:

> [25] Charles A. Reich, <u>The Greening of America</u>, quoted in Carl H. Madden, "The Greening of Economics," <u>Virginia Quarterly Review</u>, 50 (Spring 1974), 161.

In this example, Madden's article is what you read. If Madden had given the place, publisher, date, and page of Reich's book, you would have included all that material in your footnote; but he didn't, so you give only as much as you can. In any case, honesty requires you to cite Madden as well as Reich. And not only honesty, but self-protection: if it turns out that Madden has quoted Reich inaccurately, the blame falls not on you, but on Madden.

FOOTNOTING INTERVIEWS, LECTURES, LETTERS

The following notes can serve as models:

> [26] Interview with Rose Moss, novelist, Wellesley College, Wellesley, Mass., 1 March 1983.

> [27] Howard Saretta, "Buying College Athletes," lecture delivered at Atlantic College, Hudson, N.Y., 3 March 1983.

> [28] Information in a letter to the author, from William Takayanagi of Atlantic College, Hudson, N.Y., 28 February 1983.

BIBLIOGRAPHY

A bibliography is a list of the works cited in the piece of writing or, less often, a list of all the relevant writing. (There is rarely much point in the second sort; if you haven't made use of a particular book or article, why list it?) Normally a bibliography is given only in a long manuscript such as a research paper or a book, but instructors may require a bibliography even for a short paper if they wish to see at a glance the material that the student has used. In this case, a heading such as "Works Consulted" or "Works Cited" is less pretentious than "Bibliography."

Because a bibliography is arranged alphabetically by author, the author's last name is given first. If a work is by more than one author, it is given under the first author's name; his last name is given first, but the other author's or authors' names follow the normal order of first name first. (See the entry under "Brown," below.) Anonymous works are sometimes grouped at the beginning, arranged alphabetically under the first word of the title (or the second word, if the first word is an article, that is, *A, An,* or *The*), but the recent tendency has been to list them at the appropriate alphabetical place, giving the initial article, if any, but alphabetizing under the next word. Thus, an anonymous article entitled "A View of Freud" would retain the "A" but would be alphabetized under V.

In addition to giving the last name first, a bibliographic entry differs from a footnote in several ways. For example, a bibliographic entry does not put parentheses around the place of publication, the publisher, and the date. In typing an entry, begin flush with the left-hand margin; if the entry runs over the line, indent the subsequent lines of the entry five spaces. Double-space between entries. (Some manuals suggest double-spacing throughout.)

A book by one author:

Aries, Philippe.   <u>Western Attitudes Toward Death</u>: From the Middle Ages to the Present.   Trans. Patricia M. Ranum.   Baltimore: Johns Hopkins Univ. Press, 1974.

A book by more than one author:

Brown, Roger, and Richard J. Herrnstein.   <u>Psychology</u>.   Boston: Little, Brown, 1975.

Notice, in this last entry, that the book is alphabetized under the *last name* of the *first* author, but that the name of the second author is given in the ordinary way, first name first.

An essay or other work within an edited volume:

Bush, Douglas. "Wordsworth: A Minority Report," in <u>Wordsworth</u>: <u>Centenary Studies</u>. Ed. Gilbert T. Dunklin. Princeton: Princeton Univ. Press, 1951, pp. 3–22.

Two or more works by the same author:

Frye, Northrop. <u>Fables of Identity</u>: <u>Studies in Poetic Mythology</u>. New York: Harcourt, 1963.

‗‗‗‗‗‗. <u>The Secular Scripture</u>. Cambridge, Mass.: Harvard Univ. Press, 1976.

The horizontal line (six underscore marks followed by a period and two spaces) indicates that the author (in this case Northrop Frye) is the same as in the previous item; multiple titles by one author are arranged alphabetically, as here where *Fables* precedes *Secular*. By the way, the reason that the second of these entries includes "Mass." is to distinguish Cambridge, Massachusetts, from Cambridge, England. Indicate the state only if two cities share a name, or if the name of the city is not likely to be known.

Encyclopedia articles:

"Journalism." <u>Encyclopaedia Britannica</u>: <u>Micropaedia</u>. 1978 ed.

Lang, Andrew. "Ballads." <u>Encyclopaedia Britannica</u>. 11th ed.

The first of these two encyclopedia articles is unsigned, so the article is listed under its title. The second of the articles is signed, so it is listed under its author. Note that an encyclopedia article does not require volume or page, or place or date of publication; the edition, however, must be identified somehow, and usually the date is the best identification.

An introduction to a book by another author:

MacCaffrey, Isabel Gamble. Introd. to John Milton, <u>Samson Agonistes and the Shorter Poems</u>. New York: New American Library, 1966.

The last entry suggests that the student made use of the introduction, rather than the main body, of the book; if the body of the

book were used, the book would be alphabetized under M for
Milton, and the form would resemble that of the next item, with
"Ed. Isabel Gamble MacCaffrey" following the title.

An edition:

Pope, Alexander. The Correspondence of Alexander Pope. Ed. George
      Sherburn. 5 vols. Oxford: Clarendon, 1956.

A periodical:

Reynolds, Lloyd G. "Making a Living in China." Yale Review, 53 (June
      1974), 481-97.

A newspaper:

Romero, Juanita. "Panda Rejects Spouse." Washington Post, 18 March
      1979, p. 6, col. 4.

"Shakespeare Proved Not Bacon." New York Times, 21 January 1979, Sec.
      D, p. 29, col. 2.

The first of these newspaper articles is signed, so it is listed under
the author's last name. The second article is unsigned, so it is listed
under the first word of the title.

An anthology:

Valdez, Luis, and Stan Steiner, eds. Aztlan, An Anthology of Mexican
      American Literature. New York: Knopf, 1972.

This entry lists the anthology alphabetically under the editor's
name, but an anthology may be entered either under the editor's
name or under its title. See below, *Victorian Poetry.*

A book review:

Vendler, Helen. Review of Essays on Style, ed. Roger Fowler. Essays in
      Criticism, 16 (1966), 457-63.

An anthology (this one listed by title rather than by editor):

Victorian Poetry and Poetics, 2nd ed., ed. Walter E. Houghton and G.
      Robert Stange. Boston: Houghton Mifflin, 1968.

DOCUMENTATION IN FIELDS OTHER THAN THE HUMANITIES

We have given the system of documentation (footnotes and bibliography) used in the humanities, but the sciences and some of the social sciences use different systems. If you are writing a paper for a course other than one in the humanities, history, or political science, follow the style set forth in the appropriate manual.

Biology:

Council of Biology Editors, Committee on Form and Style. *CBE Style Manual.* 3rd ed. Washington, D.C.: American Institute of Biological Sciences, 1972.

Chemistry:

American Chemical Society. *Handbook for Authors of Papers in the Journals of the American Chemical Society.* Washington, D.C.: American Chemical Society, 1978.

Engineering:

Engineers Joint Council, Committee of Engineering Society Editors. *Recommended Practice for Style of References in Engineering Publications.* New York: Engineers Joint Council, 1966.

Geology:

U.S. Geological Survey. *Suggestions to Authors of Reports of the United States Geological Survey.* 6th ed. Washington, D.C.: Department of the Interior, 1978.

Mathematics:

American Mathematical Society. *Manual for Authors of Mathematical Papers.* 4th ed. Providence, R.I.: American Mathematical Society, 1973.

Medicine:

American Medical Association, Scientific Publications Division. *Stylebook.* 6th ed. Acton, Mass.: Publishing Sciences Group, 1976.

Physics:

American Institute of Physics, Publications. *Style Manual.* Rev. ed. New York: American Institute of Physics, 1973.

Psychology:

American Psychological Association. *Publication Manual of the American Psychological Association.* 2nd ed. Washington, D.C.: American Psychological Association, 1974.

19

Punctuation

Speakers can raise or lower the volume or pitch of their voices; they can speak a phrase slowly and distinctly and then (making a parenthetical remark, perhaps) quicken the pace. They can wave their arms, pound a table, or pause meaningfully. But writers, physically isolated from their audience, have only paper and ink to work with. Nevertheless, they can embody some of the tones and gestures of speech — in the patterns of their written sentences, and in the dots, hooks, and dashes of punctuation that clarify those patterns.

Punctuation clarifies, first of all, by removing or reducing ambiguity. Consider this headline from a story in a newspaper:

SQUAD HELPS DOG BITE VICTIM

Of course there is no real ambiguity here — only a laugh — because the stated meaning is so clearly absurd, and on second reading we supply the necessary hyphen in *dog-bite*. But other ill-punctuated sentences may be troublesome rather than entertaining. Take the following sentence:

He arrived late for the rehearsal didn't end until midnight.

Almost surely you stumbled in the middle of the sentence, thinking that it was about someone arriving tardily at a rehearsal, and then, since what followed made no sense, you probably went back and mentally added the comma (by pausing) at the necessary place:

He arrived late, for the rehearsal didn't end until midnight.

Punctuation helps to keep the reader on the right path. And the path is your train of thought. If your punctuation is faulty, you unintentionally point the reader off your path and toward dead end streets and quagmires. Let's look at an example.

> Once more, with feeling.
> Once more with feeling.

Is there a difference between these two sentences or do they have identical meanings? Well, if punctuation is not just ink on paper, the first sentence means something like "Let's do it again, but this time do it with feeling," while the second sentence means "The last performance had feeling, and so let's do it once more, keeping the feeling."

Even when punctuation is not the key to meaning, it usually helps you to get your meaning across neatly. Consider the following sentences:

> There are two kinds of feminism — one is the growing struggle of women to understand and change the shape of their lives and the other is a narrow ideology whose adherents are anxious to clear away whatever does not conform to their view.

This is clear enough, but by changing the punctuation it can be sharpened. Because a dash usually indicates an abrupt interruption — it usually precedes a sort of afterthought — a colon would be better. The colon, usually the signal of an amplification of what precedes it, here would suggest that the two classifications are not impromptu thoughts but carefully considered ones. Second, and more important, in the original version the two classifications are run together without any intervening punctuation, but since the point is that the two are utterly different, it is advisable to separate them by inserting a comma or a semicolon, indicating a pause. A comma before "and the other" would do, but probably a semicolon — without the "and" — is preferable because it is a heavier pause, thereby making the separation clearer. Here is the sentence, revised:

> There are two kinds of feminism: one is the growing struggle of women to understand and change the shape of their lives; the other is a narrow ideology whose adherents are anxious to clear away whatever does not conform to their view.

The right punctuation enables the reader to move easily through the sentence.

Now, although punctuation helps a reader to move through a sentence, it must be admitted that some of the rules of punctuation do not contribute to meaning or greatly facilitate reading. For example, in American usage a period never comes immediately after quotation marks; it precedes quotation marks, thus:

> She said, "Put the period inside the quotation marks."

If you put the period after the closing quotation mark, the meaning remains the same, but you are also informing your reader that you don't know the relevant convention. Since a misspelled word or a misplaced period often gives the impression of laziness, ignorance, or incompetence, why not generate as little friction as possible by learning the chief conventions?

THREE COMMON ERRORS: FRAGMENTS, COMMA SPLICES, AND RUN-ON SENTENCES

Fragments and How to Correct Them

A fragment is a part of a sentence set off as if it were a complete sentence: *Because I didn't care. Being an accident. Later in the week. For several reasons. My oldest sister.* Fragments are common in speech, but they are used sparingly in writing, for particular effects (see pages 314–15). A fragment used carelessly in writing often looks like an afterthought — usually because it *was* an afterthought, that is, an explanation or other addition that really belongs to the previous sentence. With appropriate punctuation (and sometimes with no punctuation at all) a fragment can usually be connected to the previous sentence.

1. *Incorrect*

Many nineteenth-century horror stories have been made into films. Such as *Dracula* and *Frankenstein.*

Correct

Many nineteenth-century horror stories have been made into films, such as *Dracula* and *Frankenstein.*

2. *Incorrect*

Many schools are putting renewed emphasis on writing. Because SAT scores have declined for ten years.

Correct

Many schools are putting renewed emphasis on writing because SAT scores have declined for ten years.

3. *Incorrect*

He practiced doing card tricks. In order to fool his friends.

Correct

He practiced doing card tricks in order to fool his friends.

4. *Incorrect*

She wore only rope sandals. Being a strict vegetarian.

Correct

Being a strict vegetarian, she wore only rope sandals.
She wore only rope sandals because she was a strict vegetarian.

5. *Incorrect*

A fragment often looks like an afterthought. Perhaps because it *was* an afterthought.

Correct

A fragment often looks like an afterthought — perhaps because it *was* an afterthought.

6. *Incorrect*

He hoped to get credit for two summer school courses. Batik and Hang-Gliding.

Correct

He hoped to get credit for two summer school courses: Batik and Hang-Gliding.

Notice in the examples above that, depending upon the relationship between the two parts, the fragment and the preceding statement can be joined by a comma, a dash, a colon, or by no punctuation at all.

Notice also that unintentional fragments often follow subordinating conjunctions, such as *because* and *although*. Subordinating conjunctions introduce a subordinate (dependent) clause; such a clause cannot stand as a sentence. Here is a list of the commonest subordinating conjunctions.

after	though
although	unless
because	until
before	when
if	where
provided	whereas
since	while

Fragments also commonly occur when the writer, as in the fourth example, mistakenly uses *being* as a main verb.

Comma Splices and Run-on Sentences, and How to Correct Them

An error known as a *comma splice* or *comma fault* results when a comma is mistakenly placed between two independent clauses that are not joined by a coordinating conjunction: *and, or, nor, but, for, yet, so.* If the comma is omitted, the error is called a *run-on sentence.*

Examples of the two errors:

Comma splice (or *comma fault*): In the second picture the man leans on the woman's body, he is obviously in pain.

Run-on sentence: In the second picture the man leans on the woman's body he is obviously in pain.

Run-on sentences and comma splices may be corrected in five principal ways.

1. Use a period. Write two sentences.

In the second picture the man leans on the woman's body. He is obviously in pain.

2. Use a semicolon.

In the second picture the man leans on the woman's body; he is obviously in pain.

3. Use a comma and a coordinating conjunction (and, or, not, but, for, yet, so).

> In the second picture the man leans on the woman's body, and he is obviously in pain.

4. Make one of the clauses dependent (subordinate). Use a subordinating conjunction such as *after, although, because, before, if, since, though, unless, until, when, where, while.*

> In the second picture the man leans on the woman's body because he is in pain.

5. Reduce one of the independent clauses to a phrase, or even to a single word.

> In the second picture the man, obviously in pain, leans on the woman's body.

Run-on sentences and comma splices are especially common in sentences beginning with transitional words or phrases such as the following:

also	however
besides	indeed
consequently	in fact
for example	nevertheless
furthermore	therefore
hence	whereas

When these words join independent clauses, the clauses cannot be linked by a comma.

> Incorrect: She argued from faulty premises, however the conclusions happened to be correct.

Here are five correct revisions, following the five rules we have just given. (In the first two revisions we place "however" after, rather than before, "the conclusions" because we prefer the increase in emphasis, but the grammatical point is the same.)

1. She argued from faulty premises. The conclusions, however, happened to be correct. (Two sentences)
2. She argued from faulty premises; the conclusions, however, happened to be correct. (Semicolon)
3. She argued from faulty premises, but the conclusions happened to be correct. (Coordinating conjunction)
4. Although she argued from faulty premises, the conclusions happened to be correct. (Subordinating conjunction)

    5. She argued from faulty premises to correct conclusions. (Reduction of an independent clause to a phrase)

It should now be evident that the following sentence contains a comma splice:

    The husband is not pleased, in fact, he is embarrassed.

And the ways of repairing it are equally evident.

THE PERIOD

    1. Periods are used to mark the ends of sentences (or intentional sentence fragments) other than questions and exclamations.

    A sentence normally ends with a period.

    She said, "I'll pass."

    Yes.

    Once more, with feeling.

But a sentence within a sentence is punctuated according to the needs of the longer sentence. Notice, in the following example, that periods are *not* used after "pass" or directly after "said."

    "I'll pass," she said (but meant she hoped she would).

If a sentence ends with a quotation, the period goes *inside* the quotation marks unless parenthetic material follows the quotation.

    Brutus says, "Antony is but a limb of Caesar."

    Brutus says, "Antony is but a limb of Caesar" (*Julius Caesar*, II.i.165).

    2. Periods are used with abbreviations of titles and terms of reference.

    Dr., Mr., Mrs., Ms.

    p., pp. (for "page" and "pages"), i.e., e.g., etc.

But when the capitalized initial letters of the words naming an organization are used in place of the full name, the periods are commonly omitted:

    CBS, CORE, IBM, NBA, UCLA, UNICEF, USAF

3. Periods are also used to separate chapter from verse in the Bible.

Genesis iii.2, Mark vi.10

For further details on references to the Bible, see page 359.

THE COLON

The colon has three chief uses: to introduce a list or series of examples; to introduce an amplification of what precedes the colon; and to introduce a quotation (though a quotation can be introduced by other means). A fourth, less important, use is in the indication of time.

1. The colon may introduce a list or series.

Students are required to take one of the following sciences: biology, chemistry, geology, physics.

Note, however, that a colon is *not* used if the series is introduced by *such as, for example,* or a similar transitional phrase.

2. As a formal introduction to an amplification, the colon is almost equivalent to *namely*, or *that is*. What is on one side of the colon more or less equals what is on the other side. The material on either side of the colon can stand as a separate sentence.

She explained her fondness for wrestling: she did it to shock her parents.

The forces which in China created a central government were absent in Japan: farming had to be on a small scale, there was no need for extensive canal works, and a standing army was not required to protect the country from foreign invaders.

Many of the best of the Civil War photographs must be read as the fossils of earlier events: The caissons with their mud-encrusted wheels, the dead on the field, the empty landscapes, all speak of deeds already past.

— John Szarkowski

Notice in this last example that the writer uses a capital letter after the colon; the usage is acceptable when a complete sentence follows the colon, as long as that style is followed consistently throughout a paper. But most students find it easier to use lowercase letters after colons, the prevalent style in writing today.

3. The colon, like the comma, may be used to introduce a quotation; it is more formal than the comma, setting off the quotation to a greater degree.

> The black sculptor Ed Wilson tells his students: "Malcolm X is my brother, Martin Luther King is my brother, Eldridge Cleaver is my brother! But Michelangelo is my grandfather!"
>
> — Albert E. Elsen

4. A colon is used to separate the hour from the minutes when the time is given in figures.

> 9:15, 12:00

Colons (like semicolons) go outside of closing quotation marks if they are not part of the quotation.

> "There is no such thing as a free lunch": the truth of these words is confirmed every day.

THE SEMICOLON

Typographically a semicolon is part comma, part period; and it does indeed function as a strong comma or as a weak period. It can never function as a colon.

1. As a strong comma, the semicolon can be used as follows:

> Only in countries touching on the Mediterranean has the nude been at home; and even there its meaning was often forgotten.
>
> In the greatest age of painting, the nude inspired the greatest works; and even when it ceased to be a compulsive subject it held its position as an academic exercise and a demonstration of mastery.

As a strong comma, it can be used to separate a series of phrases or clauses with internal commas.

> He had a car, which he hadn't paid for; a wife, whom he didn't love; and a father, who was unemployed.

But:

> He had a car, a wife, and a father.

2. As a weak period, the semicolon joins independent statements that the writer wishes to bring together more closely than a period allows. Lewis Thomas puts it thus: "The period tells you that that is that; if you didn't get all the meaning you wanted or expected, anyway you got all the writer intended to parcel out and now you have to move along. But with a semicolon there you get a pleasant little feeling of expectancy; there is more to come; read on; it will get clearer." Here are some examples of a semicolon joining independent but related statements.

> When a cat washes its face it does not move its paw; it moves its face.
>
> Others merely live; I vegetate.
>
> All the windows seemed to be in the wrong places; it was a house designed to hold the darkness.
>
> — Sharon R. Curtin
>
> The catacombs were not underground churches where Christians secretly worshiped; they were burial chambers connected by long passages, and they were well known to official Rome.
>
> He never complained; he knew it wouldn't do any good.

With short clauses, such as those in the last example, a comma could be used, but some purists would object, saying that joining even short clauses with a comma would produce a run-on sentence of the sort known as a comma splice or a comma fault (see pages 382–84).

Use a semicolon also before a conjunctive adverb (that is, a transitional word such as *also, consequently, furthermore, however, moreover, nevertheless, therefore*) connecting independent clauses, and put a comma after the conjunctive adverb.

> Her hair was black and wavy; however, it was false.

Semicolons (like colons) go outside of closing quotation marks if they are not part of the quotation.

> He said, "I do"; moreover, he repeated the words.

THE COMMA

A comma (from a Greek word meaning "to cut") indicates a relatively slight pause within a sentence. If after checking the rules you are still uncertain of whether or not to use a comma in a given sentence, read the sentence aloud and see if it sounds better with or without a pause, and then add or omit the comma. A women's shoe store in New York has a sign on the door:

NO MEN PLEASE.

If the proprietors would read the sign aloud, they might want to change it to

NO MEN, PLEASE

In typing, always follow a comma with a space.

We outline below the correct uses of the comma. For your reference, here is a table of contents for the following pages:

1. with independent clauses, pages 388–89
2. with introductory subordinate clauses or long phrases, page 389
3. with tacked-on subordinate phrases or long clauses, pages 389–90
4. as parentheses, page 390
5. with nonrestrictive modifiers, pages 390–92
6. with a series, pages 392–93
7. with direct discourse, page 393
8. with "yes" and "no," page 393
9. with words of address, page 393
10. with geographical locations, page 393
11. with dates, page 393

   A note on the position of the comma with other punctuation, pages 393–94

1. Independent clauses (unless short) joined by a coordinating conjunction (*and, or, nor, but, for, yet, so*) take a comma before the conjunction.

> Most students see at least a few football games, and many go to every game of the season.

> Most students seem to have an intuitive sense of when to use a comma, but in fact the "intuition" is the result of long training.

If the introductory independent clause is short, the comma is usually omitted:

> She dieted but she continued to gain weight.

2. An introductory subordinate clause or long phrase is usually followed by a comma.

> Having revised his manuscript for the third time, he went to bed.
>
> In order to demonstrate her point, the instructor stood on her head.

If the introductory subordinate clause or phrase is short, say four words or fewer, the comma may be omitted, provided no ambiguity results from the omission.

> Having left he soon forgot.

But compare this last example with the following:

> Having left, the instructor soon forgot.

If the comma is omitted, the sentence is misread. Where are commas needed in the following sentences?

> Instead of discussing the book she wrote a summary.
>
> When Shakespeare wrote comedies were already popular.
>
> While he ate his poodle would sit by the table.
>
> As we age small things become killers.

3. A subordinate clause or long modifying phrase tacked on as an afterthought is usually preceded by a comma.

> I have decided not to be nostalgic about the 1950's, despite the hoopla over Elvis.
>
> Buster Keaton fell down a flight of stairs without busting, thereby gaining his nickname from Harry Houdini.
>
> By the time he retired Hank Aaron had 755 home runs, breaking Babe Ruth's record by 41.

With afterthoughts, the comma may be omitted if there is a clear sequence of cause and effect, signaled by such words as *because, for,* and *so.* Compare the two following examples:

In 1601 Shakespeare wrote *Hamlet*, probably his best-known play.

In 1601 Shakespeare wrote *Hamlet* because revenge tragedy was in demand.

4. A pair of commas can serve as a pair of unobtrusive parentheses. Be sure not to omit the second comma.

Doctors, I think, have an insufficient knowledge of acupuncture.

The earliest known paintings of Christ, dating from the third century, are found in the catacombs outside of Rome.

Medicare and Medicaid, the chief sources of federal support for patients in nursing homes, are frequently confused.

Under this heading we can include a conjunctive adverb (a transitional adverb such as *also, besides, consequently, however, likewise, nevertheless, therefore*) inserted within a sentence. These transitional words are set off between a pair of commas.

Her hair, however, was stringy.

If one of these words begins a sentence, the comma after it is optional. Notice, however, that the presence of such a word as "however" is not always a safeguard against a run-on sentence or comma splice; if the word occurs between two independent clauses and it goes with the second clause, you need a semicolon before it and a comma after it.

Her hair was black and wavy; however, it was false.

(See the discussion of comma splice on pages 382–84.)

5. Use a comma to set off a nonrestrictive modifier. A nonrestrictive modifier, as the following examples will make clear, is a sort of parenthetical addition; it gives supplementary information about the subject, but it can be omitted without changing the subject. A restrictive modifier, however, is not supplementary but essential; if a restrictive modifier is omitted, the subject becomes more general. In Dorothy Parker's celebrated poem,

Men seldom make passes
At girls who wear glasses,

"who wear glasses" is a restrictive modifier, narrowing or restricting the subject down from "girls" to a particular group of girls, "girls who wear glasses."

Here is a *non*restrictive modifier:

> For the majority of immigrants, who have no knowledge of English, language is the chief problem.

Now a restrictive modifier:

> For the majority of immigrants who have no knowledge of English, language is the chief problem.

The first version says — in addition to its obvious message that language is the chief problem — that the majority of immigrants have no knowledge of English. The second version makes no such assertion; it talks not about the majority of immigrants but only about a more restricted group — those immigrants who have no knowledge of English.

Other examples:

> Shakespeare's shortest tragedy, *Macbeth*, is one of his greatest plays.

In this sentence, "*Macbeth*" is nonrestrictive because the subject is already as restricted as possible; Shakespeare can have written only one "shortest tragedy." That is, "*Macbeth*" is merely an explanatory equivalent of "Shakespeare's shortest tragedy" and it is therefore enclosed in commas. (A noun or noun phrase serving as an explanatory equivalent to another, and in the same syntactical relation to other elements in the sentence, is said to be in apposition.) But compare

> Shakespeare's tragedy *Macbeth* is one of his greatest plays.

with the misleadingly punctuated sentence,

> Shakespeare's tragedy, *Macbeth*, is one of his greatest plays.

The first of these is restrictive, narrowing or restricting the subject "tragedy" down to one particular tragedy, and so it rightly does not separate the modifier from the subject by a comma. The second, punctuated so that it is nonrestrictive, falsely implies that *Macbeth* is Shakespeare's only tragedy. Here is an example of a nonrestrictive modifier correctly punctuated:

Women, who constitute 51.3 percent of the population and 53 percent of the electorate, constitute only 2.5 percent of the House of Representatives and 1 percent of the Senate.

In the next two examples, the first illustrates the correct use of commas after a nonrestrictive appositive, and the second illustrates the correct omission of commas after a restrictive appositive.

Houdini, the American magician, died in 1926.

The American magician Houdini died in 1926.

6. Words, phrases, and clauses in series take a comma after each item except the last. The comma between the last two items may be omitted if there is no ambiguity.

Photography is a matter of eyes, intuition, and intellect.

— John Szarkowski

She wrote plays, poems, and stories.

He wrote plays, sang songs, and danced jigs.

She wrote a wise, witty, humane book.

But adjectives in a series may cause difficulty. The next two examples correctly omit the commas.

a funny silent film

a famous French professor

In each of these last two examples, the adjective immediately before the noun forms with the noun a compound that is modified by the earlier adjective. That is, the adjectives are not a coordinate series (what is funny is not simply a film but a silent film, what is famous is not simply a professor but a French professor) and so commas are not used. Compare:

a famous French professor

a famous, arrogant French professor

In the second example, only "famous" and "arrogant" form a coordinate series. If in doubt, see if you can replace the commas with "and"; if you can, the commas are correct. In the example given, you could insert "and" between "famous" and "arrogant," but not between "famous" and "French."

Commas are not needed if all the members of the series are connected by conjunctions.

> He ate steak for breakfast and lunch and supper.

7. Use a comma to set off direct discourse.

> "It's a total failure," she said.
> She said, "It's a total failure."

But do not use a comma for indirect discourse.

> She said that it is a total failure.
> She said it is a total failure.

8. Use a comma to set off "yes" and "no."

> Yes, he could take Freshman English at ten o'clock.

9. Use a comma to set off words of address.

> Look, Bill, take Freshman English at ten o'clock.

10. Use a comma to separate a geographical location within another geographical location.

> She was born in Brooklyn, New York, in 1895.

Another way of putting it is to say that a comma is used after each unit of an address, except that a comma is *not* used between the name of the state and the zip code.

11. Use a comma to set off the year from the month or day.

> He was born on June 10, 1965. (No comma is needed if you use the form "10 June 1965.")

A note on the position of the comma when used with other punctuation: If a comma is required with parenthetic material, it follows the second parenthesis.

> Because Japan was secure from invasion (even the Mongols were beaten back), her history is unusually self-contained.

The only time a comma may precede a parenthesis is when parentheses surround a digit or letter used to enumerate a series.

> Questions usually fall into one of three categories: (1) true-false, (2) multiple choice, (3) essay.

A comma always goes inside closing quotation marks unless the quotation is followed by a parenthesis.

"Sayonara," he said.

"Sayonara" (Japanese for "goodbye"), he said.

THE DASH

A dash — made by typing two hyphens without hitting the space-bar before, between, or after — indicates an abrupt break or pause. Overuse of the dash gives writing an unpleasantly explosive quality.

1. The material within dashes may be, in a sense, parenthetic, though the dashes indicate that it is less dispensable than is parenthetic material.

> The bathroom — that private place — has rarely been the subject of scholarly study.

> The Great Wall of China forms a continuous line over 1400 miles long — the distance from New York to Kansas City — running from Peking to the edge of the mountains of Central Asia.

> The old try to survive by cutting corners — eating less, giving up small pleasures like tobacco and movies, doing without warm clothes — and pay the price of ill-health and a shortened life-span.
> — Sharon R. Curtin

Notice that when two dashes are used, if the material within them is deleted the remainder still forms a grammatical sentence.

2. A dash can serve, somewhat like a colon, as a pause before a series. It is more casual than a colon.

> The earliest Shinto holy places were natural objects — trees, boulders, mountains, islands.

> Each of the brothers had his distinct comic style — Groucho's double-talk, Chico's artfully stupid malapropisms, Harpo's horse-play.

> — Gerald Mast

Especially in this last example, where the series is elaborated, a colon could have been used, but it would have been more formal; here the dash is more appropriate to the subject.

A dash is never used next to a comma, and it is used before a period only to indicate that the sentence is interrupted. When used with closing quotation marks it goes inside if it is part of the quotation, outside if it is not.

PARENTHESES

First, a caution: avoid using parentheses to explain pronouns: "In his speech he (Hamlet) says . . ." If "he" needs to be explained by "Hamlet," omit the "he" and just say "Hamlet."

1. Parentheses subordinate material; what is in parentheses is almost a casual aside, less essential than similar material set off in commas, less vigorously spoken than similar material set off in dashes.

> While guest curator for the Whitney (he has since returned to the Denver Art Museum), Feder assembled a magnificent collection of masks, totems, paintings, clothing, and beadwork.

Two cautions: avoid an abundance of these interruptions, and avoid a long parenthesis within a sentence (you are now reading a simple example of this annoying but common habit of writers who have trouble sticking to the point) because the reader will lose track of the main sentence.

2. Use parentheses to enclose digits or letters in a list that is given in running text.

> The exhibition included: (1) decorative screens, (2) ceramics, (3) ink paintings, (4) kimonos.

3. Do not confuse parentheses with square brackets, which are used around material you add to a quotation. See pages 357–58.

4. For the use of parentheses in footnotes, see pages 367–70.

A note on the position of other punctuation with a parenthesis: The example under rule number 2, of commas preceding parentheses enclosing digits or letters in a list given in running text, is the rare exception to the rule that within a sentence, punctuation other than quotation marks never immediately precedes an opening parenthesis. Notice that in the example under rule number 1, the comma *follows* the closing parenthesis:

While guest curator for the Whitney (he has since returned to the Denver Art Museum), Feder assembled a magnificent collection of masks, totems, paintings, clothing, and beadwork.

If an entire sentence is in parentheses, put the final punctuation (period, question mark, or exclamation mark) inside the closing parenthesis.

QUOTATION MARKS

1. Use quotation marks to attribute words to a speaker or writer. (Long quotations that are set off do not take quotation marks. See pages 356–57.) If your quotation includes a passage that was enclosed in quotation marks, alter these inner quotation marks to single quotation marks.

> According to Professor Hugo, "The male dragon in Chinese art has deep-set eyes, the female has bulging eyes, but as one Chinese scholar put it, 'This is a matter of interest only to dragons.'"

British quotation marks are just the reverse: single for ordinary quotations, double for inner quotations. If you are quoting from a passage that includes such quotation marks, change them to the American form.

2. Use quotation marks to indicate the title of unpublished works, like dissertations, and of short works — for example, a lecture, speech, newspaper article, essay, chapter, short story, or song, as well as a poem of less than, say, twenty pages. (But magazines and pamphlets, like books, are underlined.)

3. Use quotation marks to identify a word or term to which you wish to call special attention. (But italics, indicated by underlining, may be used instead of quotation marks.)

> By "comedy" I mean not only a funny play, but any play that ends happily.

Do *not* use quotation marks to enclose slang or a term that you fear is low; use the term or don't use it, but don't apologize by putting it in quotation marks, as in these examples.

Incorrect

"Streaking" was first popularized by Lady Godiva.

Incorrect

Because of "red tape" it took three years.

Incorrect

At last I was able to "put in my two cents."

In all three of these sentences the writers are signaling their uneasiness; in neither the first nor the second is there any cause for uneasiness, but probably the third should be rewritten to get rid of the cliché.

Be sparing, too, in using quotation marks to convey sarcasm, as in

These "poets" are mere dispensers of fantasies.

Sarcasm is usually a poor form of argument, best avoided. But of course there are borderline cases when you may want to convey your dissatisfaction with a word used by others.

African sculpture has a long continuous tradition, but this tradition has been jeopardized recently by the introduction of "civilization" to Africa.

Perhaps the quotation marks here are acceptable, because the writer's distaste has not yet become a sneer and because she is, in effect, quoting. But why not change "civilization" to "western culture," omitting the quotation marks?

Commas and periods go inside closing quotation marks except when the quotation marks are followed by parentheses, in which case they follow the closing parenthesis. Colons, semicolons, and footnote numbers go outside closing quotation marks. Question marks and exclamation points go inside if they are part of the quotation, outside if they are not.

While Thelma Todd paddles the canoe, Groucho listens to her chatter, looks at a duck swimming near the canoe, and asks, "Did that come out of you or the duck?"

What is funny about Groucho saying, "Whatever it is, I'm against it"?

ITALICS

Italic type is indicated by <u>underlining.</u>

1. Underline the name of a plane, ship, train, movie, radio or television program, record album, musical work, statue, painting, play, pamphlet, and book (except sacred works such as the Bible, the Koran, Acts of the Apostles). Notice that when you write of *The New York Times,* you underline *New York* because it is part of the title, but when you write of the London *Times,* you do not underline "London" because "London" is not part of the title, only information added for clarity. Similarly, when you refer to *Time* magazine do not underline "magazine."

2. As suggested on page 307, use italics only sparingly for emphasis. Sometimes, however, this method of indicating your tone of voice is exactly right.

> In 1911 Jacques Henri Lartigue was not merely as unprejudiced as a child; he *was* a child.
>
> — John Szarkowski

3. Use italics for foreign words that have not become a part of the English language.

> Acupuncture aims to affect the *ch'i,* a sort of vital spirit which circulates through the bodily organs.

But:

> He ate a pizza.
> She behaved like a prima donna.
> Avoid clichés.

4. You may use italics in place of quotation marks to identify a word or term to which you wish to call special attention.

> Claude Lévi-Strauss tells us that one of the great purposes of art is that of *miniaturization*. He points out that most works of art are miniatures, being smaller (and therefore more easily understood) than the objects they represent.

CAPITAL LETTERS

Certain obvious conventions — the use of a capital for the first word in a sentence, for names (of days of the week, holidays, months, people, countries), and for words derived from names (such as pro-French) — need not be discussed here.

1. Titles of works in English are usually given according to the following formula. Use a capital for the first letter of the first word, for the first letter of the last word, and for the first letter of all other words that are not articles, conjunctions, or prepositions.

> *The Merchant of Venice*
>
> *A Midsummer Night's Dream*
>
> *Up and Out*
>
> "The Short Happy Life of Francis Macomber"
>
> *The New York Times*

2. Use a capital for a quoted sentence within a sentence, but not for a quoted phrase (unless it is at the beginning of the sentence) and not for indirect discourse.

> He said, "You can even fool some of the people all of the time."
>
> He said you can fool some people "all of the time."
>
> He said that you can even fool some of the people all of the time.

3. Use a capital for a rank or title preceding a proper name or for a title substituting for a proper name.

> She said she was Dr. Perez.
>
> He told President Reagan that the Vice President was away.

But:

> Why would anyone wish to be president?
>
> Washington was the first president.

4. Use a capital when the noun designating a family relationship is used as a substitute for a proper noun.

> If Mother is busy, ask Tim.

But:

> Because my mother was busy, I asked Tim.

5. Formal geographical locations (but not mere points on the compass) are capitalized.

> North America, Southeast Asia, the Far East
>
> In the Southwest, rain sometimes evaporates before touching the ground.
>
> Is Texas part of the South?
>
> The North has its share of racism.

But:

> The wind came from the south.
>
> Czechoslovakia is adjoined on the north by East Germany.

Do *not* capitalize the names of the seasons.

THE HYPHEN

The hyphen has five uses, all drawing on the etymology of the word *hyphen,* which comes from the Greek for "in one," "together."

1. Use a hyphen to attach certain prefixes from root words. *All-, pro-, ex-,* and *self-* are the most common of these ("all-powerful," "ex-wife," "pro-labor," "self-made"), but note that even these prefixes are not always followed by a hyphen. If in doubt, check a dictionary. Prefixes before proper names are always followed by a hyphen:

> anti-Semite, pro-Kennedy, un-American

Prefixes ending in *i* are hyphenated before a word beginning with *i*:

> anti-intellectual, semi-intelligible

A hyphen is normally used to break up a triple consonant resulting from the addition of a prefix:

> ill-lit, all-loving

2. Use a hyphen to tie compound adjectives into a single visual unit:

out-of-date theory, twenty-three books, long-term loan

eighteenth- and nineteenth-century novels

The sea-tossed raft was a common nineteenth-century symbol of man's tragic condition.

But if a compound modifier follows the modified term, it is usually not hyphenated, thus:

The theory was out of date.

3. Use a hyphen to join some compound nouns:

Scholar-teacher, philosopher-poet

4. Use a hyphen to divide a word at the end of a line. Because words may be divided only as indicated by a dictionary, it is easier to end the line with the last complete word you can type than to keep reaching for a dictionary. But here are some principles governing the division of words at the end of a line:

   a. Never hyphenate words of one syllable, such as *called, doubt, right, through*.
   b. Never hyphenate so that a single letter stands alone: *a-bout, hair-y*.
   c. If a word already has a hyphen, divide it at the hyphen: *anti-intellectual, semi-intelligible*.
   d. Divide prefixes and suffixes from the root: *mis-spell, pro-vide, drunken-ness, walk-ing*.
   e. Divide between syllables. If you aren't sure of the proper syllabification, check a dictionary.

5. Use a hyphen to indicate a span of dates or page numbers:

1957-59, pp. 162-68.

THE APOSTROPHE

Use an apostrophe to indicate the possessive, to indicate a contraction, and for certain unusual plurals.

1. The possessive. The most common way to indicate the possessive of a singular noun is to add an apostrophe and then an *s*.

> A dog's life, a week's work
>
> a mouse's tail, Keats's poems, Marx's doctrines

But many authorities suggest that for a proper noun of more than one syllable that ends in *s* or another sibilant (*-cks, -x, -z*), it is better to add only an apostrophe:

> Jesus' parables, Sophocles' plays, Chavez' ideas

When in doubt, say the name aloud and notice if you are adding an *s*. If you are adding an *s* when you say it, add an apostrophe and an *s* when you write it.

Pronouns do not take an apostrophe.

> his book, its fur ("it's fur" is short for "it is fur")
>
> The book is hers, not ours.
>
> The book is theirs.

(Exception: indefinite pronouns take an apostrophe, as in "one's hopes" and "others' opinions.")

For plurals ending in *s*, add only an apostrophe to indicate the possessive:

> the boys' father, the Smiths' house, the Joneses' car

If the plural does not end in *s*, add an apostrophe and an *s*.

> women's clothing, mice's eyes

Don't try to form the possessive of the title of a work (for example, of a play, a book, or a film): Write "the imagery in *The Merchant of Venice*" rather than "*The Merchant of Venice*'s imagery." Using an apostrophe gets you into the problem of whether or not to italicize the *s*; similarly, if you use an apostrophe for a work normally enclosed in quotation marks, you can't put the apostrophe and the *s* after the quotation marks, but you can't put them inside either. And the work really can't possess anything anyway — the imagery, or whatever else, is the author's.

2. Contractions. Use an apostrophe to indicate the omitted letters or numbers in contractions.

> She won't.
>
> It's time to go.
>
> the class of '87

3. Unusual plurals. Use an apostrophe to make plurals of words that do not usually have a plural, and (this is optional) to make the plurals of digits and letters.

> Her speech was full of if's and and's and but's.
>
> Ph.D.'s don't know everything.
>
> Mind your p's and q's.
>
> I got two A's and two B's.
>
> He makes his 4's in two ways.
>
> the 1920's

But if the number is written out, it does not take an apostrophe:

> In the envelope were two tens and two fives.
>
> She is in her twenties.

ABBREVIATIONS

In general, avoid abbreviations except in footnotes and except for certain common ones listed below. And don't use an ampersand (&) unless it appears in material you are quoting, or in a title. Abundant use of abbreviations makes an essay sound like a series of newspaper headlines. Usually *United States* is better than *U.S.* and *the Soviet Union* better than *U.S.S.R.*

1. Abbreviations, with the first letter capitalized, are used before a name.

> Dr. Bellini, Ms. Smith, St. Thomas

But:

> The doctor took her temperature and ten dollars.

2. Degrees that follow a name are abbreviated:

B.A., D.D.S., M.D., Ph.D.

3. Other acceptable abbbreviations include:

A.D., B.C., A.M., P.M., e.g., i.e.

(By the way, *e.g.* means *for example; i.e.* means *that is.* The two ought not to be confused. See pages 421 and 424.)

4. The name of an agency or institution (for instance, the Committee on Racial Equality; International Business Machines; Southern Methodist University) may be abbreviated by using the initial letters, capitalized and usually without periods (e.g., CORE), but it is advisable to give the name in full when first mentioning it (not everyone knows that AARP means American Association of Retired Persons, for instance), and to use the abbreviation in subsequent references.

NUMBERS

1. Write them out if you can do so in fewer than three words; otherwise, use figures.

sixteen, seventy-two, ten thousand, one sixth

10,200; 10,200,000

There are 336 dimples on a golf ball

But always write out round millions and billions, to avoid a string of zeroes.

a hundred and ten million

Some handbooks say that because a figure cannot be capitalized, if a number begins a sentence it should always be written out.

2. Use figures in dates, addresses, decimals, percentages, page numbers, and hours followed by A.M. or P.M.

February 29, 1900; .06 percent; 6 percent; 8:16 A.M.

But hours unmodified by minutes are usually written out, and followed by *o'clock.*

Executions in England regularly took place at eight o'clock.

3. To make the plural of figures (but not of numbers written out) use an apostrophe.

three 6's, two tens

Use an apostrophe to indicate omitted figures.

class of '79

But use a hyphen to indicate a span.

1975-79, pp. 162-68

EXERCISES

1. In the following sentences, decide what punctuation is needed, and then add it. If the sentence is correctly punctuated, place a check mark to the left of it.

   a. Around his neck is a scarf knotted in front and covering his head is a wide brimmed hat.
   b. Buffalo Bill radiates confidence in his bold stance and looks self assured with his head held high.
   c. The demands that men and women make on marriage will never be fully met they cannot be.
   d. The case for nuclear power has always rested on two claims that reactors were reasonably safe and that they were indispensable as a source of energy.
   e. Boys on the whole do not keep diaries.
   f. Children are unwelcome in most New York restaurants that are not Chinese.
   g. Shlomo a giraffe in the Tel Aviv zoo succumbed to the effects of falling down after efforts to raise him with ropes and pulleys were unsuccessful.
   h. Character like a photograph develops in darkness.
   i. In a grief reaction especially when the person has suffered a loss crying comes easily and produces a healthy release from pent up emotion.
   j. There is no God but Allah and Mohammed is His prophet.

2. We reprint below the fourth paragraph of Jeff Greenfield's essay, "Columbo Knows the Butler Didn't Do It," but without punctuation. Go through the paragraph, adding the punc-

tuation you find necessary. Check your work against the original paragraph on pages 57–58. If you find differences between your punctuation and Greenfield's, try to explain why Greenfield made the choices he did.

columbos villains are not simply rich they are privileged they live the lives that are for most of us hopeless daydreams houses on top of mountains with pools servants and sliding doors parties with women in slinky dresses and endless food and drink plush enclosed box seats at professional sports events the envy and admiration of the crowd while we choose between johnny carson and *invasion of the body snatchers* they are at screenings of movies the rest of us wait in line for on third avenue three months later.

3. Here are the first two paragraphs — but without punctuation — of Raymond A. Sokolov's review of a book by Sarah Stage, *Female Complaints: Lydia Pinkham and the Business of Women's Medicine.* Add the necessary punctuation.

home at the range victorian women in america suffered in shame from all manner of female complaints too intimate to name many of them were the fault of men gonorrhea or men doctors prolapsed uterus and women shrewdly kept shy of the ineffectual and often positively harmful doctors of their day instead they doctored themselves with so called patent medicines the most famous of these was lydia pinkhams vegetable compound mrs pinkham actually existed in lynn mass a center of the progressive spirit hotbed of abolition and feminism

sarah stage who has taught american history at williams college had the acuity to see that lydia pinkham was more than a quaint picture on a label that she was a paradigm of the independent woman of her day building a big business with a home remedy to save her family from bankruptcy caused by a neer do well husband she saw furthermore that many of the important themes and forces of american society before world war I clustered around the medicine itself which was largely alcoholic but respectably bitter

20
Spelling

Life would be easier if a sound were always represented by the same letter. Some modern European languages come close to this principle, but English is not among them. "You" and "ewe" are pronounced identically, but they do not have even a single letter in common. George Bernard Shaw once called attention to some of the oddities of English spelling by saying that *fish* might be spelled *ghoti*. How? *Gh* is *f,* as in *enough; o* is *i,* as in *women; ti* is *sh,* as in *notion.* So, *ghoti* spells *fish.*

This is not the place to explain why English spelling is so erratic, but it may be consoling to know that the trouble goes back at least to the Norman French Conquest of England in 1066; after the Conquest, French scribes spelled English words more or less as though the words were French. Moreover, though pronunciation kept changing, spelling became relatively fixed, so that even in Shakespeare's time spelling often reflected a pronunciation that had long been abandoned. And today the spelling of many words still reflects the long-lost medieval pronunciation. The silent *e* in *life,* and the silent consonants in *knight* and *through,* for example, were pronounced in Chaucer's day.

But medieval pronunciation accounts for only some of our spellings. There are many other reasons for the oddities: the *s* in *island* is there, for example, because scholars mistakenly thought the word came into English through the Latin *insula.* (*Isle* indeed comes from *insula,* but *island* comes from Old English *iland.*) Most rules for spelling, then, must immediately be modified with lists of exceptions. Even the most famous,

> *I* before *e* except after *c*
> Or when sounded as *a*
> In *neighbor* and *sleigh,*

No, no it's  before  except after  !

Reprinted with permission of *Diversion* and J. Kohl.

has more exceptions than cheery handbooks admit. Always *ei* after *c*? What about *ancient, efficient,* and *sufficient*? Oh, but in these words the *c* is pronounced *sh,* an easy enough exception to keep in mind. But how can we explain *financier*? And of words where a *c* does not precede the letters in question, does the rule *ie* really govern all those not "sounded as *a* / In *neighbor* and *sleigh*"? How about *counterfeit, deity, either, foreign, forfeit, heifer, height, neither, leisure, protein, seize, their, weird*?

Instead of offering rules with menacing lists of exceptions, we offer a single list of words commonly misspelled in college writing. And here are four suggestions:

1. Read the list, mark any words whose spelling surprises you, and make a conscientious effort to memorize them.

2. Keep a dictionary at hand, and consult it while you are editing your final draft. If you have not formed a habit of consulting the dictionary, you may have to work at it. Begin by noticing what words or groups of words you have trouble with. Then cultivate the habit of doubting your own spellings of these words. When in doubt, don't guess; look the word up.

3. In a notebook, keep a list of words you misspell and try to classify your errors. Most spelling errors occur in characteristic and even predictable patterns. Some errors originate in mispronunciation, or the dropping or slurring of sounds in speech. (Notice, for example, government, February, prejudiced.) On the other hand, words with a vowel in an unaccented syllable are troublesome because those vowels all sound alike. You'll have to learn to visualize the correct vowel in such words as: dist*a*nt, it*e*m, ed*i*ble, gall*o*p, circ*u*s. Still other errors stem from confusing pairs of words such as: accept/except, conscience/conscious, past/passed, capital/capitol. But you don't have to be aware of all possible errors any more than you need to know all the rules. You need only to classify the errors you do make and work on reducing those. The task is really not hopeless.

4. For words that you persistently misspell, invent some device to assist your memory. For example, if you erroneously put an *a* in *cemetery* in place of an *e,* say to yourself "people rest in a cemetery." When you next have to write the word *cemetery* you will remember the associative device (*rest*), and you will spell *cemetery* with an *e*. Another example: if you repeatedly leave out an *l* from *balloon,* say to yourself — really say it — "a balloon is a ball." The next time you have to write *balloon* you will remember *ball*. Similarly, tell yourself there's *a rat* in *separate*. A last example, for people who mistakenly put an *n* in *dilemma*: "Emma is in a dilemma." Generally speaking, the sillier the phrase, the more memorable it will be.

abridgment	acknowledgment	adolescence
absence	acquire	adolescent
accessible	across	advice (noun)
accidentally	actually	advise (verb)
accommodate	address	aggravate
achievement	adjacent	aggressive

aging
alcohol
allege
all right (*not* alright)
a lot (*not* alot)
already (*not* all ready)
alter (to change)
altogether
analysis
analyze
apparent
appearance
appreciate
arctic
argument
assassin
assistance
assistant
athlete
attendance
balloon
beggar
beginner
believe
benefit
bourgeois
bourgeoisie
Britain
bureau
bureaucracy
burglar
business
calendar
capital (noun: seat of government, money; adjective: chief)
capitol (building)
category
ceiling

cemetery
changeable
chief
choose (present tense)
chose (past tense)
chosen (participle)
commit
committee
comparative
competent
complement (noun: that which completes; verb: to complete)
compliment (praise)
conferred
congratulate
conscience
conscious
consistent
controlled
controversy
coolly
corollary
counterfeit
criticism
criticize
curiosity
deceive
decision
defendant
definite
deity
dependent
description
desirable
despair
desperate
develop, develops
development

dilemma
disappear
disappoint
disastrous
divide
divine
dormitory
eighth
embarrass
envelop (verb)
envelope (noun)
environment
equipped
equivalent
especially
essence
exaggerate
exceed
excellence
excellent
exhilarate
existence
experience
explanation
familiar
fascinate
fiend
fiery
foreign
foreword (preface)
forty
fourth
friend
gauge
genealogy
goddess
government
grammar
grievance
guarantee
height
heroes

hoping
humorous
hypocrisy
imagery
imagination
immediately
impel
incidentally
incredible
independence
independent
indispensable
insistence
insistent
intelligent
interest
interpretation
interrupt
irrelevant
irresistible
judgment
led (past tense of *to
lead*)
leisure
license
loneliness
loose (adjective)
lose (verb)
losing
maneuver
marriage
mathematics
medicine
mischievous
misspell
naive
necessary
necessity
niece
ninety
noncommittal
noticeable

occasion
occasionally
occur
occurred
occurrence
omit
omitted
original
parallel
pastime
peaceable
performance
permanent
persistent
playwright
possession
practically
precede
predominant
preferred
prejudice
prevalent
principal (adjective:
foremost; noun:
chief)
principle (noun:
rule)
privilege
probably
procedure
proceed
prominent
prophecy (noun)
prophesy (verb)
pursue
quantity
realize
really
receipt
receiving
recommend
reference

referring
relevance
relevant
relieve
remembrance
repentance
repetition
resistance
rhyme
rhythm
sacrifice
secretary
seize
sense
separate
shining
shriek
siege
significance
similar
solely
specimen
sponsor
stationary
(still)
stationery
(paper)
strength
subtlety
subtly
succeed
supersede
surprise
syllable
temperament
tendency
theories
therefore
thorough
tragedy
transferred
tried

truly

unforgettable

unnecessary

useful

usually

various

vengeance

villain

weird

wholly

who's (contraction: who is)

whose (possessive pronoun: belonging to whom)

withhold

writing

21
Usage

Some things are said or written and some are not. More precisely, anything can be said or written, but only some things are acceptable to the ears and minds of many readers. "I don't know nothing about it" has been said and will be said again, but many readers who encounter this expression might judge the speaker as a person with nothing of interest to say — and immediately tune out.

Although such a double negative today is not acceptable, it used to be: Chaucer's courteous Knight never spoke no baseness, and Shakespeare's courtly Mercutio, in *Romeo and Juliet,* "will not budge for no man." But things have changed; what was acceptable in the Middle Ages and the Renaissance (for example, emptying chamber pots into the gutter) is not always acceptable now. And some of what was once unacceptable has become acceptable. At the beginning of the twentieth century, grammarians suggested that one cannot use *drive* in speaking of a car; one drives (forces into motion) an ox, or even a person ("He drove her to distraction"), but not a machine. Some seventy years of usage, however, have erased all objections.

This chapter presents a list of expressions that, although commonly used, set many teeth on edge. Seventy years from now some of these expressions may be as acceptable as "drive a car"; but we are writing for today, and we might as well try to hold today's readers by following today's taste. If our essays are thoughtful, they will provide enough challenges to the reader; we should not use constructions that will arouse antagonism or that will allow the reader to brush us off as ignoramuses.

You may not be familiar with some of the abuses in the following list; if so, our citing them will not instruct you, but may entertain you.

A NOTE ON IDIOMS

An idiom (from a Greek word meaning "peculiar") is a fixed group of words, peculiar to a given language. Thus, in English we say "I caught a cold" but we do not say "I seized a cold." If someone who is not a native speaker of English tells us that she thought "catch" and "seize" are synonymous, we may sympathize with her problem but we can only insist that in English one cannot seize a cold. Anyone who says or writes "I seized a cold" is using *un*idiomatic English, just as anyone who says he knows a poem "at heart" instead of "by heart" is using unidiomatic English.

Probably most unidiomatic expressions use the wrong preposition. Examples:

Unidiomatic	*Idiomatic*
Comply to	Comply with
superior with	superior to

Sometimes while we write, or even while we speak, we are unsure of the idiom and we pause to try an alternative — "parallel with?" "parallel to?" — and we don't know which sounds more natural, more idiomatic. At such moments, more often than not, either is acceptable, but if you are in doubt, check a dictionary when you are editing your work. (*The American Heritage Dictionary* has notes on usage following the definitions of hundreds of its words.)

In any case, if you are a native speaker of English, when you read your draft you will probably detect unidiomatic expressions such as *superior with*; that is, you will hear something that sounds odd, and so you will change it to something that sounds familiar, idiomatic — here, *superior to*. If any unidiomatic expressions remain in your essay, the trouble may be that an effort to write impressively has led you to use unfamiliar language. A reader who sees such unidiomatic language will know that you are trying to gain stature by walking on stilts.

GLOSSARY

a, an Use *a* before words beginning with a consonant ("a book") or with a vowel sounded as a consonant ("a one-way ticket," "a university"). Use *an* before words beginning with a vowel sound, including those beginning with a silent *h* ("an egg," "an hour"). Either *a* or *an* is acceptable before an initial *h* that is pronounced (for example, in "hundred"), but *an* may sound affected, so it is better to use *a*.

above Try to avoid writing *for the above reasons, in view of the above, as above,* etc. These expressions sound unpleasantly legalistic. Substitute *for these reasons,* or *therefore,* or some such expression or word.

academics Only two meanings of this noun are widely accepted: (1) "members of an institution of higher learning," and (2) "persons who are academic in background or outlook." Avoid using it to mean "academic subjects," as in "A student should pay attention not only to academics but also to recreation."

accept, except *Accept* means "to receive with consent." *Except* means "to exclude" or "excluding."

affect, effect *Affect* is usually a verb, meaning (1) "to influence, to produce an effect, to impress," or (2) "to pretend, to put on," as in "He affected an English accent." Psychologists use it as a noun for "feeling," e.g., "The patient experienced no affect." *Effect,* as a verb, means "to bring about" ("The workers effected the rescue in less than an hour"). As a noun, *effect* means "result" ("The effect was negligible").

aggravate "To worsen, to increase for the worse," as in "Smoking aggravated the irritation." Although it is widely used to mean "annoy" ("He aggravated me"), many readers are annoyed by such a use.

all ready, already *All ready* means "everything is ready." *Already* means "by this time."

all right, alright The first of these is the preferable spelling; for some readers it is the only acceptable spelling.

all together, altogether *All together* means that members of a group act or are gathered together ("They voted all together"); *altogether* is an adverb meaning "entirely," "wholly" ("This is altogether unnecessary").

allusion, reference, illusion An *allusion* is an implied or indirect reference. "As Lincoln says" is a *reference* to Lincoln, but "As a great man has said," along with a phrase quoted from the Gettysburg Address, constitutes an *allusion* to Lincoln. The student who, in a demonstration at Berkeley, carried a placard saying "I am a human being — please do not fold, spindle, or mutilate" *referred* to himself and *alluded* to a computer card. *Allusion* has nothing to do with *illusion* (a deception). Note the spelling (especially the second *i*) in "disillusioned" (left without illusions, disenchanted).

a lot Two words (not *alot*).

among, between See *between*.

amount, number *Amount* refers to bulk or quantity: "A small amount of gas was still in the tank." Use *number*, not *amount*, to refer to separate (countable) units: "A large number of people heard the lecture" (not "a large amount of people"). Similarly, "an amount of money," but "a number of dollars."

analyzation Unacceptable; use *analysis*.

and/or Acceptable, but a legalism and unpleasant-sounding. Often *or* by itself will do, as in "students who know Latin or Italian." When *or* is not enough ("The script was written by Groucho and/or Harpo") it is better to recast ("The script was written by Groucho or Harpo, or both").

and etc. Because *etc.* is an abbreviation for *et cetera* ("and others"), the *and* in *and etc.* is redundant. (See also the entry on *et cetera*.)

ante, anti *Ante* means "before" (*antebellum*, "before the Civil War"); *anti* means "against" (*antivivisectionist*). Hyphenate *anti* before capitals (*anti-Semitism*) and before *i* (*anti-intellectual*).

anthology, collection Because an *anthology* is a collection of writings by several authors, one cannot speak of "an anthology of poems by Robert Frost"; one can speak of a "collection of poems by Robert Frost."

anxious Best reserved for uses that suggest anxiety ("He was anxious before the examination"), though some authorities now accept it in the sense of "eager" ("He was anxious to serve the community").

anybody An indefinite pronoun, written as one word; if two words (*any body*), you mean any corpse ("Several people died in the fire, but the police cannot identify any body").

anyone One word, unless you mean "any one thing," as in "Here are three books; you may take any one."

area of Like *field of* and *topic of* ("the field of literature," "the topic of politics"), *area of* can usually be deleted. "The area of literature" equals "literature."

around Avoid using *around* in place of *about*: "He wrote it in about three hours." See also *centers on*.

as, like *As* is a conjunction; use it in forming comparisons, to introduce clauses. (A clause has a subject and a verb.)

> You can learn to write, as you can learn to swim.
>
> Huck speaks the truth as he sees it.
>
> He is as tall as I.

In "He is as tall as I," notice that the clause introduced by the second "as" consists of the subject "I" and the implied verb "am."

> He is as tall as I (am).

As can also introduce a clause in which both the subject and the verb are implied:

> Rose distrusts him as much as (she distrusts) me.

But notice that the last sentence means something different from the next:

> Rose distrusts him as much as I (do).

Like is a preposition; use it to introduce prepositional phrases:

> He looks like me.
>
> Like Hamlet, Laertes has lost a father.
>
> She thinks like a lawyer.

Writers who are fearful of incorrectly using *like* resort to cumbersome evasions: "He eats in the same manner that a pig eats." But there's nothing wrong with "He eats like a pig."

as of now Best deleted, or replaced by *now*. Not "As of now I don't smoke" but "Now I don't smoke" or "I don't smoke now" or "I don't smoke."

aspect Literally, "a view from a particular point," but it has come to mean *topic*, as in "There are several aspects to be considered." Try to get a sharper word; for example, "There are several problems to be considered," or "There are several consequences to be considered."

as such Often meaningless, as in "Tragedy as such evokes pity."

as to Usually *about* is preferable. Not "I know nothing as to the charges," but "I know nothing about the charges."

bad, badly *Bad* used to be only an adjective ("a bad movie"), and *badly* was an adverb ("she sings badly"). In "I felt bad," *bad* describes the subject, not the verb. (Compare "I felt happy." After verbs of appearing, such as "feel," "look," "seem," "taste," an adjective, not an adverb, is used.) But today "I feel badly" is acceptable and even preferred by many. Note, however, this distinction: "This meat smells bad" (an adjective describing the meat), and "Because I have a stuffed nose I smell badly" (an adverb describing my ability to smell something).

being Do not use *being* as a main verb, as in "The trouble being that his reflexes were too slow." The result is a sentence fragment. See pages 380–82.

being that, being as A sentence such as "Being that she was a stranger . . ." sounds like an awkward translation from the Latin. Use *because*.

beside, besides *Beside* means "at the side of." Because *besides* can mean either "in addition to" or "other than," it is ambiguous, as in "Something besides TB caused his death." It is best, then, to use *in addition to* or *other than*, depending on what you mean.

between Only English teachers who have had a course in Middle English are likely to know that it comes from *by twain*. And only English teachers and editors are likely to object to its use (and to call for *among*) when more than two are concerned, as in "among the three of us." Note, too, that even conservative usage accepts *between* in reference to more than two when the items are at the moment paired: "Negotiations *between* Israel and Egypt, Syria, and Lebanon seem stalled." *Between*, a preposition, takes an object ("between you and me"); only people who mistakenly think that "me" is vulgar say "between you and I".

biannually, bimonthly, biweekly Every two years, every two
months, every two weeks (*not* twice a year, etc.). Twice a year
is *semiannually*. Because *biannually, bimonthly,* and *biweekly* are
commonly misunderstood, it is best to avoid them and to say
"every two . . ."

Black, black Although one sometimes sees the word capitalized
when it refers to race, most publishers use a lowercase letter,
making it consistent with *white*, which is never capitalized.

can, may When schoolchildren asked "Can I leave the room,"
their teachers used to correct them thus: "You *can* leave the
room if you have legs, but you *may not* leave the room until
you receive permission." In short, *can* indicates physical possibility, *may* indicates permission. But because "you may not"
and "why mayn't I?" sound not merely polite but stiff, *can* is
usually preferred except in formal contexts.

centers on, centers around Use *centers on*, because *center* refers
to a point, not to a movement around.

collective nouns A collective noun, singular in form, names a
collection of individuals. Examples: *audience, band, committee,
crowd, jury, majority, minority, team*. When you are thinking
chiefly of the whole as a unit, use a singular verb (and a singular
pronoun, if any): "The majority rules"; "The jury is announcing
its verdict." But when you are thinking of the individuals, use
a plural verb (and pronoun, if any): "The majority are lawyers";
"The jury are divided and they probably cannot agree." If the
plural sounds odd, you can usually rewrite: "The jurors are
divided and they probably cannot agree."

compare, contrast To *compare* is to note likenesses or differences:
"Compare a motorcycle with a bicycle." To *contrast* is to emphasize differences.

complement, compliment *Complement* as a noun means "that
which completes"; as a verb, "to fill out, to complete." *Compliment* as a noun is an expression of praise; as a verb it means
"to offer praise."

comprise "To include, contain, consist of": "The university
comprises two colleges and a medical school" (not "is comprised
of"). Conservative authorities hold that "to be comprised of"
is always incorrect, and they reject the form one often hears:

"Two colleges and a medical school comprise the university."
Here the word should be *compose*, not *comprise*.

concept Should often be deleted. For "The concept of the sales
tax is regressive" write "The sales tax is regressive."

contact Because it is vague, avoid using *contact* as a verb. *Not* "I
contacted him" but "I spoke with him" or "I wrote to him," or
whatever.

continual, continuous Conservative authorities hold that *continuous* means "uninterrupted," as in "It rained continuously for
six hours"; *continually* means "repeated often, recurring at short
intervals," as in "For a year he continually wrote letters to her."

could have, could of See *of*.

criteria Plural of *criterion*, hence it is always incorrect to speak of
"a criteria," or to say "The criteria is . . ."

data Plural of *datum*. Although some social scientists speak of "this
data," "these data" is preferable: "These data are puzzling."
Because the singular, *datum*, is rare and sounds odd, it is best
to substitute *fact* or *figure* for *datum*.

different from Prefer it to *different than*, unless you are convinced
that in a specific sentence *different from* sounds terribly wrong,
as in "These two books are more different than I had expected."
(In this example, "more," not "different," governs "than." But
this sentence, though correct, is awkward and therefore it
should be revised: "These two books differ more than I had
expected.")

dilemma A situation requiring a choice between equally undesirable alternatives; not every difficulty or plight or predicament
is a *dilemma*. Not "Her dilemma was that she had nowhere to
go," but "Her dilemma was whether to go out or to stay home:
one was frightening, the other was embarrassing." And note
the spelling (two *m*'s, no *n*).

disinterested Though the word is often used to mean "indifferent," "unconcerned," "uninterested," reserve it to mean "im-
partial": "A judge should be disinterested."

due to Some people, holding that *due to* cannot modify a verb (as
in "He failed due to illness"), tolerate it only when it modifies
a noun or pronoun ("His failure was due to illness"). They also
insist that it cannot begin a sentence ("Due to illness, he failed").

In fact, however, daily usage accepts both. But because it almost always sounds stiff, try to substitute *because of,* or *through.*

due to the fact that Wordy for *because.*

each Although many authorities hold that *each,* as a subject, is singular, even when followed by "them" ("Each of them is satisfactory"), some authorities accept and even favor the plural ("Each of them are satisfactory"). But it is usually better to avoid the awkwardness by substituting *all* for *each*: "All of them are satisfactory." When *each* is in apposition with a plural subject, the verb must be plural: "They each have a book"; "We each are trying." *Each* cannot be made into a possessive; you cannot say "Each's opinion is acceptable."

effect See *affect.*

e.g. Abbreviation for *exempli gratia,* meaning "for example." It is thus different from *i.e.* (an abbreviation for *id est,* meaning "that is"). E.g. (not italicized) introduces an example; i.e. (also not italicized) introduces a definition. Because these two abbreviations of Latin words are often confused, it may be preferable to avoid them and use their English equivalents.

either . . . or, neither . . . nor If the subjects are singular, use a singular verb: "Either the boy or the girl is lying." If one of the subjects joined by *or* or *nor* is plural, most grammarians say that the verb agrees with the nearer subject, thus: "A tree or two shrubs are enough," or "Two shrubs or a tree is enough." But because the singular verb in the second of these sentences may sound odd, follow the first construction; that is, put the plural subject nearer to the verb and use a plural verb.

enthuse Objectionable to many readers. For "He enthused," say "He was enthusiastic." Use *enthuse* only in the sense of "to be excessively enthusiastic," "to gush."

et cetera, etc. Latin for "and other things"; if you mean "and other people," you need *et al.,* short for *et alii.* Because *etc.* is vague, its use is usually inadvisable. Not "He studied mathematics, etc." but "He studied mathematics, history, economics, and French." Or, if the list is long, cut it by saying something a little more informative than *etc.* — for example, "He studied mathematics, history, and other liberal arts subjects." Even *and so forth* or *and so on* is preferable to *etc.* Confine *etc.* (and most other abbreviations, including *et al.*) to footnotes, and even in footnotes try to avoid it.

everybody, everyone These take a singular verb ("Everybody is here"), and a pronoun referring to them is usually singular ("Everybody thinks his problems are suitable topics of conversation"), but use a plural pronoun if the singular would seem unnatural ("Everybody was there, weren't they?"). To avoid the sexism of "Everybody thinks his problems . . ." revise to "All people think their problems . . ."

except See *accept*.

exists Often unnecessary and a sign of wordiness. Not "The problem that *exists* here is" but "The problem here is."

expound Usually pretentious for *explain* or *say*. To *expound* is to give a methodical explanation of theological matters.

facet Literally "little face," especially one of the surfaces of a gem. Don't use it (and don't use *aspect* or *factor* either) to mean "part" or "topic." It is most acceptable when, close to its literal meaning, it suggests a new appearance, as when a gem is turned: "Another *facet* appears when we see this law from the taxpayer's point of view."

the fact that Usually wordy. "Because of the fact that boys played female roles in Elizabethan drama" can be reduced to "Because boys played female roles in Elizabethan drama."

factor Strictly speaking, a *factor* helps to produce a result, but students commonly use it in the sense of "point": "Another factor to be studied is. . . ." Used with the sense of "point" it usually sounds pretentious: "The possibility of plagiarism is a factor that must be considered" simply adds up to "The possibility of plagiarism must be considered." *Factor* is almost never the precise word: "the factors behind Gatsby's actions" are, more precisely, "Gatsby's motives."

farther, further Some purists claim that *farther* always refers to distance and *further* to time ("The gymnasium is farther than the library"; "Let us think further about this").

fatalistic, pessimistic *Fatalistic* means "characterized by the belief that all events are predetermined and therefore inevitable"; *pessimistic,* "characterized by the belief that the world is evil," or, less gloomily, "expecting the worst."

fewer, less See *less*.

field of See *area of.*

firstly, secondly Acceptable, but it is better to use *first, second.*

former, latter These words are acceptable, but they are often annoying because they force the reader to reread earlier material in order to locate what *the former* and *the latter* refer to. The expressions are legitimately used in order to avoid repeating lengthy terms, but if you are talking about an easily repeated subject — say, Lincoln and Grant — don't hesitate to replace *the former* and *the latter* with their names. The repetition will clarify rather than bore.

good, well *Good* is an adjective ("a good book"), *well* is usually an adverb ("She writes well"). Standard English does not accept "She writes good." But Standard English requires *good* after verbs of appearing, such as "seems," "looks," "sounds," "tastes": "it looks good," "it sounds good." *Well* can also be an adjective meaning "healthy": "I am well."

graduate, graduate from Use *from* if you name the institution or if you use a substitute word as in "She graduated from high school"; if the institution (or substitute) is not named, *from* is omitted: "She graduated in 1983." The use of the passive ("She was graduated from high school") is acceptable but sounds fussy to many.

he or she, his or her These expressions are awkward, but the implicit male chauvinism in the generic use of the male pronoun ("A citizen should exercise his right to vote") may be more offensive than the awkwardness of *he or she* and *his or her.* Moreover, sometimes the male pronoun, when used for males and females, is ludicrous, as in "The more violence a youngster sees on television, regardless of his age or sex, the more aggressive he is likely to be." Do what you can to avoid the dilemma. Sometimes you can use the plural *their:* "Students are expected to hand in their papers on Monday" (instead of "The student is expected to hand in his or her paper on Monday"). Or eliminate the possessive: "The student must hand in a paper on Monday." See also *man, mankind.*

hopefully Commonly used to mean "I hope" or "It is hoped" ("*Hopefully,* the rain will stop soon"), but it is best to avoid what some consider a dangling modifier. After all, the rain itself is not hopeful. If you mean "I hope the rain will soon stop," say exactly that. Notice, too, that *hopefully* is often evasive; if the president of the college says, "Hopefully tuition will not rise next year," don't think that you have heard a promise to fight against an increase; you only have heard someone evade making a promise. In short, confine *hopefully* to its adverbial use, meaning "in a hopeful manner": "Hopefully he uttered a prayer."

however It is preferable not to begin a sentence with *however* unless it is an adverb meaning "to whatever extent or degree," as in "However hard he studied, he couldn't remember irregular verbs." When *however* is a conjunctive adverb, it usually gains emphasis if you put it later in the sentence, between commas: "He failed the examination, however, and didn't graduate." (Compare, "However, he failed the examination and didn't graduate.") Unless *however* is set off in commas it usually sounds insufficiently emphatic. If you want to begin a sentence with a sharp contrast, use *but* or *nevertheless*. Note too that you cannot link independent clauses with a *however* preceded by a comma; you need a semicolon ("He tried; however, he failed"). Even here, however, *but* is usually preferable, without a semicolon.

the idea that Usually dull and wordy. Not "The idea that we grow old is frightening," but "That we grow old is frightening," or (probably better) "Growing old is frightening."

identify When used in the psychological sense, "to associate oneself closely with a person or an institution," it is preferable to include a reflexive pronoun, thus: "He identified himself with Hamlet," *not* "He identified with Hamlet."

i.e. Latin for *id est,* "that is." The English words are preferable to the Latin abbreviation. On the distinction between *i.e.* and *e.g.,* see *e.g.*

immanent, imminent *Immanent,* "remaining within, intrinsic"; *imminent,* "likely to occur soon, impending."

imply, infer The writer or speaker *implies* (suggests); the perceiver *infers* (draws a conclusion): "Karl Marx implied that . . . but his modern disciples infer from his writings that . . ." Although *infer* is widely used for *imply,* preserve the distinction.

individual Avoid using the word to mean only "person": "He was a generous individual." But it is precise when it implicitly makes a contrast with a group: "In a money-mad society, he was a generous individual"; "Although the faculty did not take a stand on this issue, faculty members as individuals spoke out."

instances Instead of *in many instances* use *often*. Strictly speaking an *instance* is not an object or incident in itself but one offered as an example. Thus "another instance of his failure to do his duty" (not "In three instances he failed to do his duty").

irregardless Unacceptable; use *regardless.*

it is Usually this expression needlessly delays the subject: "It is unlikely that many students will attend the lecture" could just as well be "Few students are likely to attend the lecture."

its, it's The first is a possessive pronoun ("The flock lost its leader"); the second is a contraction of *it is* ("It's a wise father that knows his child.") You'll have no trouble if you remember that the possessive pronoun *its,* like other possessive pronouns such as *our, his, their,* does *not* use an apostrophe.

kind of Singular, as in "That kind of movie bothers me." (*Not:* "Those kind of movies bother me.") If, however, you are really talking about more than one kind, use *kinds* and be sure that the demonstrative pronoun and the verb are plural: "Those kinds of movies bother me."

latter See under *former.*

lay, lie To *lay* means "to put, to set, to cause to rest." It takes an object: "May I lay the coats on the table?" The past tense and the participle are *laid*: "I laid the coats on the table"; "I have laid the coats on the table." To *lie* means "to recline," and it does not take an object: "When I am tired I lie down." The past tense is *lay,* the participle is *lain*: "Yesterday I lay down"; "I have lain down hundreds of times without wishing to get up."

lend, loan The usual verb is *lend*: "Lend me a pen." The past tense and the participle are both *lent. Loan* is a noun: "This isn't a gift, it's a loan." But, curiously, *loan* as a verb is acceptable in past forms: "I loaned him my bicycle." In its present form ("I often loan money") it is used chiefly by bankers.

less, fewer *Less* (as an adjective) refers to bulk amounts (also called mass nouns): less milk, less money, less time. *Fewer* refers to separate (countable) items: fewer glasses of milk, fewer dollars, fewer hours.

lifestyle, life-style, life style All three forms are acceptable, but because many readers regard the expression as imprecise and faddish, try to find a substitute such as *values*.

like, as See under *as*.

literally It means "strictly in accord with the primary meaning; not metaphorically." It is not a mere intensive. "He was literally dead" means that he was a corpse; if he was merely exhausted, *literally* won't do. You cannot be "literally stewed" (except by cannibals), "literally tickled pink," or "literally head over heels in love."

loose, lose *Loose* is an adjective ("The nail is loose"); *lose* is a verb ("Don't lose the nail").

the majority of Usually a wordy way of saying *most*. Of course if you mean "a bare majority," say so; otherwise *most* will usually do. Certainly "The majority of the basement is used for a cafeteria" should be changed to "Most of the basement is used for a cafeteria."

man, mankind Because these words strike many readers as sexist, expressions such as "man's brain" and "the greatness of mankind" should be revised where possible. Consider using such words as *human being, person, humanity, people*.

may, can See under *can*.

me The right word in such expressions as "between you and me" and "They gave it to John and me." It is the object of verbs and of prepositions. In fact, *me* rather than *I* is the usual form after any verb, including the verb *to be*; "It is me" is nothing to be ashamed of.

medium, media *Medium* is singular, *media* is plural: "TV is the medium to which most children are most exposed. Other media include film, radio, and publishing." It follows, then, that *mass media* takes a plural verb: "The mass media exert an enormous influence."

most Although it is acceptable in speech to say "most everyone" and "most anybody," it is preferable in writing to use "almost everyone," "almost anybody." But of course: "Most students passed."

nature You can usually delete *the nature of*, as in "The nature of my contribution is not political but psychological."

needless to say The reader may well wonder why you go on to say it. Of course this expression is used to let readers know that they are probably familiar with what comes next, but usually *of course* will better serve as this sign.

Negro Capitalized, whether a noun or an adjective, though *white* is not. In recent years *Negro* has been replaced by *black*.

neither . . . nor See *either . . . or,* page 421.

nobody, no one, none *Nobody* and *no one* are singular, requiring a singular verb ("Nobody believes this," "No one knows"); but they can be referred to by a plural pronoun: "Nobody believes this, do they?" "No one knows, do they?" *None,* though it comes from *no one,* almost always requires a plural verb when it refers to people ("Of the ten people present, none are freshmen") and a singular verb when it refers to things ("Of the five assigned books, none is worth reading").

not . . . un- Such an expression as "not unfamiliar" is useful only if it conveys something different from the affirmative. Compare the frostiness of "I am not unfamiliar with your methods" with "I am familiar with your methods." If the negative has no evident advantage, use the affirmative. See pages 265–66.

notorious Widely and unfavorably known; not merely famous, but famous for some discreditable trait or deed.

a number of requires a plural verb: "A number of women are presidents of corporations." But when *number* is preceded by *the* it requires a singular verb: "The number of women who are presidents is small." (The plural noun after *number* of course may require a plural verb, as in "women are," but *the number* itself remains singular, hence its verb is singular, as in "is small.")

of Be careful not to use *of* when *have* is required. Not "He might of died in the woods," but "He might have died in the woods." Note that what we often hear as "would've" or "should've" or "must've" or "could've" is "would have" or "should have" or "must have" or "could have," *not* "would of," etc.

off of Use *off* or *from:* "Take it off the table"; "He jumped from the bridge."

often-times Use *often* instead.

old-fashioned, old-fashion Only the first is acceptable.

one British usage accepts the shift from *one* to *he* in "One begins
to die the moment he is born," but American usge prefers "One
begins to die the moment one is born." A shift from *one* to *you*
("One begins to die the moment you are born") is unacceptable.
As a pronoun, *one* can be useful in impersonal statements such
as the sentence about dying, at the beginning of this entry,
where it means "a person," but don't use it as a disguise for
yourself ("One objects to Smith's argument"). Try to avoid *one*;
one *one* usually leads to another, resulting in a sentence that, in
James Thurber's words, "sounds like a trombone solo" ("If one
takes oneself too seriously, one begins to . . ."). See *you*, pages
435–36.

one of Takes a plural noun, and if this is followed by a clause,
the preferred verb is plural: "one of those students who are,"
"one of those who feel." Thus, in such a sentence as "One of
the coaches who have resigned is now seeking reinstatement,"
notice that "have" is correct, for it agrees with its subject,
"coaches." Coaches have resigned, though "one . . . is seeking
reinstatement." But in such an expression as "one out of a
hundred," the following verb may be singular or plural ("One
out of a hundred is," "One out of a hundred are").

only Be careful where you put it. The classic textbook example
points out that in the sentence "I hit him in the eye," *only* can
be inserted in seven places (beginning in front of "I" and ending
after "eye") with at least six different meanings. Try to put it
just before the expression it qualifies. Thus, not "Presidential
aides are only responsible to one man," but "Presidential aides
are responsible to only one man" (or "to one man only"). See
page 295.

other Often necessary in comparisons. "No American president
served as many terms as Franklin Roosevelt" falsely implies that
Roosevelt was not an American president. The sentence should
be revised to "No other American president served as many
terms as Franklin Roosevelt."

per Usually it sounds needlessly technical ("twice per hour") or
disturbingly impersonal ("as per your request"). Preferable:
"twice an hour," "according to your request," or "as you re-
quested."

per cent, percent, percentage The first two of these are interchangeable; both mean "per hundred," "out of a hundred," as in "Ninety per cent (or percent) of the students were white." *Per cent* and *percent* are always accompanied by a number (written out, or in figures). It is usually better to write out *per cent* or *percent* than to use a per cent sign (12%), except in technical or statistical papers. *Percentage* means "a proportion or share in relation to the whole," as in "A very large percentage of the student body is white." Many authorities insist that *percentage* is never preceded by a number. Do not use percentage to mean "a few," as in "Only a percentage of students attended the lecture"; a percentage can be as large as 99.99. It is usually said that with *per cent, percent,* and *percentage,* whether the verb is singular or plural depends on the number of the noun that follows the word, thus: "Ninety percent of his books are paperbacks"; "Fifty percent of his library is worthless"; "A large percentage of his books are worthless." But some readers (including the authors of this book) prefer a singular verb after *percentage* unless the resulting sentence is as grotesque as this one: "A large percentage of the students is unmarried." Still, rather than say a "percentage . . . are," we would recast the sentence: "A large percentage of the student body is unmarried," or "Many (or "Most," or whatever) of the students are unmarried."

per se Latin for "by itself." Usually sounds legalistic or pedantic, as in "Meter per se has an effect."

pessimistic See *fatalistic.*

phenomenon, phenomena The plural is *phenomena*; thus, "these phenomena" but "this phenomenon."

plus Unattractive and imprecise as a noun meaning "asset" or "advantage" ("When he applied for the job, his appearance was a plus"), and equally unattractive as a substitute for *moreover* ("The examination was easy, plus I had studied") or as a substitute for *and* ("I studied the introduction plus the first chapter").

politics Preferably singular ("Ethnic politics has been a strong force for a century") but a plural verb is acceptable.

prejudice, prejudiced *Prejudice* is a noun: "It is impossible to live entirely without prejudice." But use the past participle *prejudiced* as an adjective: "He was prejudiced against me from the start."

preventative, preventive Both are acceptable but the second form is the form now used by writers on medicine ("preventive medicine"); *preventative* therefore has come to seem amateurish.

prior to Pretentious for *before*.

protagonist Literally, the first actor, and, by extension, the chief actor. It is odd, therefore, to speak of "the protagonists" in a single literary work or occurrence. Note also that the prefix is *proto*, "first," not *pro*, "for"; it does *not* mean one who strives for something.

quite Usually a word to delete, along with *definitely, pretty, rather,* and *very*. See page 259. *Quite* used to mean "completely" ("I quite understand") but it has come also to mean "to a considerable degree," and so it is ambiguous as well as vague.

quotation, quote The first is a noun, the second a verb. "I will quote Churchill" is fine, but not "these quotes from Churchill." And remember, you may *quote* one of Hamlet's speeches, but Hamlet does not *quote* them; he says them.

rather Avoid use with strong adjectives. "Rather intelligent" makes sense, but "rather tremendous" does not. "Rather brilliant" probably means "bright"; "rather terrifying" probably means "frightening," "rather unique" probably means "unusual." Get the right adjective, not *rather* and the wrong adjective.

the reason . . . is because Usually *because* is enough (not "The reason they fail is because they don't study," but simply "They fail because they don't study"). Similarly, *the reason why* can usually be reduced to *why*. Notice, too, that because *reason* is a noun, it cannot neatly govern a *because* clause: not "The reason for his absence is because he was sick," but "The reason for his absence was illness."

rebut, refute To rebut is to argue against, but not necessarily successfully. If you mean "to disprove," use *disprove* or *refute*.

in regard to, with regard to Often wordy for *about, concerning,* or *on*, and sometimes even these words are unnecessary. Compare: "He knew a great deal in regard to jazz"; "He knew a great deal about jazz." Compare: "Hemingway's story is often misunderstood with regard to Robert Wilson's treatment of Margot Macomber"; "In Hemingway's story, Robert Wilson's treatment of Margot Macomber is often misunderstood."

relate to Usually a vague expression, best avoided, as in "I can relate to Hedda Gabler." Does it mean "respond favorably to," "identify myself with," "interact with" (and how can a reader "interact with" a character in a play?). Use *relate to* only in the sense of "have connection with" (as in "How does your answer relate to my question?"); even in such a sentence a more exact expression is preferable.

repel, repulse Both verbs mean "to drive back," but only *repel* can mean "to cause distaste," "to disgust," as in "His obscenities repelled the audience."

sarcasm Heavy, malicious sneering ("Oh, you're really a great friend, aren't you?" addressed to someone who won't lend the speaker ten dollars). If the apparent praise, which really communicates dispraise, is at all clever, conveying, say, a delicate mockery or wryness, it is irony, not sarcasm. The passages by Szarkowski on pages 324–25 are ironic, not sarcastic.

seem Properly it suggests a suspicion that appearances may be deceptive: "He seems honest (but . . .)." Don't say "The book seems to lack focus" if you believe it does lack focus.

shall, will, should, would The old principle held that in the first person *shall* is the future indicative of *to be* and *should* the conditional ("I shall go," "We should like to be asked"); and that *will* and *would* are the forms for the second and third persons. When the forms are reversed ("I will go," "Government of the people . . . shall not perish from the earth"), determination is expressed. But today almost nobody adheres to these principles. Indeed, *shall* (except in questions) sounds stilted to many ears.

simplistic Means "falsely simplified by ignoring complications." Do not confuse it with *simplified,* whose meanings include "reduced to essentials" and "clarified."

since Traditional objections to *since,* in the sense of "because," have all but vanished. Note, however, that when *since* is ambiguous and may also refer to time ("Since he joined the navy, she found another boyfriend") it is better to say *because* or *after,* depending on which you mean.

situation Overused, vague, and often unnecessary. "His situation was that he was unemployed" adds up to "He was unemployed." And "an emergency situation" is probably an emergency.

split infinitives The infinitive is the verb form that merely names the action, without indicating when or by whom performed ("walk," rather than "walked" or "I walk"). Grammarians, however, developed the idea that the infinitive was "to walk," and they held that one cannot separate or split the two words: "to quickly walk." But James Thurber says this idea is "of a piece with the sentimental and outworn notion that it is always wrong to strike a lady." Notice, however, that often the inserted word can be deleted ("to really understand" is "to understand"), and that if many words are inserted between *to* and the verb, the reader may get lost ("to quickly and in the remaining few pages before examining the next question conclude").

stanza See under *verse*.

than, then *Than* is used chiefly in making comparisons ("German is harder than French"), but also after "rather," "other," "different," and "else" ("I'd rather take French than German"; "He thinks of nothing other than sex"). *Then* commonly indicates time ("She took German then, but now she takes French"; "Until then, I'll save you a seat"), but it may also mean "in that case" ("It's agreed, then, that we'll all go") or "on the other hand" ("Then again, she may find German easy"). The simplest guide: use *than* after comparisons and after "rather," "other," "different," "else"; otherwise use *then*.

that, which, who Many pages have been written on these words; opinions differ, but you will offend no one if you observe the following principles. (1) Use *that* in restrictive (that is, limiting) clauses: "The rocking chair that creaks is on the porch." (2) Use *which* in nonrestrictive (in effect, parenthetic) clauses: "The rocking chair, which creaks, is on the porch." (See pages 390–92.) The difference between these two sentences is this: in the first, one rocking chair is singled out from several — the one that creaks; in the second, the fact that the rocking chair creaks is simply tossed in, and is not added for the purpose of identifying the one chair out of several. (3) Use *who* for people, in restrictive and in nonrestrictive clauses: "The men who were playing poker ignored the women"; "The men, who were playing poker, ignored the women." But note that often *that, which,* and *who* can be omitted: "The creaky rocking chair is on the porch"; "The men, playing poker, ignored the women." In general, omit these words if the sentence remains clear. See pages 266–68.

their, there, they're The first is a possessive pronoun: "Chaplin and Keaton made their first films before sound tracks were developed." The second, *there,* sometimes refers to a place ("Go there," "Do you live there?"), and sometimes is what is known in grammar as an introductory expletive ("There are no solutions to this problem"). The third, *they're,* is a contraction of "they are" ("They're going to stay for dinner").

this Often refers vaguely to "what I have been saying." Does it refer to the previous sentence, the previous paragraph, the previous page? Try to modify it by being specific: "this last point," "This clue gave the police all they needed."

thusly Unacceptable; *thus* is an adverb and needs no adverbial ending.

till, until Both are acceptable, but *until* is preferable because *till* — though common in speech — looks literary in print. The following are *not* acceptable: *til, 'til, 'till.*

topic of See *area of.*

toward, towards Both are standard English; *toward* is more common in the United States, *towards* in Great Britain.

type Often colloquial (and unacceptable in most writing) for *type of,* as in "this type teacher." But *type of* is not especially pleasing either. Better to write "this kind of teacher." And avoid using *type* as a suffix: "essay-type examinations" are essay examinations; "natural-type ice cream" is natural ice cream. Sneaky manufacturers make "Italian-type cheese," implying that their domestic cheese is imported and at the same time protecting themselves against charges of misrepresentation.

unique The only one of its kind. Someone or something cannot be "rather unique" or "very unique" or "somewhat unique," any more than a woman can be somewhat pregnant. Instead of saying "rather unique," then, say *rare,* or *unusual,* or *extraordinary,* or whatever seems to be the best word.

U.S., United States Generally, *United States* is preferable to *U.S.;* similarly, *the Soviet Union* is preferable to *the U.S.S.R.*

usage Don't use *usage* where *use* will do, as in "Here Vonnegut completes his usage of dark images." *Usage* properly implies a customary practice that has created a standard: "Usage has eroded the difference between 'shall' and 'will.'"

use of The use of *use of* is usually unnecessary. "Through the use of setting he conveys a sense of foreboding" may be reduced to "The setting conveys . . ." or "His setting conveys . . ."

utilize, utilization Often inflated for *use* and *using,* as in "The infirmary has noted that it is freshmen who have most utilized the counseling service."

verbal Often used where *oral* would be more exact. *Verbal* simply means "expressed in words," and thus a *verbal agreement* may be either written or spoken. If you mean spoken, call it an *oral agreement.*

verse, stanza A *verse* is a single line of a poem; a *stanza* is a group of lines, commonly bound by a rhyme scheme. But in speaking or writing about songs, usage sanctions *verse* for *stanza,* as in "Second verse, same as the first."

viable A term from physiology, meaning "capable of living" (for example, referring to a fetus at a stage of its development). Now pretentiously used and overused, especially by politicians and journalists, to mean "workable," as in "a viable presidency." Avoid it.

we If you mean *I,* say *I.* Not "The first fairy tale we heard" but "the first fairy tale I heard." (But of course *we* is appropriate in some statements: "We have all heard fairy tales"; "If we look closely at the evidence, we can agree that. . . .") The rule: don't use *we* as a disguise for *I.* See pages 290–91.

well See *good.*

well known, widely known Athletes, performers, politicians, and such folk are not really *well known* except perhaps by a few of their friends and their relatives; use *widely known* if you mean they are known (however slightly) to many people.

which Often can be deleted. "Students are required to fill out scholarship applications which are lengthy" can be written "Students are required to fill out lengthy scholarship applications." Another example: "*The Tempest,* which is Shakespeare's last play, was written in 1611"; "*The Tempest,* Shakespeare's last play, was written in 1611," or "Shakespeare wrote his last play,

The Tempest, in 1611." For the distinction between *which* and *that,* see the entry on *that.*

while Best used in a temporal sense, meaning "during the time": "While I was speaking, I suddenly realized that I didn't know what I was talking about." While it is not wrong to use *while* in a nontemporal sense, meaning "although" (as at the beginning of this sentence), it is better to use *although* in order to avoid any ambiguity. Note the ambiguity in: "While he was fond of movies he chiefly saw westerns." Does it mean "Although he was fond of movies," or does it mean "During the time when he was fond of movies"? Another point: do not use *while* if you mean *and*: "Freshmen take English 1–2, while sophomores take English 10–11" (substitute *and* for *while*).

who, whom Strictly speaking, *who* must be used for subjects, even when they look like objects: "He guessed who would be chosen." (Here *who* is the subject of the clause "who would be chosen.") *Whom* must be used for the objects of a verb, verbal (gerund, participle), or preposition: "Whom did he choose?"; "Whom do you want me to choose?"; "To whom did he show it?" We may feel stuffy in writing "Whom did he choose?" or "Whom are you talking about?" but to use *who* is certain to annoy some reader. Often you can avoid the dilemma by rewriting: "Who was chosen?"; "Who is the topic of conversation?" See also the entry on *that.*

whoever, whomever The second of these is the objective form. It is often incorrectly used as the subject of a clause. "Open the class to whomever wants to take it" is incorrect. The object of "to" is not "whomever" but is the entire clause — "whoever wants to take it" — and of course "whoever" is the subject of "wants."

who's, whose The first is a contraction of *who is* ("I'm everybody who's nobody"). The second is a possessive pronoun: "Whose book is it?" "I know whose it is."

would "I would think that" is a wordy version of "I think that." (On the mistaken use of *would of* for *would have,* see *of,* page 427.)

you In relatively informal writing, *you* is ordinarily preferable to the somewhat stiff *one*: "If you are addicted to cigarettes, you may find it helpful to join Smokenders." (Compare: "If one is addicted to cigarettes, one may . . .") But because the direct address of *you* may sometimes descend into nagging, it is usually better to write: "Cigarette addicts may find it helpful . . ." Certainly a writer (you?) should not assume that the reader is guilty of vices ("You should not molest children") unless the essay is clearly aimed at an audience that admits to these vices, say a pamphlet directed to child molesters who are seeking help. Thus, it is acceptable to say, "If you are a poor speller," but it is not acceptable to say, to the general reader, "You should improve your spelling"; the reader's spelling may not need improvement. And avoid *you* when the word cannot possibly apply to the reader: "A hundred years ago you were faced with many diseases that now have been eradicated." Something like "A hundred years ago people were faced . . ." is preferable.

your, you're The first is a possessive pronoun ("your book"); the second is a contraction of *you are* ("You're mistaken").

LAST WORDS

A rich patron once gave money to the painter Chu Ta, asking him to paint a picture of a fish. Three years later, when he still had not received the painting, the patron went to Chu Ta's house to ask why the picture was not done. Chu Ta did not answer, but dipped a brush in ink and with a few strokes drew a splendid fish. "If it is so easy," asked the patron, "why didn't you give me the picture three years ago?" Again Chu Ta did not answer. Instead, he opened the door of a large cabinet. Thousands of pictures of fish tumbled out.

(Continued from page iv)

Robert Bly, "Love Poem." From *Silence in the Snowy Fields* (Middletown, Conn.: Wesleyan University Press, 1962), p. 41. Copyright © 1962 by Robert Bly. Reprinted by permission of the author.

Susan Brownmiller, "With the Weathermen," *The New York Times*, 15 June, 1975. © 1975 by The New York Times Company. Reprinted by permission.

Leonard Cammer, M.D. "How to Deal with the Crying," from *Up From Depression*. Copyright © 1969 by Leonard Cammer, M.D. Reprinted by permission of Simon & Schuster, a Division of Gulf & Western Corporation.

Bruce Catton, "Grant and Lee: A Study in Contrasts" from *The American Story*. Earl Schenck Miers, editor. © 1956 by Broadcast Music, Inc. Reprinted by permission.

Joan Didion, "Los Angeles Notebook." Reprinted by permission of Farrar, Straus and Giroux, Inc. "Los Angeles Notebook" from *Slouching Towards Bethlehem* by Joan Didion. Copyright © 1967, 1968 by Joan Didion.

Paul Diederich, pages 21–22 from *Measuring Growth In English*. Copyright © 1974 National Council of Teachers of English. Reprinted by permission of the publisher.

Jim Doherty, "How Cemeteries Bring Us Back to Earth," *The New York Times*, May 31, 1982. © 1982 by The New York Times Company. Reprinted by permission.

Mamie Duff, "Dedication Doth Not a Good Teacher Make," by Mamie Duff, staff, Lockwood Press. Reprinted by permission of the author.

Bergen Evans, "Sophistication." *The New York Times Book Review*, 7 September 1961. © 1961 by The New York Times Company. Reprinted by permission.

Margaret Gooch, "Library Exercises," (after research paper in Chapter 10), reprinted by permission of Margaret Gooch, Wessell Library, Tufts University.

Jeff Greenfield, "Columbo Knows the Butler Didn't Do It," *The New York Times*, 22 April 1973. © 1973 by The New York Times Company. Reprinted by permission.

"In Search of the Elusive Pingo" (Ideas and Trends), *The New York Times* 5 May 1974. © 1974 by The New York Times Company. Reprinted by permission.

George Kane, "Traveler's Diarist," March 14, 1981, *The New Republic*. Reprinted by permission of *The New Republic*, © 1981 The New Republic, Inc.

Chuck Kraemer, "Indecent Exposure," *The Real Paper*, 4 June 1975. Reprinted by permission of *The Real Paper*.

Barbara Lawrence, "Four Letter Words Can Hurt You," (original title, "——— isn't a dirty word") *The New York Times*, 27 October 1973. © 1973 by The New York Times Company. Reprinted by permission.

"Letter to the Editor" by Leonard S. Charlap, *The New York Times*, 19 December 1977. © 1977 by The New York Times Company. Reprinted by permission.

"Letter to the Editor" by Ruth H. Cohn, *The New York Times*, 20 July 1978. © 1978 by The New York Times Company. Reprinted by permission.

W. T. Lhamon, Jr. "Family Man," *The New Republic*, 1 June 1974, pp. 27–28. Reprinted by permission of *The New Republic*, © 1974 by The New Republic, Inc.

Walter Lippmann, excerpt from column, *The New York Times*, February 20, 1942. © 1942 by The New York Times Company. Reprinted by permission.

Anne Hebald Mandelbaum, "It's the Portly Penguin That Gets the Girl, French Biologist Claims," *Harvard University Gazette*, 30 January 1976, pp. 3, 5. Reprinted by permission of the *Harvard University Gazette*.

Jack Margolis, "And All Those Others," *The Poetry of Richard Milhous Nixon* (Los Angeles: Cliff House Books, 1974). Reprinted by permission.

Sister Lynda Martin-Boyle, H.O.O.M., "Adman's Atlanta." Reprinted by permission of the author.

Gerald Mast, *The Comic Mind*, pp. 281–282, 282–283. Copyright © 1973 by Gerald Mast. Reprinted by permission of the publisher.

Anne Moody, "Coming of Age in Mississippi." Excerpted from the book *Coming of Age in Mississippi* by Anne Moody. Copyright © 1968 by Anne Moody. Reprinted by permission of The Dial Press. From page 5.

Joseph Morgenstern, "On the Road," *Newsweek*, 21 July 1969, p. 95. Copyright © 1969 by Newsweek, Inc. All rights reserved. Reprinted by permission of Newsweek, Inc.

"Notes and Comment," *The New Yorker Magazine*, 10 January 1970. Reprinted by permission; © 1970 The New Yorker Magazine, Inc.

"Notes and Comment," *The New Yorker Magazine*, 22 September 1975. Reprinted by permission; © 1975 The New Yorker Magazine, Inc.

George Orwell, from "England Your England," *The Collected Essays, Journalism and Letters, Vol. II: My Country Right or Left, 1940–1943*, Angus, Ian and Sonia Orwell, eds. (New York, Harcourt Brace Jovanovich, Inc., 1968) pp. 61–62. Reprinted by permission of Harcourt Brace Jovanovich, Inc., the estate of the late Sonia Brownell Orwell and Martin Secker & Warburg Ltd.

George Orwell, "Shooting an Elephant," *Shooting an Elephant and Other Essays*, copyright 1945, 1946, 1949, 1950, by Sonia Brownell Orwell; renewed 1978 by Sonia Pitt-Rivers. Reprinted by permission of Harcourt Brace Jovanovich, Inc., the estate of the late Sonia Brownell Orwell and Martin Secker & Warburg Ltd.

Dorothy Parker, "News Item." From *The Portable Dorothy Parker*. Revised and enlarged edition. Copyright 1936, copyright © renewed 1964 by Dorothy Parker. Reprinted by permission of Viking Penguin, Inc.

Robert M. Pirsig, "Mechanic's Feel." Excerpts from p. 14 and pp. 323–4 in *Zen and the Art of Motorcycle Maintenance* by Robert M. Pirsig. Copyright © 1974 by Robert M. Pirsig. By permission of William Morrow and Company.

Susan Pope, "Tennis Tips to a Beginner." Reprinted by permission of the author.

Charles T. Powers, "Say One Word and I'll Cut Your Throat," *Los Angeles Times*, 13 January 1974 by Charles T. Powers. Copyright, 1974, Los Angeles Times. Reprinted by permission.

Paul Reps, No. 29 from "The Gateless Gate," *Zen Flesh, Zen Bones* (Tokyo: Charles E. Tuttle Co. 1957). Reprinted by permission of Charles E. Tuttle Co., Tokyo, Japan, publishers.

Reuters, "Fish Eat Brazilian Fishermen," *The Boston Globe*, 17 January 1971. Reprinted by permission of Reuters.

Philip Roth, "The Newark Public Library" (original title, "Topics: Reflections on the Death of a Library"), *The New York Times*, 1 March 1969 © 1969 by The New York Times Company. Reprinted by permission.

David Royce, "Moby Balloon," *The New York Times Magazine*, 26 May 1974. © 1974 by The New York Times Company. Reprinted by permission.

"Science and the Citizen: Hyperactivity and Drugs," *Scientific American*, July 1974. Reprinted by permission of W. H. Freeman and Company.

Sei Shōnagon, "The Pillow Book of Sei Shonagon." From *The Pillow Book of Sei Shonagon* translated and edited by Ivan Morris and published by Oxford University Press (1967). Reprinted by permission of the publisher. Reprinted in the United States by permission of Columbia University Press.

Gary Snyder, "Hitch Haiku," *The Back Country*. Copyright © 1968 by Gary Snyder. Reprinted by permission of New Directions Publishing Corporation.

Raymond A. Sokolov, excerpt from book review, *The New York Times*, 22 April 1979. © 1979 by The New York Times Company. Reprinted by permission.

Time, excerpt from "Lord, They've Done It All," May 6, 1974. Copyright 1974 Time Inc. All rights reserved. Reprinted by permission from *Time*.

William Butler Yeats, "The Balloon of the Mind." Reprinted with permission of Macmillan Publishing Co., Inc., N.Y., M. B. Yeats, Anne Yeats, and Macmillan London Ltd. From *Collected Poems* by William Butler Yeats. Copyright 1919 by Macmillan Publishing Co., Inc., renewed 1947 by Bertha Georgie Yeats.

William Butler Yeats, "The friends that have it I do wrong." Reprinted with permission of Macmillan Publishing Co., Inc., N.Y., M. B. Yeats, Anne Yeats, and Macmillan London Ltd. From *The Variorum Edition of the Poems of W. B. Yeats*, Allt and Alspach, eds. Copyright 1957 by Macmillan Publishing Co., Inc.

Art

Pieter Brueghel, *The Painter and the Connoisseur*. From the Graphic Collection of the Albertina Museum, Vienna. Reprinted by permission.

Buddha, Sakyamuni. Japan, Heian Period, late 10th century. Katsura Wood with Gold and Traces of Polychromy, H.: 83.5 cm. 09.72, Gift of Denman Waldo Ross. Courtesy, Museum of Fine Arts, Boston.

The Bodhisattva Avalokitesvara (Kuan Yin). China, Sung Dynasty, 12th century, Wood, H.: 14.1 cm., W.: 88 cm. 20.590, Harvey Edward Wetzel Fund. Courtesy, Museum of Fine Arts, Boston.

William Notman, *Buffalo Bill and Sitting Bull*. From the Notman Photographic Archives, McCord Museum, McGill University. Reprinted by permission.

Photographer unknown. *Picasso's Son Paul on a Donkey*, c. 1923. Photograph, Collection Pablo Picasso. From Van Deren Coke, *The Painter and the Photographer* (Albuquerque: University of New Mexico Press, 1962). © SPADEM, Paris/VAGA, New York, 1982.

Pablo Picasso, *Paul, Son of the Artist*. 1923. Gouache, 40 × 32 inches. Collection of Pablo Picasso, Grasse, France. Permission © S.P.A.D.E.M., Paris/V.A.G.A., New York.

Love and Death. Francisco y Lucientes Jose de Goya. Spanish 1746–1828, Aquatint, 1973.700a, the Gift of Frederick I. Kennedy Memorial Foundation. Courtesy, Museum of Fine Arts, Boston.

Francisco Goya, *El amor y la muerte*. Courtesy, Museo del Prado, Madrid.

Leonardo da Vinci, *Mona Lisa*. Courtesy, Musée de Louvre, Paris. Reprinted by permission, Alinari/Editorial Photocolor Archives.

Spaghetti, reprinted from *Mazes 2* by Vladimir Koziakin. Copyright © 1972 by Vladimir Koziakin. Used by permission of Grosset & Dunlap, Inc.

Atlanta advertisement reprinted by permission of Atlanta Chamber of Commerce.

Index

a/an, 415
abbreviations, 403–04
above, 415
academics, 415
accept/except, 415
active voice, 289–90
adjectives in series, 392
"Adman's Atlanta," 172
adverb, conjunctive, 387, 390
affect/effect, 415
aggravate, 415
agreement
  noun and pronoun, 298–99
  subject and verb, 299–300
all ready/already, 415
all right/alright, 415
all together/altogether, 415
allusion/illusion, 416
almost/most, 426
a lot/alot, 416
already/all ready, 415
alright/all right, 415
altogether/all together, 415
ambiguity, 295, 298
among/between, 416
amount/number, 416
an/a, 415
analogy, 146
analysis, 30–49, 167–69
analyzation/analysis, 416
"And All Those Others," 340
and etc., 416
and/or, 416

ante/anti, 416
anthology/collection, 416
anti/ante, 416
anticlimax, 308–09
anxious, 416
anybody/any body, 416
anyone/any one, 417
apostrophe, 401–03
apposition, appositive, 390–91
area of, 417
argument, 137–51
  organization of, 149–51
argumentum ad hominem, 145–46
around, 417
as/like, 417
as of now, 417
aspect, 418
as such, 418
as to, 418
assumptions, 146–48
audience, 14–17, 47–49
authority, false, 142

bad/badly, 418
"Balloon of the Mind, The," 1, 234
because/since, 431
begging the question, 144–45
being, 418
being that/being so, 418
Bellanca, Pat
  "Jimmy Buffett is Going Coconuts?!," 241

Bellow, Saul, 170
Benjamin Franklin's exercise, 334–35
Bergman, Barbara R.
  "Here Is Why You Lost Your Job," 157
beside/besides, 418
between/among, 418
biannually/semiannually, 419
Bible, references to, 359, 385
bibliographic notes, 206–10
bibliography, 203, 373–77
bimonthly/semimonthly, 419
biweekly/semiweekly, 419
Black/black, 419
Bly, Robert
  "Love Poem," 304
book review(s)
  indexes to, 201–03
  references to, 370, 375
  writing a, 236–40
brackets, 357–58

Cammer, Leonard
  "How to Deal with the Crying," 123
can/may, 419
capital letters, 399–400
card catalog, 198–201
cats are dogs, 292–93
Catton, Bruce
  "Grant and Lee: A Study in Contrasts," 59
cause and effect, 130–32
centers on/centers around, 419
choppiness, 309–12
circular reasoning, 144–45
circumlocutions, 259–60
clarity, 17–19, 272–306, 332–33
classification, 32–33
clauses
  cutting, 267–68

  dependent (subordinate), 313
  extra, 266–68
  independent (main), 313–16
  introductory, 389
  who, which, that, 267–68
clichés, 284–85
coherence
  in paragraphs, 79–80
  in sentences, 292–302
collection/anthology, 416
collective nouns, 419
colon, 385–86
"Columbo Knows the Butler Didn't Do It," 57
comma, 388–94
  as parentheses, 390
  with a series, 392–93
  with direct discourse, 393
  with independent clauses, 388–89
  with introductory material, 389
  with nonrestrictive modifiers, 390–92
  with tacked on material, 389–90
  position with other punctuation, 393–94
comma fault, 380–84
comma splice, 380–84
common knowledge, 362–63
compare/contrast, 39, 419
comparison, 39–45
complement/compliment, 419
complex sentence, 314
compliment/complement, 419
compound-complex sentence, 314
compound sentence, 314
comprise, 419–20
computers, 231–33
"Conceit," 310
concept, 420
conciseness, 253–71
concluding paragraphs, 95–97
conclusions, empty, 262

concrete (specific) details, 17–19
conjunctions
    coordinating, 314, 382–83, 388–89
    subordinating, 381–82, 383
conjunctive adverb, 387, 390
connotation, 276–78
contact, 420
continual/continuous, 420
contractions, 403
contrast/compare, 419
coordinating conjunction, 314, 382–83, 388–89
corrections in manuscript, 354–55
could have/could of, 427
criteria/criterion, 420
cumulative sentence, 337–39

dangling modifiers, 296
dash, 394–95
data/datum, 420
"Dedication Doth Not a Good Teacher Make," 21
deduction, 148–49
definitely, 259
definition, 102–17
    in introductory paragraphs, 93–94
deletions, 355
denotation, 275–76
dependent clause, 313
description, 160–77
details, 17–19
dictionary, 102n
Didion, Joan
    "Los Angeles Notebook," 174
different from/different than, 420
dilemma, 420
disinterested/uninterested, 420
"Dodgers Keep Perfect Record in Knocking Out Southpaws," 282

Doherty, Jim
    "How Cemeteries Bring Us Back to Earth," 167
Donne, John
    "The Flea," 153
Doyle, Arthur Conan
    "The Science of Deduction," 46
draft, 5–6, 25–27
due to, 420–21
due to the fact that, 421

each, 421
editing, 351–436
effect/affect, 415
e.g./i.e., 421
either . . . or, 421
elegant variation, 300
ellipsis, 358
emphasis, 307–18
    false, 307
empty conclusions, 262
empty words, 257–59
encyclopedias, 202–03
    footnote to, 368–69
    bibliographic reference to, 374
endnotes, 363–72
enthuse, 421
essay examinations, 243–49
et cetera/et alii, 421–22
euphemisms, 286–87
euphony, 301–02
Evans, Bergen
    "Sophistication," 115
everybody/everyone, 422
evidence
    presenting, 136–37
    suppressing, 143
examinations, 243–49
examples/instances, 425
examples, use of, 280–81
except/accept, 415
exclamation mark, 307
exists, 422

explication, 234–36
exposition, 118–35
expound/explain, 422
extra clauses, 266–68
extra words, 257–59

facet, 422
factor, 422
fact that, the, 422
fallacies, 142–47
false series, 293–94
"Family Man," 237
famous/notorious, 427
"Farm Picture, A," 161
farther/further, 422
fatalistic/pessimistic, 422
fewer/less, 425
field of, 417
first/firstly, 423
first person, use of, 290–91
"Fish Eat Brazilian Fisherman," 88
"Flea, The," 153
fluency, 342–49
focus, 12–14, 24–25
footnotes, 363–72
formal outline, 65–67
formal writing, 325–29
former/latter, 423
found poems, 340–41
"Four Letter Words Can Hurt You," 154
fragment, sentence, 314–15, 380–82
Franklin, Benjamin, 334–35
"friends that have it I do wrong, The," 251
further/farther, 422

general, 17–19
generalization, 143–44
genetic fallacy, 144
Glossary of Usage, 415–36

good/well, 423
graduate/graduate from, 423
"Grant and Lee: A Study in Contrasts," 59
Greenfield, Jeff
"Columbo Knows the Butler Didn't Do It," 57
Groucho Marx complex, 23–24

he or she/his or her, 423
"Here Is Why You Lost Your Job," 157
his or her/he or she, 423
"Hitch Haiku," 317
hopefully/I hope, 423–24
"How Cemeteries Bring Us Back to Earth," 167
however, 387, 424
"How to Deal with the Crying," 123
"How to Grow an Avocado," 124
hyphen, 400–01

"I," 290–91
idea that, the, 424
identify, 424
idioms, 414
i.e./e.g., 421, 424
I hope/hopefully, 423–24
illusion/allusion, 416
imitation, 334–35, 337–38
immanent/imminent, 424
imply/infer, 424
"Indecent Exposure," 130
independent clause, 313–16
indexes, 203–06
individual, 424–25
induction, 143–44, 149
infer/imply, 424
infinitive, 432
informal writing, 325–29
"In Search of the Elusive Pingo," 119

instances/examples, 425
instant prose, 254–57
intensifiers, weak, 259
introductory clauses, 389
introductory paragraphs, 90–95
irony, 431
irregardless/regardless, 425
italics, 359, 398
it is, 268, 425
its/it's, 425
"It's the Portly Penguin that Gets
    the Girl, French Biologist
    Claims," 132

jargon, 281–84
"Jimmy Buffett Is Going
    Coconuts?!," 241
journal, 342–49

Kael, Pauline, 330–31
kind of, 425
Kraemer, Chuck
    "Indecent Exposure," 130

latter/former, 423
Lawrence, Barbara
    "Four Letter Words Can Hurt
        You," 154
lay/lie, 425
lend/loan, 425
less/fewer, 425
"Lesson, A," 19
levels of usage, 325–28
Lhamon, W. T., Jr.
    "Family Man," 237
library card, 198–201
lie/lay, 425
lifestyle/life-style/life style, 426
like/as, 417
literally, 426
literature, examinations in, 245–47
loan/lend, 425
logic, 137–38, 142–49

loose/lose, 426
"Los Angeles Notebook," 174
"Love Poem," 304

main clause, 313–16
majority, 426
man/mankind, 426
Mandelbaum, Anne Hebald
    "It's the Portly Penguin that
        Gets the Girl, French Biol-
        ogist Claims," 132
manuscript form, 353–54
margins, 354
Margolis, Jack
    "And All Those Others," 340
Martin, Lynda
    "Adman's Atlanta," 172
mathematics, examinations in,
    248–49
may/can, 419
me, 426
"Mechanic's Feel," 113
media/medium, 426
metaphors, mixed, 285–86
misplaced modifiers, 294–95
misquotation, 142–43
mixed metaphors, 285–86
modifiers
    dangling, 296
    misplaced, 294–95
    nonrestrictive, 390–92
    restrictive, 390–91
    squinting, 295
most/almost, 426

narration, 165–67, 178–93
nature of, the, 426
needless to say, 427
negative constructions, 265–66,
    427
Negro, 427
neither . . . nor, 421
Nemerov, Howard, 329

"Newark Public Library, The," 7
"News Item," 390
Nixon, Richard, 340
nobody/no one/none, 427
nonrestrictive modifier, 390–92
notes, taking, 206–10
not . . . un-, 427
notorious/famous, 427
number/amount, 416
number of, a, 427
numbers, 403, 404–05

obscurity, 272–75
of/have, 427
off of/off, 427
often-times, 427
old-fashioned/old-fashion, 427
one/he, 428
one of, 428
only, 295, 428
oral/verbal, 434
organization
    of arguments, 149–51
    of book reviews, 236–37
    of comparisons, 39–45
    of descriptions, 161–62
    of essays on a process, 123–26
    of expository essays, 126
    of narration, 182–85
    of paragraphs, 76–79
    of persuasive essays, 149–51
    of research papers, 211–13
Orwell, George
    "Shooting an Elephant," 186
other, 428
outline, 36, 64–67, 215–16

page, abbreviation for, 367
pagination of manuscript, 353–54
paragraphs, 68–101
    concluding, 95–97
    introductory, 90–95

length of, 86–90
organization of, 76–79
outline, 65
symbol for, 355
transitions between, 84–86
transitions in, 80–82
parallel construction, 302–05
paraphrase, 209, 335–37, 361
parentheses, 395–96
Parker, Dorothy
    "News Item," 390
Parsons, Talcott, 329
particular, 17–19
passive voice, 289–90
per, 428
per cent, percent, percentage, 429
period, 384–85
periodicals, indexes to, 203–06
per se, 429
persona, 322
persuasion, 136–59
pessimistic/fatalistic, 422
phenomena/phenomenon, 429
physical sciences, examinations in
    248–49
Pillow Book of Sei Shōnagon, The,
    346
Pirsig, Robert M.
    "Mechanic's Feel," 113
plagiarism, 360–63
plays, citations of, 364–65
plurals, unusual, 403
plus, 429
point of view, 163–65
politics, 429
Pope, Susan
    "Tennis Tips to a Beginning
        Player," 120
possessive, 402
post hoc ergo propter hoc, 145
predicate(s), 313–14
prejudice/prejudiced, 429

premises, 148–49
preventative/preventive, 430
primary material, 195–96
prior to, 430
process, 123–26
pronouns
  possessive, 402
  reference of, 296–98
  shift in, 297–98
proofreading, 354–55
protagonist, 430
punctuation, 378–406

qualifiers, weak, 259
questions, asking and answering,
  6–7, 11–12
quite, 259, 430
quotation/quote, 430
quotation marks
  as apologies, 278, 396–97
  with other punctuation, 359,
    397
  with titles, 359, 396
  single, 359, 396
quotations, form of, 356–58
  edited, 357–58
  embedded, 357
  set off, 356–57, 365

rather, 259, 430
reader, 14–17, 47–49
reading and taking notes, 207–10
reasoning, 137–38, 142–51
reason . . . is because, the, 430
rebut/refute, 430
redundancy, 264–65
reference books, 201–07
reference of pronouns, 296–98
refute/rebut, 430
regardless, irregardless, 425
regard to, 430
relate to, 431

repel/repulse, 431
repetition, 82–84, 264–65
  and variation, 300–01
  emphasis by, 312–13
research paper, 194–233
restrictive modifier, 390–91
reviews, writing, 236–43
revising, 26–27, 251–318
revisions in manuscript, 354–55
Roth, Philip
  "The Newark Public Library,"
    7
run-on sentence, 382–84

sarcasm, 141–42, 397, 431
satire, 322
"Science of Deduction, The," 46
scratch outline, 64–65
secondary material, 195–96
second/secondly, 423
seem, 431
Sei Shōnagon
  The Pillow Book of Sei Shōnagon,
    346
self, writing about, 19–21
semiannually/biannually, 419
semicolon, 386–87
semimonthly/bimonthly, 419
semiweekly/biweekly, 419
sentence(s)
  cumulative, 337–39
  defined, 313–15
  extra, 266–68
  fragment, 314–15, 380–82
  kinds of, 313–15
  run-on, 380–84
  short and long, 309–12
  structure, 302–05
series, true and false, 293–94
sexism in language (see *he or she*
  and *man/mankind,* 423, 426)
shall/will, 431

"Shooting an Elephant," 186
should/would, 431
simple sentence, 313
simplistic/simplify, 431
since/because, 431
situation, 431
Snyder, Gary
  "Hitch Haiku," 317
social sciences, examinations in,
  247–48
"Sophistication," 115
sorting, 30–38
sources, acknowledging, 360–63
specific, 17–21, 278–80
spelling, 407–12
split infinitives, 432
squinting modifiers, 295
stanza/verse, 434
stipulative definition, 106–07
style, 321–31, 334–41
subject, 12–14, 196–98
  of a sentence, 313–14
  versus topic, 12
subordinate clause, 313
subordinating conjunction, 381–
  82, 383
subordination, 266–69, 315–18
  emphasis, 313–18
summary, 38–39, 126–28, 209,
  335, 361
syllabification, 401
syllogism, 148–49
"Symbolism," 340

teacher, writer as, 15–17
technical language, 281–84
"Tennis Tips to a Beginning
  Player," 120
texture, 332–33
than/then, 432
that, 267
that/which/who, 432–33

their/there/they're, 433
then/than, 432
there is, there are, 268
thesis, 12–13, 45–46, 196–98, 211
this, 433
this is, 268
thus/thusly, 433
till/until, 433
title(s)
  capitalization of, 399
  choosing a, 25–26
  form at head of manuscript,
    353–54
  italicization of, 398
  of parts of the Bible, 359, 385
  use of quotation marks with,
    396
title page, 214, 354
to be, problems with the verb,
  262–64, 268
to have, problems with the verb,
  262–64
to make, problems with the verb,
  262–64
tone, 323–25
topic, 12
topic ideas, 70–74
topic of/area of, 437
topic sentences, 70–74
toward/towards, 433
transformations, 339
transitions, 80–82, 302
  common words and phrases,
    80–81
type/type of, 433
typographical errors, revision of,
  354–55

underlining, 398
uninterested/disinterested, 420
unique, 259, 433
unity (in paragraphs), 70–76

until/till, 433
U.S./United States, 433
usage, 413–46
  levels of, 325–28
usage/use, 433–34
use of, 434
utilize/utilization, 434

variation, 300
variety, in sentences, 309–12, 313–
  17
verbal/oral, 434
verse/stanza, 434
very, 259
viable, 434
voice, active and passive, 289–90

we, 434
well/good, 423
well-known/widely known, 434
whereas, 382
which, 267, 434–35
which/that/who, 432–33
while, 435
Whitehead, Alfred North, 330

Whitman, Walt
  "A Farm Picture," 161
who, 267
who/that/which, 432–33
who/whom/whomever, 435
whoever/whomever, 435
who's/whose, 435
widely known/well-known, 434
will/shall, 431
wit, 139–41
with regard to, 430
wordiness, 253–76
would, 435
would/should, 431
writer as teacher, 15–17

Yeats, William Butler
  "The Balloon of the Mind," 1,
    234–36
  "The friends that have it I do
    wrong," 251
you, 435–36
your/you're, 436

Zen anecdote, 319
zonkers, 254–57

To the Student

Please help us make *Barnet & Stubbs's Practical Guide to Writing* an even better book. To improve our textbooks, we revise them every few years, taking into account the experiences of both instructors and students with the previous edition. At some time, your instructor will most likely be asked to comment extensively on *Barnet & Stubbs's Practical Guide to Writing*. Now we would like to hear from you.

Complete this questionnnaire and return it to:

College English Developmental Group
Little, Brown and Company
34 Beacon St.
Boston, MA 02106

School _____
City, State, Zip Code _____
Course title _____
Instructor's full name _____
Other books required _____
_____

1. Did you like the book? _____

2. Was it too easy? _____Too difficult? _____

   Did you read it all? _____

   Which chapters were most useful? Why? _____

   _____

   Which chapters were least useful? Why? _____

   _____

3. Were the exercises useful? _____

4. Did you like the examples? _____

5. Do you feel the professor should continue to assign this book next year?

   _____ Did you tell her or him? _____

6. Please give us your reactions to the following selections:

	Keep	Drop	Didn't Read
Jeff Greenfield, "Columbo Knows the Butler Didn't Do It"	___	___	___
Bruce Catton, "Grant and Lee: A Study in Contrasts"	___	___	___
Robert M. Pirsig, "Mechanic's Feel"	___	___	___
Bergen Evans, "Sophistication"	___	___	___
Chuck Kraemer, "Indecent Exposure"	___	___	___
Anne Hebald Mandelbaum, "It's the Portly Penguin That Gets the Girl, French Biologist Claims"	___	___	___
Barbara R. Bergman, "Here Is Why You Lost Your Job"	___	___	___
Barbara Lawrence, "Four Letter Words Can Hurt You"	___	___	___
Joan Didion, "Los Angeles Notebook"	___	___	___
Lynda Martin, "Adman's Atlanta"	___	___	___
George Orwell, "Shooting an Elephant"	___	___	___
"The Pillow Book of Sei Shōnagon"	___	___	___

7. Will you keep this book for your library? _____

8. What would you have us change next time? _____

_____

_____

_____

9. Please add any comments or suggestions. _____

_____

_____

10. May we quote you in our promotion efforts for this book?

_____Yes _____No

_____

Date   Signature

_____

Mailing address

SYMBOLS COMMONLY USED
IN MARKING PAPERS

All instructors have their own techniques for annotating essays, but many instructors make substantial use of the following symbols.

ab   faulty or undesirable abbreviation (see pages 403–04)

agr   faulty agreement between subject and verb (pages 299–300) or between pronoun and antecedent (page 299)

apos   apostrophe (pages 401–03)

awk (k)   awkward

cap   use a capital letter (pages 399–400)

cf   comma fault (pages 382–84)

choppy   too many short sentences — subordinate (pages 309–12)

cl   cliché (pages 284–85)

coh   paragraph lacks coherence (pages 79–84); sentence lacks coherence (pages 292–302)

cs   comma splice (pages 382–84)

dev   paragraph poorly developed (pages 68–79)

dm   dangling modifier (page 294, 296)

emph   emphasis obscured (pages 307–17)

good   a good point; or, well expressed

frag   fragmentary sentence (pages 314–15, 380–82)

id   unidiomatic expression (page 414)

ital   underline to indicate italics (page 398)

k (awk)   awkward